Seed Wars

Seed Wars

Controversies and Cases on Plant Genetic Resources and Intellectual Property

Keith Aoki

CAROLINA ACADEMIC PRESS

Durham, North Carolina

ISBN-10: 1-59460-050-3
ISBN-13: 978-1-59460-050-0
LCCN: 2006936994

CAROLINA ACADEMIC PRESS

700 Kent Street
Durham, North Carolina 27701
Telephone (919) 489-7486
Fax (919) 493-5668
www.cap-press.com

Printed in the United States of America.

To Mona

for her patience

and unstinting support and love

Contents

Acknowledgments

In the production of this book, many people have played crucial roles. I wish to extend my special thanks and gratitude to my friend and colleague Dr. John Shuford, whose editorial acumen, research contributions, and keen judgement have been invaluable. I want to thank Professors Anupam Chander, Margaret Chon, Madhavi Sunder and Peter Yu, who have been supportive in a multitude of ways. Thanks are also due to my research assistants over the past few years: Tanya Bessera, Will Glasson, J.J. Haapala, Anne Kelson, Kennedy Luvai, Jessica McDonald, Charlotte Nisser, Claire Reichstein, and John-Paul Vallejo, each of whom played key roles in completing aspects of this project. I also wish to extend my thanks to Director Margaret Hallock and Professor Caroline Forell of the Wayne Morse Center for Law and Politics at the University of Oregon School of Law. The Morse Center provided research support and hosted the April 2004 conference "Malthus, Mendel and Monsanto: The Law and Politics of Intellectual Property and Global Food Supply"—both of which propelled this project forward. Finally, I want to acknowledge my deep intellectual debt to the work of Stephen Brush, Cary Fowler, Laurence Helfer, Jack Kloppenburg, and Pat Mooney. Their respective contributions in this area have played crucial roles in forming my thinking on the subject.

Introduction

Contemporary debate over the legal treatment of plant genetic resources (PGRs) has been described as the "Seed Wars." The phrase "Seed Wars" as it is used here comes from a *Wall Street Journal* report that refers to the conflict implicating "access to, control over, and preservation of [PGRs]."[1] This book seeks to provide an abbreviated history of events that precede and surround the "Seed Wars" of the past two and a half decades.

Chapter One gives an overview of the major tensions in this area: loss of crop genetic diversity in the 20th century; the rise of industrial agriculture; globalization with the so-called "Green Revolution;" and the intersection of these trends with intellectual property law in the 20th and early 21st centuries. This chapter also raises questions about the relation between technological advances in plant breeding, traditional crop development, and the effect of commodification of plant germplasm (or genotype).

Chapter Two gives a brief overview of plant and seed cultivation, focusing on the treatment of germplasm. The first period is from the 16th through the early 19th centuries, when European colonial powers eagerly sought out exotic plants and seeds to underwrite plantation economies in the equatorial regions of the globe. The key point here is that plants and seeds were not considered the private 'property' of individuals, but were instead "owned" (or at least "possessed") by sovereign nations.

The second period is from the early 19th through the early 20th centuries, when U.S. state and federal governments heavily subsidized the crop plant cultivation and seed distribution. In the last third of the 19th century, through institutions like land grant colleges (LGCs) and state agricultural experimental stations (SAESs), state and federal governments funded research that focused on plant improvement and dissemination of research results to farmers. The USDA used Congressional free franking privileges to send millions of seed samples to constituent farmers annually.

The third period is from the early 1900s to the 1930s, when the primacy of publicly funded breeding and research in this area came under pressure with the re-discovery of Gregor Mendel's work on plant genetics and the development of crop hybridization to induce higher yields. Private seed companies such as Pioneer Hi-Bred took center stage, as LGC-housed public plant breeding programs were eclipsed and relegated to a complementary role, thus leaving the private seed industry without competition. Finally,

---

1. *See* Jack R. Kloppenburg, Jr. & Daniel Kleinman, *Preface, Plant Genetic Resources: The Common Bowl, in* SEEDS AND SOVEREIGNTY: THE USE AND CONTROL OF PLANT GENETIC RESOURCES [hereinafter SEEDS AND SOVEREIGNTY] 1, 2 (Jack Kloppenburg ed., 1988); Jack Kloppenburg, Jr. & Daniel Lee Kleinman, *Seed Wars: Common Heritage, Private Property, and Political Strategy,* 95 SOCIALIST REV. 6 (1987). This book uses the term "plant genetic resources" in a broad sense, encompassing anything that contributes to the development or improvement of a new or existing plant variety. This book also uses the terms "seed germplasm" or "germplasm" to refer to seeds, roots, and other plant tissue containing genetic materials.

this chapter discusses the so-called "Green Revolution" brought about by higher-yielding crops and the rise of industrial agriculture as well as the costs in terms of genetic erosion that such high-input agriculture entails.

Chapter Three shifts from developments in the seed cultivation area to developments in intellectual property law. First, this chapter briefly describes the structure of U.S. patent law. To receive a utility patent, an inventor must show that her invention falls within the realm of "patentable subject matter." The inventor must also show that the invention is "non-obvious," "useful," and "novel"—that is, not part of "prior art" in the area. Before 1930, plants (either their genotype or phenotype) were not considered "patentable subject matter" because they were considered "products of nature." This changed in 1930, when the Plant Patent Act (PPA) passed into law. The PPA made asexually reproduced plants (i.e., reproduced by grafting or cloning) into legally protectable intellectual property matter. Just as importantly, the PPA specifically excluded sexually reproduced crop plants from its scope. The chapter goes on to describe the Plant Variety Protection Act of 1970 (PVPA) that did grant intellectual property protection to sexually reproduced plants that were "novel," "uniform," and "stable." The 1970 PVPA included important exceptions that allowed farmers to save seeds for planting and resale as well as for research.

Both the PPA and the PVPA limited intellectual property rights. In terms of exclusivity of ownership, a utility patent is much stronger—giving (at the time) the patent holder an exclusive right to "make, use or sell" the patented invention for 17 years from the date of issue. Unlike the PVPA, a utility patent does not have exemptions. The issues that the courts would decide next pertained to the scope of patentable subject matter and the eligibility of selectively bred (or genetically engineered) plants for utility patents.

Against this backdrop, the third chapter then describes the development of a series of cases that changed the juridical scope in North America of intellectual property protection for plants. Beginning in 1980, the U.S. Supreme Court held that living organisms could receive utility patents if they met prerequisite requirements. In 1985, the U.S. Patent and Trademark Office Board of Appeals held that genetically modified maize could receive a utility patent and that the enactment of the PVPA did not foreclose this legal option. In 2001, the U.S. Supreme Court once again revisited this area, holding that selectively bred plants could receive utility patents. These cases represent a sea change in the legal treatment of plants. At the beginning of the 20th century, plants (including selectively bred plants produced by farmers and breeders) were legally "products of nature" and part of the public domain. Legally speaking, the genetic information contained in plants was openly accessible. By the turn of the 21st century, however, if a plant breeder met the criteria, she could receive a utility patent in her selectively bred plant variety, which could include particular genomic characteristics of the plant. In other words, intellectual property rights (IPR) could extend not only to the plant phenotype, but to the genotype as well.

Chapter Four describes the emergence from the 1980s of several overlapping legal regimes that attempted to address the status of PGRs. There was a striking shift in the legal treatment of PGRs from the early 1980s to the 1990s. In 1980, with the exception of asexually reproduced varieties protected by the PPA or sexually reproduced varieties protected by PVP certificates, PGRs were considered to be part of the "common heritage of mankind," and as such were freely appropriable. However, "worked" germplasm was treated as the intellectual property of an individual or a firm. By the mid-1990s, legal treatment of germplasm as "common heritage" had been largely rejected, due in significant part to critics in the developing world that decried PGR appropriation from their countries, and PGRs were treated as "sovereign national property"—an ironic return to the de facto treatment of such resources during European colonialism.

This fourth chapter also describes and explores the several international fora that affect the legal status of PGRs. These include the UN Food and Agriculture Organization's (FAO) attempt from 1983 to secure a multilateral agreement regarding PGRs, culminating in the 2001 International Treaty on Plant Genetic Resources (ITPGR) that became effective in 2004. These also include the International Union for the Protection of New Varieties of Plants (UPOV), as outlined in its four major iterations in 1961, 1972, 1978 and 1991, the Convention on Biological Diversity (CBD) in 1992, and the Trade Related Aspects of Intellectual Property (TRIPS) of 1994. The CBD and TRIPS have a particularly complex and contentious relationship, which is explored in this chapter. Finally, the chapter also discusses the relationship between changes in U.S. intellectual property law and these overlapping, international regimes.

The fifth and concluding chapter reviews competing theories of property and intellectual property in order to explore which, if any, may help us find acceptable ways to treat PGRs in terms of promoting *in situ* genetic conservation and encouraging more open PGR exchange between seed banks, farmers, and plant breeders. This chapter suggests that the rejection of "common heritage" protection may have been both premature and overbroad. Such treatment in the 21st century may be beneficial, rather than detrimental to the countries of the developing world. Furthermore, this chapter contends that use of "open source" licensing for PGRs, influenced by its success in the software arena, may be an ironic yet highly beneficial way for seed banks to use "private" contract mechanisms to keep open access to PGRs by treating them as a form of "limited" commons.

Seed Wars

Chapter One

Malthus, Mendel, and Monsanto: Ownership of Plant Genetic Resources and Intellectual Property

Given material abundance, scarcity must be a function of boundaries. If there is plenty of air in the world but something blocks its passage to the lungs, the lungs do well to complain of scarcity. The assumptions of market exchange may not necessarily lead to the emergence of boundaries, but they do in practice. Under the assumption of exchange trade, property is plagued with entropy and wealth can become scarce even as it increases. When trade is "clean" and leaves people unconnected, when the merchant is free to sell when and where he will, when the market moves mostly for profit and the dominant myth is not "to possess is to give," but "the fittest survive," then wealth will lose its motion and gather in isolated pools.[1]

A. Prelude to the "Seed Wars"[2]

The roots of the "Seed Wars" over the past two decades lie in the early 20th century. Four converging trends intersected in the battles over the legal treatment of PGRs. The first is the rediscovery of Gregor Mendel's mid-19th century work on plant genetics at the beginning of the 20th century. This gave plant breeders a key to unlock the secrets of genetic heredity in plants. By the 1920s, using insights gained from Mendel's work, some public agricultural Land Grant Colleges (LGCs) and private companies began experimenting with hybrid corn.[3] In the latter part of the same decade two significant events occurred. First, a private firm, Pioneer Hi-Bred, began marketing higher yielding hybrid corn and, second, the division of research labor between the public and private sectors began shifting in favor of private seed companies (that held the parent lines for

---

1. Lewis Hyde, THE GIFT: IMAGINATION AND THE EROTIC LIFE OF PROPERTY, at 23 (1979) [hereinafter Hyde].

2. *See* Jack R. Kloppenburg, Jr. FIRST THE SEED: THE POLITICAL ECONOMY OF PLANT BIOTECHNOLOGY, 1492–2000 (1988, 2d ed. 2004) [hereinafter Kloppenburg, FIRST THE SEED]; Cary Fowler, UNNATURAL SELECTION: TECHNOLOGY POLITICS, AND PLANT EVOLUTION (1994)[hereinafter Fowler, UNNATURAL SELECTION]; *see generally* INTERNATIONAL PUBLIC GOODS AND TRANSFER OF TECHNOLOGY UNDER A GLOBALIZED INTELLECTUAL PROPERTY REGIME (Keith E. Maskus & Jerome H. Reichman eds., 2005)[hereinafter INT'L PUBLIC GOODS].

3. Kloppenburg, FIRST THE SEED, *supra* note 2, at 94.

C. Particular Types of Inventive Human Agency

Contemporary scientific, legislative, and judicial understandings of genetic engineering (including selective breeding based on genomic data) make human agency and intervention the benchmark for conferring intellectual property rights (IPR) in germplasm. Advances in molecular biology and genetic engineering allow us to isolate a particular moment and an individual responsible for an invention. Then, traditional intellectual property justifications and understandings come into play. The standard intellectual property cliché is that if innovative individuals do not receive exclusive rights in their innovations, they lose incentives to innovate.[24] These taken-for-granted notions ironically and simultaneously minimize the human agency and interventions of thousands of farmers and cultivators throughout history. One effect of such asymmetrical and individualized accounting of innovative human agency is that contemporary scientists-inventors are constructed legally as "Promethean" bringers of "value" to otherwise prosaic "naturally"-occurring subject matter.[25] Once such "Promethean" labor is documented and made the subject of a patent application, it is a relatively small matter for the legal system to make accommodation to reward those who "discovered" or "created" the valued innovation, with the line between "discovery" and "creation" elided. Genetic technologies make possible human intervention into the chromosomal structure of plants. The legal systems of the U.S. and other countries of the developed world construct, recognize, and reward this kind of scientific activity by granting (intellectual) property rights in the results of such intervention.

The commodification of germplasm is a story of the transformation and privatization of agriculture from an economic sector where the state primarily supplied seeds and subsidized agricultural plant-and-seed research to benefit farmers into a global economic enterprise effectively controlled by a handful of multinational corporations. Notably, those "Promethean" value-bringers rewarded with expansive intellectual property rights tend to be employees of large corporations that benefit from the conferral of such patents.

---

24. James Boyle, SHAMANS, SOFTWARE AND SPLEENS: LAW AND THE CONSTRUCTION OF THE INFORMATION SOCIETY (1996) (hereinafter Boyle, SHAMANS) (discussing the pervasiveness of the image of the romantic author in Anglo-American copyright laws, privileging clearly individualized, strongly originary work and devaluing collaborative, incremental work).
25. For example, U.S. patent law explicitly treats as prior art any invention that was "described in this or a printed publication in this or a foreign country or in public use or on sale in this country" more than one year before filing for a patent application. See 35 U.S.C. § 102 (b).

Chapter Two

From Hunter-Gatherers to Industrial Farmers: A Brief History of Seed Cultivation

This chapter gives a brief overview of the changing legal treatment of seeds, focusing on three particular periods. The first period is from the beginning of agriculture to the age of European colonialism that entailed characterizing plant germplasm as both a type of "national" property and at the same time something "freely appropriable." The second period is the last third of the 19th century through the early 20th century, when U.S. federal and state governments heavily subsidized the collection, cultivation, and distribution of seeds to U.S. farmers. The extent of the public farming subsidy may surprise a contemporary person, as government mailed millions of seed packets out to farmers for "free" and undertook the research that led to the lucrative hybrid crop industry. The third period is from the 1930s on, when the private seed industry, driven by the success of higher yielding hybrid crops, transformed the public agricultural infrastructure of Land Grant Colleges (LGCs) and State Agricultural Experimental Stations (SAESs) from competitors into roles supporting the pervasive rise of private industrial agriculture.

Humans began cultivating plants approximately twelve thousand years ago, as they transitioned from hunter-gatherers to agriculturalists.[1] While the move to cultivation entailed a focus on a relatively small number of plant species, within those species genetic diversity thrived as crops traveled with different groups and were adapted through mass selection to new pests, diseases, soils, climates, and human cultures. This genetic diversity has been crucial for the continued viability of major agricultural crops. Farmers, plant breeders, and biologists draw upon it to adapt crop species to new pests, diseases, and other environmental changes.

Yet the treatment of crop genetic diversity changed drastically over the course of the past century. The major food crops of the world have genetic components that are traceable to many local varieties developed by small subsistence farmers and farming communities around the globe.[2] From the 19th century until the late 1970s, these genetic resources were characterized legally as the "common heritage of mankind,"[3]

---

1. Fowler & Mooney, SHATTERING, *supra* Chapter One, note 11, at 8.
2. Kloppenburg, FIRST THE SEED *supra* Chapter One, note 1, at 175.
3. Until very recently, plant genetic resources (PGRs) enjoyed the distinction of being considered the "common heritage of mankind," or in other terms, humanity's collective "genetic estate." As a result, PGRs have been available as an openly accessible good. The only costs associated with their acquisition have been expenses inherent in their collection. Resources such as coal, oil, and valuable minerals do not share this distinction. Even water is ownable by nations, as wrangling over the "Law of the Sea" shows. While countries such as the United States have been reluctant to confer "common heritage" status to resources falling outside their boundaries, this reluctance does not seem to have

which meant that farmers, plant breeders, and agricultural researchers had largely unrestricted and open access to genetic resources. Many of the procedures and norms of 20th century agricultural research and breeding institutions were designed to facilitate open access to and the exchange of PGRs with the goal of promoting crop improvement available across borders.[4] However, as Professors Anupam Chander and Madhavi Sunder point out, open access to particular resources equates neither to *equality of access* nor to *equality of ability* to utilize such resources.[5] Nations with a colonial history of widespread collection of exotic germplasm, such as the U.S. and the European colonial powers, were able to exploit and benefit from the "common heritage" treatment of PGRs. Conversely, the "common heritage" regime over the past five hundred years disadvantaged those countries subject to colonial domination in which PGRs had been located. PGRs, in contrast to other extractable resources such as coal, timber, and oil, could be expropriated surreptitiously because PGRs are not taken in bulk—one plant could be sufficient to secure the PGR.

Control over plant genetic diversity is no less controversial now than it was two hundred years ago, when colonial powers vied for control of plantation crops. What are the consequences of characterizing plant genetic resources as the "common heritage of mankind?" In this context, "common heritage" may be a misnomer because it seems to imply some type of common ownership; however, resources characterized as such are available for entrepreneurs to use as the "raw materials" for intellectual property. In other words, in the case of "common heritage" resources, no one has the right to exclude anyone else from using them. Should private individuals and firms be allowed to claim exclusive ownership in assorted aspects and elements of plant genetic resources? If we allow such private claims to be made, as indeed we do at present, how do we define, qualify, and tailor those newly minted rights? To what extent should national or supranational governments be involved in establishing frameworks and rules regarding PGRs? Control and ownership are critical to questions of conservation of such PGRs. To understand contemporary control and ownership of PGRs, this chapter looks back at understandings of germplasm during the era of Western colonialism.

A. Colonialism, Germplasm Flow, and Selective Breeding: 16th–18th Centuries

The question is how does the historically uneven distribution of crop genetic diversity relate to the present uneven distributions of the benefits of such crop genetic diversity.

---

extended to PGRs. *See* Kloppenburg, FIRST THE SEED, *supra* Chapter One, note 1, at 152. For a comprehensive discussion of the concept of "common heritage" *see* Anthony J. Stenson & Tim S. Gray, THE POLITICS OF GENETIC RESOURCE CONTROL 136–53 (1999).

4. Plant viruses claim up to four-fifths of all cultivated crops. With increasing global population calling for increased agricultural output, it has been argued that making immune and disease-resistant crops is vital for the well-being of future generations. It has been further argued that crop improvement through biotechnology, among other means, leads to efficiency, productivity, and stability to an industry that is susceptible to pests, insects, and in most parts of the world, local weather conditions. *See* Karen M. Graziano, *Biosafety Protocol: Recommendations to Ensure the Safety of the Environment*, 7 COLO. J. INT'L ENVTL L. & POL'Y 179, 183–84 (1995).

5. Anupam Chander & Madhavi Sunder, *The Romance of the Public Domain*, 92 CAL. L. REV. 1331 (2004) [hereinafter Chander & Sunder, *Romance of the Public Domain*].

Wide diffusion of domesticated plant varieties has been ubiquitous throughout human history. Crop transplantation and adaptation into geographically distant, but hospitable, areas has been a frequent if nonsystemic practice.[6] However, beginning in the 16th century with nascent European colonialism, the flow of plant germplasm shifted dramatically following European contact between the "Old" and "New" Worlds.[7] Plant "wealth"—that is, germplasm—moved along with mineral wealth from empire's peripheries to enrich its core. Colonial plantation economies were an attempt to replace costly and distant sources in the "East" with a supply of valuable plant "wealth" such as tea, sugar, and spices. As Jack Kloppenburg points out, "plant germplasm is a resource that reproduces itself, and a single 'taking' of germplasm could provide the material base upon which whole new sectors of production could be elaborated."[8] Thus, unlike timber or mineral resources, the value of germplasm to the colonial powers was not proportional to the physical amount taken.

Central and South America and the Caribbean provided a cornucopia of immensely valuable plants such as tobacco, cocoa, quinine, sisal, and rubber, as well as geographically suitable sites for new plantation economies driven by chattel slavery cultivating bananas, tea, coffee, sugar, and indigo imported from other outposts of empire.[9] European powers vying for supremacy desperately sought to maintain exclusive control over plant resources such as nutmeg, clove, and indigo seeds.[10] Columbus brought maize seeds back to Europe in 1493; beans, potatoes, squash, sweet potatoes, cassava, and peanuts followed in subsequent years.[11] Kloppenburg describes how new crops from the Americas figured prominently in feeding a European population that nearly doubled between 1750 and 1850, even as the Industrial Revolution swept people off the land and into Marx's "dark, satanic mills."[12] Acquisition and transfer of plant germplasm by the European empires not only created the basis of plantation economies but also lowered the costs of feeding the swelling numbers of dispossessed European *lumpenproletariat*.

The European powers also created global networks of botanical gardens,[13] about which Lucile Brockway writes:

> As important as the physical removal of the plants was their improvement and development by a corps of scientists serving the Royal Botanic Gardens, a network of government botanical stations radiating out of Kew Gardens and

6. Wilkes, *Plant Genetic Resources, supra* Chapter One, note 23, at 67, 68.

7. Karl Marx, Capital, Vol. I at 915, 918 ("the discovery of gold and silver in America, the extirpation, enslavement and entombment in mines of indigenous population of that continent, the beginnings of the conquest and plunder of India, and the conversion of Africa into a preserve for the commercial hunting of blackskins, are all things which characterize the dawn of the era of capitalist production.... The Treasures captured outside Europe by undisguised looting, enslavement and murder flowed back to the mother-country and were turned into capital there."); *see also* Pat R. Mooney, The Law of the Seed, Development Dialogue, Vol. 1, No. 2 (1983) [hereinafter Mooney, Law of the Seed]; Lucille H. Brockway, Science and Colonial Expansion: The Role of the British Royal Botanical Gardens (1979)[hereinafter Brockway, Colonial Expansion].

8. Kloppenburg, First the Seed, *supra* Chapter One, note 1, at 154.

9. Brockway, Colonial Expansion, *supra* note 7.

10. Kloppenburg, First the Seed, *supra* Chapter One, note 1, at 154.

11. What A.W. Crosby called the "Columbian Exchange" went both ways, with germplasm transfers from Europe to the Americas of crops such as wheat, rye, and oats. *See* A.W. Crosby, The Columbian Exchange: Biological and Cultural Consequences of 1492 (1972).

12. Kloppenburg, First the Seed, *supra* Chapter One, note 1, at 156.

13. Brockway, Colonial Expansion, *supra* note 7.

stretching from Jamaica to Singapore to Fiji ... [and] regulated the flow of botanical information from the metropolis to the colonial satellites, and disseminated information emanating from them.[14]

Some governments responded to the imperial powers' germplasm appropriation and collection practices by trying to protect their native agricultural industries. Brazil prohibited the export of rubber tree germplasm in the late 19th century. At the time, Brazil held 95 percent of the world rubber market. However, British agents evaded the Brazilian rubber tree export ban by smuggling out a few seedlings. Britain subsequently established successful rubber plantations in their equatorial colonies of Ceylon and Singapore. The consequences of this colonial "biopiracy" reverberate in today's markets, where British and U.S. companies dominate the global rubber industry through raw latex supplies drawn from former colonial possessions such as Liberia and Malaysia.[15]

It is ironic that nations once treated plant germplasm as a strategic resource waiting to be exploited freely by any party who managed to appropriate a sample of that resource, given that multinational corporations looking to national patent law today view their patented seeds as legally protected from free appropriation. In fact, in the 19th century, any suggestion that the nation of Brazil "owned" rubber tree germplasm and possessed exclusive rights to produce latex would have been met with incredulity by the botanists at Royal Kew Gardens; the rubber produced by the rubber tree was a commodity but, at the time, the genotype of rubber tree itself was not. Likewise, any suggestion that 18th and 19th century (or for that matter, 20th century) European and U.S. industrialists "owed" compensation to indigenous communities in the Americas for the nourishment that potatoes provided to their workers would have seemed similarly ludicrous.

B. Government Subsidy: 19th through Early 20th Centuries

Kloppenburg has written that "[t]he introduction of plants into America has been much more than a great service; it has been an absolute imperative, a biological *sine qua non* upon which rests the whole complex edifice of American industrial society."[16] Because of the relative poverty in terms of plant genetic diversity successful European colonization of North America depended upon germplasm importation and adaptation, which in turn established a stable and growing food base for colonial American society.[17] Imported crop germplasm for some varieties of wheat, rye, oats, peas, peaches, cabbage, turnips, spinach, radishes, and onions successfully transplanted to

---

14. *Id.* at 6–7; Kloppenburg, FIRST THE SEED, *supra* Chapter One, note 1, at 301 n. 2 (noting the subsidiary gardens of the Royal Botanical Garden in Adelaide, Auckland, Bangladore, Barbados, Bombay, Brisbane, British Guiana, Calcutta, Cawnpore, Darjeeling, Dominica, Dublin, Edinburgh, Fiji, Glasgow, Gold Coast, Granada, Hong Kong, Jamaica, Lagos, Lucknow, Madras, Malacca, Malta, Mauritius, Melbourne, Mungpoo, Natal, Niger, Penang, Port Darwin, Saharanpur, Singapore, St. Lucia, Tasmania, Trinidad, and Wellington).

15. Brockway, COLONIAL EXPANSION, *supra* note 7, at 42; Kloppenburg, FIRST THE SEED, *supra* Chapter One, note 1, at 157.

16. Kloppenburg, FIRST THE SEED, *supra* Chapter One, note 1, at 50.

17. *Id.* at 46.

the new continent.[18] Farmers engaged in "simple mass selection" by picking out the best individual plants from one season and saving their seed for the following planting season. Successive waves of colonists brought additional varieties and natural cross-pollination between varieties provided additional genetic variety.

While botanical germplasm collection was ostensibly a genteel scientific pursuit, governments played a key role in its collection, transfer, and exploitation. Thomas Jefferson was an avid seed collector, receiving and growing rice varieties from China, Egypt, and Africa. Jefferson also belonged to seed exchange societies that helped distribute and introduce new varieties from other regions into new geographic areas.[19] These societies solicited aid from the new federal government in their project of testing to determine which crop varieties were capable of surviving in the American climate. Of course, this type of project engendered many failures in order to find the rare successful variety. Kloppenburg observes that the testing and introduction of new species

> was not a game that could be played successfully by the individual entrepreneur. True, Jefferson might have access to Chinese and Middle East rice, and Elkanah Wilson might use his wealth to funnel some of the world's germplasm back to his farm in Massachusetts, but neither individual altruism nor individual wealth could sustain plant collection over the time and at the scale needed to provide the country with the adapted base of germplasm it required for rapid agricultural development.[20]

Aware of the importance of establishing a stable agricultural foundation and the role that "exotic" plant germplasm played in that base, the U.S. government undertook various projects to support seed collection around the world. In 1819, the U.S. Treasury Department issued a directive requesting that consular and naval officials begin systematically collecting plant germplasm abroad.[21] By 1836, the U.S. Patent Office took interest in establishing a federally sponsored repository for the germplasm samples that were beginning to arrive as the Navy began overseeing official plant expeditions.[22] From 1839 onward, plant expeditions brought back seeds and cuttings from an increasing variety of plant breeds to a botanical greenhouse in Washington, D.C. The Patent Office in 1857 established a garden specifically designed to propagate and multiply seeds for widespread public distribution.[23]

At the time, private entrepreneurs were not particularly interested in making the investment necessary to search, find, cultivate, and select new breeds of plants, due to the difficulty of recouping investment. This situation presented a classic "public goods" problem.[24] The genetic information contained in the germplasm is present in the phe-

---

18. Conrad Zirkle, *Plant Hybridization and Plant Breeding in Eighteenth Century America*, 55 (1) AGR. HIST. 25 (1969).

19. Kloppenburg, FIRST THE SEED, *supra* Chapter One, note 1, at 52–53; *see also* Calestous Juma, THE GENE HUNTERS: BIOTECHNOLOGY AND THE SCRAMBLE FOR SEED, at 55 (1989)(referring to Thomas Jefferson as a "botanist-king")[hereinafter Juma, GENE HUNTERS].

20. Kloppenburg, FIRST THE SEED, *supra* Chapter One, note 1, at 54.

21. *Id.* at 53; Juma, GENE HUNTERS, *supra* note 19, at 57.

22. Kloppenburg, FIRST THE SEED, at 55; Norman Klose, AMERICA'S CROP HERITAGE: THE HISTORY OF FOREIGN PLANT INTRODUCTION BY THE FEDERAL GOVERNMENT, at 29 (1950) [hereinafter Klose]; *See also* Stephen B. Brush, FARMERS' BOUNTY: LOCATING CROP DIVERSITY IN THE CONTEMPORARY WORLD, at 22 (2004)[hereinafter Brush, FARMERS' BOUNTY].

23. Kloppenburg, FIRST THE SEED, *supra* Chapter One, note 1, at 55; Juma, GENE HUNTERS, *supra* note 19, at 57–58, 59.

24. Generally, economists define "public goods" as goods that are nonexcludable and nondepletable. *See* Andreu Mas-Colell et al., MICROECONOMIC THEORY 359–60 (1995); Joseph E. Stiglitz, ECONOMICS OF THE PUBLIC SECTOR 79–80 (3d ed., 2000). A "public good" has two characteristics:

notype of a plant variety. Furthermore, one who possesses a plant seed cannot, agriculturally speaking, foreclose others from reproducing seeds of the same plant variety. Once a seed was sold, the means of reproducing the seed went with it. This was also clear to many in the U.S. government in the 19th century. Yet the absence of private action and the importance of food security as state interest led to governmental action in building a broad and stable agricultural base.[25] This required collection, cultivation, wide selection, and propagation of exotic seed varieties that, in turn, would be widely distributed to U.S. farmers.[26]

The U.S. Patent Office lacked the resources in the 1840s to embark on an extensive breeding and agricultural research agenda. Instead, Patent Commissioner Henry Ellsworth arranged to have congressmen sympathetic to the Patent Office's seed distribution program send farmers packets of "exotic" seed specimens. By 1849, more than 60,000 packages were sent out annually to constituents.[27] Kloppenburg notes that

> [t]he development of the adapted base of germplasm on which American agriculture was raised is the product of thousands of experiments by thousands of farmers committing millions of hours of labor in thousands of diverse ecological niches over a period of many decades. Introductions might or might not be successful, but in any case they had an opportunity to cross naturally with land races, so that, even when they failed, they might leave a legacy of genetic variability … Individual farmers were responsible for developing improved cultivars, among the most famous being Red Fyfe wheat, Grimm alfalfa, and Rough Purple Chili potato, the germplasm sources being, respectively, Poland, Germany and Panama.
>
> The breeding method used by farmers was essentially no different from that employed by their Neolithic forbears.… [T]he nation's farmers employed simple mass selection to improve the land races of the crops they grew by screening out poorly adapted types and saving superior individuals and population for seed.[28]

Also aiding the creation of a stable and diverse agricultural base for American industrial capitalism was the establishment of agricultural schools *via* the 1862 Morrill Act authorization of Land Grant Colleges (LGCs).[29] The sale of public lands funded the

---

(1) jointness of supply, and (2) impossibility of exclusion. Jointness of supply means that consumption of one unit of the good does not foreclose others from using/consuming the good. Impossibility of exclusion means that because one may possess one unit of the good, one cannot prevent others from reproducing that particular good. Importantly, private parties will undersupply "public goods" because they cannot recoup their investment. Thus, government subsidy is a partial solution to the undersupply of important "public goods." For discussion of global public goods issues in the 21st century, *see* Peter M. Gerhart, *Distributive Values and Institutional Design in the Provision of Global Public Goods*, in INT'L PUBLIC GOODS, *supra* Chapter One, note 2, at 69. *See also* Margaret Chon's insightful discussion of the global public goods theory, Margaret Chon, *Intellectual Property and the Development Divide*, 27 CARDOZO L. REV. 2821, 2878–84 (2006)[hereinafter Chon, *Development Divide*].

25. Juma, GENE HUNTERS, *supra* note 19, at 57 ("At this moment [the 1830s] in the history of the U.S., the interpretation of national security clearly encompassed the need to to respond to the growing complexity of agriculture and its links with the rest of the economy.").

26. Kloppenburg, FIRST THE SEED, *supra* Chapter One, note 1, at 54; Klose, *supra* note 22, at 43.

27. Kloppenburg, FIRST THE SEED, *supra* Chapter One, note 1, at 56.

28. *Id.* at 56–57.

29. *Id.* at 58; Jim Hightower, HARD TOMATOES, HARD TIMES: A REPORT OF THE AGRIBUSINESS ACCOUNTABILITY PROJECT ON THE FAILURE OF AMERICA'S LAND GRANT COLLEGE COMPLEX, 8 (1973); David B. Danbom, THE RESISTED REVOLUTION: URBAN AMERICA AND THE INDUSTRIALIZA-

LGCs, which in turn supported agricultural education and research.[30] Congress also created the USDA in 1862 to administer agricultural activities previously held under Patent Office's Division of Agriculture.[31] In particular, the USDA was charged with responsibilities for collecting and disseminating plant germplasm. By the time the Hatch Act passed in 1887, thus establishing and funding a network of State Agricultural Experiment Stations (SAESs),[32] a U.S. system for collecting, propagating, evaluating, selecting, introducing, and distributing new varieties of plant germplasm was well in place.

A key feature of the public seed distribution program was that seeds were distributed "free" of charge. The program was tax-funded, but there was no assurance that crops grown from the free seeds would have any market value. Meanwhile, a small private seed industry that specialized in selling European vegetable varieties to home gardeners had begun developing, and commercial farmers generally produced their own seeds, which they traded amongst and between themselves.[33] But the public seed distribution program gained widespread popularity such that, "[b]etween 1850 and 1856 the Patent Office agricultural division budget increased from $4,500 to $75,000.... By 1861, a total of 2,474,380 packages of seed, the bulk of which contained common vegetable and flower varieties were being distributed through congressmen to their constituents."[34]

By the 1890s, the private seed industry had begun organizing opposition to the government seed-giveaway program. The American Seed Trade Association (ASTA) formed in 1883 in order to lobby for discontinuation of the government distribution program.[35] The ASTA found a sympathetic audience with J. Sterling Morton, President Grover Cleveland's Secretary of Agriculture, who also sought to discontinue the seed-distribution program. Morton observed:

TION OF AGRICULTURE, 17 (1979); Lawrence Busch & William B. Lacy, SCIENCE, AGRICULTURE, AND THE POLITICS OF RESEARCH (1983).

30. Kloppenburg, FIRST THE SEED, supra Chapter One, note 1, at 58–59 ("Most farmers were even less enthusiastic about the prospect of agricultural colleges. Their uneasiness about the hybridization of these two words centered on a fear that education would teach them nothing about farming that they did not already know and yet cost them much.... Little wonder, then, that an eastern senator, Justin Morrill of Vermont, introduced the land-grant legislation and that it was in the states where agriculture was least important that the bill found its principal support.... [I]n 1862, with secession removing southern resistance and a Homestead Act assuaging western worries, the Land Grant College Act was approved.").

31. Gladys L. Baker, W.D. Rasmussen, V. Wiser, & J.M. Porter, CENTURY OF SERVICE: THE FIRST ONE HUNDRED YEARS OF THE DEPARTMENT OF AGRICULTURE (1963); Kloppenburg, FIRST THE SEED, supra Chapter One, note 1, at 59–60; Klose, supra note 21, at 43; Juma, GENE HUNTERS, supra note 19, at 60–61.

32. Kloppenburg, FIRST THE SEED, supra Chapter One, note 1, at 60; Frederick H. Buttel & Jill M. Belsky, Biotechnology, Plant Breeding and Intellectual Property—Social and Ethical Dimensions [hereinafter Buttel & Belsky] at 113, in OWNING SCIENTIFIC AND TECHNICAL INFORMATION, VALUE AND ETHICAL ISSUES (Vivien Weil & John W. Snapper eds., 1989); Richard S. Kirkendall, SOCIAL SCIENTISTS AND FARM POLITICS IN THE AGE OF ROOSEVELT (1982); Juma, GENE HUNTERS, supra note 19, at 63–64.

33. Juma, GENE HUNTERS, supra note 19, at 60 ("During this period, the government seemed to make it difficult for private seed companies to operate. Some people used government seed for planting their regular vegetable gardens and not for experimental purposes.").

34. Kloppenburg, FIRST THE SEED, supra Chapter One, note 1, at 61, 63. Ultimately, the top volume of USDA-distributed seed reached 22.2 million packages in 1897. Because each package contained five packets of different varieties, the actual total of seed packets sent out by the USDA reached 1.1 billion that year.

35. Buttel & Belsky, supra note 32, at 113. The ASTA finally achieved its goal their goal in 1924, when Congress ended the seed distribution program.

the seed trade was no longer an infant industry and that private enterprise could put new plant varieties into the hands of farmers and consumers two to three years more quickly than could the government.... [and] the seed was being disseminated 'gratuitously,' that is, without charge, *in a manner antagonistic to the seed as a commodity-form and in direct competition with the private seed trade.*[36]

Although Morton opposed the program's continuation, widespread popular support for the program translated into staunch Congressional backing, which prevented any diminution of government seed distribution.[37] However, while "free" seed distribution programs were politically popular, other structural changes in the agricultural economy would ultimately lead to the program's demise. One such change was the 20th century transformation of plant breeding from a practical "art" into a profitable "science."

C. Hybrid Vigor: 1900–1930s

Today, Gregor Mendel (1822–1884) is widely considered "the father of genetics." However, the Augustinian monk's studies on trait heritability in plants remained largely ignored until plant breeders rediscovered his work around 1900[38] and began the transformation of plant breeding into a lucrative "science."[39] This transformation moved plant breeding away from the centuries-old simple mass selection techniques for varietal development employed by the SAESs, LGCs, and farmers, toward selection as the targeted manipulation of select isolated traits. By the 1890s, some public plant breeders in the SAESs and LGCs had already developed interest in the phenomenon of heterosis, or hybridization, which they regarded as a way to get beyond simple mass selection to achieve varietal development. At the time, hybridization "meant the cross-breeding or sexual combination of two varieties of plant or animal [and a] hybrid was simply the product of such a union."[40] However, the U.S. state-sponsored public seed sector was not in position to fully explore and develop the implications of Mendelian genetics, in part because of the pressure from farmers to continue and expand the seed distribution program.[41] Additionally, government would not distribute publicly-bred seed unless it had reached a point of superiority relative to existing cultivars.

---

36. Kloppenburg, FIRST THE SEED, *supra* Chapter One, note 1, at 62–63.

37. Kloppenburg, FIRST THE SEED, *supra* Chapter One, note 1, at 64 ("[T]he department insisted on purchasing seed of good quality.... The department became increasingly discriminating in its purchase of seed, and by 1886 had established testing procedures to assess germination rates and cleanliness and was requiring the seed it bought meet particular standards of quality ... [and] was very likely to be fresh seed of top quality ... [contrasting] sharply with that for much of the seed purveyed by the commercial seed trade.").

38. *Id.* at 69; Ernst Mayr, THE GROWTH OF BIOLOGICAL THOUGHT (1982); Charles E. Rosenberg, NO OTHER GODS: ON SCIENCE AND AMERICAN SOCIAL THOUGHT, at 90 (1976).

39. Kloppenburg, FIRST THE SEED, *supra* Chapter One, note 1, at 77; Edward M. East, THE RELATION OF CERTAIN BIOLOGICAL PRINCIPLES TO PLANT BREEDING (1908); Juma, GENE HUNTERS, *supra* note 19, at 80; Fowler, UNNATURAL SELECTION, *supra* Chapter One, note 2, at 118–19.

40. Kloppenburg, FIRST THE SEED, *supra* Chapter One, note 1, at 68. (Noting that "after 1935, the term "hybridization" assumed a much narrower meaning in reference to a combination of two inbred lines, as in hybrid corn.").

41. *Id.* at 77 ("If Mendel was necessary for rapid progress he was not sufficient, and despite the hopes of some, there was to be no swift outpouring of markedly superior new plant varieties."); *see*

The nascent private seed industry was similarly slow, at least initially, to apprehend the implications of Mendelian genetics. At the turn of the 20th century, private seed companies focused on establishing market share for private seeds and eliminating the governmental seed distribution system. Private industry's primary inroad came through vegetables and forage grasses, which are harvested for leafy growth or immature fruit rather than for seed. The private seed market for grains was almost nonexistent at this time, due largely to free government seed distribution and the widespread practice of farmer seed saving.[42] As previously mentioned, there was also the matter of qualitative disparity between government-distributed seed and seed sold by private companies. In the early 20th century, a number of state legislatures passed laws regulating the labeling and marketing of seeds, thereby limiting the degree to which private seed companies could engage in branding and product differentiation through advertising,[43] thus adding to the sense of struggle that the private seed industry experienced.[44]

Despite the lack of widespread practical acceptance for hybridization, some public plant breeders began paying attention to the insights of Mendelian genetics in conjunction with their single-line selection experiments—namely, "segregating and reproducing seed from single plants, applying continuous selection to subsequent generations, and paying attention to the value of variance revealed in the populations."[45] This meant that "[t]wo varieties would be cross-bred, [producing] new genetic variability ... [and] [s]ingle line selection was then applied to the progeny of the cross," thereby transferring individual characteristics from one variety to another.[46] Plant breeders' growing understanding of hybridization shifted their focus from merely collecting and cultivating "exotic" varieties to looking for particular traits in "exotic" germplasm samples.[47] These plants could be backcrossed with existing varieties, then subjected to single line selection. The significance of which came in how plant breeders' goals changed from trying to adapt exotic germplasm to U.S. soil and climate conditions to "improving" existing varieties by backcrossing disease resistance, higher yield, or other beneficial traits from exotic germplasm.[48]

---

also Jean-Pierre Berlan & Richard C. Lewontin, *Breeders' Rights and Patenting Life Forms*, 322 NATURE 785–8 (1986) [hereinafter Berlan & Lewontin, *Breeders' Rights*].

42. Farmers' abilities to provide for their own seed requirement effectively excluded private industry from the most widely grown and therefore potentially most lucrative crops in wheat. For example, 97 percent of the seed used in 1915 was sown on the farm where it was produced. Sales between farmers almost entirely accounted for the remaining three percent. *See* John Seabrook, *Annals of Agriculture: Sowing for Apocalypse*, THE NEW YORKER 60 (August 27, 2007) [hereinafter Seabrook, *Sowing for Apocalypse*].

43. Willard Cochrane, THE DEVELOPMENT OF AMERICAN AGRICULTURE: A HISTORICAL ANALYSIS at 352 (1979); Kloppenburg, FIRST THE SEED, *supra* Chapter One, note 1, at 39; Richard C. Lewontin, *Agricultural Research and the Penetration of Capital*, 14 SCIENCE FOR THE PEOPLE 12 (1982); James K. Feibleman, *Pure Science, Applied Science, and Technology: An Attempt at Definitions*, 4 (2) TECH. & CULT. 305 (1961).

44. Kloppenburg, FIRST THE SEED, *supra* Chapter One, note 1, at 72–73.

45. *Id.* at 78.

46. *Id.* at 79.

47. *Ibid.* ("Breeders no longer sought in plant introductions new varieties that might be superior to current ones; they looked at exotic germplasm for *specific traits* that could be transferred to established varieties.").

48. Fowler, UNNATURAL SELECTION, *supra* Chapter One, note 2, at 62 ("The science of plant breeding could not be separated from the economy of plant breeding and commercial agriculture.... Hybrid corn was a proprietary product. Farmers could not know what inbred lines had been used to produce the hybrid, nor did they have access to the privately developed lines. Private breeders could thus 'own' the variety by controlling the inbreds that constituted it and the knowledge of how the hybrid was produced.").

Much of this early experimental work took place at the publicly-funded LGCs and SAESs that also created seed certification programs in order to ensure seed quality. However, seed certification programs undermined private seed companies' attempts to enlarge market share by cutting down on the latter's ability to engage in product differentiation and by focusing buyer attention on certification rather than brand.[49] Thus, by the 1920s three important institutional obstacles to private capital investment and accumulation in the plant seed-breeding and sales industry existed:

(1) publicly-funded development and nonexclusive release of improved seed varieties;

(2) seed certification programs that moderated prices by allowing farmers to buy seeds from the lowest priced supplier; and

(3) governmental assurance that seed varieties that were sold and merchandised under their original names.

This meant that "finished" varieties "created" and distributed by public agencies competed directly in the marketplace with those varieties produced by private plant breeders. This public presence structured and disciplined the seed market for quality and price, thereby limiting the private ability to increase market share. Thus, the private seed industry argued for ending the free government distribution of seeds,[50] citing the facts of drastic agricultural price slides in the 1920s and stagnant agricultural yields from 1900 to 1920 as justification. In 1924, Congress finally heeded ASTA's decades-long lobbying and voted to cut the USDA's seed distribution program, which had been in place in one form or another since the 1830s and had taken approximately ten percent of the agency's budget in 1921.[51]

The Great Depression also spurred criticism of the USDA's agricultural research results and its budget allocations that had not produced increased agricultural yields. Although Congress became concerned by these criticisms, it instead focused on enacting agricultural price supports and loan programs.[52] Meanwhile, President Roosevelt's Secretary of Agricultural Henry A. Wallace (former president of the Hi-Bred Corn Company; son of Henry C. Wallace, President Harding's Secretary of Agriculture) lobbied for and received increased federal support for agricultural research into plant genetics, targeted towards increasing crop yield.[53] Secretary Wallace also strengthened the infrastructure of public agricultural research at SAESs and LGCs, with a clear change of emphasis from using traditional selective breeding techniques to experimenting with Mendelian genetics as providing a foundation for hybridization in the name of plant "improvement."[54]

---

49. *Id.* at 81 ("Seed companies were welcome to purchase certified seed from crop improvement association growers, but public breeders had no intention of permitting the seed trade to become an exclusive conduit for dissemination of their work to the farming community.... Public breeders were in effect setting benchmarks of quality, and the association of certification with quality leveled prices among different varieties.... [and] greatly reduced the possibilities for product differentiation.").

50. *Id.* at 84 ("[P]roductivity was static between 1900 and 1934. Despite advances made in plant breeding, yields were also static during this period.").

51. Buttel & Belsky, *supra* note 32, at 113.

52. Kloppenburg, FIRST THE SEED, *supra* Chapter One, note 1, at 87 ("Political struggle in the agricultural sector during the Depression focused not on research but on product markets and on issues such as price support, loans, land tenure and parity.").

53. *Id.* at 86 (discussing the Bankhead-Jones Act of 1935, under which Secretary Wallace received federal support for plant genetic research, "[T]he Bankhead-Jones Act was principally the product of an articulate scientific elite allied with private interests and represented by agricultural journals and corporations."). Hi-Bred Corn later became Pioneer Hi-Bred. *See also* Seabrook, *Sowing for Apocalypse*, *supra* note 42, at 66.

54. Fowler, UNNATURAL SELECTION, *supra* Chapter One, note 2, at 87–88.

Two other developments in the 1930s produced shifts that would mark the transformation of the 20th century agricultural industry. First, private seed companies became interested in germplasm, particularly as techniques to improve plant varieties became available. The biological barrier that seeds had presented to private investment was about to fall. As a product, the seed also contained the means of its own reproduction, making it particularly difficult for private industry to recoup investments made in seed improvement; a buyer/farmer could simply replant reproduced saved seed. Hybridization takes care of this "problem." Although first-generation hybrids produce very high yields, second- and third-generation hybrid progeny produce drastically lower yields.[55] Thus, the farmer who bought high-yield hybrid seed had to return to the seed company the next season if (s)he wanted continued high yields.

The second transformative development came as the focus of public agricultural research conducted at SAESs and LGCs moved into "basic" research and away from experimenting with non-proprietary open-line hybrids.[56] This shift left the "application" (creating seed "products") of "basic" research to private seed companies, which began building a market among farmers for improved closed-line proprietary hybrid seed that were unavailable elsewhere.

Corn was the first major hybrid success from the late-1930s onward.[57] Corn yields had been in decline in the U.S. prior to the introduction of hybrid corn varieties, but by 1965, high-yield hybrid seed covered over 95 percent of corn acreage.[58] Kloppenburg notes that

> [d]espite a reduction of 30 million acres on which grain corn was harvested between 1930 and 1965, the volume of production increased by over 2.3 billion bushels.... [a]nd hybrid corn's 700 percent annual return on investment remains the much cited and archetypical example of the substantial returns society enjoys from agricultural research.[59]

Before the mid-1930s farmers had been the main breeders of corn, planting a mix of the Northern Flint and Southern Dent corn land-races, both derived from Native American maize germplasm.[60] The genetic diversity in the mix of these two land-races combined with the open-pollinated nature of corn created conditions of genetic dynamism and fluidity.[61] Corn's open-pollinating nature originally vexed plant breeders and resulted in

---

55. *Id.* at 99 ("[S]eed saved from the double cross [hybrid] cannot be saved and replanted without substantial yield reduction ...").

56. *Id.* at 109 ("private-sector spokesmen urged public breeders to concentrate on the development of inbred lines and to leave the decision as to particular combinations of inbreds to be marketed as commercial hybrids to private breeders.").

57. *Id.* at 91–94; Norman W. Simmonds, PRINCIPLES OF CROP IMPROVEMENT at 161–2 (1979); Leonard Steele, *The Hybrid Corn Industry in the United States*, at 29 *in* MAIZE, BREEDING AND GENETICS (D.B. Walden ed., 1978); *See also* Fowler, UNNATURAL SELECTION, *supra* Chapter One, note 2, at 52 ("The first commercial hybrid was Funk's "Pure Line Double Cross no. 250" developed in 1922 and introduced in 1928 ... [while][i]t was not adopted on a wide scale.... hybrid corn [went] from 0.4 percent of corn acreage in 1933 to 90 percent in 1945.").

58. Kloppenburg, FIRST THE SEED, *supra* Chapter One, note 1, at 91.

59. *Id.* at 92.

60. *Id.* at 94.

61. *Id.* at 94–95 ("[G]enetic variability in corn varieties was constantly enhanced as a result of the sexual morphology of the corn plant itself. Unlike most other principal crops, corn is an outbreeder (allogamus) rather than an inbreeder (autogamous). It is open- or cross-pollinated rather than self-fertilized, and each kernel on an ear of corn may be fertilized with pollen from a different plant.... in corn nearly every plant is a product of a unique cross.").

unpredictable yields. Even if farmers found a superior variety, it was very difficult to stabilize it from season to season. Yet by 1918, a plausible method for creating a corn hybrid emerged from the Connecticut SAES.[62] This method, called "double-cross" in-breeding (self-fertilization), produced a high-yield seed with low-yield offspring. The advantage to a private plant breeder was obvious: farmers could not easily duplicate the hybrid vigor via seed saving. In 1919, Edward M. East and Donald F. Jones, the public plant breeders from the Connecticut SAES, published "Inbreeding and Outbreeding: Their Genetic and Sociological Significance." East and Jones described their hybridiza-tion method, noting both the emergence of the seed as a commodity and alluding to in-tellectual property rights in their method:

> [Our method of producing hybrid corn] is the first time in agricultural history that a seedsman is enabled to gain the full benefit from a desirable origination of his own or something that he has purchased. The man who originates de-vices to open boxes of shoe polish or to autograph our camera negatives, is able to patent his product and gain the full reward for his inventiveness. The man who originates a new plant which may be of incalculable benefit to the whole country gets nothing—not even fame—for his pains, as the plants can be propagated by anyone.... the utilization of first generation hybrids enables the originator to keep the parental types and give out only the crossed seeds, which are less valuable for continued propagation.[63]

By the 1920s, the USDA had abandoned its work on open-pollinated breeding and se-lection of corn varieties. Instead, the USDA focused on self-fertilized lines producing hy-brid offspring. Driven by demands for increased crop yields and funded by the Purnell Act of 1925, the USDA created a national corn-breeding program, the goal of which was to develop a viable double-cross corn hybrid.[64] By 1935, public agencies had developed hybrid varieties that were some ten- to fifteen-percent better yielding than their open-pollinated counterparts. Still, as Kloppenburg notes, "hybrid corn required a reorienta-tion of the farmer ... [who] would have to be taught to accept the hybrid seed."[65]

D. The Shifting Emphasis between Public and Private Seed Research

By the 1930s, hybridization had breached the biological barrier against the com-modification of germplasm. Still, the fact that government had long been an ex-tremely efficient competitor with private seed companies presented another obstacle.[66] Yet the hybrid corn seed market proved extremely lucrative. Private firms

---

62. *Id.* at 99.

63. *Ibid.*; Edward M. East & Donald F. Jones, INBREEDING AND OUTBREEDING: THEIR GENETIC AND SOCIOLOGICAL SIGNIFICANCE (1919).

64. Kloppenburg, FIRST THE SEED, *supra* Chapter One, note 2, at 103 (This was a formidable task, "given only 100 inbred lines, there are 11,765,675 possible double-cross combinations.").

65. *Id.* at 104; *see also* Seabrook, *Sowing for Apocalypse*, note 42.

66. *Id.* ("[T]he 'miracle of hybrid corn' is certainly impressive, but hardly miraculous. It was the product of political machination, a solid decade of intensive research effort, and the application of human and financial resources.... Two decades before the Manhattan Project, the agricultural sec-tor had already witnessed the birth of big science.").

began producing their own hybrids and worked to reinvigorate a costive commercial seed market. Initially, private seed companies produced publicly developed open-line varieties such as USDA Hybrid 13.[67] For obvious reasons, private firms disliked the open-pedigree lines and moved quickly toward developing proprietary closed-pedigree lines.[68] Yet, when faced with high research and development costs, very few could compete effectively with the USDA's long-standing hybrid development programs.

During the 1940s, relations between the two sectors grew increasingly antagonistic, as each engaged in the directly competitive business of developing and marketing hybrid corn. Professional associations such as the International Crop Improvement Association, the American Society of Agronomy, and the American Society for Horticultural Science sought to reshape the boundary between public and private agricultural research.[69] These organizations articulated the idea that the proper place for public investment was in "fundamental" or "basic" research, while the proper role for private seed companies was to develop and bring to market closed-line proprietary hybrids. The divisions of labor between LGCs and SAESs were redrawn during this period, as well, with publicly funded institutions focusing only on "fundamental" agricultural resources that were complementary, rather than competitive with private investment:

> "Fundamental" meant moving away from the commodity-form, that is, away from the finished variety. Private-sector spokesmen urged public breeders to concentrate on the development of inbred lines and to leave the decision as to particular combinations of inbreds to be marketed as commercial hybrids to private breeders.... Private corn breeders argued that public funds should not be used to pursue activities that attract private investment, that public duplication of private efforts was wasteful, and that a reorientation of public effort would free resources for training and basic research.[70]

The publicly-funded seed development infrastructure was thus transformed during this period into a "source" of raw materials, information, and germplasm upon which private entrepreneurial firms could draw to "create" proprietary and lucrative hybrid seed products.[71] Meanwhile, the private seed industry used various breeding techniques based on "fundamental" research in order to create their own proprietary products. An example of which is D.F. Jones'[72] technique for incorporating cytoplasmic male sterility into female

---

67. *Id.* at 107.

68. *Ibid.* (quoting a USDA public corn breeder critical of private breeders from 1936: "Among the private corn breeders and producers of hybrid corn, a tendency seems to be developing to regard the information they have on their lines and the pedigrees of their hybrids as trade secrets which they are reluctant to divulge.").

69. *Id.* at 109.

70. *Id.* at 108–09.

71. *Id.* at 110–11 ("In withdrawing from the development of commercial hybrids, public corn breeding simultaneously subordinated itself to private enterprise.... With seed companies alone producing commercial hybrids, private enterprise is interposed between public research and the consumer of seed. The products of public research can enter production, and thus have value, only if seed companies choose to use them.").

72. *Id.* at 113. Interestingly, Jones applied for and received a patent in his method, which was challenged and litigated by the private seed industry, who wanted to be free to use the technique without paying royalties. *Id.* at 115 ("Jones' action threatened the seed industry with the prospect of paying for scientific work, which previously had been available as a subsidized public good."); Fowler, Unnatural Selection, *supra* Chapter One, note 2, at 51–52.

parent lines and incorporating "restorer" genes in the male parents. This technique induced cytoplasmic sterility in female corn plants and thereby eliminated the need for manual detasseling (the labor costs for which had risen sharply after World War II).[73] A public plant breeder had developed this technique, and Jones' innovation substantially reduced labor costs for private industry in developing closed-line proprietary hybrids.[74]

Initial efforts at hybridization in crops other than corn produced mixed results.[75] Crops such as sugar beets, sorghum, spinach, onions, and cucumbers had only qualified commercial success. Those crops that were more difficult to hybridize have nonetheless undergone significant modifications through mass selection to increase their compatibility with farm machinery. For example, tomato breeders produced fruit with thicker skin to facilitate mechanical harvesting. Similarly, breeders selected rice, sorghum, and cotton for traits such as uniform maturity, concentrated fruit sets, and shape, to make these crops more compatible with mechanization.[76]

E. The "Green Revolution" and Genetic Erosion

As the example of hybridization shows, rapid changes in biotechnology transformed agriculture in the 20th century. In so doing, these changes also brought serious potential threats to world food security. As discussed before, the biotech industry hearkens back to the early 20th century, when agronomists in the U.S. and Europe rediscovered the work of Gregor Mendel, the 19th century Augustinian abbot who studied heredity in pea plants.[77] Although Mendel's work was largely ignored when it was first published, it laid the groundwork for hybrid crop development in the 1920s and 1930s. From the 1930s onward technological advances and mechanization hastened the industrialization of U.S. agriculture and shifted seed research and development from the public to the private sector.

Robert Evenson has written that five interrelated "revolutions" transformed agriculture in the U.S. (and globally) in the 19th and 20th century: (1) mechanization; (2) the widespread use of agrichemicals; (3) livestock industrialization; (4) the introduction of high-yielding crops, including hybrids; and (5) recombinant DNA (the "gene revolution"). This section looks specifically at the interaction between the agrichemical "revolution" and the "Green Revolution."[78]

---

73. Kloppenburg, FIRST THE SEED, *supra* Chapter One, note 2, at 113 ("The seed industry quickly adopted the process and over the next decade incorporated [cytoplasmic male sterility] and restorer materials into its commercial lines.").

74. *Id.*

75. *Id.* at 124–25 ("[A]part from a handful of crops, hybridization has made less headway than expected, given the interest in it and the substantial resources devoted to its development.").

76. *Id.* at 126–27.

77. In 1899 the Royal Horticultural Society organized the International Conference on Hybridisation and on Cross-Breeding of Varieties featuring prominent scientists, including H.J. Webber of the USDA's Plant Breeding Laboratory and Liberty Hyde Bailey of Cornell University. Some participants predicted that science was soon to make a significant impact on plant breeding. A year later, European botanists Hugo de Vries, Carl Correns, and Erich Tschermak independently published papers detailing rules of heredity that were later found to have been proposed by Gregor Mendel thirty-five years earlier. Across the Atlantic, a Washington State Agricultural Experiment Station wheat breeder ensured the acceptance of these new theories in the United States when he came very close to an independent rediscovery of Mendelian inheritance in 1901. *See Id.* at 68–69.

78. Robert E. Evenson, *Agricultural Research and Intellectual Property Rights, in* INT'L PUBLIC GOODS, *supra* Chapter One, note 2, at 188.

By the late 1960s, widespread Malthusian fears that the world would not be able to feed its ever-increasing population, especially in the developing world, paved the way for a new trend in agriculture. The so-called "Green Revolution"[79] caused the economic dislocation of subsistence farmers around the world. High-input farming techniques and systems displaced small, local agricultural practices, bringing with them their expensive fertilizers, pesticides, herbicides, and other high-input chemical interventions which intended to allow 'one seed to feed the world.'[80] By the 1980s, many people began to see that the "Green Revolution" was causing widespread environmental degradation due to extensive agrichemical runoff, with disastrous effects on the preservation of plant genetic diversity worldwide.[81]

During the 1970s advances in molecular biology made possible the genetic engineering of crops and other living organisms. The question was whether genetic engineering was part of the problem or part of the solution.

Genetic engineering in terms of commercial crops necessarily entails decreased genetic diversity, which is detrimental. The uniformity of genetically modified seeds makes them less resistant to disease. Because plants bred from similar strands are all vulnerable to the same pests and diseases, a single instance of disease can spread rapidly, practically unchecked, amongst the entire crop. By contrast, traditional genetically diverse landraces developed their own natural defenses against disease. The genetic diversity present in farmers' landraces is an insurance policy for cultivated crops. While one

---

79. Scientists working under the auspices of the Rockefeller and Ford foundations, which funded international agricultural research centers, were the main catalysts behind the Green Revolution. These two foundations had united what were disparate, privately-funded centers into a coordinated network in the hope of sidestepping the bureaucracy of that system while, at the same time, exploiting the legitimacy that comes with the perception of being part of the U.N. system. *See* Fowler, UNNATURAL SELECTION, *supra* Chapter One, note 2, at 182–83; Seabrook, *Sowing for Apocalypse, supra* note 42.

80. The "Green Revolution" led to widespread modern agriculture worldwide. This new agriculture relied heavily on chemical inputs, machinery, technology, research and development networks, and state-supported investment. Elizabeth Bowles & Andhra Pradesh, *India as a Case Study in Perspectives on GMO's*, 34 CUMB. L. REV. 415, 415 (2004); *see also* Fowler & Mooney, *supra* Chapter 1, note 9, 130–31 (1990) (stating that due to their reliance on chemical inputs and farm machinery the seeds developed as part of the Green Revolution opened up the world to agrichemical concerns). For a comprehensive discussion on the Green Revolution, *see* Jack Doyle, ALTERED HARVEST: AGRICULTURE, GENETICS, AND THE FATE OF THE WORLD'S FOOD SUPPLY 255–81 (1985) [hereinafter Doyle, ALTERED HARVEST]; Pat Mooney, SEEDS OF THE EARTH: A PRIVATE OR PUBLIC RESOURCE?, 37–46 (1979) [hereinafter Mooney, SEEDS OF THE EARTH].

81. The success of the "Green Revolution" specifically in Punjab, India, as elsewhere, was predicated on the displacement of genetic diversity on two levels. First, mixtures of diverse crops like wheat, maize, millets, pulses, and oil seeds were replaced by monocultures of wheat and rice. Second, the wheat and rice introduced were reproduced from large-scale monocultures that were derived from a very narrow genetic base. *See* Vandana Shiva, THE VIOLENCE OF THE GREEN REVOLUTION: THIRD WORLD, AGRICULTURE, ECOLOGY, AND POLITICS 51 (1992) [hereinafter Shiva, GREEN REVOLUTION]. The well-recognized environmental costs resulting from the Green Revolution's promotion of irrigation, fertilizers, pesticides, and herbicides include fertilizer and pesticide runoff into surface waters, and greater soil erosion. *See* Michael R. Taylor & Jerry Cayford, *American Patent Policy, Biotechnology, and African Agriculture: The Case for Policy Change*, 17 HARV. J. L. & TECH. 321, 328 n. 19 (2004) (citing Gordon Conway, THE DOUBLY GREEN REVOLUTION: FOOD FOR ALL IN THE 21ST CENTURY (1997)). The increased use of pesticides specifically is significant. Of the estimated 2.5 million tons of pesticides applied annually worldwide, only 0.3 percent reaches the intended target. All the remaining tonnage enters the environment as runoff, seepage into groundwater, volatilization into the air, intake by plants and soil organisms, or retention in the soil. Paula Barrios, *The Rotterdam Convention on Hazardous Chemicals: A Meaningful Step Toward Environmental Protection?*, 16 GEO. INT'L ENVTL L. REV. 679, 688 (2004).

variety of a cultivated crop might be vulnerable to a particular pest or disease, farmer seed-saving and the availability of genetic diversity in wild and weedy relatives in landraces protects the particular variety from widespread epidemics and harvest destruction.[82] When plant breeders began selecting plants for certain characteristics (such as yield and taste) until they arrived at a "pure line" that reproduced uniformly,[83] they inadvertently and unintentionally opened a Pandora's box that led to widespread crop monoculture and increased crop vulnerability.

Two historical events illustrate the importance of genetic diversity: the Irish potato famine during the 1840s and the Southern Corn Leaf Blight during the 1970s. Though many blamed weather for the Irish potato famine, a potato blight called *Phytophtora infestans* actually caused for this disaster. Since all of the potatoes in Ireland descended from one crop line from the Andes, they had no natural resistance to the disease, and it spread rapidly amongst the potato fields.[84] Eventually a potato variety that was resistant to *Phytophtora infestans* was discovered amongst the thousands of distinct potato varieties found in the Andes and in Mexico. The Southern Corn Leaf Blight exhibited a similarly disturbing pattern. A manmade change to corn plants, designed to make a high-yield hybrid corn seed, caused it to be vulnerable to the fungus *Helminthosporium maydis.*[85] One billion bushels of corn were lost to the blight during 1970–1971. Official reports described the blight as caused by "a quirk in the technology that had redesigned the corn plants of America until, in one sense, they had become as alike as identical twins. Whatever made one plant susceptible made them all susceptible."[86]

In their natural environment, plants and their pests co-evolve as they continuously adapt to each other. This means: "[l]andraces, because they have survived so long among pests and diseases in the centers of diversity, offer a wealth of potential resistance."[87] Breeders turn to these landraces when they cannot find resistance for a particular disease among the varieties they have bred. Wild species may offer the only resistance for the most rare and serious diseases. Genetic erosion, or the loss of genetic diversity, can eliminate plants' only defense against disease.

Yet the value of genetic diversity extends beyond simply being a stopgap against diseases and pests. Without variation, some crops can cease to evolve effectively and may eventually become extinct. Modern, genetically engineered crops "would be incapable of changing, of evolving, of adapting to new conditions, or stronger pests."[88] In other words, there would be no agriculture if not for landraces.

This statement reveals how critical genetic diversity is. Decreased diversity means more than just the loss of a specific gene. It can also cause the extinction of entire varieties, as Cary Fowler explains:

> The genetic diversity being lost today is the foundation of future plant breeding, of future plant evolution. If enough diversity is lost, the ability of crops to adapt and evolve will have been destroyed. We will not have to wait for the last wheat plant to shrivel up and die before wheat can be considered extinct. It will

82. Fowler & Mooney, SHATTERING, *supra* Chapter One, note 11, at 42.
83. *Id.* at 46.
84. *Id.* at 43.
85. Doyle, ALTERED HARVEST, *supra* note 80, at 13.
86. *Id.* at 14.
87. Fowler & Mooney, SHATTERING, *supra* Chapter One, note 11, at 50.
88. *Id.* at 53; *see also* Seabrook, *Sowing for Apocalypse, supra* note 42.

become extinct when it loses the ability to evolve, and when neither its genetic defenses nor our chemicals are able to protect it. And this day might come quietly even as millions of acres of wheat blanket the earth.[89]

Production and distribution of uniform varieties and hybrids are not the only causes of genetic erosion. Habitat destruction and the abandonment of traditional varieties also contribute to the extinction of old varieties: "Dams, occasional famines that cause people to eat up their seeds, church parking lots, and oil drilling that affect certain trees, all constitute a certain degree of danger to genetic resources."[90] Genetic erosion is a danger that threatens to cause the degradation and eventual extinction of agriculture. Thousands of unknown and unidentified varieties in remote regions are lost each year. While there are no simple solutions to this problem, since the 1970s there have been systemic efforts to collect plant genetic resources (PGRs) in *ex situ* seed banks for future use.

F. Summary

This chapter provided a brief overview of the history of seed cultivation, focusing on three periods. During the Colonial era, plants were considered to be a form of national property. In the 19th century, U.S. federal and state governments heavily subsidized seed cultivation. In the period leading up to the 1930s, the private seed industry moved in to create and exploit the market for hybrids. It is important to note the crucial role that federal and state sponsored agricultural research played in the development of hybridization, as well as the way that public institutions were pushed to the margins by those interests that sought to commodify hybrids.

The success of hybrids gave rise to industrial agriculture, with characteristic high chemical inputs in the form of pesticides, herbicides, and fertilizers. By seeking to adapt monocultured seeds to new localities, industrial agriculture and the so-called "Green Revolution" reversed the traditional ideas of seed cultivation vis à vis adaptation of plants to local conditions, thereby drawing upon and contributing to broad genetic diversity.

Against the backdrop of rapid and massive investment in commodifying germplasm from a technical perspective, there was a parallel, but not synchronous, trend in legislation and cases towards conferring and protecting innovative efforts to develop and market new plant varieties. In fact, companies producing hybrid crops did not avidly seek patent protection for their plants, choosing instead to keep their parent lines as trade secrets. However, in the late 1920s, Congress began to consider patent protection for asexually reproduced plants. The next chapter discusses developments in the area of patent law and proprietary rights in plants.

---

89. *Id.* at 89.
90. *Id.* at 78.

Chapter Three

Grafting Plants into U.S. Patent Law: The Convergence of Technology and Law: 1930–2001 and Beyond

A. General Overview of U.S. Patent Law

If 20th century technological innovations removed the biological barrier to the commodification of germplasm in the context of hybrid seeds, then U.S. patent law moved to lock in that commodification. This was accomplished through the Plant Patent Act of 1930 (PPA),[1] the Plant Variety Protection Act of 1970 (PVPA),[2] and subsequent cases interpreting these acts. This chapter looks at how U.S. patent law contributed to and reinforced the commodification of germplasm, beginning with a brief summary of U.S. patent law and moving into discussion of the PPA, the PVPA, and landmark cases in North America.

U.S. patent law[3] addresses and provides legal protection for new, nonobvious and useful inventions, manufactures,[4] compositions of matter[5] and processes[6] reduced to practice by inventors, as well as designs and new breeds of plants.[7] An inventor only receives a patent[8] after meeting stringent requirements of patentable subject

---

1. Plant Patent Act, 35 U.S.C. §§ 161–164 (1930) [hereinafter PPA].

2. Plant Variety Protection Act, 7 U.S.C. § 2321 *et seq.* (1970) [hereinafter PVPA].

3. *See generally* 35 U.S.C.A. §§ 1–376 (2001).

4. *See, e.g., Bausch & Lomb, Inc. v. Barnes-Hind/Hydrocurve, Inc.,* 796 F.2d 443 (Fed. Cir. 1986); *Polaroid Corp. v. Eastman Kodak Co.,* 789 F. 2d 1556 (Fed. Cir. 1986).

5. *See, e.g., Chakrabarty, supra* Chapter One, note 6; *Schering Corp. v. Gilbert,* 153 F.2d 428 (2d Cir. 1946).

6. *See, e.g., Gottschalk v. Benson,* 409 U.S. 63 (1972) [hereinafter *Gottschalk*]; *In re Tarczy-Hornoch,* 397 F.2d 856 (C.C.P.A. 1968).

7. There are three basic types of patents that may be obtained: utility, design, and plant patents. Utility patents cover new and useful inventions and are the most common. Design patents protect new and ornamental designs. Plant patents cover new and distinct plant varieties. *See* 35 U.S.C.A. §§ 101 (utility), 171 (designs), 161 (plants) (2001).

8. A U.S. patent gives an inventor the exclusive right to make, use and sell the patented invention in the United States for a period of 20 years. *See* 35 U.S.C.A. §§ 111, 115, 116 (2001). Note that while an inventor or inventors must make a patent application, the inventor may assign patents and patent applications. *See* 35 U.S.C.A. §§ 152, 261 (2001). *See also* David F. Noble, *The Corporation as Inventor,* in AMERICA BY DESIGN: SCIENCE, TECHNOLOGY, AND THE RISE OF CORPORATE CAPITALISM, 84–109

matter,[9] novelty,[10] utility,[11] and non-obviousness.[12] A patent confers on the inventor the exclusive right to make, use, or sell the invention described in the patent claim in the U.S. for 20 years from date of application.[13] This right includes prohibiting innocent infringers who may have independently developed the same invention from practicing such invention for the term of the patent grant.[14] Upon issue of a patent, the recipient must also disclose sufficient information[15] to "enable others skilled in the art" to practice the invention. The Patent and Trademark Office (PTO) publishes this information, thus allowing others to practice disclosed inventions after their patents expire.[16] As exclusive as patent "property" may be, it is nonetheless temporally incomplete, and this incomplete exclusivity theoretically makes possible the eventual re-combinations of elements from existing inventions into new ones, thereby adding to the common pool of ideas and inventions that are ultimately in the public domain.[17]

In general, two types of subject matter have been considered unpatentable: (1) mathematical formulae (e.g. algorithms for mathematical computations)[18] and (2) nat-

---

(1977). This includes a right to prevent anyone else from using the invention, even if independently developed. *See* 35 U.S.C. §§ 154, 271 (a) (2001); Edmund W. Kitch & Harvey S. Perlman, Legal Regulation of the Competitive Process 747–48 (3d ed., 1986).

9. 35 U.S.C. § 101 (2001).

10. 35 U.S.C. § 102 (2001); Donald S. Chisum, Patents §§ 4.01–4.04 (1988) (An inventor filing a patent application must be the first person to have made that particular invention. An invention will be considered unpatentable if it was precisely described in a printed publication prior to the patent applicant's date of invention, or if it was known or used by someone else in the U.S. prior to that date.); *see generally* Donald S. Chisum & Michael A. Jacobs, Understanding Intellectual Property Law [hereinafter Chisum & Jacobs, Intellectual Property]; *see also* 35 U.S.C. § 102(b) (1982) (providing one year grace period following publication of article describing invention during which a patent application may be filed, supposedly encouraging early publication).

11. 35 U.S.C.A. § 101 (2001); *see, e.g.*, *Brenner v. Manson*, 383 U.S. 519 (1965) (inventor must discover a substantial minimal utility for an invention, in order to be eligible for a patent); *Brown-Bridge Mills, Inc. v. Eastern Fine Paper, Inc.*, 700 F. 2d 759 (1st Cir. 1983).

12. Prior art is a moving target: firms may try to protect investments through patents on other innovations made in the course of putting earlier inventions into practice—however, many of these techniques are considered standard in the art, and therefore unpatentable. *See* 35 U.S.C.A. § 103 (1991); *Graham v. John Deere*, 383 U.S. 1, 4 (1966) ("[I]nquiries into the obviousness of the subject matter are a prerequisite to patentability.").

13. 35 U.S.C.A § 154 (2001).

14. *Id.* at § 271.

15. However, this disclosure process is not without ambiguities, as patent law also emphasizes diligence in reducing the idea for an invention to practice as a prerequisite to receiving a patent. *See, e.g.*, Edwin Mansfield, *How Rapidly Does New Industrial Technology Leak Out?*, 34 J. Indus. Econ. 217, 221 (1985) (patent applications as one avenue through which new technologies leak to competitors); Harry M. Allcock & John W. Lotz, *Patent Intelligence and Technology—Gleaning Pseudoproprietary Information from Publicly Available Data*, 18 J. Chem. Info. & Comp. Sci. 65 (1978).

16. *See, e.g.*, *United States v. Dubilier Condenser Corp.*, 289 U.S. 178, 186–87 (1933) (enabling disclosure by patentee is the "quid pro quo" for legal protection); *In re Lundak*, 733 F.2d 1216 (Fed. Cir. 1985) (materials necessary to make and use invention must be freely available to the public by the time patent issues).

17. *Kewanee Oil Co. v. Bicron Corp.*, 416 U.S. 470, 481 (1974) ("[S]uch additions to the general store of knowledge are of such importance to the public weal that the Federal Government is willing to pay the high price of 17 years of exclusive use for its disclosure, it is assumed, will stimulate ideas and the eventual development of further significant advances.").

18. *See Gottschalk*, *supra* note 6, at 71–72 (Mathematical method of converting binary-coded decimals into pure binary numbers does not qualify for patent protection); *but compare In re Jones*, 573 F.2d 1007 (C.C.P.A. 1967) (while a disk for mathematical conversion of analog to digital measurements may not be patentable, a method for using disk may be patentable); *but see Parker v.*

ural laws and "products of nature."[19] As with the idea/expression distinction in copyright law, the dichotomy of patentable/unpatentable subject matter is susceptible to exceptions at the margins. It has also proven particularly difficult to apply in the realm of inventions incorporating elements of computer software or genetic modification of living organisms. For example, systems using mathematical formulae may be patentable as processes, even though a component step of such a process consists of using a digital computer program that is essentially a compilation of mathematical algorithms.[20] Similarly, while naturally occurring products cannot be patented,[21] the discoverer of a natural product may be able to claim a patent in an isolated, purified or altered form of the product.[22] Up to the late 20th century, it was generally understood that, with a few carefully drawn exceptions,[23] plants and other living organisms occurred naturally and as such were unpatentable. Yet the contours of patentable subject matter have been in substantive flux since the 1980s, particularly with regard to patents in living organisms.

The general theory underlying U.S. patent law is a utilitarian approach, justifying the temporally limited exclusive patent rights on the basis that after the patent expires, the invention enters the public domain:

> This theory posits that inventions are costly to make and are difficult to control once they are released into the world. As a result, absent patent protection inventors will not have sufficient incentive to invest in creating, developing, and marketing new products. Patent law provides a market-driven incentive to invest in innovation, by allowing the inventor to appropriate the full economic rewards of her invention.[24]

Flook, 437 U.S. 584 (1978); *but see In re Iwahashi*, 888 F.2d 1370 (Fed. Cir. 1989)(voice recognition calculation apparatus not a mere algorithim, but was patentable); *see also* Donald S. Chisum, *The Future of Software Protection: The Patentability of Algorithms*, 47 U.Pitt. L. Rev. 959 (1986). [hereinafter Chisum, *The Patentability of Algorithms*].

19. *Funk Bros. Seed Co. v. Kalo Inoculant Co.*, 333 U.S. 127 (1948) [hereinafter *Funk Bros.*].

20. *Diamond v. Diehr*, 450 U.S. 175 (1981); *see also* Chisum, *The Patentability of Algorithms*; Pamela Samuelson, *Benson Revisited: The Case Against Patent Protection for Algorithms and Other Computer Program-Related Inventions*, 39 Emory L. J. 1025 (1990); Richard S. Gruner, *Intangible Inventions: Patentable Subject Matter for an Information Age*, 35 Loy. L.A. L. Rev. 355 (2002); Julie E. Cohen & Mark A. Lemley, *Patent Scope and Innovation in the Software Industry*, 89 Cal. L. Rev. 1 (2001); *note State Street Bank & Trust Co. v. Signature Financial Group*, 149 F. 3d 1368 (Fed Cir. 1998) (upholding the patentability of a 'business method'—a method of managing mutual funds); *but see* Robert P. Merges, *As Many as Six Impossible Patents for Breakfast*, 14 Berkeley Tech. L.J. 579 (1999); John R. Thomas, *The Patenting of the Liberal Professions*, 40 B.C. L. Rev. 1139 (1999).

21. *See Funk Bros.*, *supra* note 19.

22. *Merck & Co. v. Olin Mattheison Chemical Corp.*, 253 F.2d 156, 161, n. 6 (4th Cir. 1958) (upholding the patentability of a purified form of vitamin B-12, despite the presence of B-12 in cattle livers, "There is nothing in the language of the Act which precludes the issuance of a patent upon a 'product of nature' when it is a 'new and useful composition of matter' ... The matter of which patentable new and useful compositions are composed necessarily includes naturally existing elements and materials."); *Amgen, Inc. v. Chugai Pharmaceutical Co.*, 927 F.2d 1200 (Fed. Cir. 1991) (patents granted related to a purified and isolated DNA sequence encoding human erythropoetin); *Scripps Clinic & Research Foundation v. Genentech, Inc.*, 927 F.2d 1565 (Fed. Cir. 1991) (patent granted relating to purified a genetically engineered human blood clotting factor).

23. Two such exceptions were asexually propagating plants under the PPA or certain sexually reproduced plants under the PVPA.

24. Robert P. Merges, Peter S. Menell & Mark A. Lemley, Intellectual Property in the New Technological Age, at 127 (4th ed. 2006); *see also* Edmund Kitch, *The Nature and Function of the Patent System*, 30 J. L. & Econ. 265 (1977); Mark F. Grady & Jay I. Alexander, *Patent Law and Rent*

Having sketched a rough outline of U.S. patent law, this chapter now moves on to discuss how that body of law came to consider plant germplasm as patentable subject matter over the course of the 20th century.

B. The Plant Patent Act of 1930 (PPA)

As early as the 1880s, private plant breeders advocated that the U.S. establish a plant patenting system. In 1906, a bill backed by the American Breeders Association was introduced that purported to do just that, but the bill never reported out of committee and the issue was dropped.[25] Breeders argued that plants were akin to machines and as such, innovations in the way that plants "worked" should be protected in the same way that innovations in machinery were protected, through patent law. At the time, Congress did not seem overly concerned that lack of patent protection for plant breeders stifled innovation in the field. The USDA seed-giveaway program was at its height and plant germplasm could be seen as something that properly belonged to the "public," rather than owned by a private individual or firm. The lack of financial incentives for private seed companies did not seem to slow state-sponsored institutions' innovation and distribution of new plant varieties, particularly in light of increasing government investment in seed collection and distribution activities.[26] Still, the relatively young private plant breeding industry pushed Congress for legal protection of their work. In particular, nurseries that depended on fruit trees propagated by grafting argued for the necessity of legal protection.[27] They received it from Congress, through the 1930 PPA.[28]

Nurseries during this period paralleled developments in the seed business and benefited from the growing commercialization of agriculture from the mid-19th century onward. A big difference between the seed and the nursery businesses was that fruit trees and woody ornamentals (such as roses) could be "cloned," which allowed nurseries to offer stable varieties.[29]

Dissipation, 78 VA. L. REV. 305 (1992); *but cf.* John F. Duffy, *Rethinking the Prospect Theory of Patents*, 71 CHI. L. REV. 439 (2004).

25. Kloppenburg, FIRST THE SEED, *supra* Chapter One, note 2, at 132.

26. Cary Fowler, *The Plant Patent Act of 1930: A Sociological History of Its Creation*, 82 J. PAT. & TRADEMARK OFF. SOC'Y 621 (2001)("Absent significant numbers of distinct new varieties being produced by seed companies, variety protection through something like a patent law would hardly have been considered a business necessity."); *but cf.* Seabrook, *Sowing for Apocalypse*, *supra* note 42.

27. *J.E.M. Ag Supply*, *supra* Chapter One, note 10; Klose, *supra* Chapter Two, note 22, at 98.

28. The original text of the PPA amended the then-in-effect Patent Act to read:

> Any person who has invented any new and useful art, machine, manufacture or composition of matter, or any new and useful improvements thereof, or who has invented or discovered and asexually reproduced any distinct and new variety of plant, other than a tuber-propagated plant, not known or used by others in this country, before his invention or discovery, ... may ... obtain a patent thereof. Act of May 30, 1930, 46 Stat. 376

The current version of the PPA was moved in 1952 to Chapter 15, "Plant Patents" at 35 U.S.C. §§ 161–164 and reads:

> Whoever invents or discovers and asexually reproduces any distinct and new variety of plant, including cultivated sports, mutants, hybrids, and newly found seedlings, other than a tuber propagated plant or a plant found in an uncultivated state, may obtain a patent therefore....

29. Fowler, UNNATURAL SELECTION, *supra* Chapter One, note 2, at 76.

In 1893, the Stark Brothers (founded in 1816) purchased the rights to the original "Delicious" apple tree for $6,000 and over the course of the first half of the 20th century sold millions of copies "cloned" from the original tree, in the process, becoming the largest nursery in the U.S. at the time.[30]

Significantly, the Stark Brothers' "involvement in breeding was practically nil."[31] Because of the ease of "cloning," Stark Brothers faced the likelihood that competing nurseries would simply buy a single tree from the Starks and "clone" copies. The Starks unsuccessfully tried using a contract printed on their catalog order form that supposedly obligated customers not to propagate and offer for sale Stark Brothers' varieties.[32] Cary Fowler writes,

> The PPA ... helped Stark Brothers become the biggest retail nursery in the country. Thirty percent of all apple patents, 15 percent of plum patents and 10 percent of peach patents have gone to the company. Jenkins & Perkins and Hill Brothers dominate rose patents. Concentration levels by crop are high — never have the top ten companies accounted for fewer than a third of the more than 5,000 patents granted since passage of the Act.[33]

The PPA extended patent-like protection to asexually propagated species, i.e., plants that propagated by grafting or cuttings.[34] Note that the PPA also allowed protection for a "discovery" and the party that propagated that "discovery." Nursery professionals at the time did not engage in breeding. By comparison, farmers and plant breeders engage in origination, selection, propagation — a wider range of activities than nursery professionals — but note that they did not gain protection under the PPA. Plants that reproduced sexually (such as hybrid corn) were excluded, perhaps because some members of Congress at the time felt uncomfortable granting monopoly-like patent protection to staple food crops.[35] Tuber propagated plants were also specifically excluded from protection. Farmers opposed the inclusion of any sexually propagated species, as did the USDA.[36] Despite their opposition, the American Seed Trade Association lobbied (unsuccessfully) to have sexually reproducing species included in the 1930 Act.[37] Ultimately, plant breeders were more interested in establishing the principle that they could gain proprietary rights in certain species, even if such rights were relatively circumscribed.[38]

---

30. *Id.* at 79 ("[T]he 'Starking Double-Red Delicious' apple was discovered as a bud mutation on a Delicious apple tree growing in New Jersey ... [and] the 'original' Delicious apple was a chance seedling growing on [an] Iowa farm in 1868.").

31. *Id.*

32. *Id.* at 74; *see also* Dickson Terry, The Stark Story: Stark Nurseries 150th Anniversary (1966).

33. *Id.* at 90–91 (citing Mooney, Law of the Seed, *supra* Chapter Two, note 7, at 160).

34. S. Rep. No. 315, 71st Cong., 2nd Sess. 3 (1930) ("All such plants must be asexually reproduced in order to have their identity preserved. This is necessary since seedlings either of chance or self-pollination from any of these would not preserve the character of the individual."); *see also* Nicholas O. Seay, *Protecting the Seeds of Innovation: Patenting Plants*, 16 A.I.P.L.A. Q. J. 418 (1989).

35. Kloppenburg, First the Seed, *supra* Chapter One, note 2, at 132–33.

36. *Id.* at 133.

37. *Id.* at 132.

38. *Id.* at 133; *see also* Fowler, Unnatural Selection, *supra* Chapter One, note 2, at 83 (noting that Paul Stark, of Stark Brothers, and Chair of the American Association of Nurserymen, writing about the draft bill that eventually became the PPA of 1930: "[it] seemed to be the wise thing to get established the principle that Congress recognized the rights of the plant breeders and originator. Then ... effort could be made to get protection for seed propagated plants ...").

The PPA requirements language departed from the underlying U.S. patent statute. To receive a utility patent, an inventor needed to show that an invention was: useful, novel, non-obvious (or their equivalents in the then-in-effect Patent Act), accompanied by an enabling description, and within the scope of patentable subject matter.[39] Under the PPA, the only showing necessary to gain protection was that the asexually reproduced plant was "new" and "distinct."[40] Additionally, plant patents were partially exempt from the written description requirement of the Patent Statute, provided that the applicant's description was as complete as was reasonably possible.[41]

As of 1930, there was a valid argument that because Congress had considered making sexually reproduced crops patentable, but had failed to do so, then sexually reproduced staple crops were therefore excluded from patent protection.[42]

The economic and social upheavals of the Depression and World War II made the 1930s and 1940s decades of transition for the plant breeding industry. Hybrid corn rose to agricultural prominence during this period. Even in the absence of the express statutory protection of the PPA, private plant breeders moved to closed-line hybrids, effectively holding them as a proprietary "trade secret" by withholding their knowledge of what combination of parent inbred corn lines produced a particular hybrid.[43] Along with the postwar reconfiguration of public funds allocations toward basic/fundamental agricultural research (e.g. producing publicly available inbred lines for breeders' use in creating proprietary products and developing labor-saving breeding techniques in hybrid production), private plant breeders continued expanding their markets, even in the absence of patent protection.

However, public seed certification programs remained as obstacles to the private seed industry because they imposed a framework for governmental inspection and regulation of seed production and distribution. In contrast with the nursery industry, the seed sector during this period faced the problem of breeding for uniformity in crop varieties. There were thousands of farmer varieties at the time, inbreeding and re-crossing were experimental, and "[s]eed companies were still typically dealing in the varieties bequeathed them from earlier days by farmers and market gardeners."[44] Problems with fly-by-night seed dealers from the late-19th century onward had triggered a move to regulate the seed business, beginning with the Federal Seed Law of 1912,[45] providing for

---

39. The 1793 amendments to the original U.S. patent statute listed as patentable subject: "any art, machine, manufacture, or composition of matter or any new and useful improvement." Prior to the PPA of 1930, there was a judicial presumption that a "product of nature" was not patentable subject matter. *See* F.K. Beier & J. Strauss, *Patents in a Time of Rapid Scientific and Technological Chane: Inventions in Biotechnology*, at 25, *in* BIOTECHNOLOGY AND PATENT PROTECTION (F.K Beier, R.S. Crespi & J. Strauss eds., 1985).

40. *See* PPA, *supra* note 17; *see also Yoder Bros., Inc. v. California-Florida Plant Corp.*, 537 F 2d 1347 (5th Cir. 1976), *cert. denied*, 429 U.S. 1094 (holding that "distinctness" is assess by looking at the characteristics of a plant clearly distinguishable from other plants).

41. *See* 35 U.S.C. § 162.

42. *But cf. J.E.M. Ag Supply, supra* Chapter One, note 10 (holding that the absence of legal protection for sexually reproduced plants in the PPA of 1930 did not mean that they were excluded from utility patent protection).

43. Kloppenburg, FIRST THE SEED, *supra* Chapter One, note 1, at 107 (quoting public plant breeder Merle T. Jenkins, "among the private corn breeders and producers of hybrid corn, a tendency seems to be developing to regard the information they have on their lines and pedigrees of their hybrids as trade secrets which they are reluctant to divulge.").

44. Fowler, UNNATURAL SELECTION, *supra* Chapter One, note 2, at 100.

45. The Federal Seed Law was amended in 1916 and 1926. A different Federal Seed Law was passed in 1939, and was amended in 1956 and 1958. *Id.*

inspections of interstate seed shipments, as well as a plethora of state seed laws. The Federal Seed Act prohibited seed companies from making misleading statements about the pedigree or quality of seeds advertised in their catalogs. There was even an organization of seed regulators, the Association of American Seed Control Official, that favored compulsory registration of new seed varieties.[46]

Needless to say, the seed companies opposed what they saw as intrusive governmental interference with their businesses. Larger seed companies were ambivalent toward such regulation, because efforts to clean up the seed industry also reduced their ability to control the release of their seed varieties.[47] Jack Kloppenburg writes that in the 1920s,

> [s]eed companies were welcome to purchase certified seed from crop improvement association growers, but public breeders had no intention of permitting the seed trade to become an exclusive conduit for dissemination of their work to the farming community. The certification program was built around commitment to quality; certification became almost synonymous with superior varieties, genetic purity, and high seed quality standards.... Public breeders were in effect setting benchmarks of quality, and the association of certification with quality leveled prices among different varieties.[48]

As the focus of the USDA programs shifted during the 1940s and 1950s, government seed certification activities decreased, thereby creating a market space for private seed companies to engage in product differentiation through branding and advertising.[49] Private companies also began moving into selling seeds for vegetable, forage, and field crops unsuitable to hybridization, now free from competition by public seed distribution programs that were in place at the beginning of the 20th century. As hybrid corn demonstrated, when private seed companies and public agencies came into competitive conflict, the private sector was effective at channeling public agencies into a complementary, rather than a competitive posture.[50] Having channeled public agricultural research in the direction of "fundamental" research, the private seed industry secured for itself the ability to be the exclusive conduit of seeds to the market.

In terms of governmental seed certification programs, private seed companies argued that varietal purity should be the only relevant criteria, effectively decoupling public plant breeders' earlier successful establishment of association between certification and quality.[51] This also swept away the related leveling effect that seed certification had on prices.

By the late 1950s, brand name seed products had largely supplanted certified seeds and U.S. agriculture was in the midst of multilevel restructuring into a large-scale industrial enterprise. A key point to note is that large seed companies reaped economic power and high profit margins on their hybrid corn and sorghum products without holding patent

---

46. *Id.* at 100–01 (under proposed compulsory seed registration laws, either the state or federal government would have been able to require that registered seeds would be different and of higher quality than those already being sold).

47. *Id.* at 101.

48. *Id.* at 81.

49. *Id.* at 135–36.

50. *Id.* at 103 ("Initially, private sector breeding programs were largely staffed by scientists recruited from the public sector.... During this period, seed companies gradually made the transition out of the simple selection and 'strain' development work which had characterized the early days and began to engage in more rigorous, scientific varietal work ...").

51. *Id.*

rights in their sexually reproduced germplasm. However, developments in Europe aimed at conferring a form of intellectual property rights on plant breeders produced an ambivalent response in U.S. plant breeders. Fowler writes that while,

> [i]n Europe, variety protection had begun to take shape ... [i]n the minds of American seedsmen [those proposed] laws were linked with ... strict compulsory registration systems, ... and [were] abhorrent to American seedsmen."[52]

In the major redrafting of the U.S. Patent Act of 1952, Congress moved the PPA from the section governing utility patents into a separate section, where it is currently codified at 35 U.S.C. § 161. As the 2001 U.S. Supreme Court case *J.E.M. Ag Supply v. Pioneer Hi-Bred* demonstrates, there has been considerable ambiguity about what Congress intended to accomplish by such a move.

C. The Plant Variety Protection Act of 1970 (PVPA)[53]

The Union for the Protection of New Varieties of Plants (UPOV),[54] entered by six European nations in 1961, served as a prelude to the PVPA in the U.S. The UPOV required that plant breeders seeking legal protection had to demonstrate that their cultivars were superior to existing varieties.[55] Anticipating the eventual push for plant breeders' rights (PBRs) in the U.S., the USDA in the late 1960s began drafting a proposed amendment to the Federal Seed Act that would have imposed quality control requirements (i.e. a showing of superiority to existing varieties) as a prerequisite for receiving a Plant Variety Protection (PVP) certificate.[56] The U.S. seed industry vigorously opposed such quality control and Kloppenburg notes that "[t]he decade of the 1960s was marked by a process of negotiation between public and private breeders as to the shape that PBR legislation might take—if, in fact, it was necessary at all."[57]

As mentioned earlier, many private seed companies vigorously opposed and undermined the idea of compulsory public certification, particularly as to quality, preferring instead to rely on advertising to build and maintain consumer loyalty. This reliance on branding reflected a type of informal "trademarking" of plant varieties that contrasts

---

52. *Id.* at 103.

53. *See generally* J.M. Strachan, *Plant Variety Protection in the U.S.A.*, *in* Intellectual Property Rights in Agricultural Biotechnology, (F.H. Erbisch & K. M. Maredia eds., 2004) [hereinafter IP Rights].

54. *See discussion, infra*, in Chapter Four, Union Internationale pour la Protection des Obtentions Végétales. Six countries were the original UPOV parties: Belgium, Denmark, West Germany, the Netherlands, Italy, and the United Kingdom. The UPOV was amended and revised in 1972, 1978, and again in 1991 and is *available at* http://www.upov.int; J. Sneep, B.R. Murray & H.F. Utz, *Current Breeding Methods*, *in* Plant Breeding Perspectives (J. Sneep, A.J.T. Hendrickson eds., 1979); N.L. Innes, *Patents and Plant Breeding*, 298 Nature 786 (August 1982); Berlan & Lewontin, *Breeders' Rights, supra* Chapter Two, note 41, at 785.

55. Kloppenburg, First the Seed, *supra* Chapter One, note 2, at 137.

56. Fowler, Unnatural Selection, *supra* Chapter One, note 2, at 106 ("Seed companies wanted no part of a system which might have the government allowing access to market only to varieties deemed by the government to be an improvement over existing ones.").

57. *Id.*

with the type of formal utility patent protection that arose during the 1980s. As the seed industry increased research and development expenditures, debate over PGRs shifted to arguments about protecting and promoting private investment in varietal development, with some form of intellectual property rights functioning as incentive. The seed industry criticized the use of public funds for varietal research as wasteful and duplicative.[58] However, public plant breeders voiced serious concerns about strong PBRs. They worried that PBRs would adversely affect breeder willingness to exchange germplasm freely and place limits on use of private varieties for scientific research.[59] As such, public breeders were adamant about the importance of including an exemption for farmer seed saving.[60]

During this period, different companies were trying out various extra-legal methods to protect their so-called "proprietary" varieties. There was the biological lock-out/trade secrets approach of the hybrid sector. Cary Fowler writes that many companies "were experimenting with breeder-grower contracts whereby the grower acknowledged ownership of the variety by the breeder and agreed to provide royalties ... [that exposed] a fight between the breeder who does not discover [a valuable mutation] and the discoverer who does not breed."[61]

By 1967, Congress had already begun work on revising the PPA. The American Seed Trade Association (ASTA) had proposed an amendment to the PPA that involved adding "or sexually" to all relevant sections, thereby expanding the Act's coverage to useful, "sexually" reproducing varieties.[62] This amendment would have brought virtually all major crops under PPA protection. The USDA, LGC agronomists, farmers and public plant breeders at SAESs opposed this move and effectively killed the proposed amendment.[63] Despite this legislative defeat, it seemed clear that some type of statutory protection was inevitable. From 1967 to 1969, ASTA representatives, the USDA, public plant breeders, and members of Congress negotiated the outlines of the PVPA.[64] The

---

58. *Id.* at 138. ("To the extent that PBR encouraged private investment in varietal development, public activities in such applied work could be regarded as 'duplicative' and 'redundant' ... PBR could provide an argument for the emasculation of public breeding and its relegation to 'basic' research complementary to rather than competitive with private enterprise.").

59. *Id.* at 139.

60. *Id.*; W.M. Myers, *Germ Plasm Control as It Would Affect Variety Improvement and Release of Field Crops, in* PLANT BREEDERS' RIGHTS (American Society of Agronomy ed. 1964); Hearings Before the Subcommittee on Agricultural Research and General Legislation of the Committee on Agriculture and Forestry, U.S. Senate, Ninety-first Congress, 2nd Sess. on Plant Variety Protection Act, S. 3070, June 11.

61. Fowler, UNNATURAL SELECTION, *supra* Chapter One, note 2, at 105.

62. Kloppenburg, FIRST THE SEED, *supra* Chapter One, note 1, at 139.

63. *Id.*

64. *Id.* at 139–40 ("The seed industry succeeded in its principal objective of obtaining [p]roprietary rights to new varieties unhampered by any consideration as to quality.... The public agencies introduced language ensuring that products of their breeding plots were eligible for protection, that farmers could save and replant protected seed (and even sell to neighbors) without infringement, and that protected varieties could be used for research purposes."). Interestingly, a representative of Campbell's Soup Co. testified at Congressional Hearings in 1970 that the PVPA would "severely impede progress in the development of new varieties of plants ... [and] ... would essentially eliminate exchange of valuable germplasm and severely curtail the development of new varieties." To accommodate Campbell's objections, the Committee excluded 6 vegetables from coverage under the PVPA: carrots, celery, cucumbers, peppers and tomatoes. Fowler, UNNATURAL SELECTION, *supra* Chapter One, note 2, at 112–13 (citing Eldrow Reeve, Statement to the Subcommittee on Departmental Operation, Committee on Agriculture, U.S. House of Representatives, Hearing on the Proposed PVPA, June 10, 1970).

seed industry wanted explicit patent rights in sexually reproduced varieties without any inquiry into seed "quality."[65]

Congress enacted the PVPA in December 1970 with little fanfare.[66] The PVPA dropped the PPA's criterion of "usefulness"; PVPA protection for sexually propagated plants and tubers was obtainable upon demonstration of "novelty," "distinctness,"[67] "uniformity," and "stability" (consistent reproducibility).[68] If a variety met these requirements, then a PVP "certificate of protection" would be issued, giving the holder exclusive use of that variety for seventeen years from date of issue.[69]

The Act also contained three important exemptions as pertained directly to farmers and public plant breeders. Farmers were granted a "brown-bag" exemption that allowed them (subject to certain restrictions) to save, replant and resell PVPA-protected seed to neighboring farmers (the resale exemption was eliminated by Congress in 1994).[70] Furthermore, the Act included a research exemption and an exemption for sales of crops produced with PVPA seed.[71] Interestingly, the USDA, not the PTO, administers the PVPA, with its Plant Variety Protection Office of the USDA Agriculture Marketing Service issuing PVP certificates.[72]

---

65. *Id.* at 107 ("Talks had been underway with the public sector for a decade over public/private relations and over the questions of protection, seed certification, and registration. Most seed companies probably wanted some form of protection, but without the burden of proving or having certified that their varieties were better or represented improvements over old varieties.").

66. Doyle, ALTERED HARVEST, *supra* Chapter Two, note 80, at 62–63 ("When Congress finally moved to 'consider' the [PVPA] for final passage, it was under the worst circumstances; a pre-holiday, end-of-Congress, lame-duck session in December 1970, with mountains of left-over business to attend to.... Final House approval occurred under a suspension of the rules, and the measure was passed on a voice vote.").

67. Courts have held that "distinctness" requires that the plant variety "clearly differs by one or more identifiable morphological, physiological, or other characteristics." *See In re Bergy*, 596 F. 2d 952 (C.C.P.A. 1979); 7 U.S.C. § 1201.

68. PVPA, *supra* note 2, § 2402 (1)–(4) (2001).

69. *Id.* § 2483; *see also* 7 C.F.R. § 97.140 (2004)("Upon filing an application for protection of a variety and payment of the proscribed fee, the owner, or his or her designee, may label the variety or containers of the seed of the variety or plants produced from such seed substantially as follows: Unauthorized Propagation Prohibited—U.S. Variety Protection Applied For. Where applicable, 'PVPA 1994' or 'PVPA 1994—Unauthorized Sales for Reproductive Purposes' may be added to the notice.").

70. PVPA, *supra* note 2, § 2543 ("Right To Save Seed; Crop Exemption. Except to the extent that such action may constitute an infringement under subsections (3) and (4) of section 111, it shall not infringe any right hereunder for a person to save seed produced by the person from seed obtained, or descended from seed obtained, by authority of the owner of the variety for seeding purposes and use such saved seed in the production of a crop for use on the farm of the person, or for sale as provided in this section. A bona fide sale for other than reproductive purposes, made in channels usual for such other purposes, of seed produced on a farm either from seed obtained by authority of the owner for seeding purposes or from seed produced by descent on such farm from seed obtained by authority of the owner for seeding purposes shall not constitute an infringement. A purchaser who diverts seed from such channels to seeding purposes shall be deemed to have notice under section 127 that the actions of the purchaser constitute an infringement.") Note that this reflects the 1994 Amendments to the PVPA that eliminated the farmer exemption for reselling saved seeds to neighbors. *See* Pub. L. 103-349, 108 Stat. 3142, Oct. 6, 1994, which struck the proviso that allowed the sale of "saved seed" to other persons. Compare *Delta and Pine Land Co. v. Peoples' Gin Co.*, 694 F. 2d 1012 (5th Cir. 1983) (holding that Congress intended the farmers' exemption to be read narrowly to apply only to farmer to farmer sales).

71. PVPA, *supra* note 2, § 2544 (2001).

72. 7 U.S.C. §§ 2321–2322.

It is important to note that the *scope* of intellectual property rights under the PVPA may be seen as a curious blend of trademark and patent ideas. PVPA protection covers the *phenotype* of a particular variety, not the underlying genetic structure (the *genotype*).[73] A PVP certificate protects the exclusivity of its holder as the *source* of a protected variety. This resembles the way that trademark law protects the integrity of source-indicative trademarks.

One major consequence of the PVPA was that it made fine-tuned branding strategies available to private seed companies. However, what ends these private branding strategies may have facilitated or accomplished remains the subject of debate. Kloppenburg argues that the

> PVPA was pursued by the seed industry primarily as a mechanism for permitting differentiation of its products.... Five crops account for 62 percent of new and protected varieties, and half those are soybean or wheat cultivars.... [M]ost plant breeding involves a genetic "fine-tuning" of elite adapted species ... [and because] eligibility for protection under the PVPA requires no demonstration of economic utility over existing species means this fine-tuning can be used to create "pseudo-varieties." ... [and] the PVPA has not resulted in the development of private varieties significantly superior in yield or quality.... [but] has been associated with a proliferation of varieties and greater choice. But that choice is more apparent than real.[74]

Congress renewed the PVPA in 1980, following a decade of a seismic shifts in the seed industry. Transnational corporations Ciba-Geigy, ARCO, Pfizer, Shell, W.R. Grace, Monsanto and others were involved in a dizzying array of mergers and acquisitions, buying up smaller seed firms to augment their agribusiness, chemical, and pharmaceutical divisions.[75] The division of labor between government sponsored agricul-

---

73. Fowler, Unnatural Selection, *supra* Chapter One, note 2, at 122 ("The property rights established by the PVPA are property rights over varieties of plants, in biological terms, over certain combinations of genes. [The PVPA defined] new relationships between the owners of these rights and other actors, particularly those companies that previously multiplied and resold varieties bred by others. This practice was made illegal under the PVPA and civil remedies ... were provided under the Act. This gave legitimacy to the ownership of varieties (thus formalizing the illegitimacy of 'piracy') and changed the nature of marketing, the security of market position and enforcement of rights.").

74. Kloppenburg, First the Seed, *supra* Chapter One, note 2, at 143, 144, 146; *see* C.S. Gasser & R.T. Fraley, *Genetically Engineered Plants for Crop Improvement*, 244 Science 1293 (16 June 1998)("Although no one disputes that companies that have invested heavily in R & D to isolate, test and commercialize genes are entitled to protection, there is considerable debate within the seed industry concerning how much protection is deserved and what impacts patents will have on the cooperative nature of the seed industry itself."); W. Lesser & R. Masson, An Economic Analysis of the Plant Variety Protection Act, at 123 (1985)(finding that the PVPA was generally a positive stimulus to the seed industry); *but compare* Julian M. Alston & Raymond J. Venner, *The Effects of the U.S. Plant Variety Protection Act on Wheat Genetic Improvement*, 31 Research Pol'y 527 (2002) (finding the PVPA had little or no effect on wheat yields); *see also* Mark A. Janis & Jay P. Kesan, *U.S. Plant Variety Protection: Sound and Fury ... ?*, 39 Hous. L. Rev. 727 (2002) (arguing that more utility patents will be sought for plant varieties following the *J.E.M. Ag Supply* decision); Katherine E. White, *An Efficient Way to Improve Patent Quality for Plant Varieties*, 3 Nw. J. of Tech. & Intell. Prop. 79 (2004)(arguing that the PVPO databases should be considered 'prior art' by the PTO for purposes of utility patent applications for plant varieties).

75. On growing concentration in the agrichemical and seed industry, *see* ETC Group (Action group on Erosion, Technology and Concentration, formerly RAFI, Rural Advancement Foundation International), *Communique, Seed Industry Consolidation: Who Owns Whom?* (July 30, 1998) *available at* http://www.etc.org/article.asp?newsid=186 (last visited August 21, 2006); *see also* Kloppenburg, First the Seed, *supra* Chapter One, note 1, at 147 ("[A]n astounding wave of acquisitions

tural research that began in the 1930s also became more pronounced during this period, with public research programs focusing on plant population improvement and germplasm enhancement, and ultimately phasing out all governmental varietal releases during the 1980s.

D. Opposition to Expanded Intellectual Property Protection for Plants

By the late 1970s, agricultural activists and authors in Europe and North America began voicing concerns that "the genetic base of the world's food supply was quickly disappearing and that restrictive legislation was making it possible for agribusiness to gain control of this vital segment of the total food system."[76] These concerns provided the genesis of newly emerging non-governmental organizations (NGOs) against the spread of industrialized agriculture in the so-called "Third World,"[77] with a particular focus on plant breeding and crop improvement.[78]

NGOs advanced their cause by employing several arguments. First, they argued that industrial crop development policies and agricultural practices were destroying the genetic base essential to plant breeding.[79] The global erosion of plant genetic diversity was causally related to the Rockefeller Foundation-sponsored "Green Revolution" as the spread of new, high-yielding, uniform varieties replaced traditional farmer landraces and their wild and weedy relatives. Second, these activist NGOs argued that there was a serious problem: the uncompensated appropriation of plant genetic diversity from the developing countries of the global South to the industrialized countries of the global North. This appropriation went uncompensated, these NGOs argued, because plant genetic resources (PGRs) were treated legally as the "common heritage of mankind."[80] Third, these NGOs argued that throughout the last third of the 20th century, multinational chemical, pharmaceutical, and food processing corporations had produced, through a spate of mergers and acquisitions of smaller seed supply companies, a striking economic concentration in the seed sector.[81] As these corporations merged with or acquired smaller companies, they gained control and access to unique seed and gene libraries, which they converted into proprietary resources used to create new plant vari-

---

and mergers ... has swept the American seed industry since 1970. Many of the corporations are large transnational corporations with established agricultural (often agrichemical) interests. The principal factors contributing to this consolidation trend ... include the rising commodity prices and export markets of the 1970s, the opportunity to rationalize and coordinate the marketing of agricultural inputs, and of course, the passage of the PVPA.").

76. Meeting in Canada under the aegis of the International Coalition for Development Action (ICDA), these authors and activists expressed concern about crop development and the world food supply in general and seed in particular. The book, SEEDS OF THE EARTH authored by Pat Mooney, resulted from this conference. The concerns vocalized in the conference and articulated in SEEDS OF THE EARTH were developed further by other authors. Robin Pistorius & Jeroen van Wijk, THE EXPLOITATION OF PLANT GENETIC INFORMATION: POLITICAL STRATEGIES IN CROP DEVELOPMENT 8 (1999) [hereinafter Pistorius & van Wijk].

77. *See* Pistorius & van Wijk.

78. *Id.* at 8–10.

79. *Id.* at 9.

80. *Id.*

81. *Id.*

eties suited to industrialized agriculture. In many instances, plant breeders' rights or patents protected these proprietary resources, which meant that in many circumstances farmers could not legally reproduce the seeds beyond the first sale.[82]

The final set of NGO claims focused on the rise of intellectual property rights in PGRs for food and agriculture. NGOs raised concerns over how these technological and legal shifts had slowed down or stopped the transfer of new crop development technology to farmers and plant breeders in the developing world. Because the seeds and chemicals in "agricultural technology systems" contained technology protected by intellectual property rights, farmers risked intellectual property infringement simply by using them without proper authorization.[83] However, if they did not, they risked being driven out of their markets by farmers who would use the seeds, the chemicals, and their latent technologies.[84] Additionally, NGOs were concerned with the way that such intellectual property rights could be used to create dependence on agrichemical companies, thereby leading to striking declines in farmer seed-saving and other traditional subsistence farming practices in the developing world.[85]

Many of the concerns discussed above came to a focus around the proposed 1980 amendments to the PVPA.

Unlike the 1970 passage of the PVPA, the 1980 amendments were fraught with controversy. The 1980 amendments were adopted ostensibly to "make the U.S. requirements compatible with the requirements of the [UPOV]. This would allow the U.S. to join the UPOV and thus facilitate international trade."[86]

The 1980 amendments added the six crops excluded from the 1970 PVPA and, as mentioned above, the seed industry had undergone significant concentration through an exceptional number of mergers. By strengthening the PVPA and desiring to pare back on the farmer exemption for seed-saving, companies such as Monsanto, Ciba-Geigy and others sought to enhance the value of their recent acquisitions.

---

82. *Id*. at 10.

83. While these new varieties were developed using genetic resources acquired from developing nations, these nations are precluded from exploiting the new varieties without the consent of the respective developers. Some have seen this situation as not only being unfair, but also a hindrance to agricultural development in these poorer countries. *Id*.

84. This is just one of the criticisms leveled against the technology transfer provisions under TRIPS, *see* discussion *infra* Chapter Four, 77–85, note 87, from the perspective of the developing world. *See also* Donald P. Harris, *TRIPS' Rebound: An Historical Analysis of How the TRIPS Agreement Can Ricochet Back Against the United States*, 25 Nw. J. INT'L L. & BUS. 99, 108–09 (2004) (stating that while the long-term positive effects of TRIPS' technology transfer provisions are yet to come to fruition in addition to being questionable, the short-term negative effects are fully apparent).

85. The extension of intellectual property rights to PGRs threatens to eliminate farming as it has been practiced over the last ten millennia. For instance, patents protecting "Terminator Technology"—technology that renders seeds infertile—have led to the dependence on the ever expensive modified seed and chemical inputs from a handful of global biotechnology companies at the expense of farmers' ability to save and share the seed. Consequently, family and indigenous farmers risk being driven off the land owing to the march toward "bioserfdom" whereby farmers have no choice but to license, or conceivably "lease," the crops they wish to cultivate from the conglomerates. *See* Verlyn Klinenborg, *Biotechnology and the Future of Agriculture*, NEW YORK TIMES, at A18, December 8, 1997; *see also* Ronnie Cummins, *Hazards of Genetically Engineered Foods and Crops: Why We Need a Global Moratorium*, *available* at http://www.inmotionmagazine.com/geff4.html (last visited February 8, 2007).

86. Fowler, UNNATURAL SELECTION, Chapter One, *supra* note 2, at 137 (quoting then-USDA Director for Economic Policy Analysis and Budget, Howard Hjort).

Unlike the 1970 passage of the PVPA, the 1980 amendments generated opposition that included environmental activists, clergy and farmers.[87] During 1979–1980, the seed industry and activists clashed over the proposed PVPA amendment. Writer-activists such as Francis Lappé,[88] Joseph Collins, Cary Fowler, Jack Harlan[89] and Pat Mooney[90] criticized the proposed amendment and its connection to "loss of genetic diversity consolidation of the seed industry, difficulty with enforcing the law, increasing seed prices for farmers, the proposed joining of the UPOV, and the spectre of illegal vegetal varieties."[91]

Opponents of the amendment included clergy from the Baptist, Presbyterian, and Catholic Churches who issued a statement that read:

> The control of seeds because it implies also the control of food production and indeed of life itself, should not be appropriated to itself by any company or nation. We therefore urge a careful review of present and pending seed patent legislation.[92]

Other opponents of the amendments raised the question of how to apportion rewards under the PVPA. Professor Kenneth Dahlberg said, "90 percent of all plant breeding has been done by nature itself and 9.9 percent by subsistence farmers and our Neolithic ancestors. Should modern plant breeders doing 0.1 percent of the work reap all the credit and the rewards?"[93]

The coalition of environmental, farming, gardening and clergy managed to catch the public's attention and the bill temporarily stalled.[94] A representative of ASTA told the *New York Times*: "It's the most insignificant piece of legislation. It allows you to patent six little vegetables, when you've already got 222 other food crops covered. So what?"[95]

In the end, the seed companies prevailed. The amendment went through the House on a voice vote, went through the Senate without debate and was signed by President Jimmy Carter in December 1980.[96]

However, the PVPA still contained a farmers' seed-saving exemption for replanting and even for resale. An important distinction is that the PVPA protected varieties (that is, the phenotype), but not the underlying genotype. It would be for the U.S. patent system—a much stronger form of intellectual property than a PVP certificate—to grant protection to a plant's genotype and genetic sequences within.

---

87. *Id.* at 145 (noting the opposition to the 1980 amendments included the Sierra Club, the Environmental Defense Fund, the Consumers Federation of America, Rural America, Inc., the Interreligious Task Force, the National Farmers' Union, the National Sharecroppers' Fund, and the Resources Agency of the State of California, among others).

88. Francis Moore Lappé, Joseph Collins & Cary Fowler, FOOD FIRST: BEYOND THE MYTH OF SCARCITY (1977); *see also* Francis Moore Lappé, DIET FOR A SMALL PLANET (1971).

89. Jack Harlan, *Genetics of Disaster*, 1 J. ENVTL QUALITY 213 (1977).

90. Pat Mooney, SEEDS OF THE EARTH: A PRIVATE OR PUBLIC RESOURCE? (1979).

91. Fowler, UNNATURAL SELECTION, *supra* Chapter One, note 2, at 135.

92. *Id.* at 141.

93. *Id.* at 145 (citing Kenneth Dahlberg, Testimony before the House Subcommittee on Department Investigations Oversight and Research on H.R. 999, April 22, 1980).

94. *Id.* at 144.

95. Ann Crittenden, *Plan to Widen Plant Patents Stirs Conflict*, NEW YORK TIMES, at A1 (June 6, 1980).

96. Fowler, UNNATURAL SELECTION, *supra* Chapter One, note 2, at 144.

E. Recent Skirmishes in the "Seed Wars"

Given the PPA, the PVPA, their somewhat complex legislative histories, and the numerous compromises that went into drafting each Act, it is not surprising that different aspects of these statutes have spawned litigation that has reached the U.S. Supreme Court. This part of this chapter surveys key cases that shed light on different aspects of the "Seed Wars" since 1980.

a. 1980: *Diamond v. Chakrabarty*

Living organisms have long been considered "ownable" in terms of possession, in the ways that one may own a dog, livestock, or a tree growing on one's land. But with the exceptions encompassed by the PPA and the PVPA, historically an organism's genetic structure, or genotype, has not been considered legally ownable. The "product of nature" doctrine would have excluded a plant's germplasm from patent protection, at least up until 1980. The Patent Act in 35 U.S.C. § 101 states that property rights embodied in a utility patent (limited in time and geography) go to a person that invents "any new and useful process, machine, manufacture, or composition of matter, or any new and useful improvement thereof." Into this categorical scheme, where do living organisms and organism genotype fall?

Traditionally, the idea that living organisms would be patentable intellectual property would be far-fetched, indeed.[97] In 1948, using imagery evoking a "commons," Justice William O. Douglas wrote in *Funk Bros. Seed Co. v. Kalo Inoculant Co.*,[98] which determined the invalidity of a patent for a combination of nitrogen-fixing bacteria:

> ... patents cannot issue for the discovery of the phenomena of nature.... The qualities of these bacteria, like the sun, electricity, or the qualities of metals, are part of the storehouse of knowledge of all men. They are manifestations of laws of nature, free to all men and reserved exclusively to none ... [The bacteria at issue] serve the ends nature originally provided and act quite independently of any effort of the patentee.[99]

For a number of reasons, the legal conception of unpatentable products of nature has undergone striking transformation. Not the least of these reasons has been the persuasiveness of a vision of "private" property. The core legal question raised in the landmark case *Diamond v. Chakarabarty*[100] is whether living organisms are patentable subject matter. Chief Justice Warren Burger, writing the majority opinion for a 5-4

---

97. *But note Parke-Davis & Co. v. H.K. Mulford*, 189 F. 95 (C.C.S.D.N.Y. 1911)(Hand, J.)(upholding the patentability of an isolated and purified substance from the suprarenal glands of animals, adrenaline); *but compare* Parke-Davis with cases finding patent claims over metal compounds found in nature invalid. *See General Electric Co. v DeForest Radio Co.*, 28 F. 2d 641 (3d Cir. 1928); *see also* Linda J. Demaine & Aaron Xavier Fellmeth, *Reinventing the Double Helix: A Novel and Nonobvious Reconceptualization of the Biotechnology Patent*, 55 STAN. L. REV. 303 (2002).

98. *Funk Bros.*, *supra* note 19.

99. *Id.* at 130–31.

100. *Chakrabarty*, *supra* Chapter One, note 8.

Supreme Court, held that genetically altered living organisms (in this case, a genetically engineered oil-eating bacterium) were patentable as "manufactures" or "compositions of matter." The Court majority reasoned that "a live, human-made organism is patentable subject matter"[101] because human agency (*via* newly developed genetic engineering techniques) had effectively removed such organisms from the category of items occurring in nature. In the Court's view, the scientist's discovery was "not nature's handiwork, but his own; accordingly it is patentable subject matter."[102] While the case dealt with the patentability of a bacterium, the Court opened the door to patents in other living organisms by its focus on human intervention as a crucial factor in determining patentability. Thus, *Chakrabarty* held implications for utility patents in plant germplasm and other living organisms well.

Chakrabarty emphasized a very *particular* form of human agency, and simultaneously eclipsed and obscured other types of human agency that the genetic structure of the major food crops grown by traditional agriculture represents.[103] Namely, human agency that is collectively generated, generally anonymous and incremental over long periods of time. This type of human agency produced multiple varieties of corn and wheat from an almost unrecognizable common ancestor variety of grass over thousands of years.

Following *Chakrabarty*, the Plant Variety Protection Office (which is administered by the USDA) began warning applicants for "certificates of protection" that PVPA varieties might also be protected concurrently under a utility patent (which are administered by the PTO).[104] However, substantial uncertainty and confusion remained about whether PVPA protection was concurrent with or exclusive of utility patent protection. The Patent Office argued unsuccessfully in *Chakrabarty* that because Congress had expressly protected plants, it had not considered living organisms to be patentable subject matter. However, the Court held that the PVPA and the PPA did not exclude living organisms from patentability, thus leaving to be worked out any substantive, interpretive, and procedural problems with the overlapping regimes and regarding the eligibility of plants for protection under the PVPA as well as under a utility patent. Initially following *Chakrabarty*, the PTO rejected all utility patent applications for non-hybrid plants, justifying its rejection on grounds that Congress had intended to create separate property rights regimes for plants under the PPA and the PVPA.[105]

b. 1985: *Ex Parte Hibberd*

Against the backdrop of post-*Chakrabarty* uncertainty, the U.S. Board of Patent Appeals and Interferences issued the *Ex Parte Hibberd* opinion in 1985.[106] Dr. Kenneth

---

101. *Id.* at 303.

102. *Id.* at 310.

103. *See generally* Kloppenburg, FIRST THE SEED, *supra* Chapter One, note 2.

104. *Id.* at 262 ("In view of the implications of *Chakrabarty*, the Plant Variety Protection Office took the precaution of appending to its list of abandoned applications the warning that 'Varieties published in this list may possibly be protected under the Patent Act'.").

105. Stephen A. Bent, *Protection of Plant Material under the General Patent Statute: A Sensible Policy at the PTO?* BIOTECH. L. REP. 105 (March 1985); C.H. Neagly, D.D. Jeffery, & A.R. Diepenbrock, *Genetic Engineering Patent Law Trends Affecting Development of Plant Patents*, 4 GENETIC ENGINEERING NEWS 10 (April 1984); Sidney B. Williams, *Protection of Plant Varieties as Intellectual Property*, 225 SCIENCE 18 (July 6, 1984).

106. *Ex Parte Hibberd*, *supra* Chapter One, note 9.

Hibberd, a scientist with Molecular Genetics, had applied for a patent on the tissue culture, seeds, and whole plant of a maize line selected from that tissue culture. The PTO
initially rejected Hibberd's patent application on grounds that the availability of protection under the PPA and the PVPA preempted its authority and prevented Hibberd from
receiving a utility patent. Hibberd appealed the denial and the Board of Patent Appeals
reversed the PTO's decision, holding that the PPA and the PVPA did *not* limit Hibberd's
ability to seek utility patent protection for plants that otherwise met the Patent Act's requirements of novelty, non-obviousness, and usefulness.

The *Hibberd* decision opened the door to a wide variety of utility patents for plants
and their component structures.[107] As between a PVPA "certificate of protection" and a
utility patent, the latter offers the more expansive protection:

> For several reasons, utility patents are likely to be preferred to PVP certificates
> and to plant patents.... The PVPA and the Plant Patent Act permit only a sin-
> gle claim for the new plant variety as an indivisible whole. Utility patents may
> encompass claims not only to multiple varieties but also to the individual com-
> ponents of those varieties: DNA sequences, genes, cells, tissue cultures, seed,
> and specific plant parts, as well as the entire plant. The *Hibberd* application,
> for example, included over 260 separate claims. The ability to make multiple
> claims significantly broadens the protection afforded the invention. It also per-
> mits the licensing of particular components—e.g., a gene for herbicide toler-
> ance to transformations at the cellular and molecular levels, utility patents pro-
> vide a significant advantage over PVP certificates, which can provide property
> rights only in the whole organism.[108]

The significance of the *Hibberd* case is that an administrative agency—the PTO
through its adjudicatory arm, the Board of Patent Appeals—made a very important
policy decision: *plants are eligible for utility patents as well as PVP certificates.* This policy
decision was not the product of Congressional legislation; in many ways, it flies in the
face of the PVPA's legislative history. Congress intended the PVPA to be the sole avenue
of intellectual property protection available for sexually reproduced plants. Although
the dicta in *Chakrabarty* may provide some support for the PTO's decision, the problem
of how to interpret Congressional silence or ambiguity is vexing.

The PTO granted more than 1,800 utility patents over the next fifteen years, covering
various aspects of plant germplasm.[109] When coupled with the growing tendency in the
seed industry towards consolidation via mergers and acquisition, the commodification
of plant germplasm was well on its way, awaiting only the introduction of genetic engineering on a mass scale.

From the 1930s on, seed companies made enormous strides in overcoming the biological barrier that had previously discouraged private investment in the seed sector.
Hybridization and selective breeding afforded the seed industry the ability to separate
the product from the means of (re)production. However, hybridization and selective

---

107. Note that following *Chakrabarty* and *Hibberd*, the PTO began issuing patents on animals,
including mammals. *See Ex Parte Allen*, 2 U.S.P.Q. 2d 1425 (Bd. Pat. App. & Int. 1987) (a genetically
engineered oyster was found to fall within patentable subject matter, but patent was found to be
"obvious"); *see* U.S. patent No. 4,736,866 (April 12, 1988) (patent for the Harvard "OncoMouse®"
issued for a "Transgenic Non-Human Mammal,") discussed *infra* note 162), *but see* Eileen M. Kane,
Splitting the Gene: DNA Patents and the Genetic Code, 71 Tenn. L. Rev. 707 (2004).

108. Kloppenburg, First the Seed, *supra* Chapter One, note 2, at 263–264.

109. *See J.E.M. Ag Supply, supra* Chapter One, note 10.

breeding only worked with traits *within* species, and involved considerable expertise, time, and effort in order to yield a marketable hybrid seed variety. This all changed with the post-*Chakrabarty* rise of genetic engineering, which created the possibility of targeted manipulation *on the genetic level* of a plant's specific traits. It also created the practical possibility of introducing cross-species genetic material. One such example was the "Verminator," a cross-species seed variety that utilized rodent DNA to render a plant sterile.[110] Farming, which had been steadily undergoing industrialization for much of the 20th century, was now set for an even more fundamental and profound transformation: crop seeds that needed to be purchased anew every season.

c. 1995: *Asgrow Seed Co. v. Winterboer*

Asgrow Seed v. Winterboer[111] attempted to clarify an unusually opaque provision of the PVPA. In this case, Asgrow Seed sued an Iowa farming couple, the Winterboers, for violating the PVPA[112] by selling one of Asgrow's PVPA-protected seed varieties. The PVPA provides that an owner of a "certificate of protection" for a variety of a sexually reproduced plant may "exclude others from selling the variety, or offering it for sale, or reproducing it, or importing it, or exporting it, or using it in producing (as distinguished from developing) a hybrid or different variety there from" for an 18 year term of protection.[113]

At the time this lawsuit commenced, the PVPA also contained a farmers' exemption from infringement liability for making sales of protected seed.[114] The relevant language stated that, "it shall not constitute infringement, subject to subsections (3) and (4) of the Act, for a farmer to save seed which was obtained from the owner of the variety to be used in the production of a crop for use on his farm, or for sale."[115] Furthermore, seed sales to other persons could be for reproductive or non-reproductive purposes.[116] Notably, this seed-saving exemption seemed to permit farmers to obtain protected PVPA seed from a company like Asgrow, and plant, grow, harvest, and then save or sell the seed to other farmers (such sales were known as "brown bag" sales).

Asgrow alleged that the Winterboers were making substantial income from their "brown bag" sales to neighboring farmers at below-market prices. For example, during 1990, the Winterboers planted 265 acres of soybean using PVPA-protected varieties bought from Asgrow and sold their entire soybean crop to neighboring farmers at about 50 percent of Asgrow's price.[117] Asgrow claimed that the Winterboers' sales infringed Asgrow's rights under 7 U.S.C. §§ 2541(1), (3), and (6) of the PVPA.[118] The Winterboers

---

110. ETC Group, *Communique, 2001: A Seed Odyssey, available at* http://www.etcgroup.org/documents/com_2001.pdf (last visited August 20, 2006).

111. *Asgrow Seed Co. v. Winterboer* 513 U.S. 179 (1995) [hereinafter *Asgrow Seed*].

112. PVPA, *supra* note 2.

113. *Id.* § 2483.

114. *Delta and Pine Land Co. v. Peoples' Gin Co.*, 694 F.2d 1012 (5th Cir. 1983)(holding that the PVPA farmers' exemption should be construed narrowly and only contemplated farmer-to-farmer transaction that didn't involve intermediaries).

115. PVPA. *supra* note 2, § 2543.

116. *Id.*

117. *Asgrow Seed, supra* note 111, at 182.

118. *Id.*, 33 U.S.P.Q.2d at 1431–32. As noted above, under subsection (1) it is an infringement to "sell the novel variety, or offer it or expose it for sale, deliver it, ship it, consign it, exchange it, or solicit an offer to buy it, or any other transfer of title or possession of it." PVPA, § 2541(1) (1988). Under subsection (3), it is also an infringement to "sexually multiply the novel variety as a step in marketing (for growing purposes) the variety." PVPA, § 2541(3) (1988). Additionally, under subsec-

counter-argued that the PVPA's "brown bag" exemption gave them the right to sell seed from a PVPA-protected variety, since the buyers and the seller alike were "farmers" within the meaning of the PVPA's exemption.

At trial, Asgrow argued—and the District Court agreed—that the PVPA exemption only allowed a farmer to save and resell to other farmers the amount of seed needed to replant one's own fields.[119] However, the Federal Circuit disagreed and reversed, holding that nothing in the language of the PVPA's § 2543 limited the amount of seed that a farmer may sell.[120] Additionally, the Federal Circuit held the PVPA "brown bag" exemption permitted one farmer to sell up to one-half of every crop produced from PVPA-protected seed to another farmer for planting, as long as the remaining half of the crop was sold for non-reproductive purposes only, such as animal feed or as food.[121] Asgrow appealed. The Supreme Court granted certiorari and reversed the Federal Circuit's decision.[122]

Writing for the majority, Justice Scalia's opinion focused on the convoluted character of PVPA § 2543, about which he observed, "it is quite impossible to make complete sense of [this] provision."[123] Nonetheless, the Court attempted to parse the confusing statutory language. Justice Scalia noted that "the first sentence of § 2543 allowed seed that had been preserved for reproductive purposes ('saved seed') to be sold for [reproductive] purposes."[124] Analyzing the structure of that sentence, Scalia reasoned that the authorization "to sell for reproductive purposes did *not* extend to saved seed that was grown *for the very purpose* of sale ('marketing') for replanting."[125] Justice Scalia continued puzzling through the statutory language, reasoning that if that were the case, then

> § 2541(3) would be violated, and the above-discussed exception to the exemption would apply. Since § 2541(1) prohibited all unauthorized transfer of title to or possession of the protected variety, this meant that the only seed that can be sold under the exception in the first sentence was seed that was saved by the farmer to replant her own acreage.[126]

Justice Scalia interpreted the statutory language of the PVPA to mean that if a farmer saved seeds to replant her acreage, but for some reason changed plans, the farmer could instead choose to sell those seeds for "replanting" under the terms set forth in the first sentence (or, of course sell them for "nonreproductive" purposes, i.e., as crops, under the crop exemption).[127]

Asgrow is exemplary of a growing number of situations where the holder of a PVP certificate (or a utility patent) does not sue a market competitor (i.e., another seed company infringing on their protected variety), but instead brings a lawsuit against an end user—the farmer as the *consumer*, or user, of the seed. *Asgrow* is also yet another marker in the fundamental transformation of seed as a good purchased with no strings

---

tion (6), it is an infringement to "dispense the novel variety to another, in a form which can be propagated, without notice as to being a protected variety under which it was received." PVPA, § 2541(6) (1988).

119. *Asgrow Seed, supra* note 111, at 183.
120. *Ibid.*
121. *Ibid.*
122. *Id.* at 196.
123. *Id.* at 192.
124. *Id.* at 186.
125. *Ibid.*
126. *Ibid.*
127. *Ibid.*

attached into a good subject to numerous statutory and contractual conditions attached. Seed is now not only a commodity; it is, more importantly, a licensed (as opposed to purchased) commodity. This effectively turns farmers from "owners" of the seeds they grow into "renters/tenants," with agrichemical corporations operating as and holding rights analogous to "landlords."

d. 2001: *J.E.M. Ag Supply, Inc. et al., v. Pioneer Hi-Bred Int'l.*

J.E.M. Ag Supply, Inc. et al., v. Pioneer Hi-Bred Int'l[128] was the first direct challenge to the legality of the PTO's administrative decision in 1985 to issue utility patents for germplasm in the *Hibberd* case,[129] coming more than 15 years and 1,800 granted utility patent later. *J.E.M. Ag Supply* involved patented, but not genetically engineered, hybrid corn.[130] In February 1998, Pioneer Hi-Bred International brought a patent infringement lawsuit against Farm Advantage, a small Iowa seed supply company. Pioneer Hi-Bred claimed that Farm Advantage had infringed seventeen Pioneer Hi-Bred hybrid corn seed patents by purchasing hybrid seed from authorized Pioneer Hi-Bred seed dealers and then reselling it, thereby violating Pioneer Hi-Bred's exclusive right to make, use, and sell its own proprietary hybrid seed during the patent term.[131]

Farm Advantage responded to Pioneer Hi-Bred's lawsuit, claiming in its defense that its resale of the hybrid corn seeds did not constitute infringement because Pioneer Hi-Bred's utility patents were invalid as a matter of law. Farm Advantage argued that in light of the PPA and the PVPA, the PTO had illegitimately extended the scope of utility patent rights under § 101 of the Patent Act[132] because it was done without express Congressional approval.[133] Farm Advantage further claimed that by explicitly providing protection for asexually reproduced plants in the PPA and for sexually reproduced varieties under the PVPA, Congress intended to exclude and foreclose utility patent protection for plants and their seeds under 35 U.S.C. § 101.

The Court upheld the validity of the Pioneer Hi-Bred seed utility patents. Writing for a majority of six, Justice Thomas assessed and dismissed the defendant's arguments. Thomas began by invoking *Chakrabarty* to support broad construction of "manufactures" and "compositions" of matter in § 101 of the Patent Act to include plants as potentially patentable subject matter.[134] Justice Thomas then addressed six of the defendant's arguments, three relating to the PPA and three relating to the PVPA.

First, Farm Advantage had argued that prior to the PPA's enactment, the general utility patent statute did not cover plants.[135] Justice Thomas responded that as of 1930, two

---

128. *J.E.M. Ag Supply*, *supra* Chapter One, note 10 (Thomas, J.).

129. *Id.* at 144.

130. Note that the *J.E.M. Ag Supply* case did *not* involve the question of the scope of utility patent rights over a plant variety. In *Imazio Nursery, Inc. v. Dania Greenhouses*, 63 F. 3d 1560, at 1566–67 (Fed. Cir. 1995), the Federal Circuit held that while there are no research or seed saving exemptions under a U.S. utility patent, sexual crosses and seed propagation are outside the scope of patent rights in plants.

131. 534 U.S. at 127.

132. 227 U.S.P.Q. 443 (1985)(Bd. Pat. App. & Int.).

133. 534 U.S. at 133.

134. *Id.*

135. *Id.* at 127.

factors removed plants from the patent statute: (1) plants were thought of as "products of nature," and (2) plants were thought not amenable to the "written description" requirement of the patent statute (that enables a person skilled in the art to "make and use" the invention).[136] However, Thomas argued that while Congress at the time of enacting the PPA may have considered plants to be outside the scope of patentable subject matter and therefore included a relaxed written description in the PPA, to recognize of the value of plant breeders' innovations, times have changed. For Justice Thomas, the relevant line between patentable and unpatentable subject matter after *Chakrabarty* is the line between "products of nature" and human inventions.[137] Furthermore, advances in biological knowledge and breeder expertise make it possible to meet the written description requirement in many cases.[138]

Second, Farm Advantage argued that limiting the PPA to asexually reproduced plants made no sense if it were possible to obtain a general utility patent for sexually reproduced plants.[139] Justice Thomas responded that during the 1920s, grafting or some other asexual method of reproduction had been the best way to make a true-to-type plant. Sexually reproduced plants were too unstable to constitute true-to-type plants, and Congress sought merely to protect the extant market created by nurseries that propagated asexually reproduced fruit trees. Furthermore, Thomas alluded to the "free" USDA public seed distribution program as a reason why there was virtually no private seed industry that needed congressionally-conferred patent protection for its products.[140]

Third, the defendants argued that in the major rewriting of patent law that constituted the 1952 Patent Act, Congress had moved plant patents out of § 101 into a separate § 161, thereby indicating legislative intent to create patent protection for plants apart and separate from general utility patents.[141] Justice Thomas dismissed the move of plants from the utility patent section to another separate section as mere congressional housekeeping, noting that he could find no statement in the language of the Patent Act which indicated that protection for plants was exclusively available under § 161.[142]

Fourth, Farm Advantage argued that the enactment of the PVPA in 1970 evinced congressional intent to deny broader protection available through §101 to sexually reproduced plants that met the PVPA requirements of being new, distinct, uniform, and stable.[143] Justice Thomas once again bemoaned the absence of any express indication that Congress had intended that PVPA "certificates of protection" be the "exclusive" protection available to breeders of sexually reproduced plants. Thomas

---

136. *Id*. at 132.

137. Stephen Brush makes a similar point when he discusses the distinction between 'products *of* nature' (unpatenable) and 'products *from* nature' (patentable). Brush, FARMERS' BOUNTY, *supra* Chapter Two, note 22, at 231 ("Legal discourse in industrial countries with a long record of intellectual property accepted the coexistence of the public domain and intellectual property by acceding to the difference of 'products of nature' and 'products from nature.' This distinction rests on the conception that genetic resources are public goods in the public domain that can be manipulated into novel and unique forms by skilled persons.").

138. 534 U.S. at 133.

139. *Id*. at 134.

140. *Id*. at 135–36.

141. *Id*. at 136.

142. *Id*. at 136–37.

143. *Id*. at 137.

argued that the different levels of requirements and protections available under a PVPA certificate[144] and the § 101 general utility patent were complementary rather than contradictory.[145]

Fifth, Farm Advantage argued that the PVPA altered by implication the meaning of "patentable subject matter" under the general patent statute.[146] Thomas rejected this argument, stating that repeal by implication was only applicable in cases where an earlier statute and a later one are irreconcilable. Justice Thomas reasoned that the PVPA and the general patent statute were not irreconcilable, particularly given the requirements for a § 101 utility patent that the invention be "novel," "nonobvious," and "useful," and the accompanying, relatively stringent written description and public deposit requirements. To Justice Thomas, there are two categories of protectable plants. The first are those plants that satisfy the utility patent requirements of § 101.[147] The second are those that satisfy PVPA requirements[148] but do not meet § 101 requirements.

Sixth, the defendants argued that when two statutes protected the same commercial attribute of a thing, such dual protection should not exist as a matter of statutory interpretation.[149] Justice Thomas also rejected this argument, reciting examples of coexisting dual protection for the subject matter of trade secrets law and patent law, as well as for copyright and patent law.[150]

Finally, Justice Thomas mentioned the over 1,800 utility patents that the PTO had issued since *Ex Parte Hibberd* in 1985, as well as the absence of Congressional intervention in terms of overruling the PTO's issuance of utility patents in plants. In light of this, Thomas held that the 17 Pioneer Hi-Bred patents were valid and that Farm Advantage's unauthorized resale of patented hybrid corn seeds infringed those patents.[151]

Criticisms of the Court's decision in *J.E.M. Ag Supply* have focused on how Justice Thomas de-emphasized (to the point of ignoring) Congressional intent as evidenced by the legislative history behind the PVPA.[152] Thomas took the historically difficult to defend view that passage of the PVPA was an *alternative* to granting utility patents in sexually reproduced plants, but was *not* a specific rejection by Congress of the PTO's ability to grant seed patents. The District Court, the Federal Court of Appeals, and even the plaintiff, Pioneer Hi-Bred, had all conceded that enactment of the PVPA indicated Congress' clear rejection of the option of allowing utility patents for sexually-reproduced plants in the 1970 statute. Nonetheless, Justice Thomas viewed the PVPA as an alternative, not a foreclosure of utility patent protection for sexually reproduced plants.

---

144. These included a research exemption, a farmer seed saving exemption as narrowed by *Asgrow*, and the lack of "nonobviousness" or "usefulness" requirements.

145. *Id.* at 137–140.

146. *Id.* at 140.

147. *Id.* at 140–143.

148. That is, plants that are "new," "distinct," "uniform," and "stable," and that meet a relaxed description requirement (describing the breeding program, if available, and setting forth that the variety indeed meets the aforementioned criteria).

149. *Id.* at 143.

150. *Id.* at 143–44.

151. *Id.* at 144.

152. *See* analysis by the International Center for Technology Assessment, *available at* http://www.icta.org/intelprop/FarmAdAnalysis.pdf (last visited August 21, 2006), as well ICTA's amicus brief in the *J.E.M. Ag Supply* case, *available at* http://www.icta.org/intelprop/SupremeBrief.pdf (last visited August 21, 2006). *See also* Joseph Mendelson III, *Patently Erroneous: How the U.S. Supreme Court's Decision in Farm Advantage Ignores Congress and Threatens the Future of the American Farmer*, 32 ENVTL L. REV. 10698 (June 2002).

Justice Thomas' majority opinion seems to say that because the text of the PPA and the PVPA do not explicitly indicate that general utility patents *cannot* be issued for germplasm, this constituted legislative permission for the PTO to extend utility patent protection to sexually reproduced plants and seed germplasm. However, as Justice Breyer noted in a pointed dissent, the majority opinion ignores the clear legislative history of Congressional understandings about the scope of intellectual property rights in plants during the PVPA drafting process. Breyer argued that the legislative history showed that in 1968, Congress rejected the option of extending utility patents to sexually reproduced plants. Instead, Congress negotiated compromises with and among the public breeders, the seed industry, and farmers, and incorporated those understandings into the draft legislation that ultimately became the PVPA, in order to grant plant breeders a weaker form of intellectual property protection. Justice Breyer argued that providing farmer seed saving and research exemptions under the PVPA when no such exemptions exist under the general utility patent statute would render congressional intent a nullity if the seed industry was able to concurrently seek utility patents along with PVPA certificates. Nonetheless, Justice Breyer's arguments did not prevail, and he wrote as part of a three-justice dissent.

e. 2004: *Monsanto Canada, Inc. v. Percy Schmeiser*

Monsanto Canada v. Schmeiser[153] is an ambivalent decision that contains a troubling precedent, one that continues the North American legal trends in favor of commodifying the seed and protecting the interests of large agribusiness at farmers' expense. In a 5-4 split decision, the Supreme Court of Canada upheld a lower court ruling[154] that Percy Schmeiser, a third-generation Saskatchewan farmer who has farmed canola for more than 55 years,[155] had infringed Monsanto's Canadian utility patent[156] on its genetically modified Roundup Ready® canola seed.[157] By its interpretation of the Canadian Patent Act,[158] the Court concluded that the owner of genetically modified seed has exclusive right to that seed. The Court also upheld the strictly liability standard for patent infringement, focusing not on what Schmeiser might have intended to do, but rather on what he did in fact.[159] Although Monsanto seeds invaded Schmeiser's fields and outcrossed with his crops, thereby destroying his custom-bred canola plants and seeds, the Court reasoned that Schmeiser's unlicensed use, storing, and re-planting of Monsanto's genetically modified canola seed[160] in pursuit of his own commercial interests deprived Monsanto of its monopoly on the patented seed. Yet the Court limited the scope of Monsanto's utility patent to the cells and genes that confer herbicide resistance in canola plants, thereby drawing what may seem an arbitrary line between cells and genes as

---

153. *Monsanto Canada, Inc. v. Schmeiser* [2004] 1 S.C.R. 902. McLachlin C.J. with Major, Binnie, Deschamps and Fish JJ. concurring; Arbour J., writing for Iacobucci, Bastarache, and LeBel JJ., dissented in part. [hereinafter *Schmeiser* [2004]].

154. *Schmeiser*, [2004] at 937.

155. *Profile of Percy and Louise Schmeiser, available at* http://percyschmeiser.com/profile.htm (last visited December 10, 2006).

156. Can. Patent No. 1,313,830 (issued August 6, 1986).

157. *Schmeiser*, [2004] at 937.

158. Patent Act, R.S.C., ch. P-4, §44 (1985) (Can.)

159. *Schmeiser*, [2004] at 920–21.

160. *Id.* at 930, 935, 991–92.

patentable "technology"[161] and plants as unpatentable subject matter.[162] The Court also limited the scope of Schmeiser's liability and denied Monsanto's claim to damages,[163] court costs and technology fees, on grounds that "Schmeiser did not benefit from the Roundup Ready® gene because he did not use Roundup® on his crops, thus [he] made no more profit than he would have if he did not use the patented seeds."[164]

Some background information is useful. GMO (genetically modified organism) farming has become widespread now that it is possible to manipulate the characteristics of plant species at the molecular and genetic levels. Biotechnology and agrichemical companies have made massive capital investments in the genetic modification of germplasm with eyes toward a practically-limitless global GMO market. Monsanto, which is the world's largest biotechnology company, exercises near-total control over the global GMO-farming industry.[165] Two of Monsanto's most important products are Roundup® and Roundup Ready®. The tandem comprises what the company markets as a full agricultural technology system.[166] Today, Monsanto sells Roundup Ready® Corn 2, Roundup Ready® Soybeans, and Roundup Ready® Canola,[167] all of which are meant to be used in tandem with Roundup®, Monsanto's patented broad-spectrum, non-selec-

---

161. Stephanie M. Bernhardt, *High Plains Drifting: Wind-Blown Seeds and the Intellectual Property Implications of the GMO Revolution*, 4 Nw. J. of Tech. & Intell. Prop. 1, 1 at 7 (Fall 2005) [hereinafter Bernhardt].

162. *Monsanto Canada, Inc. v. Schmeiser*, [2001] F.C.J. 436; *President and Fellows of Harvard College v. Canada* (Commissioner of Patents) [hereinafter *Harvard College*] [2000] 4 F.C. 528 (F.C.A.) (reversing an earlier denial of a utility patent application in the OncoMouse®, a transgenic mammal genetically engineered for predisposition to certain cancers) [2002] 4 S.C.R. 45 (overturned). The reasoning of the Canadian Supreme Court's dissent in *Schmeiser* follows the majority opinion from the Federal Court of Appeals in *Harvard College*. There, the court concluded that though a company can patent products and processes, they cannot patent higher forms of life such as a whole plant itself. That is, "the plant cell claim cannot extend past the point where the genetically modified cell begins to multiply and differentiate into plant tissues, at which point the claim would be for every cell in the plant" (¶ 138), which would extend the patent too far. The patent can only be for the founder plant and not necessarily its offspring.

163. *Schmeiser*, [2004] at 939.

164. *Id.* at 938–39.

165. Bernhardt, *supra* note 161, at 7; *Monsanto Co., Achievements in Plant Biotechnology—Evaluation: Canola, available at* http://www.biotechknowledge.com/biotech/bbasics.nsf/biotech01_canola.html (last visited December 10, 2006); ETC Group, *Communique, Bioserfdom, Technology, and the Erosion of Farmers' Rights in the Industrialized World* (March 30, 1997), *available at* http://www.etcgroup.org/article.asp?newsid=193 (last visited August 20, 2006). By 2000, Monsanto's genetically engineered seed comprised 94 percent of the global area sown with genetically modified seed, with Roundup Ready® seed planted on approximately 41.6 million hectares (103 million acres) globally. Roundup Ready® canola was introduced in Canada in 1996, and by 1998, Roundup Ready® crops represented 25 percent of Canada's canola-planted area. As of 2005, more than 600,000 acres of Roundup Ready® canola had been planted in the United States and more than 4,000,000 acres had been planted in Canada. Other genetically engineered canola technology systems are Liberty Link® (resistant to glufosinate ammonium); Navigator/Compas® (resistant to bromoxynil) and SMART® canolas (resistant to certain ALS inhibitors).

166. David Barboza, *A Weed Killer is a Block to Build On*, New York Times, August 2, 2001, *available at* http://www.nytimes.com/2001/08/02/business/02CHEM.html (last visited December 17, 2006) ("Monsanto has maintained and even souped up Roundup's status by forging what analysts say was a brilliant strategy of dropping its price years ahead of patent expiration and tying its use to the early growth of genetically modified crops—crops made to work in tandem with the herbicide.").

167. *Monsanto Canada: Products: Roundup Ready, available at* http://www.monsanto.ca/products/rounduprready/index.shtml (last visited December 10, 2006).

tive herbicide. The major active ingredient of Roundup® is glysophate, an enzyme inhibitor that alters plant metabolism and prevents root development.[168] Around the same time that it introduced Roundup®, Monsanto acquired general utility patents in several countries for Roundup Ready® (glysophate-resistant) seeds. Farmers who purchase and use Roundup® and Roundup Ready® seed can spray an entire field for weeds without worrying about harming the glysophate-resistant crops, thereby eliminating weeds more easily and cutting associated costs.[169]

Monsanto has gone to great lengths to protect its legal interests in these proprietary genetic interventions. Roundup Ready® seeds are accompanied by extensive and complicated contractual licensing provisions which make farmers who use the seed licensees for an annual fee.[170] This contract grants Monsanto personnel permission to monitor and test farmers' crops to make sure that the terms of agreement are being followed.[171] Monsanto has robustly patrolled its rights, making numerous investigations and reaching out-of-court settlements with farmers to pay licensing fees, all the while steadily increasing its market share.[172]

Yet Monsanto knows that efforts to control the distribution and use of Roundup Ready® canola seed literally fly in the face of nature. Like conventional plants, genetically modified plants produce pollen that bears the plant's genetic material. Reproductive isolation of germplasm, whether pre- or post-harvest, is difficult if not impossible. In comparison to plants like corn and wheat, which have been domesticated by more than 10,000 generations of breeding, canola is a relatively "primitive" crop that retains many of its wild characteristics. Because canola pods mature unevenly, canola farmers must place the crop in "wind rows" to allow green seed to dry prior to mechanical combining. Just like their conventional counterparts, genetically modified canola seed can spread accidentally over significant distances due to wind, insects and wild animals, harvesting and hauling equipment (e.g. combines and trucks), or commingling whilst in storage.[173] Although incidents of cross-contamination via accidental seed dispersal are thought to be relatively isolated, seed dormancy and accidental cross-pollination present more significant and costly problems.[174] Once genetically-modified canola

168. *History of Monsanto's Glyphosate Herbicides*, *available at* http://www.monsanto.com/monsanto/content/products/productivity/roundup/back_history.pdf (last visited August 20, 2006).

169. *Schmeiser*, [2004] at 915–16.

170. The licensing agreement specifies that users must purchase new seed from Monsanto every year and they are not permitted to save and replant any of the Roundup Ready® seeds in subsequent seasons—in other words, there are no "brown bag" exemptions for farmers.

171. ETC Group, *Communique, Enclosures: Alternate Mechanisms to Enhance Corporate Monopoly and Bioserfdom in the 21st Century* (November 19, 2001) [hereinafter ETC Group, *New Enclosures*], *available at* http://www.etcgroup.org/article.asp?newsid=271 (last visited August 20, 2006).

172. *Id.*

173. Bernhardt, *supra* note 161, at 7; E. Ann Clark, *The Implications of the Schmeiser Decision*, *available at* http://percyschmeiser.com/crime.htm (last visited December 10, 2006); Drew L. Kershen, *Of Straying Crops and Patent Rights*, 43 WASBURN L. J. 575, 579 n. 66 (2004). Canola is an oilseed that works well in rotation with crops like wheat, oats, and barley. Canola seeds are round, smooth, and very small. Because of its shape and the necessity of windrowing, windblown canola seed can travel easily to adjacent fields. Some estimates show that at least 800 meters of buffer are required to isolate canola from windblown cross-contamination. Canola seed can also be dispersed by hauling equipment (e.g. blowing off the top or falling over the edges of an uncovered truck). However, some studies indicate that the frequency and amount of gene flow through such accidental seed dispersal across adjacent fields is less than one percent.

174. Bernhardt, *supra* note 161, at 7.

pollen and seed are released into the environment, plant reproduction—and any reproductive consequences—lay beyond the pale of human control.[175] Because self-fertilizing
crops like canola can outcross in a variety of ways[176] or remain dormant for as long as a
decade,[177] even the most diligent farmer's efforts to remove unwanted genetically modified plants may prove insufficient. Furthermore, it is impossible to distinguish conventional canola from the Roundup Ready® variety either without the aid of scientific testing or inspection or without using Roundup® to reveal whether crops are glysophate-
resistant. Thus, even for those canola farmers who do not wish to use Monsanto's seeds
and who would prefer not to have Monsanto's patented technology contaminate their
fields, it is highly likely that: (1) genetically-modified seeds or pollen will infiltrate the
farmer's crops, (2) some genetically-modified seeds will remain dormant, and (3) some
of these seeds will eventually germinate[178] and release their pollen into the environment,
producing hybridized seed and other unintended consequences.[179]

To complicate matters for farmers, Monsanto has successfully distributed to non-li-
censees many costs (not to mention the burden of farmers' resultant lost profits) of
policing patent-infringement prevention, even when infringement occurs accidentally
and against farmers' wishes (and property interests). Monsanto's utility patent rights
and licensing agreements put those who are accidental users due to natural forces in the
position of patent infringement.[180] Its corporate policy is to remove cross-contaminated
and other unlicensed plants upon farmers' request.[181] This places the burden on farmers
to identify infringing canola plants and to initiate the removal request. Yet removal efforts might well result in the uncompensated destruction of a farmer's non-infringing
plants.[182] Furthermore, in order to be effective such removal processes would require
the destruction of *all* canola plants on a farmer's land. Even so, the realities of seed dormancy and pollen dispersal mean that *total* crop destruction cannot ensure against accidental patent infringement in the future. Only total replacement of soil—an extremely
costly proposition—might insure non-infringement, and then for only as long as the
soil remains free from contamination by Monsanto's patented germplasm.[183]

In order to protect its invention from unlicensed use, Monsanto also monitors the
crops of farmers who have *not* bought Roundup Ready® seeds. This is what happened

---

175. Carlos Scott Lopez, *Intellectual Property Reform for Genetically Modified Crops: A Legal Imperative*, 20 J. CONTEMP. HEALTH & POL'Y 367, 377 (2004) [hereinafter Lopez] ("once [genetically-
modified] seeds are released into the environment, the consequences of their uncontrolled reproduction ... cannot be predicted.").

176. Phil Thomas, *Outcrossing between Canola Varieties—A Volunteer Canola Control Issue*,
available at http://mindful.org/GE/Outcrossing-Canola-Alberta.html (last visited October 23,
2006). While canola is a self-fertilizing species, canola outcrosses in the range of 20–30 percent. Al-
berta Agriculture estimates that even at a low outcrossing rate of .2 percent, a crop yielding 25
bushels per acre would deposit 10,000 outcrossed seed per acre in one season. The outcrossing rates
increase with every season, factoring in the lengthy dormancy period of canola seed. Under the no-
till conditions favored in prairie areas such as Saskatchewan, canola can remain dormant for as long
as ten years.

177. Keith Aoki, *Recent Skirmishes in the Seed Wars*, 11 CARDOZO J. INT'L & COMP. L. 247, 294
(2003) [hereinafter Aoki, *Skirmishes*].

178. *Schmeiser*, [2004] at 933–34.

179. Lopez, *supra* note 175, at 377; Bernhardt, *supra* note 161, at 7.

180. *Schmeiser*, [2004] at 910–11; Aoki, *Skirmishes*, *supra* note 177, at 292–93.

181. Clark, *supra* note 173.

182. Aoki, *Skirmishes*, *supra* note 177, at 297; Hilary Preston, *Drift of Patented Genetically Engineered Crops: Rethinking Liability Theories*, 81 TEX. L. REV. 1153, 1159–60 (2003) [hereinafter Pre-
ston].

183. Preston, *supra* note 182, at 1172.

to Percy Schmeiser, whose own custom strain of canola seed[184] was invaded and destroyed by Monsanto's genetically-modified canola. Based on an anonymous tip, Monsanto sent in investigators to survey and sample canola plants on Schmeiser's property.[185] Monsanto also contacted Humboldt Flour Mill, where Schmeiser had his canola seed milled, which provided Monsanto with glysophate-resistant samples in Schmeiser's seeds. After confirming the presence of canola plants bearing their patented gene, Monsanto sued Schmeiser for infringement of their utility patent, as well as injunctive relief, delivery of all infringing seeds and crops in his possession, plaintiff's costs, actual damages, and exemplary (or punitive) damages.[186]

Although Schmeiser did not adopt Monsanto's canola seed technology system, windblown pollen from Roundup Ready® canola carried onto his fields and outcrossed with his plants.[187] Schmeiser first discovered the presence of Monsanto's seed in 1997, after spraying Roundup® to kill weeds around the power poles and ditches next to the public road that runs by one of his fields. When Schmeiser noticed that some of the canola plants that had been sprayed did not die, he then tested a larger area by spraying Roundup® on approximately four acres of the same field. He discovered that 60 percent of the canola plants survived numerous sprayings,[188] thus meaning that these plants were glyphosate-resistant and that Monsanto's patented germplasm had invaded his crops. However, Schmeiser took no action to contact Monsanto, remove the glyosphate-resistant plants himself, or become one of Monsanto's licensed users.[189] He instead instructed a farmhand to harvest the test field and store its seed separate from the rest of the harvest. Schmeiser used seed from the glysophate-resistant canola plants to plant approximately 1,000 acres of canola in 1998, and sold that harvest for feed.

At trial, and later on appeal, Schmeiser advanced several (albeit unsuccessful) alternative defenses to Monsanto's allegations of patent infringement and even attempted (again, unsuccessfully) to turn the tables on the corporate gene giant. First, he argued that the Monsanto seeds were on his fields without his intent or invitation.[190] However, at trial Judge Andrew McKay pointed out "the source of the Roundup resistant canola ... is really not significant for the resolution of the issue of infringement."[191] The trial court found that, on the balance of probabilities, the presence of the patented gene in Schmeiser's fields could not be attributed solely to accidental

---

184. *Monsanto Canada, Inc. v. Schmeiser*, [2001] F.C.J. 436 ¶¶ 7, 29–30 [hereainafter *Schmeiser* [2001]]. Schmeiser practiced "brown bagging" for many years, which allowed him to develop a custom crop from a conventional seed variety called Argentine canola. Schmeiser had selected seed based on his choice of desirable genetic characteristics.

185. *Schmeiser*, [2004] at 912; *Schmeiser*, [2001] F.C.J. 436, ¶ 37–58.

186. *Schmeiser*, [2001] F.C.J. 436, ¶ 9; *Monsanto Canada, Inc. v. Schmeiser*, [2003] F.C. 165, 205 [hereinafter *Schmeiser* [2003]]; *Schmeiser*, [2004], ¶ 98–105 (damages overturned). The Federal Court of Appeals had affirmed the trial court's decision on the matter of Monsanto's receipt of injunctive relief and money damages. The trial court had ordered Schmeiser to deliver all of the Roundup Ready® canola seeds or plants held in his possession. It had also awarded Monsanto $153,000 CDN in judiciary costs, $19,832 CDN in actual damages (for Schmeiser's patent infringement at the rate of $15 CDN per acre containing Monsanto genetics, plus lost licensing fees), and $25,000 CDN in exemplary (or punitive) damages.

187. By 1998 five of Schmeiser's neighboring farmers—and approximately 40 percent of all western Canadian farmers—had adopted the Roundup® and Roundup Ready® system. Schmeiser's fields were located near a major hauling road and in the direction of the area's prevailing winds.

188. *Schmeiser*, [2001] C.P.R. (4th) 204, [2001] F.C.J. 436 (QL), ¶ 38–39.

189. *Id.* ¶ 40.

190. *Schmeiser*, [2001] F.C.J. 436, ¶ 12; Bernhardt, *supra* note 161, at 5–6.

191. Clark, *supra* note 173.

causes—between 95–98 percent of the 1,000-plus acres involved were contaminated. Although the fact that the presence of Monsanto's product in his crops destroyed his custom strain canola seed (and thereby damaged his overall farming enterprise) supports Schmeiser's claim that he never intended to cultivate the patented plants, he could not rebut the presumption of intent to cultivate—and therefore deprive Monsanto of its monopoly—because he had continued saving and re-planting seeds after receiving notice from Monsanto that his actions had infringed upon their patent rights.[192]

Second, Schmeiser argued that the outcrossed germplasm belonged to him. Schmeiser based his claim upon an analogy he drew between the Roundup Ready® gene and a "stray bull" as the latter is dealt with under admixture law.[193] Schmeiser contended that he was entitled to ownership of *any* seed on his land, including seed from volunteer plants that resulted from Roundup Ready® germplasm invading his land and outcrossing with his crops. However, the trial court disagreed with Schmeiser and distinguished plant germplasm subject matter from admixture law on the grounds that Monsanto's utility patent extended only to the gene's use, not to plants.[194]

Relatedly, Schmeiser argued that the patent was invalid for improper subject matter on grounds that the seed was neither caused nor controlled by human intervention.[195] The trial court rejected Schmeiser's argument and upheld Monsanto's rights to the gene as recognized by law, but limited specifically to genetically-modified seeds and cells and not extended to plants.

Fourth, Schmesier argued that he did not use the patented gene because he did not use Roundup® on his fields. The argument here is based on the tandem status of Roundup® and Roundup Ready® as a total agricultural technology system. Schmeiser contended that, within the terms of the licensing agreement, in order to have used the Monsanto system on the 1,000-plus acres involved in this case, Schmeiser would have had to spray that area with Roundup®, which he did not.[196] Anticipating that he did not have the right to use the patented gene, Schmeiser also argued that he had not benefited from the Roundup Ready® gene sequences. He explained that although he had used Roundup® to spray around telephone poles on his property, and had planted some of his acreage with outcrossed seed to see the extent of genetic contamination caused by the wind-blown pollen, he sold his crop for grain (rather than as seed) and that he never used (and therefore did not benefit from) Roundup® to protect his canola crop.

On appeal, Schmeiser even contended that the corporate gene giant had failed to control the spread of its product, thereby contaminating and genetically polluting his crops via an "unconfined release." Therefore, Monsanto should either lose its monopoly or be liable for damages. The tension between positions here is akin to an old adage, with a slight twist: *one man's treasure is another man's trash.* In this case, a powerful multinational corporation's patented, genetically engineered seed was, at least to Schmeiser, a nuisance and an invasive pollutant. Monsanto countered that, through its infringement notification

192. *Schmeiser*, [2004] at 933–34.
193. *Schmeiser*, [2001] F.C.J. 436, ¶ 19; Bernhardt, *supra* note 161, at 3. Under "stray bull" case law, any reproductive offspring that result from a rancher's bull wandering onto another rancher's land belongs to the latter.
194. *Id.* ¶ 93.
195. *Id.* ¶ 78.
196. *Id.* ¶ 121; Br. of Res. ¶ 160, *Schmeiser*, [2001] F.C.J. 436.

and removal policies, it took reasonable efforts to avoid the spread of seeds to other neighbors. The Court of Appeals agreed that Monsanto was not required to do more than was reasonably necessary to prevent the inadvertent spread of its seeds by the individuals who legally purchased them.[197]

While arguing before the Supreme Court of Canada, Schmeiser revived some of these arguments but presented them with new twists. He once again raised lack-of-use and lack-of-intent based defenses, arguing that the gene's presence in his field and crops was uninvited and that he did not seek to cultivate the outcrossed plants (as evidenced by the fact that he did not possess enough Roundup® to treat his fields if necessary). Since he lacked intent and had derived no advantage from the uninvited, unwanted contaminant, Schmeiser argued that he did not infringe upon Monsanto's monopoly. The Court rejected these arguments on grounds that a patent prohibits any and all unauthorized use of an invention, not just those unauthorized uses for intended purposes and by intended processes.[198] The majority looked to whether Schmeiser's activity had "deprived the inventor, in whole or in part, directly or indirectly, of full enjoyment of the monopoly conferred by law."[199] Under the Canadian Patent Act, the definition of "use" includes not only patented products, but also patented processes and the output from such products or processes.[200] Furthermore, the Court held that the intent of an unlicensed user and whether that use results in actual benefit to the unlicensed user are irrelevant to the issue of patent infringement.[201] Schmeiser had infringed Monsanto's patent simply because Monsanto's patented genetics were present in the canola crops growing on his land. The strict liability standard applies regardless of whether infringement is accidental or intentional and regardless of how patented material finds its way into an unlicensed user's possession—*the mere opportunity to benefit is all that matters.*

Ultimately, the Court concluded that Schmeiser had not made the patented plant within the meaning of the Canadian Patent Act.[202] To support its reasoning, the majority analogized Schmeiser's outcrossed plants containing Monsanto's patented gene to a building made of Lego® blocks. From the standpoint of patent law, a user's intervening contribution is irrelevant to the matter of who is entitled to the monopoly and all of its business advantages—these rest with the patent owner.[203] Contrary to Schmeiser's assertion that a farmer's "brown bag" rights supersede Monsanto's patent rights, a farmer's rights to save and replant seed are no greater than an ordinary property owner's right to use her or his own property subject to ordinarily applicable limits and restrictions to prevent infringement. The patent holder's ownership rights foreclose the possibility of a farmer's rights to ownership in the form of seed-saving and replanting where doing so infringes upon the owner's rights.

---

197. *See Schmeiser*, [2003] F.C. at 196. The Supreme Court of Canada did not revisit this issue.
198. *See generally Schmeiser*, [2004], 921–27; Bernhardt, *supra* note 161, at 4.
199. *Schmeiser*, [2004] at 919.
200. *Id.* at 921.
201. *Id.* at 911, 930.
202. *Id.* at 917.
203. *Id.* at 991–92. *But cf. President and Fellows of Harvard College v. Canada* (Commissioner of Patents) [2002] 4 S.C.R. 45], at 73–74, 86. The *Schmeiser* majority's reliance on the Lego® metaphor is contentious in that it equates lifeforms (seeds and cells) with mechanical devices (building blocks). This is precisely the distinction that the *Harvard College* decision attempted to maintain and sought to leave in the hands of the Canadian Parliament to work out through legislation. It also parses the "higher life form" criteria of *Harvard College* and draws an arguably arbitrary line between seeds and cells on one side and whole plants on the other as patentable or unpatentable subject matter.

However, the Canadian Supreme Court's holding in *Schmeiser* is somewhat ambivalent. The majority overturned Monsanto's award of damages and costs, on the grounds that while the matters of Schmeiser's use, intent, and actual benefit were irrelevant to the issue of infringement, they were *directly relevant* to the question of Monsanto's alleged damages. Schmeiser did not benefit from the presence of the patented gene because he did not in fact use Roundup® on the 1,000-plus acres of canola crops involved in this case. Therefore, he made no more profit in the sale of these crops than he would have otherwise received. The fact that Monsanto was not entitled to receive money damages (and therefore was not entitled to reimbursement for its litigation costs) surely allowed Percy Schmeiser to avoid economic ruin.[204]

Yet in the end, the *Schmeiser* holding increases and solidifies the legal protections that agrichemical and biotechnology companies enjoy in Canada and places farmers (in Canada, at least[205]) in a very difficult position. Farmers may have to pay royalties on genetically engineered seed found on their land, even if they did not buy the seed or seek to benefit from it. The possibility of farmers' rights for crop or "brown bag" exemptions in such cases has been foreclosed. The strict liability standard for patent infringement forces those who discover plants containing patented genes in their fields into a choice between signing a licensing agreement, facing a possible patent-infringement suit, or making an adverse out-of-court settlement. Most farmers would lack the necessary resources to mount a successful legal defense against an adversary of Monsanto's means.[206] Furthermore, a patent owner is under no obligation to control or prevent accidental dispersal of, or reproduction by, its patented germplasm, despite the fact that the presence of the germplasm may force some farmers into the position of an unlicensed user. Farmers may also face additional economic hardships such as the loss of the custom-designed seed that they have cultivated over time, the loss of organic certifications (if contamination via genetic modification appears in the plant or seed),[207] and replacement costs for purchasing

---

204. Because the Canadian Supreme Court denied Monsanto's claim for damages, Schmeiser also avoided having to reimburse Monsanto for several hundred thousand dollars in litigation costs. Although Schmeiser's profits were less than $20,000 CDN, Schmeiser sustained economic losses arising from his lengthy legal defense (which cost approximately $400,000 CDN, most of which he fundraised) and his lost right to use his own strain of canola that he had developed over many decades (because he could not prove that his seed was free from the Roundup Ready® gene). As a result, Schmeiser's own strain of canola no longer exists and he has had to purchase seed anew, thus adding another economic burden arising from this situation.

205. For discussion of likely consequences of *Schmeiser* in the United States, *see* Bernhardt, *supra* note 161, 7–11.

206. *Schmeiser*, [2004] at 933; Bernhardt, *supra* note 161, 9–11; Paul Elias, *Saving Seed is Latest Tech Piracy*, Jan. 14, 2005, *available at* http://www.wired.com/news/technology/0,1282,66282,00 .html (last visited December 10, 2006); Stephen Leahy, *Monsanto's 'Seed Police' Watching Farmers* (*available* at LEXIS, IPS-Inter Press Service, January 14, 2005). Monsanto's patent compliance and investigation includes a staff of 75 investigators and has an annual operating budget of $10 million USD. Unlicensed users receive threatening letters to sign a licensing agreement and pay technology fees or face the prospect of defending themselves in court. While it is unlikely that Monsanto would go after every farmer whose crops or land contain traces of its patented germplasm, as of 2005 Monsanto had filed 100 seed piracy cases in the United States, recovering more than $15 million USD and winning in every case decided thus far. In addition to these economic disparities of power and their direct translation into disparities of legal or dispute resolution power, Monsanto's patented technology use agreements include silencing provisions. Because of these provisions, it is difficult to say with certainty how many of the approximately 500 investigations Monsanto conducts each year ultimately result in licensing agreements.

207. Preston, *supra* note 182, at 1161.

new seed and new soil. Farmers who do not want to use a seed technology system must either switch to another line of business or sell their farms to those who will use those systems.

f. Other Cases

The *Schmeiser* case, the status of GMOs, and controversial issues regarding the patentability of both the genotype and the phenotype of agricultural crops, remain influential in courtrooms throughout the U.S. and Canada. Canadian courts have addressed the patentability of genetically engineered "higher" life forms. *President of Harvard College v. Canada (Commissioner of Patents)*,[208] a 2002 Canadian Supreme Court ruling, involved a patent application for the OncoMouse®, DuPont's proprietary transgenic mammal that is genetically designed for cancer and toxicology research experiments. In reaching its decision, the court first placed mammals in the "higher" life form category and then went on to rule that "higher" life forms would not fit into any of the patentable subject matter classes.[209] The court applied this reasoning and proscribed the patenting of plants by classifying such as "higher" life forms.[210] This proscription also applies to animal life that is "more complex than microbes but less complex than mammals."[211] With its holding, the Supreme Court of Canada seemed to reject the far-reaching holding its American peer reached in *Chakrabarty*.

As noted in the previous section, *Schmeiser* upholds the patentability of "living" inventions,[212] so long as they are not expressed as a higher life form.[213] Therefore, in Canada, while a "higher" life form such as a plant is not eligible for patent protection, a patent claim to a modified plant gene or cell is.[214] Subsequent to *Schmeiser*, the Canadian Patent Office revised its position on the patentability of claims directed to plant or animal cells.[215]

Back in the United States, in *Monsanto Co. v. McFarling*,[216] a 2004 decision of the U.S. Court of Appeals for the Federal Circuit, the court unanimously found that McFarling, a farmer, infringed a Monsanto patent by saving and planting glyphosate-tolerant soybean seed without Monsanto's permission.[217] In his defense, McFarling alleged Mon-

---

208. *Harvard College*, [2002] S.C.R. 45. *supra* note 162.

209. *Id.* at 47. A "higher life form" cannot be described as an art, process, machine, manufacture, or composition of matter, the categories of patentable subject matter, because such a life form possesses qualities that transcend its mere genetic makeup. *Id.* at 45.

210. *Id.* However, it has been noted that the qualities the Court described defining higher life forms could hardly apply to plants especially in terms of displaying emotion or even responding to stimuli in a complex and unpredictable manner. *See* Adrian Zahl, *Patenting of "Higher Life Forms" in Canada*, 23 BIOTECH. L. REP. 556, 557 (2004) [hereinafter Zahl].

211. Zahl, *supra* note 210, at 557 (noting that the Court appreciated the difficulty in drawing a line between higher and lower life forms and made a conscious decision not to do so).

212. *See Schmeiser* [2004], *supra* note 153.

213. *Id.*

214. Zahl, *supra* note 210, at 558.

215. Before the *Schmeiser* decision, the Canadian Patent Office required claims to plant or animal cells to be restricted to isolated cells, cell lines, or cells in culture. The Patent Office currently permits claims to cells as long as the description does not define "cells" to include plants, animals, or tissue. *ABA Section on Intellectual Property Law Bulletin* (January 2005), *available at* http://www.abanet.org/intelprop/bulletin/January_2005.doc (last visited February 11, 2005).

216. *Monsanto Co. v. McFarling*, 363 F.3d 1336 (2004) [hereinafter *McFarling*].

217. *Id.* at 1339–40.

santo had violated the PVPA and federal antitrust laws. McFarling also invoked the patent misuse, patent exhaustion, and first sale doctrines.[218] However, unlike Schmeiser, McFarling did not challenge the underlying validity of Monsanto's patents.[219] The court rejected McFarling's patent misuse argument, which claimed that, by prohibiting seed-saving, Monsanto had extended its patent on gene technology to include the germplasm—a product that cannot be patented.[220] Citing *J.E.M. Ag Supply v. Pioneer Hi-Bred*,[221] the court also declined McFarling's invitation to reconsider an earlier ruling that the PVPA "does not demonstrate a congressional intent to preempt or invalidate all prohibitions on seed saving contained in utility-patent licenses."[222]

In cases dealing with Monsanto's "no seed-saving" licenses that farmers must sign before using Monsanto's patented "crop technology systems," the U.S. federal courts have quibbled not about infringement, but about what is the proper measure of damages that infringing farmers should pay.[223] Another case from the Eastern District of Missouri (where Monsanto is headquartered), *Monsanto v. Swann*, held that Monsanto's "crop technology" licensing agreement that limits a farmer's growing rights to a single growing season was not a form of patent misuse.[224]

F. Summary

Until the early-20th century, the self-replicating nature of the seed defied attempts of private capital to commodify seed production. As Jack Kloppenburg has pointed out, the seed was both the means of production and the product—something that, at least partially, resisted the commodity form. The public subsidy of research and free seed distribution made it difficult for private capital to commodify germplasm. With the rediscovery of Mendelian genetics at the turn of the 20th century, some private and public plant breeders began exploring the hybridization of crops such as corn through techniques that combined outcrossing and selection.

By the 1930s, however, commercially viable hybrids appeared and the "problem" (at least to private entrepreneurs) of how to separate the product (seed) from the means of production (again, seed) began to be addressed by a combination of technological

---

218. *Id.* at 1340.
219. *Id.*
220. *Id.* at 1341–43.
221. *See J.E.M. Ag Supply, supra* Chapter One, note 10.
222. *McFarling, supra* note 216, at 1344.
223. See *Monsanto v. Byrd*, 200 U.S. Dist. LEXIS 22793 (E.D. Mo. 2000) (holding that PVPA §2543—the provision of the PVPA that allows farmers to save and replant seeds—does not provide a defense for a farmer from patent infringement liability in which damages will be calculated as no less than a reasonable royalty; *Monsanto v. Ralph*, 38 F. 3d 1374 (Fed. Cir. 2004) (holding that patent infringement damages are not limited to the anticipated profits of the infringer; however, where a liquidated damages provision in a "technology fee agreement" providing for 120 times the price of the technology fee assessed per bag violated a state law prohibition on "one-size-fits-all" liquidated damages clause.).
224. *Monsanto v. Swann*, No.4:00-CU-1481 CEJ, 2003 WL 1487095 (E.D. Mo. 2003)(holding that while Monsanto's crop technology agreement may have the effect of compelling a grower to repurchase seeds in subsequent growing seasons, it does not require the purchase of Monsanto's seeds and therefore does not constitute patent misuse.); *see generally* Center for Food Safety, MONSANTO v. U.S. FARMERS (2004), *available* at http://percyschmeiser.com/MonsantovsFarmerReport/3.05.pdf.

advances in plant breeding and changes in the legal regime governing property in germplasm. Hybrid lines were kept from the public and were held as proprietary "trade secrets."

The PPA was an initial legislative recognition of the value that nursery professionals brought to the plants that they worked upon. The PPA granted limited rights against unauthorized reproduction of nurserymen's work with asexually reproduced plants. From the PPA to the PVPA there were deep changes in the U.S. seed industry, with massive investments in hybridization but with varying degrees of success.

Judicial changes have shaped and reshaped understandings of intellectual property rights in plants from the *Chakrabarty* to *Schmeiser* and beyond. In the arc of these cases, one sees a steady but accelerating trend toward legal acceptance of the commodification of PGRs. Against the ambiguous backdrop of the PPA and the PVPA, *Chakrabarty* redrew the line of patentable subject matter along the "products *of* nature"/"products *from* nature" axis, inveighing for broad interpretation of what might be considered "manufacture" or "composition of matter" under § 101 of the Patent statute. The PPA and the PVPA expressly recognized the innovative human intervention (albeit of a particular and partial sort) necessary to produce cultivated varieties of plants, whether through asexual reproduction or sexual reproduction as embodied by germplasm. With recognition of human intervention as a touchstone of patent protection in *Chakrabarty*, the PPA, and the PVPA also went the granting of property rights—namely, the right to exclude others from the product of that intervention.

Chakrabarty left a lacuna: if living organisms transformed by human agency were patentable subject matter under the Patent Statute, 35 U.S.C. § 101, what was the relation of the PPA and the PVPA? If *Chakrabarty* helped lay the foundation for the biotech industry by creating the possibility that genetically engineered organisms could be commodified (and done so lucratively), then *Hibberd* helped complete the commodification of germplasm by allowing owners of genetically manipulated plants and hybrids to exercise the strong property rights of a utility patent. Utility patents grant their holders the exclusive right to "make, use, and sell" the patented invention for the patent term, without exceptions and exemptions such as those for seed saving or research under the PVPA. Utility patents also allowed the patenting of particular molecular and genetic characteristics of plants as opposed to the PVPA protection of the whole plant, not its isolated traits.

In the decade between *Hibberd* and *Asgrow* the U.S. seed industry accelerated its transformation into a concentrated industrial enterprise dominated by multinational agrichemical corporations like Monsanto (Pharmacia), Novartis (Sygenta), Ciba-Geigy, and DuPont. The early 1990s saw the advent of seed technology systems, such as Monsanto's Roundup® crops, that possessed a patented genetic sequence making them resistant to Monsanto's broad band herbicide Roundup®. Beyond herbicide resistance, it became possible to target specific traits within germplasm such as thicker husks, pest-resistance, shape, color, higher vitamin content, or even induced sterility in a way and on a scale that inbreeding and hybridization never allowed. An unusual feature of these patented seed technology systems was that the target of patent infringement lawsuits was not other competitors, but the end users—the farmers who purchased or licensed the seed technologies. These lawsuits challenged farmers' traditional practices of seed saving and selection, as companies asserted their patent rights in commodified germplasm.

Asgrow and Schmeiser embody the legal consequences of treating the patented seed as a paradigm commodity and of treating the farmer as an end user. In *Asgrow*, the

Supreme Court interpreted the PVPA's seed-saving exemption narrowly, disallowing farmer-to-farmer "brown bag" sales. *Schmeiser* carries disturbing implications, particularly given its facts. An agrichemical corporation successfully sued for patent infringement a Canadian farmer who had never purchased or planted any of its patented seed on his land. Monsanto sued on the basis that the genetically-modified patented pollen blew onto his property, out-crossing with his non-genetically engineered plants. The farmer is liable for license fees, profits from sales of the crops for milling as well as having his entire crop confiscated. In the U.S., farmers are prevented from saving and re-selling PVPA-protected seed. Furthermore, farmers must now return to the seed industry to buy seeds anew each year. What was once unowned and available cheaply and renewably—the genetic and molecular structure of germplasm and the practices of seed saving and selection—are fast on their way to becoming scarce, costly commodities with expanding markets premised on ever-renewed demand for product.

J.E.M. Ag Supply finally, if problematically, clarifies the post-*Chakrabarty* lacunae. *J.E.M. Ag Supply* held that the PVPA and § 101 general utility patents are not mutually exclusive avenues for protection of property rights in germplasm, even if the legislative history underlying both the PPA and the PVPA appeared to contradict an interpretation of such protection as concurrent. One can note a distinct irony brought about by the commodification of germplasm. In the early 19th century, the U.S. Patent Office began to collect, catalog, and make seeds freely available. By the beginning of the 21st century, the utility patent system has become a primary means by which the ages-old practice of farmer seed-saving is under serious legal attack.

In light of these decisions, it is time to consider the following propositions: the germplasm that provided the foundation for germplasm's commodification originated as a resource obtained for "free" via voraciously collected seed and plant samples appropriated from regions and peoples around the world. This "free" resource was then selected and distributed to U.S. farmers "free" of charge, first by the U.S. Patent Office and then by the USDA until 1924. Indeed, there is an irony that the U.S. Patent Office, which in the 19th century was responsible for starting germplasm collection, propagation, and distribution until the time of the USDA's creation, is today a key institutional actor in promoting laws and practices that prohibit seed saving. Where does this leave us when considering ways to protect and conserve traditional knowledge and global bio-agricultural resources?

Chapter Four

Overlapping International Legal Regimes for Plant Genetic Resources: From "Common Heritage" to "Sovereign Property"

The past two decades of legal and technological development reflect the heavy influx of investment into biotechnology following the *Chakrabarty* decision and the subsequent rise of recombinant DNA technology. These innovations allowed corporate plant breeders to manipulate plant genetic sequences and acquire an exclusive (though temporally limited) monopoly in those sequences that expressed particular plant traits.[1] This shift occurred contemporaneously with passage of the Bayh-Dole Act,[2] which (1) mandated the patenting of all inventions produced at federally-funded public research universities and (2) triggered new trade secrecy policies regarding any potentially patentable inventions, including possible patents in living organisms.

Yet in order to understand the complex contemporary state of intellectual property protection for food- and agriculture-based PGRs,[3] one needs also to understand the

---

1. New genetic information can now be incorporated into an organism's DNA structure through gene splicing or other recombinant techniques. Through gene splicing, scientists use restrictive enzymes to isolate the gene responsible for the trait they would like to transfer to the target organism. Once the enzymes break the DNA into fragments, the next step is to transfer the isolated gene, for example, through infection of the target organism via a weakened bacterium. If all goes as planned, the bacterium transfers the new DNA into the chromosomes of the host. Cynthia C. Urbano, *Gene Splicing: How Does It Work and What Can It Do?* Am. Nurseryman Oct. 15, 2004, at 44; *see also* Seabrook; *Sowing for Apocalypse, supra* Chapter Two, note 42.

2. Bayh-Dole University and Small Business Patent Procedures Act, Pub. L. No. 96-517, §6(a), 1980 U.S.C.C.A.N. 3015, 3018–29 (1980) (codified at 35 U.S.C. §200–212 (2000)). For a discussion on the impact of the Bayh-Dole Act on University-based research in the scientific realm, *see* Arti K. Rai & Rebecca S. Eisenberg, *Bayh-Dole Reform and the Progress of Biomedicine*, 66 Law & Contemp. Probs. 289 (2003).

3. For discussions of the complex contemporary state of intellectual property protection for food- and agriculture-based PGRs, *see generally* IP Rights, *supra* Chapter 3, note 53; Economic & Social Issues in Agricultural Biotechnology (R.E. Evenson, V. Santaniello & D. Zilberman eds., 2002) [hereinafter Economic & Social Issues]; Derek Byerlee & Ruben G. Echeverria, Agricultural Research Policy in an Era of Privatization (2002); Sheldon Krimsky, Science in the Private Interest: Has the Lure of Profits Corrupted Biomedical Research? (2003); Joseph Henry Vogel, Genes for Sale: Privatization as a Conservation Policy (1994); Robert E. Evenson, Science for Agriculture: A Long Term Perspective (1993); Crop Variety Improvement and Its Effect on Productivity: the Impact of International Research (Robert E. Evenson & D. Gollin eds., 2002).

controversies over PGR exploitation that occurred in the early 1980s and related developments in international law. This chapter analyzes those controversies and critiques developments such as: the 1992 "Earth Summit" and the resulting Convention on Biological Diversity (CBD), the 2001 Cartegena Protocol,[4] the creation of the World Trade Organization (WTO), and the ongoing implementation of the Agreement on Trade Related Aspects of Intellectual Property (TRIPS),[5] as well as the 2001 Doha Round[6] (which collapsed in the summer of 2003 at Cancún).[7] The chapter also focuses on the network of international agricultural research stations and seed conservation banks administered by the Rockefeller Foundation-funded Consultative Group on International Agricultural Research (CGIAR)[8] and the role of the Food and Agriculture Organization of the United Nations (FAO).[9]

---

4. For a study on the achievements, limitations, and implications of the United Nations CBD, *see* MICHAEL GRUBB et al., THE EARTH SUMMIT AGREEMENTS: A GUIDE AND ASSESSMENT 75–82 (1993) On the Cartegena Protocol, *see* Secretariat of the Convention on Biological Diversity, Contegena Protocol on Biological Safety (text and annexes), *available at* http://www.cbd.int/biosafety/protocol.shtml (effective September 2003).

5. Marrakech Agreement Establishing the World Trade Organization, Apr. 15, 1994, Annex 1C: Agreement on Trade-Related Aspects of Intellectual Property Rights Including Trade, 33 I.L.M. 81, 84 [hereinafter TRIPS]. *See also* "The Final Act Embodying the Results of the Uruguay Round of Multilateral Trade Negotiations," 1867 U.N.T.S. 14. This agreement was meant to clarify the results of the negotiations since the Round was launched in Punta del Este, Uruguay, in September 1986. A summary of the Final Act of the Uruguay Round is available online at the WTO website at http://www.wto.org/english/docs_e/ legal_e/ursum_e.htm#nAgreement (last visited March 9, 2005). For a comprehensive analysis of the TRIPS agreement and its history, *see* DANIEL GERVAIS, THE TRIPS AGREEMENT: DRAFTING HISTORY AND ANALYSIS (2003); *see also* INTELLECTUAL PROPERTY AND INTERNATIONAL TRADE: THE TRIPS AGREEMENT (Carlos M. Correa & Abdulqawi A. Yusuf, eds., 1998) [hereinafter TRIPS AGREEMENT]; Graeme Dinwoodie & Rochelle Cooper Dreyfus, *TRIPS and the Dynamics of Intellectual Property Lawmaking*, 36 CASE W. RES. J. INT'L L. 95 (2004); Jayashree Watal, INTELLECTUAL PROPERTY RIGHTS IN THE WTO AND DEVELOPING COUNTRIES 11–47 (Jayashree Watal ed., 2001) [hereinafter Watal, IP RIGHTS].

6. In November 2001, the WTO meeting in Doha, Qatar set in motion discussion meant to liberalize global trade, this time bearing in mind the needs of poorer nations. However, there were sticking points that were not ultimately resolved, mainly agricultural subsidies. The Doha Round was meant to "reduce trade-distorting farm support, slash tariffs on farm goods and eliminate agricultural-export subsidies in areas poor countries cared about, such as textiles." *The WTO under Fire—The Doha Round*, THE ECONOMIST (U.S. Edition), September 18, 2003, at 26 [hereinafter *WTO under Fire*]. For documents relating to the Doha Round, visit http://www.wto.org/english/tratop_e/dda_e.htm (last visited March 9, 2005).

7. The Cancún negotiations were doomed from the start, as countries seemed to disavow significant parts of the Doha Round. The E.U., for example, denied it had agreed to get rid of export subsidies. Poorer countries for their part denied they assented to participating in talks on new rules. Agriculture was the biggest issue dividing negotiators. To ease the stalemate, the E.U. and the U.S. proposed a framework to free farm trade. This framework, however, was rejected by poor nations who felt it did not go far enough. Export subsidies would remain in place, for instance. *See WTO under Fire, supra* note 6, at 26-27.

8. Fowler, UNNATURAL SELECTION, *supra* Chapter One, note 2, at 182–83. *See also infra* note 20 ("In 1974, the [CGIAR] founded the International Board for Plant Genetic Research (IBPGR). The IBPGR, a self-described 'purely scientific and technical body,' was to serve as a 'catalyst' for plant genetic resource conservation activities. CGIAR is the parent body of a network of agricultural research centers (IARCs) … [that] have been major collectors and storage sites for germplasm and have played a key role in the breeding of new varieties for the Third World.").

9. The FAO is a United Nations agency mandated to lead international efforts in the fight against hunger. It is meant to be a neutral forum where all member nations meet as equals to debate policy and negotiate agreements in addition to aiding developing countries in their transition towards modern agriculture, forestry, and fisheries practices. More information on the FAO and its activities is available at http://www.fao.org/UNFAO/about/index_en.html (last visited March 9, 2005).

A. The International Union for the Protection of New Varieties of Plants: 1961, 1972, 1978, and 1991

In the 1950s, the U.S. Congress created and funded a National Seed Storage Laboratory[10] as part of a network of gene banks to house the U.S. government's global germplasm collection.[11] This indicated a growing awareness of the importance of conserving plant genetic resources in the face of genetic erosion brought about by "Green Revolution" farming practices. Against this backdrop, some countries in Europe met to consider some type of protection for plant breeders that produced cultivated plant varieties.[12]

In 1961, a group of European nations met to create the UPOV, which was designed to provide a legal basis for plant breeders' rights in privately bred plant varieties.[13] The UPOV protections went farther than the PPA, which protected only asexually reproduced plants.[14] The UPOV protected all varieties of plants, including sexually reproduced varieties, as long as they were (1) new,[15] (2) distinct,[16] (3) uni-

---

10. Kloppenburg, First the Seed, *supra* Chapter One, note 2, at 172 (quoting a 1977 Agricultural Research Service letter to the chairman of the IBPGC to the effect that deposits made at the NSSL pursuant to IBPGR became the property of the U.S. government); *see also* Fowler, Unnatural Selection, *supra* Chapter One, note 2, at 242 ("[T]he U.S. Department of Agriculture established the [NSSL] in 1958.... The NSSL sought to collect and store genetic diversity for future use in plant breeding [and] ... operated much the way botanical gardens had in previous centuries.").

11. Kloppenburg, First the Seed, *supra* Chapter One, note 2, at 159 ("[By the 1950s][t]he need for effective storage facilities for acquired plant genetic materials became acute. Improved understanding of seed physiology and advances in seed preservation technology made long-term storage feasible. In 1956, Congress appropriated funds for the construction of a National Seed Storage Laboratory (NSSL) at Fort Collins, Colorado. The NSSL was completed in 1958 and is the flagship of the network of gene banks that now serves as the repository for the fruits of global germplasm collection.").

12. Fowler, Unnatural Selection, *supra* Chapter One, note 2, at 241–242.

13. *See* UPOV, *supra* Chapter Three, note 54. Union Internationale pour la Protection des Obtensions Végétales (International Union for the Protection of New Varieties of Plants), December 16, 1961, 33 U.S.T. 2703, 815 U.N.T.S. 89. For a discussion on the first plant breeders' protection systems in Europe, the conflicts between industry and plant breeders, the adoption of UPOV, and the introduction of plant breeders' rights in the U.S., *see* Pistorius & van Wijk, *supra* note Chapter 3, note 52, at 79–85. The UPOV has been amended several times since 1961 when the original convention was finalized. These amendments include those of 1972, 1978, and 1991. Currently, different countries apply different versions of the UPOV convention as provided by the amendments. Steven M. Ruby, *Note, The UPOV System of Protection: How to Bridge the Gap Between 1961 and 1991 in Regard to Breeders' Rights*, 2 Okla. J.L. & Tech 19, 19 (2004). For a list of the 61 member nations (as of April 2006) and the respective versions of UPOV the member nations currently apply *see States Party to the International Convention for the Protection of New Varieties of Plants, available at* http://www.upov.int/en/about/members/index.htm (last visited August 21, 2006).

14. *See supra* Chapter Three, Section C.

15. A variety is deemed new if "at the date of filing of the application for a breeder's right, propagating or harvesting material of the variety has not been sold or otherwise disposed of to others, by or with the consent of the breeder, for purposes of exploitation of the variety." UPOV Convention, ch. 3, art. 6(1).

16. A variety is distinct

if it is clearly distinguishable from any other variety whose existence is a matter of common knowledge at the time of the filing of the application.... [T]he filing of an application for the granting of a breeder's right or for the entering of another variety in an official register of varieties, in any country, shall be deemed to render that other variety a matter of common knowledge from the date of the application, provided that the application form,[17] and (4) stable.[18] As discussed in Chapter Three, the U.S. passed its own form of plant variety protection in 1970, at the height of the so-called "Green Revolution." The Rockefeller Foundation collaborated with the U.S. government to create agricultural programs and International Agricultural Research Centers to "improve" crops in different regions of the world,[19] which included collecting and cataloging germplasm samples.[20] Then, the Rockefeller and Ford Foundations, along with the U.S. and the World Bank, created the Consultative Group on International Agricultural Research (CGIAR) to coordinate the global network of International Agricultural Research Centers (IARC).[21] The United Nations-backed Food and Agriculture Organization (FAO) organized two conferences in 1961 and 1967. Those present for the FAO conferences decided to undertake a coordinated global germplasm collection and conservation program.[22] These pieces of legislation and public-private collaborations indicated that private breeders increasingly dominated plant breeding in North America and Europe and were eager to introduce their varieties into Latin America and Asia.

The IARCs provided a framework for the transformation of agriculture in the developing world. The IARCs introduced new varieties that were double-edged. They were higher yielding, but they were also high-input because of the necessity of high-use fertilizers, herbicides and water. Cary Fowler writes that these new varieties

> spread over Latin America and Asia with astonishing speed. In the process ancient centers of crop genetic diversity nearly disappeared.... In the twinkling of the evolutionary eye, the effects of thousands of years of crop evolution were wiped out.... Over 100 million acres of new uniform rices and wheats were soon being grown where tens of thousands of farmer varieties had once been found.[23]

---

leads to the granting of a breeder's right or to the entering of the said variety in the official register of varieties....
UPOV Convention, ch. 3, art. 7.

17. A variety is uniform if "subject to the variation that may be expected from the particular features of its propagation, it is sufficiently uniform in its relevant characteristics." UPOV Convention, ch. 3, art. 8.

18. To be stable, a variety's relevant characteristics must remain unchanged after repeated propagation or in case of a cycle of propagation, at the end of that cycle. UPOV Convention, ch. 3 art. 9.

19. Kloppenburg, FIRST THE SEED, *supra* Chapter One, note 2, at 159 ("'[T]he early initiatives sponsored by the Rockefeller Foundation and the U.S. government spawned a whole series of secondary agricultural programs that encompassed an increasingly broad number of crops, countries and funding agencies. These programs spread to other countries during the 1960s.").

20. *Id.* at 160–61 ("[T]he IARCS perform a dual role in the processing of plant germplasm. They necessarily collect and evaluate indigenous land races and primitive cultivars that are the raw material from [high-yielding varieties] are bred. And because their "imported" agricultures are based on the very species that the IARCS are mandated to improve (i.e., corn, wheat, potato), such collection and evaluation are of direct value to the developed nations.... [and] are also vehicles for the efficient extraction of plant genetic resources from the Third World and their transfer to the gene banks of Europe, North America and Japan.").

21. *Ibid.*

22. *Id.* at 161("At these [FAO] meetings, in 1961 and 1967, there developed a consensus that a coordinated global program of collection and conservation was necessary to ensure that the essential raw materials of plant improvement would not be lost to humanity."); *see also* Sir Otto H. Frankel, *Genetic Resources: The Founding Years*, 7 DIVERSITY 26 (Fall 1985); *Genetic Resources: The Founding Years—Part Two: The Movement's Constituent Assembly*, 8 DIVERSITY 30 (Winter 1986); *Genetic Resources: The Founding Years—Part Three: The Long Road to the International Board*, 9 DIVERSITY 30 (1986).

23. FOWLER, UNNATURAL SELECTION, *supra* Chapter One, note 2, at 241–42.

Thus, farmer varieties were being avidly collected and stored *ex situ* in places like the NSSL, while at the same time a legal regime was being constructed that would treat uniform varieties bred for industrial agriculture as intellectual property.

Under the 1978 UPOV, farmer-grown local varieties and landraces were considered to be openly accessible because they lacked the uniformity and stability required for protection.

The UPOV was also similar to the PVPA in having a "farmers' exemption," that allowed any farmer who purchased seeds of a protected variety to save seeds from those crops for subsequent replanting without paying additional royalties.[24] Subsequently, the seed industry lobbied governments in many UPOV-member countries to limit the "farmers' exemption."[25] In the 1991 UPOV, the rights of farmers were curtailed as follows: (1) article 15.2 made "farmers' rights" optional and allowed each UPOV member nation to decide whether or not to extend such rights;[26] (2) plant breeders' exemptions were narrowed in articles 14 and 15.1, so that "essentially derived" varieties cannot be marketed without permission from the original plant breeders;[27] and

---

24. The so-called "farmers' exemption" in the 1978 UPOV is implicit. The actual language of the 1978 UPOV art. 5(1) states that:

The effect of the right granted to the breeder is that his prior authorization shall be required for:
- the production for purposes of commercial marketing
- the offering for sale
- marketing

of the reproductive or vegetative propagating material as such, of the variety.

Thus the 1978 UPOV, in limiting the rights of plant breeders to only prevent the commercial exploitation of their varieties, indirectly extended to farmers the right to save seed for their own personal (i.e., non-commercial) purposes.

25. The global seed and biotechnology industries continue to pressure developing countries to adopt the 1991 version of UPOV with its stronger monopoly rights and watered-down farmers' exemption. *See, e.g.* Nadine Barron & Ed Couzens, *Intellectual Property Rights and Plant Variety Protection in South Africa: An International Perspective*, 16 J. ENVIRONMENTAL LAW 19, 36 (2004).

26. The farmer's exemption is contained in the 1991 UPOV Convention art. 15 which reads as follows:

(2) [*Optional exception*] Notwithstanding Article 14, each Contracting Party may, within reasonable limits and subject to the safeguarding of the legitimate interests of the breeder, restrict the breeders' right in relation to any variety in order to permit farmers to use for propagating purposes, on their own holdings, the product of the harvest which they have obtained by planting, on their own holdings, the protected variety or a variety covered by Article 14(5)(a)(i) or (ii).

27. Ch. 4, art. 14 reads as follows:

(5) [essentially derived and certain other varieties] (a) The provisions of paragraphs (1) to (4) shall also apply in relation to (i) varieties which are essentially derived from the protected variety, where the protected variety is not itself an essentially derived variety, (ii) varieties which are not clearly distinguishable in accordance with Article 7 from the protected variety and (iii) varieties whose production requires the repeated use of the protected variety.

The convention itself defines essentially derived varieties as "predominantly derived ... while retaining the expression of essential characteristics," "clearly distinguishable," or "conforming to the initial variety in the expression of the essential characteristics that result from the genotype or combination of genotypes in the variety." These definitions rely on an understanding of the phrases "essential characteristics" and "clearly distinguishable." While the UPOV protects PBRs over "essentially derived" varieties, the convention itself fails to define what "essentially derived" may entail. It therefore leaves this interpretation to the UPOV signatory states to determine, through such vehicles as domestic legislation, judicial interpretation, or contractual negotiations between private parties. *See* Mark Hanning, *An Examination of the Possibility to Secure Intellectual Property Rights for Plant Ge-*

(3) unlike the 1978 UPOV, which did not allow member nations to grant utility patents for sexually reproduced varieties, article 35(2) of the 1991 UPOV seemed to do just the opposite.[28]

The long-term status of the UPOV remains to be seen. In particular, it is unclear what effect TRIPS (the subsequent intellectual property treaty discussed later in this chapter) will have on developing countries' abilities to enter into the UPOV. Arguably, developing countries may accede to the 1978 UPOV (which allows farmer seed saving) and stay out of the 1991 agreement; however, this is only possible if developed countries like the U.S. allow lower 1978 levels of UPOV protection for protected varieties, which is doubtful.

B. The CGIAR System

The Consultative Group on International Agricultural Resources (CGIAR) is the parent institution of an international network of agricultural research centers (IARCs).[29] For example, the International Maize and Wheat Improvement Center (CIMMYT) in Mexico focuses on collection, storage and breeding of barley, maize, wheat and triticale.[30] The International Rice Research Institute (IRRI) focuses its work on varieties of rice.[31]

The CGIAR is governed by a board representing donors of funds such as the Rockefeller and Ford Foundations. These foundations, in part, created and funded the CGIAR to try and unite privately or nationally funded gene banks into an international network. The CGIAR is headquartered in Washington, D.C.[32]

---

netic Resources Developed by Indigenous People of NAFTA States: Domestic Legislation Under the International Convention for Protection of New Plant Varieties, 13 ARIZ. J. INT'L & COMP. L. 175, 241–42 (1996) (footnotes omitted).

28. Article 35 of the 1991 UPOV states:

(2) [*Optional exception*] (a) Notwithstanding the provisions of Article 3(1), any State which, at the time of becoming party to this Convention, is a party to the Act of 1978 and which, as far as varieties reproduced asexually are concerned, provides for protection by an industrial property title other than a breeder's right shall have the right to continue to do so without applying this Convention to those varieties.

One commentator noted that the 1991 Act aided plant breeders in that it removed "the prohibition against double protection of varieties, found in Article 2, which had prevented UPOV members from offering both breeders' rights protection and patents for plant varieties. The U.S. had previously been exempted from the ban on double protection, but its removal creates the opportunity for the rapid expansion of both forms of protection in other countries, especially some in Europe. Under the present European Patent Convention, a specific prohibition for patenting was created for 'plant or animal varieties or essentially biological processes for the production of plants or animals; this provision does not apply to microbiological processes or the products thereof.' While the provision appears to prevent all patenting of plants, it has been interpreted as applying only to varieties *per se*. As a result, the European Patent Office now examines and grants utility patents on plants when the claims are not directed at a variety." Neil D. Hamilton, *Who Owns Dinner? Evolving Legal Mechanisms for Ownership of Plant Genetic Resources*, 28 TULSA L.J. 587, 606–07 (1993) (footnotes omitted) [hereinafter Hamilton, *Who Owns Dinner?*].

29. *CGIAR Research: Genebanks and Plant Genetic Resources, available at* http://www.cgiar.org/impact/genebankssdatabases.html (last visited March 17, 2007). The CGIAR centers "together maintain over 700,000 samples of crops, forages and agro-forestry genetic resources in the public domain."

30. Fowler, UNNATURAL SELECTION, *supra* Chapter One, note 2, at 182.

31. *Id.*

32. *Id.*

In 1974, the CGIAR formed the International Board for Plant Genetic Resources (IBPGR) whose scientific experts would serve as a spur to PGR conservation activities. While the rhetoric surrounding the founding of the IBPGR was shot through with talk of "neutrality" and "expertise," Cary Fowler notes that proponents of the "Green Revolution" and others with a unilinear view of international development were on the IBPGR.[33] Fowler notes that Richard Demuth, "a Washington lawyer for the State Department, who long had ties with the Agency for International Development ... retired ... and became the first to chair this 'purely' technical and scientific body."[34]

The IBRGR has an unusual relationship with the United Nations Food and Agriculture Organization (FAO). While the IBPGR has its headquarters at the FAO's Rome offices and the FAO pays the IBPGR's staff salaries, the IBPGR has autonomy in setting its own programmatic agenda.[35] Fowler notes that the IBPGR during this period had a "distinctly northern flavor," and pointed out that in the late 1980s, "[o]nly 15 percent of the [germplasm] samples collected [were] designated for storage in Third World collections ... [and] [f]ully 85 percent [have] been stored in industrialized countries and IARC seed banks."[36]

The IBPGR had the power to designate which crops were endangered as well as the order in which germplasm from such crops would be collected and preserved.

The legal treatment of these stored PGRs was somewhat ambiguous prior to the 1990s, but became clearer later in that decade. At the least, prior to the 1980s, PGRs would have been treated a belonging to the "common heritage of mankind," and thus,

---

33. The term "development" and terms such as "developed" and "developing" used to designate different countries are drawn from a larger debate about the United Nations and the Bretton Woods Initiatives that were created following World War II. Bretton Woods established the International Monetary Fund and the World Bank, and, in the 1990s, the World Trade Organization. *See* Richard Peet with Elaine Hardwick, THEORIES OF DEVELOPMENT (1999). Margaret Chon writes that,

"[a]ccording to the (neo)liberal world view, the development system basically works, with some minor adjustments needed as problem arise. To remedy politically unacceptable differences among the developing and developed countries, policymakers need just add a little more 'equality' and stir. Mistakes are minor and the overall direction is positive. One underlying assumption is that the short term costs of free trade will result in long term gains by pushing countries into greater economic growth. Economic growth is the sine qua non of development.... (Neo)liberalism is characterized by certain policy recommendations, including, among other things, trade liberalization, foreign direct investment and property rights." Chon, *Development Divide, supra* Chapter Two, note 24, at 2861–63.

Andy Crump defines "developing countries" as countries that

[i]nclude states which are variously labeled as ... underdeveloped countries, low income countries, Majority world, the South or the Third World. These nations have low levels of technology, basic living standards and little in the way of an industrial base.... Their economies are mainly agricultural ... Per capita incomes are below $5000 and often less than $1500. Around 70 percent of the world's population lives in developing countries. Andy Crump and Wayne Elwood, THE A TO Z OF WORLD DEVELOPMENT 78–79 (1999).

Crump goes on to describe "developed countries" as

Northern, industrialized nations, sometimes also referred to as the 'First World.'... [this category] almost always includes the 35 market-oriented countries of the Organization for Economic Co-operation and Development (OECD).... Generally, nations having a per capita income of over $10,000 are included in this group. *Id.* at 78. *See also* Chon, *Development Divide, supra* Chapter Two, note 24, at 2826.

34. Fowler, UNNATURAL SELECTION, *supra* Chapter One, note 2, at 183.

35. *Id.* at 184.

36. *Id.*

would have been subject to a principle of "open access" with a norm of reciprocity. Professor Stephen Brush writes

> Common heritage was the ex ante governance of biological resources until the last quarter of the twentieth century.... Common heritage refers to the treatment of genetic resources as belonging to the public domain and not owned or otherwise monopolized by a single group or interest. Common heritage is similar to common property regimes that anthropologists and other social scientists have described for nonmarket economies. Neither common heritage nor common property implies a lack of rules (*res nullius*) ... Rather they imply community management (*res communes*) that involves regulated access to common resources and reciprocity among users. [37]

During the mid-1980s, there was a significant shift in the legal characterization of PGRs. This shift may be seen in the way that the 1992 Convention on Biological Diversity (CBD)[38] recharacterized PGRs as being the "sovereign national property" of the country in which they are located.

This was a significant change, particularly when the IBPGR "has been particularly generous to the United States when it has come to designating sites for global and regional storage responsibility [for germplasm].... [o]f the top 15 crops, the United States ranks among the top four germplasm holders in the world."[39]

With the CGIAR system, there were marked critiques of the IBPGR channeling PGRs to U.S. gene banks in the early 1980s.[40] The U.S. also placed conditions to the IBPGR under which the U.S. would accept germplasm storage responsibilities, one of which was that accepted germplasm would "become the property of the U.S. government."[41]

"Common heritage" treatment of PGRs and "open access" came under critical pressure during this decade. Anti-colonialist critics of "common heritage" argued that it was a vestige of colonialism that facilitated a unilateral flow of genetic resources out of the poor nations of the global South.[42] Others argued for abandoning the "common heritage" principle because it led to a "Tragedy of the Commons" result—because the resources were treated as "open access," it left them open to premature degradation.[43]

---

37. Brush, FARMERS' BOUNTY, *supra* Chapter Two, note 22, at 221–22 (2004).

38. Convention on Biological Diversity, 5 June 1992, UNEP/Bio.Div./N7-INC5/4, 31 I.L.M. 818 (1993) (Opened for signature, May 1992, and entered into force, December 1993); *see also* Parties to the Convention on Biological Diversity, *available at* http://www.biodiv.org/world/parties.asp (last visited March 17, 2007).

39. Fowler, UNNATURAL SELECTION, *supra* Chapter One, note 2, at 185; *see also* Fowler & Mooney, SHATTERING, *supra* Chapter One, note 11, at 190–91.

40. Fowler, UNNATURAL SELECTION, *supra* Chapter One note 2, at 185 (describing a letter from the Institute for Tropical Agriculture's David Wood to the IBPGR criticizing the way that there seemed to be an untoward relation between the financial donations to IBPGR and the number of collections designated to that country by the IBPGR).

41. *Id.* at 186 (citing a letter from T.W. Edminste to Richard Demuth, Chairman of the IBPGR, Jan 19, 1997); *see also* Seabrook; *Sowing for Apocalypse*, *supra* Chapter Two, note 42.

42. Brush, FARMERS' BOUNTY, *supra* Chapter Two, note 22, at 231; *see also* Shiva, GREEN REVOLUTION, *supra* Chapter Two, note 81.

43. Brush, FARMERS' BOUNTY, *supra* Chapter Two, note 22, at 230 (describing the argument that "[a]s long as biological resources were common heritage goods, nations richly endowed with genetic diversity had no incentive to conserve them. Indeed the lack of ownership was seen as incentive to overexploit biological resources."); *see also* Roger A. Sedjo, *Property Rights and the Protection of Plant Genetic Resources*, at 293, *in* SEEDS AND SOVEREIGNTY, *supra* Introduction, note 1. For a fuller discussion of "Tragedy of the Commons," see Chapter 5, 99–101, *infra*.

It was against this increasingly contentious backdrop that delegates from developing countries met at the 1981 FAO Conference to express their growing discontent with the IBPGR's tilt toward the U.S. and other countries of the global North and what they saw as a generally unilateral, Northward flow of PGRs.

Concerns over the erosion of genetic diversity in major crops as well as disquiet over how industrialized nations were moving quickly to adopt intellectual property systems (such as the UPOV or the PVPA, which protect plant varieties as well as provide patent protection for gene sequences within plants) coalesced during this period.

These critiques and concerns finally crystallized at the March 1983 meeting of the FAO's Committee on Agriculture, where delegates openly argued and challenged the status quo, calling for changes in IBPGR policy and a restructuring of the CGIAR system.[44]

One of the major challenges raised focused on the basic assumption underlying both the PVPA and the UPOV—the distinction between "raw" and "worked" germplasm. This distinction provided a rationale for protecting germplasm that had been "worked" by plant breeders, and denying it to germplasm that was merely "raw." "Raw" germplasm could be further distinguished as highly variable and when "found" (generally by someone in the developed world) would be transformed from a "primitive" landrace into an elite "stable" cultivar thus protectable as intellectual property.

Needless to say, this debate was politically fraught. Countries such as the U.S. were unwilling to give an inch when a country like Mexico insisted that the "common heritage" principle should apply to both "raw" and "worked" germplasm, to elite cultivars as well as "primitive" landraces and farmers' varieties.[45]

The next section explores the consequences of the declaration that came out of the 1983 FAO Conference.

C. The 1983 International Undertaking on Plant Genetic Resources (IUPGR)[46]

As discussed above, the United Nations-backed FAO became a flashpoint for debates between Northern and Southern countries regarding PGR exploitation during the early 1980s. In 1974, a wide variety of international institutions formed the IBPGR to help fund and organize germplasm collection.[47] Over strong U.S. objections, the FAO estab-

---

44. Fowler, UNNATURAL SELECTION, *supra* Chapter One, note 2, at 188.

45. *Id.* at 185.

46. *See* INTERNATIONAL UNDERTAKING ON PLANT GENETIC RESOURCES, Report of the United Nations Food and Agriculture Organization placing Collections of Plant Germplasm under the auspices of the FAO, art. 3(a) (1994), reprinted in a booklet of the CGIAR Centre Policy Instruments, GUIDELINES AND STATEMENTS ON GENETIC RESOURCES, BIOTECHNOLOGY AND INTELLECTUAL PROPERTY RIGHTS (September 2001) (Agreement between individual CGIAR members and the FAO that PGRs are held "in trust for the benefit of the international community") [hereinafter IUPGR].

47. See Laurence R. Helfer, *Using Intellectual Property Rights to Preserve the Global Genetic Commons: The International Treaty on Plant Genetic Resources for Food and Agriculture*, at 217, in INT'L PUBLIC GOODS, *supra* Chapter One, note 2 [hereinafter Helfer, *Using IP*]; Kloppenburg, FIRST THE SEED, *supra* Chapter One, note 2, at 164–65; *see also* Fowler, UNNATURAL SELECTION, *supra* Chapter One, note 2, at 182; Hamilton, *Who Owns Dinner? supra* note 28.

lished a Commission on Plant Genetic Resources for Food and Agriculture (CPGR), which in turn adopted the International Undertaking on Plant Genetic Resources (IUPGR) in 1983.[48] A group of developing countries spearheaded the IUPGR and the CPGR, which also drew support from NGOs allied with the International Coalition for Development Action.[49]

The IUPGR was a nonbinding agreement that set out rules and standards for exchanging and conserving seeds and plant tissues.[50] Importantly, the IUPGR took the controversial position that PGRs are the "common heritage of mankind."[51] Why would

---

48. U.N.F.A.O. Res. 8/83, U.N.F.A.O., 22d Session, Nov. 5–23, 1983 ("At the 1981 FAO biennial conference, a resolution was adopted, against the vehement opposition of developed countries [especially the United States, United Kingdom, and Australia] and the seed industry, calling for the drafting of a legal convention. In 1983, the over-ambitious demand for a convention was replaced by a call for a non-binding undertaking, and for the creation of a new FAO Commission on Plant Genetic Resources (CPGRS) where governments could meet for discussion and monitor what became known as the International Undertaking on Plant Genetic Resources."). Graham Dutfield, *TRIPS-Related Aspects of Traditional Knowledge*, 33 CASE W. RES. J. INT'L L. 233, 265 (2001) [hereinafter Dutfield, *TRIPS*].

49. NGOs such as the International Coalition for Development Action were more knowledgeable on the outstanding issues than were most of the delegates from the developing world. Thus, the delegates viewed these NGOs as resources that they could consult for analysis and information. Also, the NGOs played the important role of bridging the gap between Latin American delegates and their counterparts from Africa and Asia. *See* Fowler & Mooney, SHATTERING, *supra* Chapter One, note 11, at 187; *See also* Helfer, *Using IP*, *supra* note 47, at 217–218 ("[G]overnments in developing countries pressured the [FAO's Committee on Genetic Resources] to staunch the flow of PGRs from centers of biodiversity in the developing world to plant breeding institutions in industrialized nations. The governments argued that commercial plant breeders were using PGRs to develop new proprietary plant varieties without compensating the countries that had provided the new materials for their innovations."); *see also* CFAS Consultants (Wye) Ltd., Centre for European Agricultural Studies, FINAL REPORT FOR DIRECTORATE GENERAL TRADE, EUROPEAN COMMISSION, STUDY ON RELATIONSHIP BETWEEN AGREEMENTS ON TRIPS AND BIODIVERSITY RELATED ISSUES (2000).

50. See IUPGR, *supra* note 46. The IUPGR declared that naturally occurring plants, plant genetic resources stored in gene banks and cultivars and elite varieties were *all* part of the "heritage of mankind and consequently should be available without restriction" for scientific research, plant breeding, and conservation. *See* IUPGR, Report of the Conference of the United Nations Food and Agriculture Organization, 22d Sess., U.N. Doc C/83/REP (1983), art. 5 (declaring that adherents to the IU must make germplasm available "free of charge, on the basis of mutual exchange or on mutually agreed terms").

51. The principle of "common heritage" is embodied in the IUPGR of the Food and Agriculture Organization of the United Nations, International Undertaking on Plant Genetic Resources for Food and Agriculture, U.N. Food & Agriculture Organization, 22d Sess., Annex, Res. 8/83, *available at* ftp://ext-ftp.fao.org/ag/cgrfa/Res/C8-83E.pdf (last visited March 3, 2005) ("Recognizing that (a) *plant genetic resources* are a *heritage of mankind* to be preserved, and *to be freely available for use, for the benefit of present and future generations*") (emphasis in original). The phrase "common heritage of mankind" derives from Hugo Grotius and came into contemporary usage when Avril Pardo, the Ambassador of Malta, spoke in November 1967 of the deep seabed as the "common heritage of mankind." Pardo articulated five basic points: (1) the seabed and the ocean floor, underlying the seas beyond the limits of national jurisdiction as defined in the treaty, are not subject to national appropriation in any manner whatsoever; (2) the seabed and the ocean floor beyond the limits of national jurisdiction shall be reserved exclusively for peaceful purpose; (3) scientific research with regard to the deep seas and ocean floor not directly connected with defence, shall be freely permissible and its result available to all; (4) the resources of the seabed and ocean floor beyond the limit of national jurisdiction shall be exploited primarily in the interest of mankind with particular regard to the needs of poor countries; and (5) the exploration and exploitation of the seabed and ocean floor beyond the limits of national jurisdiction shall be conducted in a manner consistent with the principles and purposes of the UN Charter and in a manner not causing obstruction of the high seas or

this be controversial, given the fact that the developed countries of the North had justified their access to and use of the genetic resources from the developing countries of the
South on just that basis? One reason why is that the IUPGR's "common heritage" principle invoked an extremely broad definition of PGRs "subject to the undertaking." Commercial plant varieties and elite cultivars protected by plant breeders' rights and plant
patents were to be treated in the same way as traditional landraces and wild plants — as
"common heritage." Therefore, farmers and breeders around the world would have free
access to these commercial plant varieties.[52] Laurence Helfer observes that

> [a]lthough the Undertaking was merely a nonbinding statement of principles, it
> was opposed by the United States and some European governments who ar-
> gued that the document conflicted with a multilateral document [the
> UPOV] ... [and] also with their national patent laws, which grant intellectual
> property rights in isolated and purified genes.[53]

A second reason why the IUPGR was so controversial may be found in its refusal to
abide by the traditional distinction between "raw" and "worked" plant germplasm. Prior
to the 1980s, "raw" germplasm was not commodified, but "worked" germplasm was
commodifiable.[54] Yet what is the source of this asymmetric distinction between "raw"
and "worked," and how coherent is it? Consider this observation by Cary Fowler:

> Third World farmers have been found to employ taxonomic systems, encour-
> age introgression, use selection, make efforts to see that varieties are adapted,
> multiply seeds, field test, record data, and even name their varieties. In short,
> they do what many northern plant breeders do, except they do not apply for
> patents.... If the actions of Third World farmers can so closely resemble the
> steps taken in more formal plant breeding programs, and if the product of
> their labors is valuable, the argument can be made that the genetic diversity of
> the Third World cannot be considered a "raw material."[55]

In terms of an international division of labor, the developing world has generally
been defined by the export of "raw" materials. As discussed in Chapter One, Northern
industrialized nations have historically and systemically acquired "raw" germplasm,
generally without compensation, from "gene-rich" regions of the equatorial Southern

---

serious impairment of the marine environment. *See* Susan J. Buck, THE GLOBAL COMMONS: AN IN-
TRODUCTION (1998).

52. It is no surprise that such an arrangement was unacceptable to industrial nations, especially
those with established private seed industries. These nations viewed the undertaking was as a veiled
attempt at undermining the principle of private property. They had good reason for concern since
the undertaking literally sought to decommodify commercial plant varieties. *See* Kloppenburg,
FIRST THE SEED, *supra* Chapter One, note 1, at 174. *See also* Jim Chen, *Webs of Life: Conservation as
a Species of Information Policy*, 89 IOWA L. REV. 495, 583 (2004) [hereinafter Chen, *Webs of Life*] (In
adopting the undertaking the "Food and Agriculture Organization of the United Nations (FAO)
provides one example of an approach repudiating private property."); Fowler, UNNATURAL SELEC-
TION, *supra* Chapter One, note 2, at 189 ("The Undertaking specified that all categories of
germplasm should be freely available and proceeded to list those categories, which predictably included patented varieties and breeding lines — a direct threat to plant variety protection ... Third
World delegates and NGOs were still promoting the principle of 'free availability' of germplasm ...
[and] had not made the leap to advocating Third World sovereignty over the material.").

53. Helfer, *Using IP*, *supra* note 47, at 218–219; *see also* Dan Leskien & Michael Flinter, *Intellectual Property Rights and Plant Genetic Resources: Options for a Sui Generis System, Issues in Genetic
Resources*, No. 6 at 8, INTERNATIONAL PLANT GENETIC RESOURCES INSTITUTE (1997).

54. The terms "commodified" and "commodifiable" here designate a partial product of intellectual property laws.

55. Fowler, UNNATURAL SELECTION, *supra* Chapter One, note 2, at 189.

hemisphere and "worked" it to produce staple crops (and, more recently, plants and seeds) that are protected by intellectual property laws. As such, one explanation as to why "worked" germplasm has been increasingly commodified may be that "none of the world's twenty most important food crops is indigenous to North America or Australia.... [and] it is clearly the West Central Asiatic and Latin American regions where germplasm resources have historically made the largest genetic contribution to feeding the world."[56]

Although it is tempting to picture a gene-poor Northern hemisphere siphoning the genetic wealth of a gene-rich Southern hemisphere, neither the North nor the South are genetically independent. Rather, there is (and has been) a deep and politically contentious genetic interdependence between the two hemispheres, and it is instructive to examine global germplasm flows. Many international institutions largely rely on existing germplasm banks for samples.[57] The banks are located primarily in the industrialized countries of North America and Europe.[58] Because most funds from the IBPGR have gone to germplasm collections in the industrialized North, these countries are now rich in gene-banked germplasm. They possess "more stored germplasm accessions than do those nations that are regions of natural diversity for the crop."[59] Indeed, Professor Brush writes that

> of the 6,159,248 accessions inventoried among all gene banks in 1996, slightly more than half (3,447,469) were held by gene banks in Europe, North America, Japan and international agricultural research centers of ... [the] CGIAR ... a large portion of the total diversity of the world's major crops has been captured and stored in gene banks of major industrial countries and agricultural research centers.[60]

As a result, the U.S., which has been characterized as "gene poor" but which developed extensive seed collections under the "common heritage" regime, is a net *exporter* of seed germplasm to supposedly "gene rich" countries.[61]

Conversely, the least developed countries (LDCs) are net *importers* of seed germplasm, left dependent on access to seed banks such as the NSSL in the industrialized nations, even though they may have been the sources of the very seeds now collected in seed banks. As a result of their germplasm dependence, Professor Brush notes that

> a slowdown in crop germplasm exchange is likely to hurt poor countries ... more than wealthy industrial countries without indigenous crop resources [because] industrial countries have established effective crop collections that are used not only by their national breeding programs but by programs else-

---

56. Kloppenburg, FIRST THE SEED, *supra* Chapter One, note 2, at 181.

57. Note that "mining" genetic resources does not directly cause the depletion of the genetic resource. The samples taken for a gene bank are *de minimis* in terms of physical quantity or size of the species. In other resources, such as coal or oil, the value of the resource is related directly to the amount extracted.

58. Kloppenburg, FIRST THE SEED, *supra* Chapter One, note 2, at 162 ("By 1970 it was apparent that such predictions were correct and that a corollary to the adoption of the new Green Revolution cultivars was the displacement and disappearance of the land races that provided breeders with the genetic variability on which their advances were founded."); Fowler, UNNATURAL SELECTION, *supra* Chapter One, note 2 at 243 ("During the green revolution, not only was an infrastructure of agricultural colleges and extension services built, but also a new market for seeds was created. This process destroyed much of the old system of seed-saving and farmer-breeding.").

59. Brush, FARMER's BOUNTY, *supra* Chapter Two, note 22, at 166 (2004).

60. *Id.* at 237–38.

61. *Id.* at 237.

where.... the poorest countries are net borrowers from other countries, including the United States.[62]

The different roles that germplasm flow has played in the Northern and Southern hemispheres further complicate whether (and, if so, in what sense) germplasm can be called a "raw" material at all. The trend in both the laws and agricultural technology in the developed countries has been to define germplasm as private intellectual property. The contradiction between characterizing "raw" germplasm as "common heritage" and "worked" germplasm as intellectual property complicates the task of creating a coherent system for addressing germplasm flows.

One partial explanation for uncompensated taking of germplasm from the countries of the Southern hemisphere is the pervasive idea that "the major food plants of the world are not owned by any one people and are quite literally a part of our human heritage."[63] This idea has allowed those germplasm collectors to attempt to justify and rationalize both the historical and contemporary practices, as well as institutional structures, of uncompensated appropriation.[64] Such difficulties and controversies are also important indicators as to why subsequent multilateral agreements have steered away from the "raw"/"worked" distinction.

The problems of genetic erosion due to monoculture agriculture in the developing world and genetic vulnerability due to uncompensated appropriation in the developed world present curious symmetry and further support for the notion that the two hemispheres are genetically interdependent. As the global seed industry expands, genetic erosion increases. The global regions that produced the genetic diversity which enabled plant breeders (both public and private) to introduce traits into cultivated varieties have also become growing markets for the introduction of proprietary plant varieties, agricultural systems, and high chemical input products. Unfortunately, uniform genetically engineered and other proprietary varieties are extremely vulnerable to new pests, diseases, and blights.

This vulnerability makes diverse germplasm more important than ever. Genetic diversity acts as a kind of "insurance policy" against problems such as the corn blight that devastated U.S. crops in the Midwest during the 1970s. That blight, which attacked a characteristic present in 90 percent of American corn varieties, cost American farmers fifteen percent of that year's harvest.[65] A subsequent National Academy of Sciences study found that American crops were "impressively uniform genetically and impressively vulnerable."[66] Though agronomists and policymakers tried addressing the genetic vulnerability of industrial agriculture from the late 1950s through the 1970s, the consensus on genetic vulnerability as a serious global problem attenuated over time. This may be due in part to a sanguine sense of genetic security that rests on the national and

---

62. *Id.* at 236.

63. H. Garrison Wilkes, *The World's Crop Germplasm—An Endangered Resource*, 33 BULL. ATOM. SCI. 8 (1977).

64. United Nations Food and Agriculture Organization, PROPOSAL FOR THE ESTABLISHMENT OF AN INTERNATIONAL GENEBANK AND THE PREPARATION OF A DRAFT INTERNATIONAL CONVENTIONAL FOR PLANT GENETIC RESOURCES (conference resolution), Document D 83/LIM/2 September (1983); Norman Myers, A WEALTH OF WILD SPECIES 24 (1983); Dominic Fuccillo, Linda Sears & Paul Stapleton, BIODIVERSITY IN TRUST: CONSERVATION AND USE OF PLANT GENETIC RESOURCES IN CGIAR CENTRES (1997); Kloppenburg, FIRST THE SEED, *supra* Chapter One, note 1, at 152–190.

65. Kloppenburg, FIRST THE SEED, *supra* Chapter One, note 2, at 163; *see also* Fowler, UNNATURAL SELECTION, *supra* note 2, at 111; Doyle, ALTERED HARVEST, *supra* Chapter Two, note 80, 1–8.

66. Kloppenburg, FIRST THE SEED, *supra* Chapter One, note 2, at 163.

international system of *ex situ* gene banks such as the NSSL and the CGIAR system. However, these gene banks are underfunded and cannot replace a global system for *in situ* preservation and related traditional agricultural knowledge and know how.[67]

Ultimately, the emerging global germplasm system has produced genetic vulnerability and genetic erosion—processes and products that further link the developed and developing world. Elite commercial varieties that provide the basis of modern industrial agriculture show a high degree of genetic uniformity because they have undergone rigorous selection in breeding. Their narrow genetic makeup renders them systematically vulnerable to diseases and pest infestations in a way that heterogeneous landraces are not. As genetic erosion drains the gene pool for an entire species, it becomes more difficult to find characteristics to combat the appearance of disease or pest epidemics that challenge the genetically vulnerable commercial cultivars.[68]

Under the legal regime in place prior to the 1990s, once "primitive" or "raw" plant germplasm was construed legally as the "common heritage of mankind," it could be removed from genetically rich regions for as little as it cost to gather a few samples. These "free" genetic resources then flowed into Northern gene banks and laboratories of agrichemical giants, where their genetic diversity was "worked" to improve and safeguard proprietary, patented varieties. Then, these "stabilized" varieties were sold at a premium in the emerging agricultural markets of the very countries and regions where the genetic resources originated, pushing formerly genetically diverse countries toward industrial agriculture and monoculture. Ironically, the last reserve of genetic diversity may reside in the developed world's gene banks, where genetic diversity has finally been priced.

The final irony here is that "common heritage" treatment for PGRs was vilified and abandoned as (1) an artifact of colonialism, or (2) as giving rise to a "Tragedy of the Commons" scenario, *precisely* at the time when developing countries were becoming net *importers* from gene banks located in countries like the U.S.

D. The Keystone Dialogues and "Farmers' Rights"

As discussed above, prior to the 1980s, PGRs were treated as the "common heritage of mankind," and as such were legally seen as freely appropriable.[69] Consensus as to whether "common heritage" treatment adequately applied to germplasm did not last.[70]

---

67. Brush, FARMERS' BOUNTY, *supra* Chapter Two, note 22, at 200–01.

68. Kloppenburg, FIRST THE SEED, *supra* Chapter One, note 2, at 162.

69. There is also the framework of international human rights norms and laws as articulated first, by the Universal Declaration of Human Rights and partially embodied by two international covenants, the International Covenant on Civil and Political Rights (ICCPR) and the International Covenant on Economic, Social and Cultural Rights (ICESCR) as discussed by Rosemary J. Coombe, *Intellectual Property, Human Rights & Sovereignty: New Dilemmas in International Law Posed by the Recognition of Indigenous Knowledge and the Conservation of Biodiversity*, 6 IND. J. GLOBAL LEG. STUD. 59 (1998). Her discussion is an excellent analysis of issues that are beyond the scope of this Chapter.

70. Kloppenburg, FIRST THE SEED, *supra* Chapter One, note 2, at 171–72 ("[I]nternationalization of the commercial seed industry has brought plant germplasm as a commodity and plant germplasm as a public good into unambiguous and contradictory juxtaposition in the Third World. Governments and companies of the advanced capitalist nations have encouraged the developing nations to adopt PBR legislation—that is, to recognize private property rights in one form of germplasm. At the same time, they had argued forcefully for the need to collect and preserve other

In the 1980s, the FAO began developing an international framework to govern the global flow of germplasm.[71] As discussed above, as they drafted a declaration, two opposing views emerged. On one hand, representatives from the developing world and the communist bloc nations wanted to apply the principles of "common heritage" and free exchange to *all* types of germplasm.[72] On the other hand, representatives from the developed countries maintained that only so-called "primitive" farmer varieties and landraces should be deemed "common heritage" and that elite breeders' lines should be excluded from this category.[73] The developing and communist bloc nations prevailed at the FAO, and the definition of "common heritage" came to include mutant lines, current breeders' lines, and genetically engineered germplasm—all subject to PVP certificates and/or utility patents. However, this victory at the 1983 FAO Conference was more symbolic than substantial, as the result was a non-binding "Undertaking" which involved voluntary adherence rather than a binding "Convention."[74]

Meanwhile, countries such as the United States flatly refused to participate in the IUPGR. The resulting stalemate lasted until 1989, when the developing and developed countries reached preliminary agreement on three principles reflected in the Keystone Dialogues.[75] First, the parties came to the consensus that plants protected by PVP/UPOV rights would *not* be considered freely accessible or treated as "common heritage"—a recognition of the validity of plant breeders' rights in plant varieties.[76] Second, the parties agreed that "common heritage" or open accessibility to farmers' lan-

forms of germplasm sich as primitive cultivars and landraces. Although the rationale for the efforts at plant genetic conservation in the Third World has emphasized the ultimate economic utility of the genetic material located there, these resources have been held to be the common heritage of humanity, a public good to be freely appropriated.").

71. *Id.* at 172 ("Mounting Third World dissatisfaction found expression in political action in the United Nations system. At the FAO's 21st biennial conference in 1981, a resolution was passed instructing FAO's director to prepare a draft of an international agreement that would provide a legal framework for controlling the flow of genetic resources.").

72. *Ibid.*

73. *Id.* at 173.

74. *Id.* ("[A]rticle 2 of the Undertaking makes a crucial addition to the range of materials that have been conventionally included under the rubric of 'plant genetic resources' [that are the common heritage of mankind]." To the primitive cultivars, land races, and wild and weedy relatives of crop plants that have long been the object of collection and have been appropriated free of charge ... the FAO Undertaking explicitly appends "special genetic stocks [including elite and current breeders' lines and mutants].").

75. Fowler, UNNATURAL SELECTION, *supra* Chapter One, note 2, at 197–199 (detailing how in the late 1980s, Ciba-Geigy and other agrichemical corporations attempted to reach out to its opponents in the fight over the IUPGR and funded a conference at the Keystone Center in Colorado as a "neutral, safe, off-the-record site for discussions among key participants in the contentious debates.... Forty people participated in the meetng. They included the heads of the government resource programs for the United States, China, Brazil, Peru, the Netherlands, Ethiopia, and the Nordic countries. Both IBPGR and the FAO Commission of Plant Genetic Resources were represented, as were the World Bank and the CGIAR system. From the corporate side, the president of Cetus, ... [executives] from Pioneer, ... Ciba-Geigy, ... [and] DeKalb-Pfizer Genetics were present.... [as were representatives from the] US National Academy of Sciences and the US Agency for International Development ... [and the head of] the [U.S. House Agriculture Committee]. NGO participation centered around the Rural Advancement Fund International ... and Third World NGOs that had participated in FAO lobbying activities. The Mexican ambassador to FAO ... was also present.... [as were several well-known academics]....").

76. The Keystone Center, FINAL CONSENSUS REPORT OF THE KEYSTONE INTERNATIONAL DIALOGUE SERIES ON PLANT GENETIC RESOURCES: MADRAS PLENARY SESSION (1990); Fowler, UNNATURAL SELECTION, *supra* Chapter One, note 2, at 199 (describing the Keystone rules: "Participants are asked to speak as individuals, not as representatives of their organizations ... All discussion are

draces and wild and weedy crop relatives did *not* mean access *free of charge*, i.e., that it might be possible to design arrangements or systems wherein plant breeders would be obligated to pay for plant tissue and seeds collected in a particular country's territory.[77] Finally, the parties averred to a vague idea of "farmers' rights."[78] Although these rights were left undefined, the FAO referred to the idea that there should be some sort of recognition for the thousands of years of farmers' efforts spent in domesticating current agricultural staple crops and varieties.[79]

"Farmers' rights" was an idea initially proposed by a Canadian NGO, the Rural Advancement Foundation International (RAFI) in 1985.[80] The notion of "farmers' rights" intended to embody concerns over genetic erosion and the North-South "gene drain." In the context of global development[81] As envisioned by RAFI, "farmers' rights" were a new

---

held off the record.... And finally, any report coming out of the meeting must be adopted by consensus.").

77. *See* Kirit K. Patel, *"Farmers' Rights" over Plant Genetic Resources in the South: Challenges and Opportunities, in* IP RIGHTS, *supra* Chapter Three, note 53) [hereinafter Patel].

78. Fowler, UNNATURAL SELECTION, *supra* Chapter One, note 2, at 199 ("[I]mportant ground was broken in two areas—in defining the notion of genetic resources as 'common heritage' and in the emerging concept of 'farmers' rights.'"); Note that "farmers' rights" are recognized in four other international instruments: (1) Chapter 14.60 (a) of the United Nations Conference on Environment and Development (UNCED) Agenda 21 that states that the appropriate UN agencies and regional organizations should 'strengthen the Global System on the Conservations of [PGRs] by ... taking further steps to realize Farmers' Rights'; (2) The Global Plan of Action (GPA) for the Conservation and Sustainable Utilization of Farmers' Rights at the national, regional and international level, as one of the objectives of the GPA re: *in situ* conservation of PGRs; (3) Resolution 3 of the Nairobi Conference for the Adoption of an Agreed Text of the UN Convention on Biological Diversity noted the realization of farmers' rights as an 'outstanding issue' for further negotiation; and (4) a June 1999 study by the UN Economic and Social Council on the Right to Food, submitted to the Commission on Human Rights, suggested that farmers' rights be promoted as part of the 'Right to Food.') See Daniel Alker & Franz Heidlues, *Farmers' Rights and Intellectual Property Rights—Reconciling Conflicting Concepts,* at 61, 71, in ECONOMIC & SOCIAL ISSUES, *supra* note 3 [hereinafter Alker & Heidlues].

79. FAO Resolution (5/89): "farmers' rights" are

[R]ights arising from the past, present and future contributions of farmers in conserving, improving and making available plant genetic resources, particularly those in centres of origin/diversity. These rights are vested in the international community, as trustee for present and future generations of farmers, for the purpose of ensuring full benefits to farmers, and supporting the continuation of their contributions.

Carol B. Thompson, *International Law of the Sea/Seed: Public Domain Versus Private Commodity*, 44 NAT. RESOURCES J. 841, 866 n.94 (2004). While the FAO formulated the concept of "farmers' rights," these rights were not defined in a legal sense because the term was considered political. *Id.*

80. Alker & Heidlues, *supra* note 78, at 61, 69. ("The term 'farmers' rights' came up in the early 1980s and was featured in debates held within the FAO on the inequality in the distribution of the benefits of plant genetic resources for food and agriculture use. While a commercial variety generates return to the breeder on the basis of plant breeder rights, no parallel appropriation mechanism to act as an incentive for the providers of germplasm *maintain* and make available these resources existed."); Brush, FARMERS' BOUNTY, *supra* note 22, at 247; *see also* Carlos M. Correa, *Options for the Implementation of Farmers' Rights at the National Level,* Working Paper No. 8, Trade Related Agenda, Development and Equity (TRADE), South Centre (2000); Susette Biber-Klemm, Phillipe Cullet & Katharina Kummer Peiry, *New Collective Policies,* at 283, 285–286, *in* RIGHTS TO PLANT GENETIC RESOURCES AND TRADITIONAL KNOWLEDGE: BASIC ISSUES AND PERSPECTIVES (Susette Biber-Klemm & Thomas Cottier eds., 2006); *see also* Seabrook; *Sowing for Apocalypse, supra* Chapter Two, note 42.

81. See Susan K. Sell, *Post-TRIPS Developments: The Tension Between Commercial and Social Agendas in the Context of Intellectual Property,* 14 FLA. J. INT'L L. 193, 216 n.50 (2002). For discussions on the social costs of development generally *see, e.g.* Denis Goulet & Charles K. Wilber, *The Human Element of Development, in* THE POLITICAL ECONOMY OF DEVELOPMENT AND UNDERDEVELOPMENT (Kenneth P. Jameson & Charles K. Wilber eds., 1996) [hereinafter DEVELOPMENT &

type of *collective* intellectual property rights meant to counter-balance plant breeders' rights as embodied by the UPOV and the PVPA. Theoretically, "farmers' rights" would allow farmers to receive compensation from an international genetic conservation fund administered by the FAO.[82]

"Farmers' rights" advocates focused on four core issues: (1) the right to grow, improve, and market local varieties and their products; (2) the right to access improved plant varieties and use farm-saved seeds of commercial varieties for planting and exchange; (3) the right to be compensated for the use of local varieties in the development of new commercial products by outsiders; and (4) the right to participate in decision-making processes related to acquiring, improving, and using PGRs.[83]

In 1989 the FAO adopted a new interpretation of the IUPGR declaring that plant breeders' rights were *not* incompatible with "common heritage." The FAO also recognized "farmers' rights" principles.[84] This was a recognition that most of the world's valuable germplasm came from the developing world; that this was the result of thousands of years of selective breeding by farmers around the world; and that some form of compensation should be paid for use of that germplasm.[85] However, neither the international fund for genetic conservation nor "farmers' rights" crystallized legally in the period after 1989, in large part because contributions to such a fund were voluntary.

E. The 1992 Convention on Biological Diversity (CBD) and the 1994 Agreement on Trade-Related Aspects of Intellectual Property (TRIPS)

The ongoing debate over PGRs must also be understood in the context of two multilateral international agreements. The first is the CBD, which was adopted at the 1992 United Nations Conference on Environment and Development (the "Earth Summit").[86] The sec-

---

UNDERDEVELOPMENT]; Peter Gall, *What Really Matters—Human Development, in* DEVELOPMENT & UNDERDEVELOPMENT.

82. Laurence Helfer defines "farmers' rights" as:

a loosely defined concept that seeks to acknowledge the contributions that traditional farmers have made to the preservation and improvement of [PGRs]. Unlike other natural resources such as coal and oil, [PGRs] are maintained and managed by humans, who cultivate the wild plant varieties that serve as raw materials for future innovations by plant breeders. But whereas breeders obtain proprietary rights in new varieties to compensate them for the time and expense of innovation, no system of remuneration rewards farmers. "Farmers' rights" thus act as a counterweight to plant breeders' rights, compensating the upstream input providers who make downstream innovations possible.

Laurence R. Helfer, *Regime Shifting: The TRIPS Agreement and New Dynamics of International Intellectual Property Lawmaking*, 29 YALE J. INT'L L. 1, 37 (2004) [hereinafter Helfer, *Regime Shifting*].

83. Patel, *supra* note 77, at 96.

84. Agreed Interpretation of the International Undertaking, Res. 4/89, adopted by FAO Conference 25th Sess. (20 Nov. 1989).

85. Annie Patricia Kameri-Mbote & Philippe Cullet, *The Management of Genetic Resources: Developments in the 1997 Sessions of the Commission on Genetic Resources for Food and Agriculture*, 1997 COLO. J. INT'L ENVTL L. & POL'Y 78, 83–84 (1997).

86. United Nations Conference on Environment and Development: Convention on Biological Diversity, 5 June 1992. UNEP/Bio.Div/N7-INC 5/4, 31 I.L.M. 818 (1993) (opened for signatures, May 1999, entered in force December 1993)[hereinafter CBD], *available at* http://www.biodiv.org/

ond is TRIPS, part of the General Agreement on Tariffs and Trade (GATT), finalized in 1994.[87] The 1983 IUPGR had taken the position that all germplasm, including elite culti-

---

convention/articles.asp. The CBD became effective on December 29, 1993. While the U.S. is a signatory, it has not ratified the CBD. The CBD's objectives are "the conversation of biological diversity, the sustainable use of its components, and the fair and equitable sharing of the benefits arising out of the utilization of genetic resources." CBD, art. 1. The CBD "echoes the International Covenant on Economic, Social and Cultural Rights on the right to self-determination and on the balance of rights and duties inherent in the protection of intellectual property rights." Intellectual Property Rights and Human Rights, Sub-commission on Human Rights Resolution 2000/07 (August 17, 2000), *available at* http://www.unhchr.ch/Huridocda/Huridoca.nsf/0/c462b62cf8a07b13c1256970 0046704e?Opendocument (last visited August 14, 2006).

87. TRIPS, *supra* note 5; TRIPS Including Trade in Counterfeit Goods of the General Agreement on Tariffs and Trade, amending the General Agreement on Tariffs and Trade and creating the World Trade Organization, signed April 15, 1994, Marrakech, Morocco, 33 I.L.M.J. 1 (1994); *see also* Article 27 ("Patentable Subject Matter") of TRIPS available at http://www.wto.org/english/tratop_e/ TRIPS_e/t_agm3_e.htm; J.H. Reichman, *From "Free Riders" to "Fair Followers": Global Competition Under the TRIPS Agreement*, 29 NYU J. Int'l L. & Pol. 11 (1996–97); David Henderson, *International Agencies and Cross-Border Liberalization: The WTO in Context*, at 97 in The WTO as an International Organization (Anne O. Kreuger ed., 1998); Miriam Latorre Quinn, *Protection for Indigenous Knowledge: An International Law Analysis*, 14 St. Thomas L. Rev. 287 (2001); Traci L. McClellan, *The Role of International Law in Protecting the Traditional Knowledge and Plant Life of Indigenous People*, 19 Wis. Int'l L. J. 249 (2001); Meetali Jain, *Global Trade and the New Millennium: Defining the Scope of Intellectual Property Protection of Plant Genetic Resources and Traditional Knowledge in India*, 22 Hastings Int'l & Comp. L. Rev. 777 (1999); Ruth L. Gana, *Prospects for Developing Countries Under the TRIPS Agreement*, 29 Vand. J. Transnat'l L. 735 (1996) [hereinafter Gana, *Prospects for Developing Countries*]; Doris Estelle Long, *The Impact of Foreign Investment on Indigenous Culture: An Intellectual Property Perspective*, 23 N.C. J. Int'l L. & Com. Reg. 61 (1998); Aoki, *Skirmishes, supra* Chapter Three, note 177; Aoki, *Malthus, supra* Chapter One, note 7 (2004); James O. Odek, *Bio-Piracy: Creating Proprietary Rights in Plant Genetic Resources*, 2 J. Intell. Prop. L. 141 (1993); Shayana Kadidal, *Plants, Poverty and Pharmaceutical Patents*, 103 Yale L. J. 223 (1993); Peter Jaszi & Martha Woodmansee, *Beyond Authorship: Refiguring Rights in Traditional Culture and Bioknowledge* at 195 in Scientific Authorship: Credit and Intellectual Property in Science (Mario Biagoli & Peter Galison eds., 2001); Angela R. Riley, *Recovering Collectivity: Group Rights to Intellectual Property in Indigenous Communities*, 18 Cardozo Arts & Ent. L.J. 175 (2000); Naomi Roht-Arriaza, *Of Seeds and Shamans: The Appropriation of the Scientific and Technical Knowledge of Indigenous and Local Communities*, 17 Mich. J. Int'l L. 919 (1996); David A. Cleveland & Stephen J. Murray, *The World's Crop Genetic Resources and the Rights of Indigenous Farmers*, 38 Curr. Anthro. 477 (1997); Mark Hennig, *An Examination of the Possibility to Secure Intellectual Property Rights for Plant Genetic Resources Developed by Indigenous Peoples of the NAFTA States—Domestic Legislation Under the International Convention for Protection of New Plant Varieties*, 13 Ariz. J. Int'l & Comp. L. 175 (1996); Graham Dutfied, *Indigenous Peoples, Bioprospecting and the TRIPS Agreement: Threats and Opportunities, available at* http://www.acts.or.ke/prog/biodiversity/TRIPS/dutfield.doc (last visited August 22, 2006); Chen, *Webs of Life, supra* note 52; Lara E. Ewens, *Seed Wars: Biotechnology, Intellectual Property and the Quest for High Yield Seeds*, 23 B.C. Int'l & Comp. L. Rev. 285 (2000); Lakshmi Sarma, Note, *Biopiracy: Twentieth Century Imperialism in the Form of International Agreements*, 13 Temp. Int'l & Comp. L. J. 107 (1999); John Ntambirweki, *Biotechnology and International Law Within the North-South Context*, 14 Transnat'l Law. 103 (2001); Charles McManis, *The Interface Between Intellectual Property and Environmental Protection: Biodiversity and Biotechnology*, 76 Wash. U. L. Q. 255 (1998) [hereinafter McManis, *Biodiversity & Biotechnology*]; Michael Halewood, *Indigenous and Local Knowledge in International Law: A Preface to Sui Generis Intellectual Protection*, 44 McGill L. J. 953 (1999); Remegius N. Nwabreze, *Ethnopharmacology, Patents and the Politics of Plants' Genetic Resources*, 11 Cardozo J. Int'l & Comp. L. 585 (2003); Ikeihi Mgbeoji, *Patents and Traditional Knowledge of the Uses of Plants: Is a Communal Patent Regime Part of the Solution to the Scourge of Biopiracy?*, 9 Ind. J. Global Leg. Stud. 163 (2001); Valuing Local Knowledge: Indigenous People and Intellectual Property Rights (Stephen B. Brush & Doreen Stabinsky eds., 1996)[hereinafter Valuing Local Knowledge]; David A. Cleveland & Stephen C. Murray, *The World's Crop, Genetic Resources and the Rights of Indigenous Farmers*, 38 Curr. Anthro. 477 (1997)[hereinafter Cleveland & Murray, *Crop Genetic Resources*]. Stephen B. Brush, *Comment:*

vars, should be treated under a "common heritage" approach. TRIPS allowed member nations to exclude plants from patentability, however, those countries must provide some equivalent intellectual property-like protection for cultivated plant varieties.[88] While not singling out agricultural crops, the CBD took the position that plant biological materials (presumably including farmer landraces and wild and weedy relatives) were "sovereign national property" of the nation in which they are located and thus were not freely appropriable "common heritage of mankind." Consequences that flowed from rejection of the IUPGR's stance on PGRs as "common heritage" will be examined later in this chapter.

The CBD was a multilateral agreement, the result of a process to address environmental concerns raised by Organization for Economic Cooperation and Development (OECD) member nations.[89] While the CBD aimed at conserving biodiversity, as discussed in this section, it also had important implications on the issue of intellectual property rights in PGRs. For example, the CBD put the idea of PGRs as "sovereign national property" on the table and established a structure for negotiating bilateral contracts as a means of effectuating "prior informed consent" and "equitable benefit sharing."

The CBD took the position that economic incentives were necessary to encourage developing countries to conserve their biodiversity rather than to seek quick gains through activities, such as deforestation, that result in its destruction.[90] While the CBD did not

---

David A. Cleveland and Stephen C. Murray, The World's Crop Genetic Resources and the Rights of Indigenous Farmers, 38 CURR. ANTHRO. 497 (1997); Stephen B. Brush, *Indigenous Knowledge of Biological Resources and Intellectual Property Rights: The Role of Anthropology,* 95 AM. ANTHRO. 653 (1993); Ruth L. Okediji, *The International Relations of Intellectual Property: Narratives of Developing Country Participation in the Global Intellectual Property System,* 7 SING. J. INT'L & COMP. L. 315 (2003) [hereinafter Okediji, *Developing Country Participation*]; *Public Welfare and the Role of the WTO: Reconsidering the TRIPS Agreement,* 17 EMORY INT'L L. REV. 819 (2003); Carlos Correa, INTELLECTUAL PROPERTY RIGHTS, THE WTO AND DEVELOPING COUNTRIES: THE TRIPS AGREEMENT AND POLICY OPTIONS (2000) [hereinafter Correa, IP RIGHTS]; Margaret Chon & Shubha Ghosh, *Joint Comment on the WIPO Draft Report: Intellectual Property Needs and Expectations of Traditional Knowledge Holders* (Fall 2000), *available at* http://www.wipo.int/tk/en/tk/ffm/fffm_report.comments/msg00008 .html (last visited August 22, 2006).

88. *See* Watal, IP RIGHTS, *supra* note 5, at 131, 134 (2001)("Article 27 of TRIPS requires that patents be made available, both for processes and products in all fields of technology. Article 27.3(b) plants and animals, and essentially biological processes may be excluded from patentability.... However, under 27.3 (b), if plants are excluded from patent protection, at least an effective *sui generis* system must be put in place for the protection of new plant varieties. In other words, plant breeders' rights are to be protected despite the optional exclusion from the patenting of plants.").

89. For background on this convention, *see* Amanda Hubbard, *Comment, The Convention on Biological Diversity's Fifth Anniversary: A General Overview of the Convention—Where Has It Been and Where is It Going?,* 10 TUL. ENVTL L.J. 415 (1997).

90. Under the terms of the CBD, developing biodiversity-rich countries are obliged to conserve, sustainably use, and guarantee access to genetic resources, in return for financial aid and a fair and equitable sharing of benefits (including royalties) arising out of corporate utilization and exploitation of these resources. The CBD included an incentive for developing nations to safeguard these resources and in the process protect against short-term ventures, the consequences of which are likely to include rapid deforestation and species destruction. However, many activists favored a stronger legal framework to protect genetic diversity in the CBD, which they viewed as far from perfect, it nevertheless provided a framework on which to build. *See* Ranee K. L. Panjabi, *Idealism and Self-Interest in International Environmental Law: The Rio Dilemma,* 23 CAL. W. INT'L L.J. 177, 191 (1992); McManis, *Biodiversity and Biotechnology,* at 260. The financial aid and royalty payment system was instituted based on the realization that most developing nations would be unable to pay for measures called for in the CBD without adequate compensation. An element of historical justice has also been proposed, with the premise that while the developed world industrialized and subsequently ensured higher standards of living for its citizenry, those same advances led to the destruc-

specifically focus on PGRs for food and agriculture, it did address general concerns relating to the conservation of all plants and other organisms in the global ecology.

Controversies dividing the countries of the global North and the global South that originally had surfaced in the FAO debates over the IUPGR resurfaced in the CBD negotiations. These included: (1) the North-South divide over distribution of the benefits of biological organisms; (2) the propriety of granting intellectual property rights over living organisms; and (3) technology transfer questions regarding access to technologies necessary to utilize the benefits of such biological organisms.[91]

However, the CBD differed from the IUPGR in at least two key respects. First, the CBD acknowledged that many nations had already granted intellectual property protection for biotechnological inventions. Second, the CBD did not take a "common heritage" approach to biological resources, but rather incorporated the idea that the *countries of origin* of biological resources exercised sovereignty over all plants, animals, and microorganisms within their national boundaries.[92] In so doing, the CBD recast PGRs within a nation's borders as "sovereign national property"[93] that provided a basis for "informed consent" (prior to extraction/exploitation) and "equitable benefit sharing."[94]

---

tion of biodiversity in the developing world. *See also* Catherine J. Tinker, *Introduction to Biological Diversity: Law, Institutions and Science*, 1 Buff. J. Int'l L. 1, 21 (1994).

91. The United States' refusal to ratify the CBD came as no surprise to many. The U.S. repeatedly voiced substantive objections in the areas of the CBD. First, it took issue with the CBD's requirement that developed countries fund environmentally conscious development in developing countries. The U.S. specifically was uncomfortable with what it perceived as the lack of definite restrictions on the amount of funds developed nations could be forced to contribute to developing nations. Second, the CBD called for essentially open technology transfer including the transfer of biotechnology. This aspect of the CBD was seen as endangering intellectual property rights since the treaty-mandated transfer of not only publicly owned but also privately owned technology. This reading, it was argued, was apparent when the CBD technology transfer provisions were analyzed in context with other provisions serving as a backdrop, which led to the conclusion that the treaty was disregarding patents and other intellectual property rights. Finally, the U.S. found it unacceptable that the CBD called for regulatory measures that applied only to biotechnology as opposed to other environmentally harmful and diversity-depleting activities. George Van Cleve, *Regulating Environmental and Safety Hazards of Agricultural Biotechnology for a Sustainable World*, 9 Wash. U. J.L. & Pol'y 245, 252 n.16 (2002). Although the first Bush Administration (1988–92) advanced these arguments, large and influential U.S.-based corporations repeated these concerns. The United States later became a signatory under the Clinton Administration. David B. Vogt, *Protecting Indigenous Knowledge in Latin America*, 3 Or. Rev. Int'l L. 12, 19 n.57 (2001).

92. The CBD treats genetic resources as "tradable commodities subject to national sovereignty rights" and envisions this developing-to-developed transfer as entailing return benefits, including technology transfer. Dutfield, *TRIPS supra* note 48, at 260. *Compare* IUPGR approach discussed *supra* note 51.

93. CBD, *supra* note 86, at art. 3 states that:

States have, in accordance with the Charter of the United Nations and the principles of international law, the sovereign right to exploit their own resources pursuant to their own environmental policies, and the responsibility to ensure that activities within their jurisdiction or control do not cause damage to the environment of other States or of areas beyond the limits of national jurisdiction.

31 I.L.M. 818, 824.

94. CBD art. 15.5 (requiring prior informed consent of the party 'owning' the natural resource); art. 8(j) (equitable sharing of benefits); Additionally, the CBD recognized the rights of subnational groups, such as indigenous and local communities to participate in "benefit sharing." For more on traditional resource knowledge and resources, and indigenous heritage, *see* Darrell A. Posey & Graham Dutfield, Beyond Intellectual Property: Toward Traditional Rights for Indigenous Peoples and Local Communities (1996) [hereinafter Posey & Dutfield, Beyond IP]; Indigenous Heritage & Intellectual Property (Silke von Lewinski ed., 2004).

The CBD contemplated that the principles of "sovereign national peoperty" and "informed consent" would give rise to, and be the backdrop for, a regime of freely entered-into bilateral contracts pertaining to PGRs and other bioresource extraction. As a marketplace-based solution, this contract regime would occur between private parties or between private parties and a government (or governmental subunit). The CBD also indicated that "common heritage" treatment of PGRs was history.

TRIPS further solidified the impression that the "common heritage" regime was over and done. In 1986, the initial focus of the Uruguay Round, and specifically TRIPS, was an ultimately successful attempt by industrialized nations to secure multilateral protection for new technologies, pharmaceuticals, and copyrighted media works against unauthorized imitation or duplication.[95] However, by 1990, intellectual property protection for biological organisms (including PGRs) had emerged as a major sticking point in negotiations over TRIPS between the developed and developing countries, just as several newly patented biotech inventions began making their way to market, such as Monsanto's patented genetically engineered crop varieties.[96] Additionally, the spate of mergers and acquisitions in the chemical and pharmaceutical economic sectors that began in the 1970s continued with these companies swiftly moving into the areas of genetically engineered crops, plant breeding, germplasm research, and crop development.[97] Companies also aggressively acted to secure some form of global intellectual property protection for their biotech innovations and projects-in-the-pipeline.[98]

---

95. TRIPS, *supra* notes 5, 87; Andrew T. Guzman, *International Antitrust and the WTO: The Lesson from Intellectual Property*, 43 Va. J. Int'l L. 933, 950 (2003) ("[T]he agreement seeks to prevent developing countries from allowing what in developed countries would be viewed as violations of intellectual property rights....").

96. The various states differed in attitudes regarding how to deal with intellectual property in genetically engineered products. These discussions formed part of the negotiations that led to the 1994 Uruguay Round agreements on trade. Interestingly, the language that emerged from these negotiations failed to address the treatment of genetically engineered products, thus leaving many questions unanswered. *See* Sean D. Murphy, *Biotechnology and International Law*, 42 Harv. Int'l L.J. 47, 67–68 (2001).

97. Kloppenburg, Seeds and Sovereignty, *supra* Introduction, note 1, at 9. More recently, according to the NGO RAFI (now known as ETC Group, an acronym for Erosion, Technology and Concentration),

> [t]he first half of 1998 witnessed a dramatic consolidation of power over plant genetics worldwide, punctuating a trend that began over three decades ago. The global seed trade is now dominated by life industry giants whose vast economic power and control over plant germplasm has effectively marginalized the role of public sector plant breeding and research.

Seed Industry Consolidation: Who Controls Whom?, Communique (July 30, 1998), *available at* http://www.etcgroup.org/article.asp?newsid=186 (last visited August 22, 2006). Other observers note that U.S. regulatory changes served as a catalyst in the recent spate of mergers resulting in corporate realignment. However, this trend is not unique to the U.S. as there have been massive mergers within the chemical and "life sciences" industries. For example, Novartis AG is one of the largest pharmaceutical companies and a global leader in crop protection chemicals. Novartis was the result of a $27 billion merger between two Swiss corporations, Ciba-Geigy SA and Sandoz Ltd. in 1996. The consummation of this merger increased the stakes in the biotechnology industry, thereby leading to a spate of mergers between large multinationals and smaller biotechnology companies. Strategic alliances between large multinationals and small biotechnology firms have also been popular arrangements. Stevan Pepa, *Research and Trade In Genetics: How Countries Should Structure for the Future*, 17 Med. & L. 437, 441 (1998).

98. *See generally* Debora Halbert, *Intellectual Property in the Year 2025*, 49 J. Copyright Soc'y U.S.A. 225, 242 (2001).

> Intellectual property law is the key component of the globalized world, allowing for corporations to enforce their property rights internationally. The ability of corporations to

However, some developing countries challenged these claims for more expansive intellectual property protection, raising concerns about being locked into permanent subordinate status in the global economy by foreign corporations via expansive patents held in staple food crops.[99] These countries advocated for the exclusion of plant or animal varieties from patent protection if required on particular public interest grounds.[100]

TRIPS was finalized in 1992 as part of the GATT, signed by 125 countries in 1994, and went into effect on January 1, 1995. TRIPS recognizes plant breeders' rights and provides that plants may be excluded from patentability, but if they are, they must be effectively protected under a *sui generis* system, if they meet nationally set standards for protectability.[101] Robert Keohane writes

---

enforce their intellectual property rights was codified into international law. TRIPS, the international trade agreement that had helped globalize intellectual property regimes, was the product of a lobbying effort by twelve American multinational corporations. By successfully equating intellectual property rights with trade these companies ensured they would remain firmly entrenched as players in the global future.

Id. (footnote omitted).

99. *See* Chon, *Development Divide, supra* Chapter Two, note 24, at 2866 (2006) ("Integrating intellectual property standards through TRIPS is supposed to result in long term economic growth through innovation across all member states, at the cost of short term decreases in access to goods because of higher prices. For developing countries, this innovation-driven growth [created primarily through foreign direct investment and accompanying technology transfer] may be an abstract or perhaps even non-existent benefit. Firms may not enter into the poorest of countries regardless of the level of intellectual property protection they offer because no profit is likely to be made where consumers cannot pay.").

100. TRIPS, *supra* note 5, at art. 27(2) (excludable if threat to public order, etc.) ("WTO members shall provide for the protection of plant varieties either by patents or by an effective *sui generis* system or by any combination thereof."). *Id.* art. 27(3)(b). *See* Susan H. Bragdon & D.R. Downes, *Recent Policy Trends and Developments Related to the Conservation, Use and Development of Genetic Resources: Issues in Genetic Resources*, IPGRI Paper No. 7, International Plant Genetic Research Institute, IPGRI (Rome 1998); TRIPS art. 27 (2)–(3) (*ordre public* or morality clause):
  2. Members may exclude from patentability inventions, the prevention within their territory of the commercial exploitation of which is necessary to protect *ordre public* or morality, including to protect human, animal or plant life or health or to avoid serious prejudice to the environment, provided that such exclusion is not made merely because the exploitation is prohibited by domestic law. 3. Members may also exclude from patentability: (a) diagnostic, therapeutic and surgical methods for the treatment of humans or animals; (b) plants and animals other than microorganisms, and essentially biological processes for the production of plants or animals other than non-biological and microbiological processes. However, Members shall provide for the protection of plant varieties either by patents or by an effective *sui generis* system or by any combination thereof. The provisions of this sub-paragraph shall be reviewed four years after the entry into force of the Agreement Establishing the WTO. 33 I.L.M. 81, *94

TRIPS, *supra* note 5, at art. 27(2)–(3).

101. To many observers, the UPOV regime, on which the European plant variety protection (PVP) measures are based, seems to be an effective *sui generis* system. However, it does fall short in important respects. To meet the TRIPS standard, all species would have to be eligible for protection, and the rights guaranteed under law in one nation would have to extend not just to other members of UPOV, but to all countries under the World Trade Organization. The general UPOV approach, nevertheless, is certainly what parties to the TRIPS agreement had in mind for an acceptable *sui generis* alternative to patents. However, UPOV does not provide for protection of traditional farmer-varieties of crops, and thus cannot substantially help meet the goals of the Convention on Biological Diversity to ensure the conservation, sustainable utilization and fair and equitable sharing of benefits arising from the use of biological diversity.

See Cary Fowler, *By Policy or Law? The Challenge of Determining the Status and Future of Agro-Biodiversity*, 3 J. Tech. L. & Pol'y 1, 36–37 (1997). In the U.S., plant variety protection is provided

Power is distributed in a highly asymmetrical fashion. The United States, the European Union, and to a lesser extent, large, rich states such as Japan have a great deal of influence in the World Trade Organization (WTO), in the stipulation and implementation of the TRIPS agreement, and in domain not regulated by international institutions. Small, poor states have little influence: They are "policy-takers," rather than "policy-shapers." [102]

On one level, the CBD and TRIPS share important similarities. Both are multilateral agreements that contemplate an economy of commodifiable intellectual property (or other) rights, underwritten by market exchange *via* private bilateral contracts. Yet on another level, many gains made by the developing countries at the 1992 Earth Summit were in tension with parts of TRIPS.[103] While the CBD promoted "informed consent" and "equitable benefit sharing" and treated PGRs as "sovereign national property," TRIPS required member nations to meet "minimum standards" of intellectual property protection, including PBRs, and ignored any type of collective rights that might have been cognizable under the Keystone Dialogue's "farmers' rights" rubric.[104] However, as the next section describes, "farmers' rights" resurfaced in the 2001 International Treaty on Plant Genetic Resources for Food and Agriculture.

---

by several means. Utility patent protection is geared towards biotechnological inventions, plant patent protection targets new and distinct asexually reproducible plant varieties, and *sui generic* protection (plant variety protection) is aimed at sexually reproduced plant varieties. McManis, *supra* note 74, at 276. The Supreme Court has previously ruled that both measures, i.e., utility patents and plant variety protection measures, do coexist. For a discussion on the options for *sui generis* protection, *see* Posey & Dutfield, INTELLECTUAL PROPERTY RIGHTS, *supra* note 94, 78–80.

102. Robert O. Keohane, *Comment: Norms, Institutions and Cooperation*, at 65, 65–66, *in* INT'L PUBLIC GOODS, *supra* Chapter One, note 2.

103. TRIPS had been construed as providing not only for international recognition, but also for the enforceability of private patents for microorganisms and even life itself. It should therefore come as no surprise that many have railed against it as legitimizing biopiracy and indigenous biodiversity-related "traditional" knowledge. *See* Shalini Bhutani & Ashish Kothari, *The Biodiversity Rights of Developing Nations: A Perspective From India*, 32 GOLDEN GATE U. L. REV. 587, 591 (2002). One view of the split between rich and poor nations has been characterized as "arrogant, cash-rich, resource-poor northern nations attempting to solidify their economic position at the expense of naive, cash-poor, resource-rich southern nations." The CBD signing was intended to mend this rift, but the U.S. refusal to join in the final agreement caused concern in the South. India, acting on behalf of the developing nations, squared off against the developed nations at a WTO meeting to plan the final agenda for the next meeting. The two sides were unable to reach a consensus on any of the outstanding issues, including how to reconcile TRIPS with the CBD. As a result, many of the developing nations traveled to the WTO meeting in Seattle ready to disavow their previous TRIPS commitments and in the process force a renegotiation of the entire TRIPS agreement. Scott Holwick, *Developing Nations and the Agreement on Trade-Related Aspects of Intellectual Property Rights*, 11 COLO. J. INT'L ENVTL L. & POL'Y 183 (2000). For more *see generally* Evelyn Su, *The Winners and the Losers: The Agreement on Trade-Related Aspects of Intellectual Property Rights and Its Effects on Developing Countries*, HOUS. J. INT'L L. 169 (2000) (providing analysis of the TRIPS Agreement and its implications for developed and developing nations); Gana, *Prospects for Developing Countries, supra* note 87 (analyzing the relationship between the TRIPS Agreement and developing nations).

104. Some subsequent international conventions have sought to advance national intellectual property rights (IPR) regimes to benefit developing nations within the context of TRIPS and other international agreements, and also to improve the international framework of rules and agreements surrounding such issues as traditional knowledge and access to genetic resources. *See, e.g.,* REPORT OF THE COMMISSION ON IPRs, INTEGRATING IPRs AND DEVELOPMENT POLICY (2002), *available at* http://www.iprcommission.org (last visited August 27, 2006).

There is a critical lacuna between the equity-conservation regime of the CBD and the intellectual property-trade regime of TRIPS that is the differential effects of "development." Professor Margaret Chon writes,

> As implemented and interpreted thus far, intellectual property globalization seems to have incorporated the standard domestic balancing test between protection of goods through intellectual property and, on the other hand, access by consumers to information embedded within these protected knowledge goods.... While severely problematic even in the domestic welfare generating context, this type of crude welfare calculation can have brutal consequences in the context of intellectual property globalization.... Over-reliance on utility-maximization ignores distributional consequences ... [however], [i]n the parallel universe of development economics, an alternative to raw utilitarianism in the measure of social welfare has gained broad consensus.... [E]conomists such as Amartya Sen began to theorize an alternate human capability approach towards the measurement of social welfare, which has been adopted by mainstream development institutions. Since 1991, the Human Development Index, composed of three variables—life expectancy at birth, educational attainment, and the standard of living measured by real per capita income—has been used by the United Nations Development Programme to measure social welfare within and across nations.... [but this approach] ... has not yet informed intellectual property globalization....
>
> ... To the extent that development encompasses not only the economic but also cultural, social, and political dimensions of national well-being, a more deliberate consideration of these newer concepts in development economics could ameliorate intellectual property's one-sided emphasis on pure wealth- or utility-maximization.[105]

Professor Chon raises the important question: how are we to understand the skirmishes that have occurred in the "Seed Wars"? These skirmishes deal with an undeniable "global public good"[106] such as the food system, however this area has been pervasively colonized by intellectual property. Chon's insights may help frame debates in this are where the developing countries and the developed countries have repeatedly clashed. Significantly, in 2002, the U.K. commissioned a Report from the Commission on Intellectual Property Rights (CIPR) entitled, "Integrating Intellectual Property Rights and

---

105. Chon, *Development Divide*, *supra* Chapter Two, note 24, at 2829–30, 2832, 2834; Okediji, *Developing Country Participation*, *supra* note 87; Correa, IP Rights, *supra* note 87; Kerry Rittich, *The Future of Law and Development: Second Generation Reforms and the Incorporation of the Social*, 26 Mich. J. Int'l L. 199 (2004); Peter M. Gerhart. *Distributive Values and Institutional Design in the Provision of Global Public Goods*, at 69, *in* Int'l Public Goods, *supra* Chapter One, note 2; Balakrishnan Rajagopal, International Law From Below: Development, Social Movements, and Third World Resistance (2003); Peter Drahos with John Braithwaite, Information Feudalism: Who Owns the Knowledge Economy? (2002), Susan K. Sell, Private Power, Public Law: The Globalization of Intellectual Property Rights (2003) [hereinafter Sell, Private Power].

106. Chon, *Development Divide*, *supra* Chapter Two, note 24, at 2833 ("Global public goods theorists include an enormous array of things as potential public goods. Indeed states themselves can be viewed as public goods, as can markets and legal regimes. To one degree or another, each of these other public goods [like all public goods] bears the characteristics of non-rivalry and non-exclusivity.... Global public goods theorists insistently who the beficiaries of public goods are—that is, who are the haves and have-nots?"); Global Public Goods: International Cooperation in the 21st Century (Inge Kaul et al. eds., 1999).

Development Policy." The CIPR was chaired by Professor John H. Barton of Stanford Law School and represented a remarkable interrogation of the interrelationship between development and intellectual property law. The CIPR Report stated,

> We therefore conclude that far more attention needs to be accorded to the needs of the developing countries in the making of international IP policy. Consistent with the recent decisions of the international community at Doha and Monterrey, the development objectives need to be integrated into the making of IP rules and practice.[107]

At the very least, raising the question of what Chon refers to as the "Development Divide" may be an important piece of the puzzle when trying to parse the complexities of the current legal treatment of PGRs.

F. The 2001 International Treaty on Plant Genetic Resources (ITPGR)[108]

The FAO's 1983 IUPGR was a non-binding "undertaking" and, therefore, of limited impact on the regulation of PGR exchange and conservation. Although the IUPGR was non-binding, "farmers' rights" were recognized in a 1989 FAO resolution that proposed "establishing a mandatory international fund to support conservation and utilization of [PGRs] through various [programs] particularly, but not exclusively, in the Third World."[109] This fund was eventually implemented in the 1990s and, as a result, the FAO

---

107. Commission on Intellectual Property Rights, INTEGRATING INTELLECTUAL PROPERTY RIGHTS AND DEVELOPMENT POLICY (2002), *available at* http//www.iprcommission.org/graphic/documents/final_report.htm; *see also* UN Millennium Development Goals, G.A. Res. 55/2, U.N. Doc. A/RES/55/2 (18 Sept. 2000), *at* http://www.un.org.millenniumgoals/index.html (committing the UN system to "eradicate extreme poverty and hunger, achieve universal primary education, promote gender equality and empower women, reduce child mortality, improve maternal health, combat [] diseases, ensure environmental sustainability and develop a global partnership for development.").

108. The ITPGR seeks to govern the international exchange of plant genetic resources. The ITPGR was opened for signatures on November 3, 2001. In November 2001, delegates from 116 countries voted to adopt the ITPGR, which was to enter into force only when at least 40 nations either ratified or acceded to it, which occurred in early 2004. The 40 nation threshold was surpassed when twelve European nations and the European Community ratified the treaty, triggering a 90 day countdown that culminated in the treaty going into effect on June 29, 2004. *See* http://www.fao.org/ag/cgrfa/IU.htm; *see also* Ali Mekouar, A Global Instrument on Agrobiodiversity: The International Treaty on Plant Genetic Resources for Food and Agriculture, FAO Legal Papers Online # 24, at 3, *available at* http://www.fao.org/Legal/prs-ol/10024.pdf (2002)(stating that the treaty was the "result of a laborious and lengthy, hard-fought, seven-year negotiating process."); Kelly Day-Rubenstein & Paul Heisey, *Plant Genetic Resources*, AMBER WAVES, June 2003, at 22. *Biodiversity Treaty Signed, Southwest Farm Press*, April 15, 2004, *available at* http://southwestfarmpress.com/mag/farming_biodiversity_treaty_signed/index.html (last visited March. 9, 2005); *see also* Seabrook, *Sowing for Apocalypse, supra* Chapter Two, note 42.

109. Patel, *supra* note 77, at 97 (citing The Keystone Center Report, *supra* note 76). It is worth noting that as applied to PGRs, the IUPGR was viewed as conflicting with the UPOV, which favored PBRs, when it came to cultivated plant varieties. However, proponent states lobbied successfully for a revision of the IUPGR, stating that PBRs were "not incompatible" with the principles underlying the IUPGR. This reconciliation had the effect of permitting unrestricted access to unimproved PGRs without the benefit of compensation to the states, communities, or institutions that maintained them. To address this imbalance, the developing states proposed that the revised IUPGR vest "farmers' rights" in the international community as trustees. A vital component of this arrangement

decided to instigate "farmers' rights" through a Global Plan of Action adopted at Leipzig in 1996.[110] However, like the IUPGR, the Global Plan of Action similarly lacked adequate funding, due in part to the voluntary nature of contributions to the fund.[111]

In 1994, the FAO initiated an intergovernmental round of negotiations meant to revise the IUPGR in order to (1) make it a legally binding treaty, and (2) harmonize its provisions with the 1992 CBD which, as mentioned earlier, was significantly at odds with the IUPGR's broad definition of "common heritage." In November 2001, 116 member nations (including the United States) signed a new agreement, the International Treaty on Plant Genetic Resources (ITPGR).

The ITPGR reaffirmed the nascent FAO commitment to "farmers' rights" as protecting traditional knowledge and farmer know-how relevant to PGRs, recognizes a right to "equitable benefit sharing," and grants the right to participate in national-level decision-making on matters related to PGR use and genetic conservation.[112] However, the ITPGR allowed the most important issue with regard to "farmers' rights"—the rights to use, exchange, and sell farm-saved seeds of traditional as well as improved varieties—to remain within the sole discretion of national governments.[113] The ITPGR sought to pro-

---

was the creation of an international fund to support conservation. However, FAO members failed to contribute in any meaningful way causing the fund to languish during the 1980s and 1990s. Helfer, *Regime Shifting, supra* note 82, at 36–37.

110. *See* David S. Tilford, *Saving the Blueprints: The International Legal Regime for Plant Resources*, 30 CASE W. RES. J. INT'L L. 373, 426–27 (1998) [hereinafter Tilford, *Saving the Blueprints*]. Creation of an international fund in support of "farmers' rights" was a controversial proposition at the FAO-sponsored Fourth Technical Conference on Plant Genetic Resources held in Leipzig, Germany in June 1996. Prior to the conference, 154 governments submitted country reports to FAO. These reports assessing the status of plant genetic resource conservation within their respective jurisdictions served as the basis for the FAO Report on the State of the World's Plant Genetic Resources. Drawing on this report, delegates from 150 countries converged in Leipzig and agreed upon the Global Plan of Action (GPA).

111. ITPGR art. 14 expressly acknowledges the Global Plan of Action:
Recognizing that the rolling Global Plan of Action for the Conservation and Sustainable Use of Plant Genetic Resources for Food and Agriculture is important to this Treaty, Contracting Parties *should promote* its effective implementation, including through national actions and, *as appropriate*, international cooperation to provide a coherent framework, inter alia, for capacity-building, technology transfer and exchange of information, taking into account the provisions of Article 13. (emphasis added)

It should not come as a surprise that the GPA seems to suffer the same fate as the revised IUPGR when it comes to the reluctance of the FAO to fund it. The language in article 14 is framed in soft terms including "should promote" when referring to effective implementation and "as appropriate" when talking about international cooperation. Such language has led to the impression that national action is discretionary rather than mandatory. *See* Gregory Rose, *International Law of Sustainable Agriculture in the 21st Century: The International Treaty on Plant Genetic Resources for Food and Agriculture*, 15 GEO. INT'L ENVTL L. REV. 583, 592 (2003).

112. Patel, *supra* note 77, at 97.

113. ITPGR art. 9.3 states that "[n]othing in this Article shall be interpreted to limit any rights that farmers have to save, use, exchange or sell farm-saved seed/propagating material, *subject to national law* and as appropriate." (emphasis added)

Note that because the Treaty leaves implementation (or not) of "farmers' rights" to national governments, there have been two examples of nations that have attempted to implement "farmers' rights" on the national level: India and the Organization of African Unity's (OAU) model legislation. India's Act 123, Act for the Protection of Plant Varieties, was enacted in 1999; the OAU's Model Legislation for the Protection of the Rights of Local Communities, Farmers, and Breeders and for Regulation of Access to Biological Resources was released in 2000. Both regimes allow farmers to register their varieties without the traditional PVP criteria of uniformity, distinctiveness and stability. Both establish a gene conservation fund funded by royalties paid by plant breeders.

mote "farmers' rights" by encouraging information exchange,[114] facilitating technology transfer and capacity building,[115] as well as encouraging benefit sharing (monetary and non-monetary alike) arising from PGR commercialization.[116] Just how well the ITPGR will meet its aspirational goals remains to be seen, particularly given the "Development Divide" between rich and poor nations.[117]

Some problems with the ITPGR's articulation of "farmers' rights" are its ambiguity regarding what the substance of those rights are; who are the titleholders of those rights; what is the subject matter covered by those rights; and their duration.[118] While the ITPGR contains salutary language on recognition of the economic benefit conferred by farmers in the past and present and the promise about benefit sharing in the future, the Treaty does not give an estimate of the value of those contributions or a method for calculating them.[119]

Both exempt farmers from PBRs—farmers may save, use, and process plant genetic material. Criticism of these regimes has centered on the low value of the registered varieties, with concomitant low funding of the gene conservation fund, as well as the difficulty of estimating the economic value of a single landrace with a complex pedigree. *See* Brush, Farmers' Bounty, *supra* Chapter Two, note 22, at 252.

114. ITPGR, *supra* note 108, art. 13.2(a).

115. *Id.* at art. 13.2(b)–(c). *Compare* with TRIPS art. 66, which mandates developed countries to provide incentives for businesses to promote and encourage technology transfer to poorer nations. For discussion on technology transfer after the TRIPS agreement, *see* Keith E. Maskus & Jerome H. Reichman, *The Globalization of Private Knowledge Goods and the Privatization of Global Public Goods*, 7 J. Int'l Econ. L. 279, 287–91 (2004); Robert E. Evenson, *Agricultural Research and Intellectual Property Rights*, at 188 *in* Int'l Public Goods, *supra* Chapter One, note 2; Michael P. Ryan, Knowledge Diplomacy: Global Competition and the Politics of Intellectual Property (1998); Sell, Private Power, *supra* note 105; Michel Petit, et al., Why Governments Can't Make Policy: The Case of Plant Genetic Resources in the International Arena (2001); Rosemary J. Coombe, *Fear, Hope, and Longing for the Future of Authorship and a Revitalized Public Domain in the Global Regime of Intellectual Property*, 52 DePaul L. Rev. 1171 (2003).

116. ITPGR, *supra* note 19, art. 13.2(d). However, for an assessment on the adverse impact of the diffusion of commodified plant genetic resources on the peasant sectors of less developed countries *see* Stephen B. Brush, *Genetically Modified Organisms in Peasant Farming: Social Impact and Equity*, 9 Ind. J. Global Leg. Stud. 135 (2001).

117. For a detailed summary of the ITPGR ministerial that took place in June 2006 in Madrid, Spain, *see* Summary of the First Session of the Governing Body of the International Treaty on Plant Genetic Resources for Food and Agriculture, 12–16 June 2006, *available at* http://www.iisd.ca/vol09/enb09369e.html (last visited August 14, 2006) (including discussion of funding strategy for a "farmers' rights" fund and the relationship between the ITPGR and the use by the CGIAR Network of revised Material Transfer Agreements (MTAs)). New implementation initiatives and strategies are underway. One is the so-called "doomsday vault," the global seed repository under construction on the permanently frozen Norwegian Island of Svalbard. Unlike other seed banks, which are working banks with uneven security and access levels, not to mention funding sources and commitments, Svalbard is meant to be off-limits and a bank-of-last-resort, both legally and geographically speaking. The seed vault is scheduled to start accepting deposits by Fall 2007, starting with those from smaller seed banks and agricultural and scientific organizations. The vault will have capacity for up to 3 million seed varieties, holding what Cary Fowler calls "the biological foundation for all of agriculture." *See* Rick Weiss, *The World's Agricultural Legacy Gets a Safe Home*, Washington Post, A01 (Monday, June 19, 2006); *see also* Seabrook, *Sowing for Apocalypse*, *supra* Chapter Two, note 42.

118. Brush, Farmers' Bounty, *supra* Chapter Two, note 22, at 249–52.

119. ITPGR art. 9, *supra* note 108; *see also* Phillipe Cullet, *The International Treaty on Plant Genetic Resources for Food and Agriculture*, IELRC, Briefing Paper, No. 2003–2 at 4, *available at* http://www.ielrc.org/content/f0302.htm ("Different types of benefit-sharing mechanisms are provided.... These include the exchange of information, access to and transfer of technology, capacity building

If stewardship and conservation are the goals of promoting "farmers' rights," then the "soft" law part of the Treaty that contemplates the use of bilateral bioprospecting contracts seems to contradict those goals because such contracts are fortuitous to a great degree, benefiting some farming communities and ignoring others.[120]

Further questions arise regarding who the ITPGR contemplates as titleholders. Are they farming communities or nation-states? Because of broad diffusion of PGRs and metapopulations crossing national boundaries, does the Treaty contemplate nations forming PGR-cartels?[121]

In terms of subject matter, there is considerable ambiguity in certain terms in the Treaty. For example, "landrace" is left undefined and subject to different interpretations. Much of traditional farmers' knowledge is "local, widely shared, changeable and orally transmitted."[122] Much of the germplasm stored *ex situ* is only minimally documented and characterized.

Finally, there is the question of the duration of "farmers' rights." Traditional intellectual property rights are finite—U.S. copyrights last for an author's life plus 70 years, U.S. patents last for 20 years from the date of application, and U.S. trademarks must be renewed at regular intervals. However, "farmers' rights" have no cut-off point and are temporally open-ended. Additionally, traditional intellectual property rights are justified as providing an incentive for innovation and balanced against an interest in promoting competition—the potentially perpetual rights under the ITPGR contradict this model.[123]

An additional feature of the ITPGR is the way that a type of "common heritage" treatment is accorded 64 crops and forages on the ITPGR Annex I[124] from the CGIAR gene banks, however "sovereign ownership" seems to be the model for all other PGRs not listed on Annex I. There is a profound lack of consensus concerning the question of intellectual property in such materials, which in turn undermines PGR collection and transfer. This lack of consensus relates to perceptions of the increased economic value of PGRs and fears of the "theft" of such resources. Indeed, the metaphor of (sovereign) property may be used by particular countries to block the characterization of PGRs as intellectual property. For example, Ethiopia stopped export of its wild coffee germplasm.[125] Meanwhile, Peru's National Institute for Natural Resources and the National Institute for Agricultural Resources allow plant collectors to only collect authorized materials, prohibit collection from local communities, and use Material Transfer Agreements (MTAs) to prevent collectors from seeking or obtaining intellectual property on material without their permission.[126]

The ITPGR partially addresses the question of granting intellectual property rights in PGRs by creating a multilateral system (MLS), where member states and their nationals will receive "facilitated access" to PGRs stored in the CGIAR gene banks.[127] Under the terms of the ITPGR Annex I list, recipients of germplasm[128] "shall not claim

and the sharing of benefits arising from commercialization."); *see also* Helfer, *Using IP, supra* note 47, at 222.

120. Brush, FARMERS' BOUNTY, *supra* Chapter Two, note 22, at 250–51.
121. *Id.* at 251.
122. *Ibid.*
123. *Ibid.*
124. *See* ITPGR, *supra* note 108 (Annex I includes 35 crops and 29 forages).
125. *Id.*
126. *See, e.g.,* Brush, FARMERS' BOUNTY, *supra* Chapter Two, note 22, at 233.
127. ITPGR, *supra* note 108, arts. 10, 13.
128. *Id.*, Annex I, List of Crops Covered under the MLS.

any intellectual property or other rights" that limit access to PGRs "in the form received from the Multilateral System."[129] Thus, these 64 crops and forages are effectively placed into a type of "limited commons," subject to conditional limitations contained in the MTAs that accompany PGRs from the MLS.[130]

This means that germplasm of crops and forages on Annex I in the original "form received" from a CGIAR gene bank may not subsequently be protected by intellectual property rights; however, any individual genes, advanced lines, cells, particular DNA sequences, and compounds derived from such germplasm may be eligible for intellectual property protection. Laurence Helfer writes that,

> [t]he core of the debate focused on whether to bar patenting of isolated and purified genes extracted from seeds placed in the common seed pool. In the final round of negotiations, governments adopted 12.3 (d) which state that ... "recipients shall not claim any intellectual property rights that limit the facilitated access to [PGRs] or their genetic parts or components, in the form received from the [MLS].[131]

Helfer points out that the U.S. wanted to strike article 12.3(d) completely. Developing countries wanted to retain the "genetic parts or components" language, whereas the U.S., failing to strike the section, wanted to keep the "in the form received language." The final version of the ITPGR kept both provisions.[132]

Helfer argues that "[t]he critical issue for interpreting article 12.3(d) is just how far a seed's genetic blueprint must be modified so that the resulting genetic materials is no longer 'in the form received' from the [MLS]."[133]

Additionally, any crops not listed in Annex I are presumably eligible for intellectual property protection.[134] Indeed, the MLS seems to assume that private entities will incorporate PGRs from the MLS into proprietary varieties and that a percentage of profits from those commercial varieties will go to promote benefit sharing and conservation, under the rubric of promoting "farmers' rights."[135]

Thus, arguably, the "in the form received" language is in tension with the "farmers' rights" provisions of the ITPGR.[136] Also, as discussed above, the ITPGR does not recognize any rights in the labor by individual farmers and breeders who develop new plant varieties through systemic practices; however, institutional public and private plant breeders continue to enjoy intellectual property protection.[137] Furthermore, while the

---

129. ITPGR, *supra* note 108, art. 12.3(d).

130. Carol M. Rose, *The Several Futures of Property: Of Cyberspace and Folk Tales, Emission Trades and Ecosystems*, 83 MINN. L. REV. 129, 132 (1998) [hereinafter Rose, *Several Futures*] (defining a "limited commons" as "property held as commons amongst the members of a group, but exclusively vis-à-vs the outside world."); see discussion *infra*, Chapter Five.

131. Helfer, *Using IP, supra* note 47, at 220–221.

132. *Id.*

133. *Ibid.*

134. *Ibid.*

135. *Ibid.* Helfer points out that "only through commercialization would [there be] sufficient revenue to fund the treaty's benefit-sharing and conservation goals. However the [MLS] itself would be threatened if large parts of the seed treasury could be privatized through the grant of [IPRs]."

136. Patel, *supra* note 77, at 98.

137. *See, e.g.,* Thomas Cottier & Marion Panizzon, *Legal Perspectives on Traditional Knowledge: The Case for Intellectual Property Protection*, 7 J. INT'L ECON. L. 371, 377–78 (2004). ITPGRS art. 12.3 is opposed to the extension of intellectual property rights to traditional knowledge and on plant genetic resources used for food or agriculture. However, the ITPGRS permitted plant breeders who utilized genetic materials from the CGIAR gene banks to obtain proprietary rights. Arts.

ITPGR is more comprehensive in its treatment of "farmers' rights," to date, it has not offered individual farmers and breeders much in terms of effective implementation or vindication of those rights.[138]

Helfer describes six challenges facing the Governing Board of the ITPGR for determining: (1) appropriate terms of its MTAs;[139] (2) whether and how to amend the crops and forages listed on Annex I;[140] (3) how to go about bringing more private entities into the MLS;[141] (4) the appropriate scope of intellectual property rights in material derived from PGRs in the MLS;[142] (5) what types of commercialization of genetic materials derived from PGRs in the MLS will trigger a duty to contribute to the Treaty's "farmers' rights" fund;[143] and, finally (6) how to track compliance with MTA obligations.[144]

G. Comparison and Comments: Two Decades of International Treaties and Agreements

The plethora of international actors, fora, principles, interests, and commitments have produced dynamic, unfolding, and contradictory consequences as the "Seed Wars" continue in the 21st century. Yet with regard to global intellectual property protection for PGRs, the nations of the developed world (which also happen to be TRIPS' most ardent backers) appear to have had the last laugh—*or have they?*

Before answering this question, it is useful to compare the different fora. The United Nations-sponsored 1983 IUPGR eventually became the 2001 ITPGR. The 1992 Earth Summit produced the CBD. The intellectual property-forum UPOV influenced the adoption of the PVPA of 1970 in the United States. The CGIAR system is largely funded

---

12.3(f) and (g) do not preclude private plant breeders or public institutions from claiming intellectual property rights on modifications of plant genetic materials; once protection is extended, only the patent holder can release control over it.

138. While ITPGR art. 9.2, *supra* note 108, recognizes the concept of "farmers' rights" with regard to plant genetic resources for food and agriculture, it places the primary responsibility of its realization on national governments. The ITPGR only calls for each signatory nation to enact legislation to protect "farmers' rights" in the areas of (1) protection of traditional knowledge; (2) the right to equitable participation; and (3) the right to participate in decision-making. Although art. 9.3 preserves the right for farmers to save, use, exchange, or sell farm-saved seed or propagating material, this right is subject to local legislation.

139. Helfer, *Using IP*, *supra* note 47, at 222; *see also* Intergovernmental Committee on Intellectual Property and Genetic Resources, Traditional Knowledge and Folklore, Second Sess. (10–14 Dec. 2001), *Operational Principles for Intellectual Property Clauses of Contractual Agreements Concerning Access to Genetic Resources and Benefit Sharing*, WIPO/GRTKF/1C/2/3 94 (10 Sept. 2001).

140. Helfer, *Using IP*, *supra* note 47, at 223 (noting that many crops were excluded from Annex I because many developing countries desired to enter into potentially lucrative bilateral bioprospecting contracts instead of having their bio-resources consigned to Annex I's "limited commons").

141. There are three types of PGRs relevant to the MLS: (1) materials under state control (parties to the ITPGR); (2) materials in *ex situ* CGIAR collections (subject to control of the Governing Board); and (3) materials in private collection that the Governing Board wants to encourage to join the MLS. *Id.*

142. *Id.* at 221.

143. *Id.* at 222.

144. *Ibid.*

by institutions of the industrialized world. Finally, TRIPS is an outgrowth of the GATT, which was the precursor to the WTO.[145] The 1989 and 1991 changes in the interpretation of the IUPGR benefited the developing world, whereas the 1991 revisions to UPOV served to strengthen the position of private plant breeders and were arguably detrimental to the interests of farmers.[146] The CBD represented important gains for the developing world: (1) recognizing of the "sovereign national property" principle with regard to bio-resources[147] and (2) obliging private entities that used developing countries' PGRs to share benefits arising from commercialization of such resources and transfer technology to host countries.[148] Additionally, under Article 19 of the CBD, developing countries receive priority access to biotech products developed from exploitation of their PGRs.[149] The CBD also linked intellectual property rights to the distribution of benefits of biotechnology, one of which is "the fair and equitable sharing of the benefits of genetic resources."[150] Yet unlike any of the aforementioned agreements, only TRIPS has "teeth."[151] TRIPS has a set of detailed, comprehensive substantive rules that are linked to

---

145. Kal Raustiala & David G. Victor, *The Regime Complex for Plant Genetic Resources, available at* http://papers.ssrn.com/sol3/papers.cfm?abstract_id=441463; Helfer, *Regime Shifting, supra* note 82.

146. The ITPGR goes beyond recognizing "farmers' rights"; one of its main aims is to facilitate the exchange of seeds and other plant materials for research, breeding, and crop development purposes. It seeks to accomplish this exchange by creating a multilateral system to which member states and their nationals will be granted "facilitated access." Helfer, *Regime Shifting, supra* note 82, at 40. In contrast, the UPOV aims at protecting breeder's rights and creates an obligation for the respective signatory states to enact legislation to further that goal. In effect, UPOV sought to harmonize property rights associated with the creation or selective breeding of plant varieties. Eric B. Bluemel, *Substance Without Process: Analyzing TRIPS Participatory Guarantees in Light of Protected Indigenous Rights*, 86 J. Pat. & Trademark Off. Soc'y 671, 695–96 (2004).

147. CBD, *supra* note 86; *see also* Sabrina Safrin, *Hyperownership in a Time of Biotechnological Promise: The International Conflict to Control the Building Blocks of Life*, 98 Am. J. Int'l L. 641, 664 (2004) ("The [CBD] essentially takes the position that genetic material is the same as any tangible natural resource, such as oil and timber, over which sovereigns exercise control and even ownership.").

148. The CBD language is framed in terms of an "equitable sharing" of the benefits resulting from the exploitation of traditional knowledge between developed and developing nations. The convention further promotes broader participation in scientific research, the exchange of information amongst the various member signatory states, the facilitation of both public and private sector technology transfer, and the equitable sharing of the results of the scientific research and the benefits of genetic resource commercialization. Wesley A. Cann, Jr., *On the Relationship Between Intellectual Property Rights and the Need of Less-Developed Countries for Access to Pharmaceuticals: Creating a Legal Duty to Supply Under a Theory of Progressive Global Constitutionalism*, 25 U. Pa. J. Int'l Econ. L. 755, 925 (1996). Therefore, the CBD creates a legal basis for the developed signatory states to bargain with the developing signatories should they require access to traditional knowledge for commercial development. Royalties or other remuneration paid to the state were envisioned as the results of such a bargaining process. These financial considerations are then in turn distributed to the community as proceeds arising from commonly-held traditional knowledge to the community. Shubha Ghosh, *Traditional Knowledge, Patents and the New Mercantilism (Part II)*, 85 J. Pat. & Trademark Off. Soc'y 885, 921 (2003).

149. *See* CBD, *supra* note 86, at art. 19(2).
Each Contracting Party shall take all practicable measures to promote and advance priority access on a fair and equitable basis by Contracting Parties, especially developing countries, to the results and benefits arising from biotechnologies based upon genetic resources provided by those Contracting Parties. Such access shall be on mutually agreed terms.
Id.

150. *Id.* at art. 1 (stating that intellectual property rights should not run counter to the objectives of the CBD).

151. Helfer, *Regime Shifting, supra* note 82, at 2. For discussion of the relationship between TRIPS and the CBD, *see* CBD Third Conference, UNEP/CBD/COP/3/23)(October 5, 1996); UNEP

the WTO's hard-edged dispute settlement system whereby treaty bargains are enforced through mandatory adjudication and backed by the threat of retaliatory sanctions.[152]

Amidst the flurry of fin-de-siécle treatymaking, two forking models regarding PGRs emerged: The first, embodied by the ITPGR, is a multilateral approach concerned with creating international institutions to address PGR transfer issues. The second is the CBD/TRIPS approach epitomized by pharmaceuticals giant Merck's contractual arrangements with Costa Rica's InBio, whereby Merck received access to a Costa Rican biological preserve for $1.13 million dollars plus an undisclosed share of future royalties.[153] This approach focuses on bilateral market transactions and is also consistent with CBD's Articles 15[154] and 16.[155]

Both models attempt to characterize indigenous knowledge of PGRs and traditional farmer "know-how" as a type of intellectual property in problematic ways.

The bilateral agreement/transactions/bio-prospecting model contemplates contracts for PGR commercialization, but does not necessarily provide for PGR conservation. This approach has three significant drawbacks. One is the difficulty of establishing the prospective value of, and setting a price for, a genetic resource at the point of collection. A second is the speculative worth of some plant genetic traits, which might be economically worthless in the present but could become valuable at some uncertain point in the future. A third drawback is that the intellectual property laws of countries like the U.S. were not designed for recognizing, let alone compensating, the types of collective, intertemporal, and anonymous innovations that PGRs such as peasant farmers' landraces represent. To the extent that this model is consistent with the CBD, obtaining *meaningful* "informed consent" is complicated by the fact that, in reality, communities from whom consent is sought are often fragmented and dynamic in composition over time rather than homogenous and stable. To the extent that the "sovereign national property" model locates the ability to "consent" at the national level, one can imagine situations where the interests of subnational groups, communities or tribes are at loggerheads with state interests.[156]

Conference of the Parties, UN Doc: UNEP/CBD/COP/3/23 (1996); Relationship Between the TRIPS Agreement and the Convention on Biological Diversity: Summary of Issues Raised and Points Made by the WTO Secretariat, IP/C/W/368 (August 8, 2002). *See also TRIPS versus CBD: Conflicts between the WTO Regime of Intellectual Property Rights and Sustainable Biodiversity Management, Global Trade and Biodiversity in Conflict*, 1 GAIA/GRAIN (April 1998), *available at* http://www.grain.org/briefings/?id=24 (last visited August 14, 2006) (TRIPS as contradicting CBD and threatening CBD implementation; proposed solutions to their contradictions).

152. Helfer, *Regime Shifting*, *supra* note 82, at 2.

153. Silvia Rodriguez & Maia Antnieta Camacho, *Bioprospecting in Costa Rica: Facing New Dimensions of Social and Environmental Responsibility, in* THE GREENING OF BUSINESS IN DEVELOPING COUNTRIES: RHETORIC, REALITY AND PROSPECTS (Petter Utting ed., 2002); *compare* Edgar J. Asebey & Jill D. Kempenaar, *The Intellectual Property Perspective on Biodiversity: Biodiversity Prospecting Fulfilling the Mandate of the Biodiversity Convention*, 28 VAND. J. TRANSNAT'L L. 703 (1995); Tom Dedeurwaerdere, *Bioprospecting: From the Economics of Contracts to Reflexive Governance*, working paper *available at* http://www.bioecon.ucl.ac.uk/Venice/dedeurwaedere.doc.

154. CBD, art. 15 (CBD "sharing in a fair and equitable way the results of research and development").

155. CBD, art. 16 (concerning "access to and transfer of technology ... under fair and reasonable terms").

156. Rosemary J. Coombe, *Intellectual Property Rights & Sovereignty: New Dilemmas in International Law Posed by the Recognition of Indigenous Knowledge and the Conservation of Biodiversity*, 6 IND. J. GLOBAL LEG. STUD. 59, 95 (1998) [hereinafter Coombe, *New Dilemmas*] (pointing out that government elites might exploit/extract PGRs in ways that impoverish local communities).

By contrast, the MLS at least provides a counterbalance to market-based bilateral transactions and allows the genetic materials listed on the ITPGR's Annex I in the CGIAR gene banks to exist unambiguously in a "limited commons" under control of an intergovernmental body. However, the ITPGR model also contains at least five distinct flaws. First, while the ITPGR contemplates a "Multilateral System of Access and Benefit Sharing," it simply pays lip service to the idea of "farmers' rights." Article 9 articulates three categories of "farmers' rights" that are so vague as to be diaphanous. Second, the ITPGR states that "farmers' rights" are "subject to national legislation" and that the responsibility for implementing those rights "rests with national governments." What does this mean to a country like the U.S. that in 1994, amended the PVPA to cut back on the farmer "seed saving" exemption? Third, while the ITPGR ostensibly creates a mechanism for sharing the benefits of commercialization, the manner of payments are not delineated, thus making the ITPGR reminiscent of the hollow FAO IU gene conservation fund. Fourth, as mentioned above, PGRs stored in gene/seed banks and listed in Annex I within the MLS have extremely ambiguous protection from being converted into intellectual property. The weakness here is that the gene bank MTAs only stipulate that people receiving PGRs listed on Annex I are prohibited from obtaining intellectual property rights in the material, but only "in the form received." This means that subsequent transformations *via* breeding or genetic engineering could be patentable. Finally, Article 13 states "benefits should flow primarily, directly and indirectly, to farmers." Yet farmers and farming communities do not receive direct financial benefits. Benefits only accrue to farmers indirectly, through "trickle down" information exchange, technology transfer, and capacity building *via* the scientific community.

The ITPGR's MLS was premised on all crops *not* on the ITPGR Annex being "sovereign national property" that invite bilateral transactions and conversion into intellectual property under national laws as required by TRIPS. Yet "common heritage" treatment exists only for the 64 crops and forages on the ITPGR Annex I list and the genetic materials in the CGIAR seed banks "in the form received." "Sovereign ownership" seems to be the model for all other PGRs. Furthermore, there is a profound lack of consensus on the question of intellectual property in such materials, which undermines all PGR collection and transfer. Related to this lack of consensus are the perception of PGRs' increased economic value and the fear of "piracy" of such resources.

The breakdown of the "common heritage" system via the CBD, TRIPS, and the ITPGR, and consequent hampering of seed germplasm collection/exchange, presents an "anticommons" problem as envisaged by Michael Heller and Rebecca Eisenberg.[157] As will be discussed further in Chapter Five, an "anticommons" is the opposite of the "tragedy of the commons" situation where overuse depletes a valuable resource (e.g. a town commons used to graze sheep) because there is no entity to exclude people wishing to exploit the particular resource. By contrast, "anticommons" problems, resulting in underutilization of particular resources, arise when too many parties possess rights to exclude with regard to a valuable resource.

Professor Brush has suggested that our legal treatment of plant genetic diversity is in the process of giving rise to conditions that constitute an "anticommons"—underutilization (or sub-optimal diffusion) of PGRs because of too many parties hold potential

---

157. Michael A. Heller, *The Tragedy of the Anticommons: Property in the Transition from Marx to Markets*, 111 HARV. L REV. 622 (1998) [hereinafter Heller, *Anticommons*]; Michael A. Heller & Rebecca S. Eisenberg, *Can Patents Deter Innovation? The Anticommons in Biomedical Research*, 280 SCIENCE 698 (1998) [hereinafter Heller & Eisenberg]. For further discussion of the problem of the "anticommons," see Chapter Five, section C, *infra*.

veto rights. Brush describes how "the domain of crop resources is crowded with real and potential claimants to the right to restrict access to genetic resources. Private parties claim ... elite breeding lines, gene fragments, genes and genotypes ... The CBD recognizes national sovereignty over biological resources.... international treaty blocs [such as the Andean Pact] have agreements on the management and exchange of crop material. Germplasm ... is stored in local, national and international gene bank[s] ..." in large because "[t]he demise of common heritage has left nations with numerous claimants to the right to restrict access to genetic resources."[158] Such scenarios privilege private parties and entities that "own" or contract to "own" genetic and genetically engineered material via trade secret law, certified UPOV varieties, or utility patents. Of this development, Brush observes:

> Recognizing genes as economic resources and intellectual property effectively foreclose[es] a return to the ex ante practices of common heritage.... [But] crop scientists believed that, by the mid-1980s, a large portion of the world's major crop species had been captured and stored in gene banks of major industrial countries and international agricultural research centers ... [and] reliance on gene banks as the sole method of conserving crop resources [is] undercut by three factors: (1) lack of secure funding, (2) need for international germplasm exchange, and (3) ecological perception of crop resources as environmental assets that require *in situ* conservation.[159]

Neoliberal encouragement of the use of "sovereign property" notions coupled with the use of bilateral contracts/transactions after the CBD may work to create scenarios in which "multiple owners each have the right to exclude others from a scarce resource and no one has an effective privilege of use." Indeed, as mentioned above, some countries have used the metaphor of (sovereign) property in order to block characterization of PGRs as *intellectual* property. Ethiopia stopped export of its wild coffee germplasm.[160] Peru's National Institute for Natural Resources and the National Institute for Agricultural Resources[161] allow plant collectors to collect only authorized materials, prohibit material collection from local communities, and use MTAs to bind collectors contractually from seeking or obtaining intellectual property on material without permission.[162]

Professor Brush states the dilemma clearly. On one hand, by creating a new form of international "property" (PGRs) that is owned by sovereign nations, we facilitate bilateral contracts to extract value and commercialize PGRs in order to facilitate "equitable benefit sharing." On the other hand, the proliferating forms of intellectual property in PGRs create the very real prospect of chilling open access and germplasm exchange that has been a hallmark of global agricultural practices until the mid-20th century. Perhaps "common heritage" treatment was properly vilified in the 1980s by *both* the developed countries that rejected the IUPGR and the developing countries that decried the exploitive extractive practices of former colonial powers that took their PGRs for free but demanded respect for PVP and patented plants developed in part from those resources. Yet the 21st century eclipse of "common heritage" treatment for PGRs seems to be falling hardest on developing countries and poor farmers, who are now dependent on PGRs held *ex situ* in countries like the U.S.[163]

---

158. Brush, Farmers' Bounty, *supra* Chapter Two, note 22, at 235.
159. *Id.* at 236–38.
160. *Ibid.*
161. *Ibid.*
162. *Ibid.*
163. *Id.* at 237.

The emphasis since the 1990s on bilateral contracts with "informed consent" between sovereign nations and private entities (as opposed to multilateral public approaches) also raises questions. Is there a way to retain the beneficial aspects of "common heritage" as a means of disseminating and maintaining genetic crop diversity? At the very least, finding a way to give some substantive legal and economic "teeth" to the idea of "farmers' rights" could produce salutary effects.

Additionally, the ITPGR's prohibition (in the MTA/license) on obtaining intellectual property protection in genetic materials (listed on Annex I) "in the form received" could be changed. One intriguing possibility, to be discussed at length in the next chapter, is to change it so that it becomes "viral" in the same way that the General Public License (GPL)[164] for open source software "infects" any software that incorporates open source, making the subsequent combined software open source as well. A "Bio-Linux" licensing scheme would use private contract law to keep a vital public good such as PGRs from becoming privatized.[165]

Meanwhile, the likelihood of ongoing inter-regime arbitrage in the Regime Complex for PGRs in the 21st century remains high. Here are three reasons why. First, it is very difficult for one set of interests (national, private corporations, NGOs, developed/developing world, North/South, etc.) to win consistently when the action of a particular issue involving PGRs can shift from fora to fora. For example, while the TRIPS' "minimum standards" of intellectual property protection seemed to vindicate the interests of the intellectual property-rich countries of the European Union and North America, TRIPS was also subsequent to the CBD's provision for "equitable benefit sharing" arising from commercialization of biological resources taken from developing countries.

---

164. For comprehensive discussions of the open source movement and ways that the General Public License (GPL) works in a "viral" fashion, see the discussion, *infra*, in Chapter Five; *see also* Yochai Benkler, *Coase's Penguin, or, Linux and the Nature of the Firm*, 112 YALE L.J. 369 (2002) [hereinafter Benkler, *Coase's Penguin*]; David McGowan, *Legal Implications of Open-Source Software*, 2001 U. ILL. L. REV. 241 (2001); Glyn Moody, REBEL CODE: THE INSIDE STORY OF LINUX AND THE OPEN SOURCE REVOLUTION (2001) [hereinafter Moody, REBEL CODE]; Sara Boettiger & Dan. L. Burk, *Open Source Patenting* 1 J. INT'L BIOTECH L. 221 (November/December 2004) [hereinafter Boettinger & Burk, *Open Source Patenting*]; Janet Elizabeth Hope, OPEN SOURCE BIOTECHNOLOGY (Ph.D. Dissertation, Australian National University, December 2004) *available at* http://opensource .mit.edu/hope.pdf (last visited August 12, 2006) [hereinafter Hope, O/S BIOTECH]; *Open Source Initiative, available at* http://www.opensource.org/ (last visited August 12, 2006); Richard P. Gabriel & Ron Goldman, *Open Source: Beyond the Fairytales* (2002), *available at* http://opensource.mit.edu/ papers/gabrielgoldman.pdf (last visited August 12, 2006); Steven Webber, THE SUCCESS OF OPEN SOURCE (2004); Joel West, *How Open is Open Enough? Melding Proprietary and Open Source Platform Strategies*, 32(7). RESEARCH POL'Y 1259 (2003).

165. *See generally* Stephen M. Maurer, Arti Rai & Andrej Sali, *Finding Cures for Tropical Diseases: Is Open Source an Answer?*, 6 MINN. J. L. SCI. & TECH. 169 (2004) [hereinafter Maurer et al., *Open Source Answer*]. BIOS, founded by Richard Jefferson, proposed a spoke and wheel approach as a means of implementing such a scheme. As envisioned:

> a BIOS group, or node, might contain a core technology, or groups of technologies, necessary for introducing new genes into plants. Such technologies would not have to be superior to existing commercial technologies. They would just need to provide a sufficiently effective tool for engaging in the basic research such that developing nations, small biotechnology companies, and public research agencies will be able to engage in research without becoming ensnared in current patent traps.

BIOS stands for Biological Innovation for Open Society and can be found on the worldwide web at http://www.bios.net/daisy/bios/home.html. *But compare* Robin Feldman, *The Open Source Biotechnology Movement: Is It Patent Misuse?* 6 MINN. J. L. SCI. & TECH. 117, 126–27 (2004) [hereinafter Feldman, *Patent Misuse*] (exploring the possibility that Open Source licenses in the biotech area may give rise to patent misuse problems).

No *meta*-global institution exists to address such interpretive conflicts between multilateral treaties like TRIPS and the CBD.

Second, the existence of overlapping and competing regimes addressing PGRs—the CBD, the UPOV, the FAO's multilateral treaties such as the 2001 ITPGR, the CGIAR system, national intellectual property laws, and TRIPS—invites governments, NGOs, and corporations to engage in forum shopping. This practice generates an increasing number of inconsistencies between regimes addressing aspects of PGRs—for example, tensions between the regimes initiated to address equity and conservation issues and those trade-related regimes intended to ensure "minimum standards" of intellectual property protection are acting to produce inconsistencies.

Third, as Helfer has described, these growing inconsistencies in the PGR regime complex cultivate a norm of "legalism." This norm can be seen in TRIPS ministerials such as the Doha Round, which attempt to "harmonize" TRIPS provisions or address any gaps, conflicts, or other inconsistencies in TRIPS, such as the failure of the original Agreement to address "traditional knowledge."

Taken together, these three factors give rise to ongoing inter-regime arbitrage on the international stage. An example is the way that the ITPGR's multilateral approach toward creating the PGR Annex[166] may be undermined by the ability of parties to shift into the bilateral contract approach consistent with the CBD's Articles 15 and 16, whereby private parties enter contracts/licenses with sovereign nations regarding their PGR "property." Yet another example of inter-regime arbitrage is discussed ahead—that is the CGIAR system gene banks' use of MTAs to impose contractual conditions on those who receive PGRs from their germplasm libraries. One plausibly positive (and ironic) intervention in this arbitrage has already been alluded to above: taking elements of the Open Source software movement's General Public License (GPL) and incorporating them into MTAs, thereby ensuring that PGRs from the seed banks may provide a way to reclaim the better aspects of the "common heritage" approach as an optimal way of assuring wider diffusion of crop improvements.

H. Summary

This chapter sought to lay out the emerging backdrop of overlapping, and sometimes contradictory, treatment of PGRs on both the national and international level. The chapter first evoked a sense of crisis at the accelerating trend toward wholesale marketplace commodification of germplasm and concentration in the global seed industry. With regard to PGRs in the international arena, the forum in which an international agreement is negotiated determines which way the pendulum swings, so to speak. As a result, there currently exists a multiplicity of overlapping PGR regimes with disparate enforceability mechanisms. The poorer nations of the developing world have generally relied on the U.N. system; the notions of sovereignty are paramount to advance their causes. The richer nations of the developed world that have primarily sidestepped the U.N. system in favor of multilateral trade and intellectual property arrangements to protect their interests. Helfer describes this situation as "Regime

---

166. The ITPGR prevents pursuit of intellectual property protection as a contractual condition of receipt of materials from the PGR Annex.

Shifting."[167] Considered as a whole, this chapter suggests that the expanding scope of intellectual property laws and international treaties over the past twenty years continues to force fundamental changes in the way we think about agriculture. While it is important not to overstate the argument, at times it seems that the expansion of intellectual property has taken on a strange but dynamic life of its own.

167. Helfer, *Regime Shifting, supra* note 82.

Chapter Five

Intellectual Property and Beyond?

A. Governing the (Limited) Commons?[1]

Terminology may be confusing when discussing an idea like the "commons," and before this chapter moves on to examine alternate property models, it is useful to look at what the relation is between private property, the "commons" and the "public domain".

If a primary goal of property models is as some suggest—to empower traditionally disenfranchised groups—it might be useful to rethink the traditional concept of property. Elinor Ostrom describes three powerful arguments for a private property model rather than an open-access regime. The first is Garrett Hardin's "Tragedy of the Commons,"[2] which explains that a resource unaccompanied by a right of exclusion is ripe for overuse and depletion. The second is the "Prisoner's Dilemma,"[3] which shows that decisions premised on maximizing short-term individual self-interest may be at odds with long-term benefits. The third is Mancur Olson's "The Logic of Collective Action,"[4] which describes the prevalence of the "free rider" problem. This problem arises from a

---

1. Elinor Ostrom, GOVERNING THE COMMONS: THE EVOLUTION OF INSTITUTIONS FOR COLLECTIVE ACTION (1990)[hereinafter Ostrom, GOVERNING THE COMMONS]; *see also* Rose, *Several Futures, supra* Chapter Four, note 130; Carol M. Rose, *The Comedy of the Commons: Custom Commerce and Inherently Public Property,* 53 U. CHI. L. REV. 711 (1986)[hereinafter Rose, *Comedy of Commons*]; LOCAL COMMONS AND GLOBAL INTERDEPENDENCE: HETEROGENEITY AND COOPERATION IN TWO DOMAINS (Elinor Ostrom & Robert Keohane eds., 1994); Robert C. Ellickson, ORDER WITHOUT LAW: HOW NEIGHBORS SETTLE DISPUTES (1991).

2. Garrett Hardin, *The Tragedy of the Commons,* 162 SCIENCE 1243 (1968) [hereinafter Hardin, *Tragedy of the Commons*] ("Therein is the tragedy. Each man is locked into a system that compels him to increase his herd without limit—in a world that is limited. Ruin is the destination toward which all men rush, each pursuing his own best interest in a society that believes in the freedom of the commons."); Ostrom, GOVERNING THE COMMONS, *supra* note 1, at 2–3.

3. Ostrom, GOVERNING THE COMMONS, *supra* note 1, at 3–5 ("[T]he prisoner's dilemma fascinates scholars. The paradox that individually rational strategies lead to collectively irrational outcomes seems to challenge a fundamental faith that human beings can achieve rational results.").

4. Mancur Olson, THE LOGIC OF COLLECTIVE ACTION: PUBLIC GOODS AND THE THEORY OF GROUPS at 1–2 (1965)("[I]f the members of the group have a common interest or object, and if they would all be better off if the objective were achieved, it has been thought to follow logically that the individuals in that group, would, if they were rational and self-interested, act to achieve that objective.... [However] unless the number of individuals is quite small, or unless there is coercion or some other special device to make individuals act in their common interest, rational, self-interested individuals will not act to achieve their common or group interests.").

lack of incentive to create or maintain a collective good, which results when access to the good, or benefit from it, is free.

These three narratives depict private property as efficient and open-access regimes as misconceived and wasteful.[5] Yet Ostrom notes that establishing private property rights is not always easy, especially when dealing with common pool resources: "In regard to nonstationary resources, such as water and fisheries, it is unclear what the establishment of private rights means."[6] If private property rights in fugitive resources are unclear, developing such rights for plant germplasm seems even more difficult.

Because "rational choice" theories of property ownership and market behavior are skeptical of cooperation between individuals and groups, the importance of alternate social practices and understandings—sometimes referred to as gift economies—are suppressed, distorted or ignored.[7] Gift economies are premised on collaborative, non-proprietary thinking and relative insulation from strict profit pressures that exist in different forms and fora, including scientific research, parks, schools, and libraries. David Bollier writes that

> [T]he commons is frequently confused with an open access regime, in which a resource is essentially open to everyone without restriction. In an open-access regime, there is no identifiable authority. No one has any recognized property rights, and the output of the commons is intended for sale on external markets, not for personal use by members of the commons.... Without the "social infrastructure" that defines a commons—the cultural institutions, norms, and traditions—the only real social value in open-access regimes is private profit for the most aggressive appropriators.[8]

Some traditional agricultural economies are sustained in important ways by non-proprietary practices that make agricultural markets possible. However, these practices and the accompanying way of thinking have come under significant pressure, due in part to the pervasiveness of the three narratives mentioned above.

Professor Carol Rose notes that Hardin's "Tragedy of the Commons" is not a transhistorical axiom; instead, it is rooted in the enclosure movement in England that is understood to have begun in the 15th century and went through several permutations until the 19th century.[9] Indeed, Yochai Benkler has shown that the actual tragedy resulted from the concentration of agricultural land in the hands of a few: By the late 19th century, less than 1 percent of England's population owned over 95 percent of the arable agricultural land.[10] Historical quibbles notwithstanding, Rose astutely questions Hardin's definition of the commons. She points out that what Hardin called a "com-

---

5. Harold Demsetz, *The Private Production of Public Goods*, 13 J. L. & ECON. 293 (1970).

6. Ostrom, GOVERNING THE COMMONS, *supra* note 1, at 13.

7. David Bollier, SILENT THEFT: THE PRIVATE PLUNDER OF OUR COMMON WEALTH (2002)[hereinafter Bollier, SILENT THEFT]. For discussion of the distinction between a gift economy and a market economy, *see generally* Hyde, *supra* Chapter One, note 1.

8. Bollier, SILENT THEFT, *supra* note 7 at 20; *see also* Charlotte Hess and Elinor Ostrom, *Ideas, Artifacts, and Facilities: Information as a Common Pool Resource*, 66 LAW & COMTEMP. PROBS. 111 (2003) [hereinafter Hess & Ostrom, *Common Pool Resource*] (discussing "the difference between property regimes that are *open-access*, where no one has the right to exclude anyone from using a resource, and *common property*, where members of a clearly defined group have a bundle of legal rights including the right to exclude non-members from using the resource.").

9. Carol Rose, PROPERTY AND PERSUASION: ESSAYS ON THE HISTORY, THEORY AND RHETORIC OF OWNERSHIP (1994); Rose, *Comedy of Commons*, *supra* note 1.

10. Yochai Benkler, *Free as the Air to Common Use: First Amendment Constraints on the Enclosure of the Public Domain*, 74 N.Y.U. L. Rev. 354, 408 (1999); *see also* Robert C. Allen, *The Efficiency and Distributional Consequences of Eighteenth Century Enclosure*, 9 ECON. J. 937 (1982); ENCLOSURE AND

mons" was actually an "open access" regime because no particular party could exclude others. Professor Rose defines a commons as a set of resources and the social practices necessary to manage them.[11] Hardin's "Tragedy of the Commons" occurred when the cooperative idea of using woodlands and pastures for subsistence was replaced with the belief that such property should be enclosed to generate increased rent. Hardin's account rests on the characterization of the commons as a regime where no one had the right to exclude others. Thus, whatever was taken from the commons could be sold outside the commons, and the most aggressive and exploitative actor could get the highest profits (which equated to getting something for almost nothing). Rose and Ostrom believe that this absence of governing institutions or customs to control the use of the "commons" is telling.

Indeed, Rose alludes to the success of common ownership of resources by recasting Hardin's title as the "Comedy of the Commons."[12] She describes how common ownership of common pool resources such as navigable waterways, beaches, roads and other water resources resulted in cooperatively maintained resources.[13] Both Ostrom and Rose describe a limited commons, where defined community members treat a resource as a commons, but outsiders view that same resource as private property. Noting the success of this method, Rose asks why Anglo-American property law has adopted land law's enclosed model rather than water law's common pool resources model.[14] For one benefit of the water model is that certain common pool resources become more valuable the more they are used. Governance regimes for such limited commons can range from informal— yet powerful—social norms, customs, understandings, and practices to formal legal rules and procedures. Such regimes rely on decentralized governance structures.[15]

Rose's work reveals the false dichotomy between exclusively owned private property and open-access commons regimes. Implicit in the limited commons concept, which acts like a commons on the inside and private property on the outside, is the idea of partial commodification. That is, despite powerful market rhetoric and narratives, commodification is not always an all or nothing proposition. Markets are valuable tools, and in many circumstances (such as in gift economies coupled with social norms), they combine with other tools to distribute and increase access to resources, thereby curbing market excesses. Yet commodification can and often does engulf and destroy the practices on which fragile gift economies rely.[16]

To analyze the commons regime, Rose turned to England, perhaps because the Blackstonian "exclusive control" model dominates the U.S. view of property.[17] However,

---

THE YEOMAN (1994) (arguing that enclosure had distributional consequences but that there were little efficiency gains); J.A. Yelling, COMMON FIELD AND ENCLOSURE IN ENGLAND, 1450–1850 (1977).

11. Rose, *Several Futures, supra* Chapter Four, note 130.

12. Rose, *Comedy of the Commons, supra* note 1.

13. Elsewhere, Rose has pointed out the Roman law roots of these ideas such as "*res communes* in tangible things [such as] *the* ocean and the air mantle, since they were impossible to own ..." Carol M. Rose, *Romans, Roads and Romantic Creators: Traditions of Public Property in the Information Age*, 66 LAW & CONTEMP. PROBS. 89 (2003).

14. Rose, *Several Futures, supra* Chapter Four, note 130.

15. Ostrom, GOVERNING THE COMMONS, *supra* note 1.

16. *See* Bollier, SILENT THEFT, *supra* note 7 at 27; *see generally* Hyde, *supra* Chapter One, note 1.

17. James Boyle, *The Second Enclosure Movement and the Construction of the Public Domain*, 66 LAW & CONTEMP. PROBS. 33, 35 (2003) ("The big point about the Enclosure Movement is that it worked; this innovation in property systems allowed an unparalleled expansion of productive possibilities ... The strong private property rights and single entity control that were introduced in the

empirical facts suggest that the majority of U.S. property is not owned by individuals, but is held in various joint ownership arrangements, many of which are forms of family property, such as traditional joint tenancies and tenancies in common.[18] Other forms of joint ownership include future interests and trust arrangements, interests in cooperatives, condominiums, and homeowner's associations.[19] A closer look at the expanding category of jointly-owned property reveals the inaccuracy of describing U.S. property with a sole ownership model.

In addition, the accountability to co-owners that is inherent in joint property ownership is reminiscent of the limited commons model. Whether it is an accounting to a joint tenant or a fiduciary duty to a shareholder, many of these situations resemble what Rose describes as a "commons on the inside, [private] property on the outside."[20] So much of our social lives occur in the shadows of institutions premised on co-ownership. Granted, the liberal presumption of corporate personality conflates co-ownership into an illusion of Blackstonian exclusive ownership, but the illusion only goes so far. Nonetheless, two important features of co-ownership are accountability and governance, albeit private.

These features are also fundamental to publicly-owned land.[21] A closer look at limited purpose institutions such as irrigation, water and fire districts, business improvement districts, and school districts reveals a plethora of limited purpose governments. Fisheries and wildlife management regimes can also be forms of limited purpose governments.[22] Even privately owned condominiums and homeowner's associations must conform to requirements set by a publicly elected legislature.[23] Additionally, numerous examples of commons, such as riparian and littoral rights, are adumbrated through common law doctrines and modified through legislative and administrative stipulations.[24] Finally, municipal, county, state, and federal property all have complex relationships with private entities to deal with their valuable commonly-owned resources.[25]

The overlap that exists between public and private ownership of land and natural resources may be instructive for intellectual property law pertaining to PGRs as well. As Professor Margaret Radin has pointed out, partial commodification regimes may "involve property or interactions in which meanings are not binary or mutually exclusive" and may require a pragmatic reconciliation of inalienable values with market forces.[26] Yet understanding that such overlap exists is only the first step. The next is to discover how to use the limited commons concept to reconcile traditional understandings of PGRs with expansive contemporary intellectual property in such a way as to prevent exploitation and despoliation.

Enclosure Movement avoided the tragedies of overuse and underinvestment."); *see also* Hannibal Travis, *Pirates of the Information Infrastructure: Blackstonian Copyright and the First Amendment*, 15 BERKELEY TECH. L. J. 777 (2000).

18. Joseph William Singer, PROPERTY LAW: RULES, POLICIES & PRACTICES (4th ed. 2005).

19. Robert C. Ellickson, *Cities and Homeowners Associations*, 130 PA. L. REV. 1519 (1988); Gerald E. Frug, *Decentering Decentralization*, 60 U. CHI. L. REV. 253 (1993).

20. *See* Rose, *Several Futures, supra* Chapter Four, note 130, at 144, 155.

21. George Cameron Coggins et al., FEDERAL PUBLIC LAND & RESOURCES (5th ed. 2002).

22. H. Scott Gordon, *The Economic Theory of a Common-Property Resource: The Fishery*, 62 J. Pol. Econ. 124 (1954); James R. Goodwin, CRISIS IN THE WORLD'S FISHERIES (1990).

23. Gregory Alexander, *Dilemmas of Group Autonomy: Residential Associations and Community*, 75 CORNELL L. REV. 1 (1989).

24. Robert E. Beck, WATER & WATER RIGHTS V.I.III. (Robert E. Beck ed., 1991).

25. Gerald E. Frug, Richard T. Ford & David Barron, LOCAL GOVERNMENT LAW (4th ed. 2005).

26. Margaret Jane Radin, CONTESTED COMMODITIES (1996).

What is the relation between Rose's idea of a "limited commons" and the intellectual "public domain"? At the very least, one should not assume that the two ideas are equivalent or interchangeable. James Boyle has articulated a worthwhile distinction between the terms.

> The term "public domain" is generally used to refer to material that is unprotected by intellectual property rights, either as a whole or in a particular context and is thus "free" for all to use — a term that is itself susceptible to multiple meanings in this context, ranging from costless access, through political liberty, to free trade ...
>
> ... The "commons" is *generally* used in the intellectual property literature to refer to material that is not subject to individual control; rather it is controlled, if at all, by some larger group ... The axis of variation here is not the "owned" versus the "free" [but is] individual versus collective control ... [27]

The question is how to operationalize a form of "limited commons" with regard to PGRs. As we have seen, the ITPGR Annex I attempts to create what can be understood as a "limited commons" for the 64 listed crops and forages. Is there a way to extend this idea by re-characterizing and re-thinking our ideas about (intellectual) property?

B. Alternate (Intellectual) Property Regimes

The asymmetric character of germplasm flow and the lack of consensus on what constitutes the commons are proof that the world has not yet discovered a sensible way of dealing with its PGRs. One possibility is to consider germplasm in the context of the emerging regimes for protecting traditional knowledge, which also implicates emerging international human rights norms.

Professor Shubha Ghosh examines the intersection of broadly defined international intellectual property law and human rights norms, as discussed in the *World Intellectual Property Organization Report on Intellectual Property Needs and Expectations of Traditional Knowledge Holders*. That report was designed to:

> Identify and explore the intellectual property needs and expectations of new beneficiaries, including the holders of indigenous knowledge and innovations, in order to promote the contribution of their intellectual property system to their social, cultural and economic development.[28]

Professor Ghosh correctly points out that promoting social, cultural, and economic development may be difficult. For example, "granting an intellectual property right to commercially exploit traditional knowledge may facilitate economic expansion," but it may also inhibit social, cultural, or economic development.[29] Because no normative

---

27. James Boyle, *Foreword: The Opposite of Property,* 66 Law & Contemp. Probs. 1, 30–31 (2003).

28. World Intellectual Property Organization, Intellectual Property Needs and Expectations of Traditional Knowledge Holders at 5 (2001); *see also* Minutes of WIPO's 26th General Assembly, Report WO/GA/26/6, available at http://www.wipo.int/eng/meetings/2002/igc/index.htm (last visited August 20, 2006); WIPO Meeting Geneva, April 30–May 3, 2001, *available at* http://www.wipo.int/eng/meetings/2001/igc/doc/grtkficl_3.doc (last visited August 20, 2006).

29. Shubha Ghosh, *The Traditional Terms of the Traditional Knowledge Debate* 11 Cardozo J. Int'l & Comp. L. 497, at 530 (2001) [hereinafter Ghosh, *Traditional Terms*]; *see also* Shubha Ghosh,

principle exists to help decision-makers choose between conflicting alternatives, Ghosh recommends "empowering traditionally subordinated groups"[30] when helping communities structure traditional knowledge rights.

Ghosh also attempts to reconcile his suggested norm with TRIPS. To do so, he offers two suggestions:

> The first proposition is that the author should be the owner of his creation that is the subject of intellectual property. The second proposition is that the owner of intellectual property should exercise complete control over its use.... [E]ven if no individual author can be found, there is no reason to preclude ownership of traditional knowledge by traditional groups themselves.[31]

Germplasm is a nettling example. One possibility is to designate indigenous crop varieties as "folk varieties"[32] and protect them under the regime proposed by the Model Provisions for National Laws on the Protection of Expressions of Folklore. Setting aside the problem of state management of folk varieties, Rosemary Coombe suggests, "it might be possible to put a moratorium on patent and plant breeders' rights applications that use or draw upon such resources until the cultural status of such resources is determined."[33] Yet even then, someone must decide how to treat the germplasm that has been systematically stored in public and private repositories of the industrialized North for over half a century.[34] That germplasm is a non-rivalrous good since storing and cataloging a sample does not preclude a traditional community from continuing to use the variety. A germplasm sample is only a small amount of plant tissue, and its value is unrelated to its physical volume.[35]

Furthermore, given the number of traditional varieties and landraces that plant breeders have used since the 1930s to introduce particular traits in cultivated varieties, it may be difficult—but not impossible—to determine an individual folk vari-

---

Pills, Patents and Power: State Creation of Gray Markets as a Limit on Patent Rights, 14 FLA J. INT'L L. 217 (2002); Adam Mossoff, *What is Property? Putting the Pieces Back Together*, 45 ARIZ. L. REV. 371 (2003); Chika B. Onwuekwe, *The Commons Concept and Intellectual Property Rights: Whither Plant Genetic and Traditional Knowledge*, 2 PIERCE L. REV. 65 (2004).

30. Ghosh, *Traditional Terms, supra* note 29, at 533. Such a goal is also consonant with the Universal Declaration of Human Rights as well as the International Covenant on Civil and Political Rights (ICCPR), Dec. 19, 1966, 999 U.N.T.S. 171 and the International Covenant on Economic, Social and Cultural Rights (ICESCR), Dec. 16, 1966, 993 U.N.T.S. 3, although there may be a tension between "the [author's] right to benefit from the protection of the moral and material interests resulting from any scientific, literary or artistic production" under the ICESCR and the right to cultural identity under the ICCPR. *See* Asbjørn Edie and Allan Rosa, *Economic, Social and Cultural Rights: A Universal Challenge*, at 15, *in* ECONOMIC, SOCIAL AND CULTURAL RIGHTS: A TEXTBOOK (Asbjorn Eide et al. eds., 1995); Bruno Simma, *The Implementation of the International Covenant of Economic, Social and Cultural Rights*, at 70 *in* THE IMPLEMENTATION OF THE INTERNATIONAL COVENANT OF ECONOMIC, SOCIAL AND CULTURAL RIGHTS: INTERNATIONAL AND COMPARATIVE ASPECTS (Engel Verlag ed., 1991); INTERNATIONAL HUMAN RIGHTS IN CONTEXT: LAW, POLITICS, MORALS (Henry J. Steiner & Philip Alston eds., 1996).

31. Ghosh, *Traditional Terms, supra* note 29, at 531.

32. Coombe, *New Dilemmas, supra* Chapter Four, note 157, at 82; *see also* Hope Shand, *There is a Conflict Between Intellectual Property and the Rights of Farmers in Developing Countries*, 4 J. AGRIC. & ENVTL ETHICS 131 (1991); Cleveland & Murray, *Crop Genetic Resources, supra* Chapter Four, note 87.

33. Coombe, *New Dilemmas, supra* note 5, at 83.

34. *See generally* Kloppenburg, FIRST THE SEED, *supra* Chapter One, note 2, at 152–89.

35. *Id.* at 187.

ety's genetic contribution to a particular variety.[36] The way patent and PBRs regimes define a protectable innovation makes the determination even more difficult. These regimes consider protectable innovations as "tangible changes in plant genetics or management which were developed by an individual or a corporation over a known period of time." This standard does not include "enhancements that have occurred largely as a result of cooperative exchanges and the elaboration of plant-specific information over generations."[37] In fact, these regimes are premised on the view that protecting a "snapshot" of existing knowledge and evolving seed heritages as one tribe's cultural legacy alone belies this incremental and serendipitous evolutionary process.[38]

Professor Coombe notes that the "snapshot" problem is not the only difficulty. She imagines a scenario where several different groups claim rights to a single variety:

> If a number of groups have engaged in similar efforts to nurture and develop similar genetic properties in a particular variety, should the group for whom the variety has cultural or religious significance be enabled, as a human right, to preclude or control the commercialization of such genetic resources for whom the plant and its qualities have no such values? ... [R]ights of religious and cultural identity may come into conflict with the rights of others to subsistence, livelihood, and to benefit from progress in the arts and sciences.[39]

Both Professors Coombe and Ghosh highlight the complexities—and the politics—of using the idea of property to address these types of issues. More often than not, a discussion of property rights results in a series of vexing questions rather than producing any answers.[40] For example, when Ghosh proposes that authors should be the owners of, and maintain exclusive control over, traditional knowledge, he also suggests that such ownership should remain with the group that produced the knowledge if no indi-

---

36. *Ibid.* ("It may be true that genetic materials present the market with some unique problems in pricing.... Useful genetic material is in fact identified and used, to the great benefit of those who have appropriated it. The inability to set a price through the 'natural' operation of the market is not itself a justification for failure to assign a value to something with recognized utility. There are various non-market strategies that could be used to establish compensation schedules for appropriation and use of raw materials if there was a willingness to do so.").

37. Gary P. Nabhan, *Sharing the Benefits of Plant Resources and Indigenous Scientific Knowledge*, *in* VALUING LOCAL KNOWLEDGE, *supra* Chapter Four, note 87, at 191–92.

38. *Id.*

39. Coombe, *New Dilemmas*, *supra* note 5, at 85.

40. *Id.* at 114 ("Intellectual property protections are becoming more extensive and more pervasive. An acknowledgement of their status as human rights instruments seems timely, if not urgent, given the contemporary hegemony of financial and trade considerations in global discussions of intellectual property.... States with international human rights commitments retain a significant power, though largely untapped, to ensure that IPRs serve larger goals of global social justice."); Ghosh, *Traditional Terms*, *supra* note 29, at 500–01 ("[T]he terms of the traditional knowledge debate are actually very traditional, the continuation of tensions between North and South in ownership and control of resources. At stake are the tensions between the growth of a market culture and a communitarian, gift-based culture.... The traditional knowledge debate occurs in the context of a culture clash between the developing and developed world, between different social structures in the South and in the North (as well as structures within those two regions).... [and implicate] issues of development, sovereignty and control over resources."); *see also* Hess & Ostrom, *Common-Pool Resource*, at 127 (" A key finding from multiple studies is that no set of property rights work equivalently well in all types of settings.... The world of property rights is far more complex than simply government, private and common property.... [Property] rights can be held by single individuals or collectivities ...").

vidual "author" could be found.[41] Issues of control, voice, and power relations within groups push us to question property rights models.[42] While Ghosh does not discuss germplasm derived from landraces and traditional varieties, he offers four models for structuring traditional knowledge rights: a "public domain" model, a commercial use model, a trust model, and an ownership model. These models help explain the direction the "Seed Wars" have taken and may take in the future.[43]

The first model is the "public domain" model, or the formal intellectual property model. Industrialized countries in North America and Europe have used this model and have pushed for its global implementation.[44] This model is rooted in the history of colonial germplasm flows; it characterizes landraces and traditional crops as "public domain" materials. As such, these supposedly "raw," naturally occurring materials are openly accessible and free to anyone who collects them, and are part of the "commons."

Two U.S. Supreme Court cases exemplify this view, albeit in different ways and separated by more than thirty years: *Funk Bros.* (1948) and *Chakrabarty* (1980). However, the reluctance of groups in industrialized countries to include genetically engineered and hybrid lines in the "commons"(as seen in the resistance to the 1983 IUPGR) reveals that the "public domain" may be merely a heuristic device to denote what is actually (or what may become) private property.[45]

Indeed, denoting germplasm as part of the "public domain" is crucial to this model if so-called "raw" materials are to be "free" to Promethean inventors and the corporations that invest in their research. Current wealth distributions might look quite different if these players had to pay individuals or groups for the germplasm they extracted. As Jack Kloppenburg suggests:

> A Turkish landrace of wheat supplied American varieties with genes for resistance to stripe rust, a contribution estimated to have been worth $50 million per year. The Indian selection that provided sorghum with resistance to greenbug has resulted in $12 million in yearly benefits to American agriculture. An Ethiopian gene protects the American barley crop from yellow dwarf disease to the amount of $150 million per annum.... And new soybean varieties developed by University of Illinois plant breeders using germplasm from Korea may

41. Ghosh, *Traditional Terms, supra* note 29, at 531.

42. *Id.*

43. Posey & Dutfield, Beyond IP, at 103–4. ("Does anyone have a better mechanism than IPR to provoke a new, more socially just and economically sound paradigm of wealth, to strengthen positions of local communities, or to recognize the intellectual contribution of indigenous peoples to human patrimony? Alternative strategies are welcome and needed. But the deadly serious race to conserve the biological and cultural diversity of the planet is on: IPR seems to be one of the most interesting intellectual, legal, economic and political tools available to us at the present time.").

44. Ghosh, *Traditional Terms, supra* note 29, at 534–37.

45. Note that there is a robust and growing literature critiquing the traditional intellectual property model, including the legal construction of the "public domain." *See, e.g.*, Boyle, SHAMANS, *supra* Chapter One, note 25; David Lange, *Recognizing the Public Domain,* 44 LAW & CONTEMP. PROBS. 147 (1981); Jessica Litman, DIGITAL COPYRIGHT: PROTECTING INTELLECTUAL PROPERTY ON THE INTERNET (2001); Jessica Litman, *The Public Domain,* 39 EMORY L. J. 965 (1990); THE CONSTRUCTION OF AUTHORSHIP: TEXTUAL APPROPRIATION IN LAW AND LITERATURE (Martha Woodmansee and Peter Jazsi eds., 1994); Siva Vaidhyanathan, COPYRIGHTS AND COPYWRONGS: THE RISE OF INTELLECTUAL PROPERTY AND HOW IT THREATENS CREATIVITY (2001); Lawrence Lessig, THE FUTURE OF IDEAS: THE FATE OF THE COMMONS IN A NETWORKED WORLD (2001); Yochai Benkler, THE WEALTH OF NETWORKS: HOW SOCIAL PRODUCTION TRANSFORMS MARKETS AND FREEDOM (2006)[hereinafter Benkler, WEALTH OF NETWORKS]; Yochai Benkler, *Free as the Air to Common Use: First Amendment Constraints on Enclosure of the Public Domain,* 74 N.Y.U. L. REV. 354 (1999).

save American agriculture an estimated \$100–500 million in yearly processing costs.... It is no exaggeration to say that the plant genetic resources received as free goods from the Third World have been worth untold *billions* of dollars to the advanced capitalist nations.[46]

However, given the agrichemical sector's global economic and political power, it seems unlikely that the "public domain" will be restructured any time soon. Even if it were, existing disparities in technology and capital might prevent the regions that have provided raw materials and sources of genetic diversity from maximizing their newly expanded access to cultivated germplasm. Furthermore, it is uncertain whether allowing those countries to access such material is ecologically or economically sound.[47]

A second model is a "commercial use" model, which is based roughly on the misappropriation norms of unfair competition law.[48] This model would grant exclusive rights to the party or parties that first made successful commercial use of the traditional knowledge. In the PGR context, this model would permit traditional communities in gene-rich regions to assert rights when *they* could demonstrate that they had cultivated "weeds" into varietal seeds. The success of North American agriculture could provide at least partial evidence of so-called primitive germplasm's vast commercial value.[49] Still, commercial value would be difficult to define, especially for crops grown for traditional subsistence use.

There is also the "proportionality" problem. Traditional knowledge communities could not lay *exclusive* claim to the success of such "improved" crops. Though the people who have historically identified and cultivated a landrace deserve some proportion of its value, so too do the plant breeders or molecular biologists who added value to the germplasm.[50] Even if a "commercial use" model applied to germplasm, historical and contemporary resource and wealth disparities between developed and developing nations, as well as internal disparities between ruling elites and traditional communities, might prevent commercial-use funds from being used to maintain genetic diversity or to compensate traditional communities.[51]

---

46. Kloppenburg, FIRST THE SEED, *supra* Chapter One, note 2, at 167–169 (emphasis in original).

47. *See* ETC Group, *available at* http://etcgroup.org (arguing that for ecological, economic, and cultural reasons, expansion of intellectual property rights are extremely problematic, no matter to whom they are assigned or for what purposes); *see also* Tilford, *Saving the Blueprints, supra* Chapter Four, note 110 ("Seed companies cannot market diversity. To protect investment, the seed industry must have intellectual property protections. To receive protection under the current intellectual property system, seed companies must develop uniform products, a task made easier through biotechnology. To financially gain from these uniform products, the seed industry must then pursue the obvious strategy of mass production of products for a public willing to buy them.... Perversely, therefore the agricultural industry must follow the typical formula for market success, it must do so by eroding the very pedestal upon which its success is built.").

48. Ghosh, *Traditional Terms, supra* note 29, at 534–35.

49. Kloppenburg, FIRST THE SEED, *supra* Chapter One, note 1, at 185–86 ("[T]he land races of the Third World are most emphatically not simple products of nature. Traditional agriculturists have made very great advances in crop productivity. Domesticated forms of a species are frequently very different from their wild or weedy relations.... It is important to recognize, as Marx did, that the germplasm of domesticated species is not a free gift of nature, but the product of millions and millions of hours of human labor. Whatever the contribution of plant scientists, they are not the sole producers of utility in the seed.").

50. *Id.* at 186.

51. Coombe, *New Dilemmas, supra* note 32, at 95 ("[T]he assumption that transnational corporations or more developed countries are unfairly exploiting local communities is exaggerated in comparison to the exploitation by the political-economic elites of less developed countries who are far more likely to be engaged in commercial extraction resulting in resource degradation that im-

A third model is a trust model, which assigns traditional knowledge rights to a party other than the community where the knowledge originated. This is the model suggested by the CBD, as discussed in the previous chapter.[52] A trust model would address situations where no clearly identifiable individual or corporate creator can be found but where a particular traditional knowledge community can be identified as a beneficiary. For example, this approach would allow the state to grant or deny access to PGRs and administer a royalty/licensing scheme to distribute the income generated from the use of agricultural know-how and traditional knowledge to the appropriate communities. This model also promotes the use of bilateral bioprospecting contracts. Professor Ghosh observes that this model "has the benefit of having an identifiable bargaining agent, typically the state, in situations where traditional knowledge holders may be far-flung and/or not familiar with formal legal rules of intellectual property and/or contract law."[53] This model attempts to address concerns that corporations are exploiting traditional knowledge communities by extracting PGRs without paying for them. Yet, as with the "commercial use" model, even if communities are compensated, further exploitation may come from "the political-economic elites of less developed countries who are far more likely to be engaged in commercial extraction resulting in resource degradation that impoverishes local communities."[54] As Ghosh points out, "one's view of the trust model depends heavily on whether one 'trusts' the trustee."[55]

The final model Ghosh examines is the "ownership" model.[56] In some ways, this model is a subset of the "public domain" model because it shifts the line between private property and the "public domain" to grant ownership rights to a person or persons within the traditional knowledge community. Instead of being seen as mere producers of "raw" materials, such individuals or groups are recast as proprietors. This model is based on the argument that property rights are empowering, which is paralleled in Anglo-American property law, where, arguably, private property rights have been a way of pushing power downward by spreading proprietorship to new classes of people.[57] Some argue that historically, the institution of private property helped liberate individuals from the feudal domination of the sovereign.[58] Similarly, private property rights assigned to individuals or groups in the germplasm context might be capable of serving as a shield against domination by states, individuals, or groups.[59] However, this shield is

---

poverishes local communities."); *see also* Michael R. Dove, *Center, Periphery, and Biodiversity: A Paradox of Governance and a Developmental Challenge*, in Valuing Local Knowledge, *supra* Chapter Four, note 87, at 57 [hereinafter Dove].

52. Ghosh, *Traditional Terms, supra* note 29, at 535–36; *see generally* Restatement (Third) of Unfair Competition, Sections 38–45 (1995); *International News Service v. Associated Press*, 248 U.S. 215 (1918); *National Basketball Association v. Motorola, Inc.*, 105 F. 3d 841 (2d Cir. 1996).

53. Ghosh, *Traditional Terms, supra* note 29, at 536.

54. Coombe, *New Dilemmas, supra* Chapter Four, note 156, at 95.

55. Ghosh, *Traditional Terms, supra* note 29, at 536.

56. *Id.* at 539–40.

57. Joseph William Singer, Entitlement: The Paradoxes of Property (2000).

58. *Id.*

59. Dove, *supra* note 51, at 56 ("Much of the support [for IPRs] seems to come from scholars and activists in the industrialized nations (with minor support coming from political-economic— including governmental—elites in less-developed countries). Notably absent from this dialogue are the voices of indigenous people and activists in these less-developed countries.... The fact that local communities are not asking for compensation in the name of their countries, coupled with the fact that their national governments are not addressing the issue of compensating local communities as distinct from the state, provides the first of several cautions against uncritical adoption of the intellectual property rights approach.").

not a permanent one. One aspect of property rights is alienability—what may be owned may also be sold. Thus, commodifying ownership rights in germplasm may actually concentrate ownership of germplasm in the private seed industry if rights-holders decide to sell their rights.

U.S. law has generally not been hospitable to "public" communal property rights of the sort asserted by traditional knowledge communities, though it is notable that for centuries, U.S. corporate law has provided ample opportunities for assertion of "private" collective rights. What option might be available to create "private" law solutions, i.e., contracts, licenses and variations on the corporate and partnership forms to protect traditional knowledge communities and vindicate the idea of "farmers' rights"? The next section examines how the "open source biotechnology" licenses, or BioLinux agreements, may provide the beginning of a solution to the loss of the open access "common heritage" system for managing plant genetic diversity.

C. "Farmers' Rights," the Open Source Software Movement and Open Access to PGRs

This section discusses what the open source software movement may have to tell us about how we legally treat PGRs. First, this section looks at some of the basic ideas of open source software. Following that, the relevance of open source approaches to PGRs and related technologies and tools is assessed by comparing and contrasting the software and the agricultural biotechnology contexts. Next, this section looks at the problem of the "anticommons" in the area of PGRs and related agricultural and plant breeding biotechnology and ways that applying open source principles in the agricultural biotechnology area may help resolve this problem. Finally, this section considers institutional challenges to operationalizing BioLinux licenses and the irony of using "private" law vehicles, such as licenses, to leverage "public" access to PGRs and related agricultural biotechnology.

The following section gives a brief overview of some of the key ideas of the Open Source Software Movement.[60]

a. Open Source Software Principles[61]

The open source software movement, in general, and the development of the Linux operating system, in particular, challenges the prevailing view (reflected in the

---

60. *See* David W. Operbeck, *The Penguin's Genome, or, Coase and Open Source Biotechnology*, at http://ssrn.com/absract:574804 (2004); Dan L. Burk, *Open Source Genomics*, 8 Boston U. J. Sci & Tech. L. 254 (2002).

61. *See, e.g.,* Benkler, Wealth of Networks, *supra* note 45; *Coase's Penguin, supra* Chapter Four, note 164; Richard Stallman, *The GNU Operating System and the Free Software Movement, in* Open Sources: Voices From the Open Source Revolution (Chris DiBona, Sam Ockman, & Mark Stone eds., 1999) [hereinafter Open Sources]; Richard Stallman, The GNU Manifesto, *available at* http://www.gnu.org/gnu/manifesto.html (last visited January 20, 2007) [hereinafter Stallman, GNU Manifesto]; Richard Stallman, The GNU Library General Public License (GPL), *available at* http://www.gnu.org/copyleft/library/txt (last visited January 20, 2007); Sam Williams, Free as in Freedom: Richard Stallman's Crusade for Free Software (2002); Steven Weber, The Success of Open Source (2004) [hereinafter Weber, Open Source]; Moody, Rebel

intellectual property laws of countries such as the U.S.) that innovation will be deterred or under-incentivized absent strong domestic and multilateral international IPR regimes.[62] Moreover, the open source software movement demonstrates the fallacy of the idea that only large companies (e.g. Microsoft) with vast capital devoted to research and development can develop fully functioning computer operating systems.[63] The open source software movement has shown that it is possible to make high quality software widely available without the prohibitively priced licenses that go hand in hand with copyrighted software.[64] Furthermore, this movement has shown that it is possible to develop open source programs to meet the needs of the various platforms currently in use.[65]

The open source software movement originated from two groups in the U.S. in the late 1970s and early 1980s.[66] On the East Coast, Richard Stallman launched the GNU project, the goal of which was to create a free operating system that duplicated the functionality of the proprietary operating system UNIX. On the West Coast, the Computer Science Research Group at UC-Berkeley—a Department of Defense-funded group under its Defense Advanced Research Projects Agency (DARPA)—was making progress in improving the UNIX system.[67]

The open source software model grew out of the "hacker" culture of U.S. computer science labs.[68] Open source software emerged three decades ago, in the era prior to the advent of the proprietary/copyright model in the software industry.[69] Open source responded to programmers' needs for sharing source code, and was premised on the General Public License (GPL) developed by Stallman.[70] The GPL provides:

> You may copy and distribute verbatim copies of the Program's source code as you receive it, in any medium, provided that you conspicuously and appropriately publish on each copy an appropriate copyright notice and disclaimer of warranty; keep intact all the notices that refer to this License and to the absence of any warranty and give any other recipients of the Program a copy of this License along with the program.[71]

CODE, *supra* Chapter Four, note 110; Eric S. Raymond, THE CATHEDRAL AND THE BAAZAR: MUSINGS ON LINUX AND OPEN SOURCE BY AN ACCIDENTAL REVOLUTIONARY (1999) [hereinafter Raymond, CATHEDRAL & BAZAAR]. Peter Wayner, FREE FOR ALL: HOW LINUX AND THE FREE SOFTWARE MOVEMENT UNDERCUT THE HIGH-TECH TITANS (2000); Eben Moglen, *Anarchism Triumphant: Free Software and the Death of Copyright*, 4 FIRST MONDAY 8 (August 2, 1999), *available at* http://first monday.org/issues/issue4_8/moglen/index.html (last visited February 12, 2007).

62. *See* K. Ravi Srinivas, *Innovations, Commons and Creativity: Open Source, Bio Linux and Seeds* [hereinafter Srinivas, *Innovations*], *available at* http://www.wacc.org.uk/wacc/content/pdf/634 (last visited June 27, 2006); THE CASE FOR BIOLINUXES AND OTHER PRO-COMMONS INNOVATIONS, THE SARAI READER 2002: THE CITIES OF EVERYDAY LIFE 325 (2002) [hereinafter Srinivas, BIOLINUXES], *available at* http://www.sarai.net/journal/02PDF/10infopol/09biolinux.pdf (last visited August 19, 2006); *see also* Hope, O/S BIOTECH, *supra* Chapter Four, note 164; Margaret E.I. Kipp, *Software and Seeds: Open Source Methods*, *available at* http://firstmonday.org/issues/issues10_9/kipp/ (last visited January 20, 2007) [hereinafter Kipp, *Software & Seeds*].

63. *See* Benkler, WEALTH OF NETWORKS, *supra* note 45.

64. Weber, OPEN SOURCE, *supra* note 61.

65. Srinivas, *Biolinuxes*, *supra* note 62.

66. Hope, O/S BIOTECH, *supra* Chapter Four, note 164.

67. Moody, REBEL CODE, *supra* Chapter Four, note 110.

68. Pekka Himanen, THE HACKER ETHIC AND THE SPIRIT OF THE INFORMATION AGE (2001); Steven Levy, HACKERS: HEROES OF THE COMPUTER REVOLUTION (1984).

69. Moody, REBEL CODE, *supra* Chapter Four, note 110.

70. *Id.*

71. *See generally* Stallman, GNU MANIFESTO, *supra* note 61.

Throughout the 1980s, open software was developed in relatively isolated groups.[72] That began changing in the early 1990s, when Linus Torvalds, building on Stallman's GNU program, began writing the first versions of the Linux kernel which resulted in many programmers collaborating and cooperating by adding functionalities and utilities.[73] The result of which was GNU/Linux, an operating system that was distributed for free.[74]

GNU/Linux is distributed under a version of the GPL and the license is described as "viral." This means that if one downloads a copy of GNU/Linux, one is bound by its terms.[75] Any modification one makes to the program is not proprietary but rather is subject to the same terms of the GPL, and so on to any person who ultimately receives a copy of one's program. The key thing about the GPL is that it contractually prevents one as user/creator from claiming intellectual property in the underlying program or subsequent modifications—it can be view as a "private" alternative to "public" copyright law as it pertains to software. This is paradoxical: by using "private" contractual terms, the GPL keeps GNU/Linux "public," or freely available. One of Richard Stallman's mottos is "Free Software, Not Free Beer," which means that one may not purchase a particular copy of open source software for cash (no "free" beer), but one is "free" to copy and modify that software, subject only to the GPL.

Eric Raymond has described GNU/Linux as produced by a commons-based peer production system that is democratically organized and comprised of a loose hierarchy of programmers.[76] Democratically-chosen project managers direct decisions about development. The project managers define goals, monitor progress, motivate participating programmers, organize people's work, and marshal resources.

So what does open source software have to do with PGRs?

b. An Intellectual Property Anticommons for PGRs and Related Technology?

Departing for a moment from discussing open source software and returning to PGRs, this section looks at the accessibility and availability of agricultural and plant breeding technologies.

One of the most important issues when assessing different property/ownership models with respect to PGRs is the question whether the increasing thicket of intellectual property rights gives rise to a "Tragedy of the Anticommons." Michael Heller has described an "anticommons" as a situation where there are too *many* parties holding a right to exclude with respect to a particular property/resource, thereby giving rise to underutilization of the property/resource. Another way of putting it is that there are too many bottlenecks or choke points (owners who can say "no") in an "anticommons" situation—in short, there is too *much* property.[77] Heller's "anticommons" is a mirror

---

72. *See* Moody, REBEL CODE, *supra* Chapter Four, note 110; Raymond, CATHEDRAL & BAZAAR, *supra* note 61.
73. Linus Torvalds, *The Linux Edge, in* OPEN SOURCES, *supra* note 61.
74. Moody, REBEL CODE, *supra* Chapter Four, note 110.
75. *Id.*
76. *See* Raymond, CATHEDRAL & BAAZAR, *supra* note 61.
77. Michael A. Heller, *Tragedy of the Anticommons, supra* Chapter Four, note 157; *see also* Heller & Eisenberg, *supra* Chapter Four, note 157.

image of Hardin's "Tragedy of the Commons," where because no one has the right to exclude, a resource is prematurely exhausted—the "commons" is denuded.[78]

Plant breeding and agricultural biotechnology use a wide variety of research tools that go beyond the question of access to PGRs. Janet Elizabeth Hope writes that most of these research tools are bundled together in what she calls "transformation technologies." These "transformation technologies" combine information "from many areas, including crop genetics, breeding, agronomy, pest control and agro-ecology" that makes "innovation ... cumulative, in the sense that each invention builds on previous inventions, and complementary, in the sense that each invention contains elements derived from more than one source."[79]

As described in Chapter Three, there has been a dramatic expansion in the scope of patentable subject matter over the past quarter century which has given rise to a substantial increase in patents on gene sequences and molecular biological techniques with applications in agricultural biotechnology.[80] As also discussed in Chapter Three, there has been an increase in the number of legal vehicles to secure intellectual property rights such as utility patents, PVP certificates, trade secrecy, contracts/license and self-help such as Genetic Use Restriction Technologies (GURTs)[81] (which render the seeds of GURT-protected plants sterile).[82] These various proprietary claims on plant phenotype, genotype, and gene sequences within the plant begin to create an "anticommons"—a situation where a particular resource is underutilized because of too many bottlenecks where permission must be obtained, due to overlapping property/ownership claims.

In the area of agricultural biotechnology, the multiple, overlapping intellectual property rights (or bottlenecks) must all be cleared before using "transformation technology" research tools relating to modern plant breeding techniques. Janet Elizabeth Hope points to some recent examples of anticommons effects:

> Depending on the complexity of a product, its development may involve the use of dozens of proprietary research tools; an often cited example is that of Golden Rice™, a genetically engineered rice variety developed using approximately 70 different patented technologies.... [A] recent survey of intellectual property rights related to Agrobacterium-mediated transformation (a key enabling technology for plant transformation) concluded that ownership of the most far-reaching patents in the area cannot be determined because the broadest patents have yet to issue.[83]

One problem, in the plant breeding and agricultural biotechnology area, as discussed in Chapter Two, had been the significant shift in research from the public sector to the

---

78. Hardin, *Tragedy of the Commons, supra* note 2.

79. Hope, O/S BIOTECH, *supra* Chapter Four, note 164.

80. Gregory Graff & Dave Zilberman, *Intellectual Property Clearinghouse, Mechanisms for Agriculture: Summary of an Industry, Academic and International Development Round Table,* 3 IP STRATEGY TODAY 15, 19–20 (2001) (noting the increase in U.S. patent applications for gene sequences increasing from 4000 in 1991 to 500,000 in 1996). For further discussion of GURTs and related use-restriction technologies, see notes 118–119, *infra.*

81. C.S. Srinivasan & Colin Thirtle, *Impact of Terminator Technologies in Developing Countries: A Framework for Economic Analysis,* at 159 in ECONOMIC & SOCIAL ISSUES, *supra* Chapter Four, note 3.

82. L.J. Butler, *Conflicts in Intellectual Property Rights of Genetic Resources: Implications for Agricultural Biotechnology,* at 17 in ECONOMIC & SOCIAL ISSUES, *supra* Chapter Four, note 3.

83. Hope, O/S BIOTECH, *supra* Chapter Four, note 164, at 48–49; C. Nottenbenburg, *Accessing Other Peoples' Technology for Non-Profit Research,* 46 AUSTRALIAN J. AGR. RESOURCE ECON. 389 (2002).

private sector. The seed sector has undergone a dramatic and pervasive restructuring since the 1980s. Alan Marco and Gordon Rausser write that

> Over the past decade the structure of the plant breeding and agricultural biotechnology industries have been transformed. Through dozens of mergers, acquisitions and strategic alliances, there has been a rapid and dramatic concentration of control over value-generating assets.... [For example] [t]he acquisition of Holder's Foundation Seeds by Monsanto may have been ... surprising. Here, a privately owned company, Holder's, with gross revenues of only $40 million, was acquired for a purchase price of $1.1 billion. A principal regulatory issue was the potential effect that arose for germplasm access by Monsanto's competitors. Holder's germplasm is widely distributed throughout the industry and at least one of its elite lines in present in most commercial maize pedigrees.[84]

Hope suggests that this merger-mania "has been driven primarily by the need to avoid high transaction costs associated with [clearing] multiple intellectual property rights," and that "the outcome is certain: most key enabling technologies are now in the hands of only a handful of firms."[85]

Additionally, with the shift in agricultural biotechnology research from the public to the private sector and the rise and expansion of intellectual property rights in PGRs, there has been a redirection of research to focus on crops that will earn high profits, with concomitant neglect of unprofitable subsistence crops. As industrial agriculture edges out more and more subsistence farmers who had relied on seed-saving, farmer landraces, and *in situ* genetic conservation, crop genetic diversity (and related farmer know-how) is being lost. There is an irony to this because, as previously discussed, the store of global crop genetic diversity is increasingly to be found in *ex situ* storage in the gene banks of countries like the U.S. Another effect is that the non-systemized knowledge of farmer landraces and their wild and weedy relatives is being lost as well.[86] Stephen Brush writes that:

> [r]apid growth of this international system [of gene banks] in a quarter of a century has led to the creation of over a thousand gene banks in 123 countries ... with collections of over 6,000,000 accessions. These gene banks include immense national facilities such as the [U.S.] NSSL with 268,000 accessions ...
>
> ... Acceptance of conservation outside of gene banks was slow and often grudging.... Several answers might be posited to the question, 'Why was *in situ* conservation delayed so long?' The most immediate and compelling answer is that on-farm conservation is incompatible with agricultural development.... Development traditionally has been perceived as a process of technological substitution—of new crops for old—that had occurred in industrialized countries and that should rightly occur in developing areas.... Another reason ... is that assumption that farmers who grow traditional crop varieties would require a direct monetary subsidy to continue this practice once improved varieties become available. Finally, crop scientists who promoted conservation were not interested in conservation alone but also in obtaining genetic resources for crop development.[87]

---

84. Alan C. Marco & Gordon C. Rausser, *Mergers and Intellectual Property in Agricultural Biotechnology*, at 119, *in* ECONOMIC & SOCIAL ISSUES, *supra* Chapter Four, note 3.

85. Hope, O/S BIOTECH, *supra* Chapter Four, note 164, at 50–51.

86. Brush, FARMERS' BOUNTY, *supra* Chapter Two, note 22, at 196 (2004).

87. *Id.* at 196–98.

As intellectual property rights expand to encompass plant phenotype, genotype, and genetic sequences, public plant breeding programs in developing countries are falling further behind the private laboratories of companies such as Monsanto, as well as the public laboratories and test fields of public and private universities in countries such as the U.S. Plant breeders in developing countries may find themselves locked in a vicious circle of dwindling resources leading to a diminished ability to innovate.

What is to be done?

Hope argues that "participatory plant breeding" may hold some of the answer. "Participatory plant breeding" consists of a set of approaches that seek to "create more relevant technology and more equitable access to technology in order to improve the service and delivery of crop improvement to the poorest and most marginalized people and areas."[88] K. Ravi Srinivas[89] and Margaret Kipp[90] have referred to such approaches as "BioLinux." The next section looks at the applicability of the Open Source Model to PGRs and then assesses some of the plusses and minuses of a BioLinux approach to PGRs.

c. Applicability of the Open Source Model to PGRs

First, the concepts of PBRs and utility patented germplasm may be seen as analogous to copyrighted software. The open source software movement was a response to expansive intellectual property claims that programmers like Stallman felt encroached on the freedom of computer programmers and users to develop, create, or use software through use of the GPL to ensure that "free" (meaning freely accessible) software stays "free." In the PGR context, "farmers' rights" groups make a similar claim with regard to plant varieties protected by utility patents or PVP certificates as well as related agricultural biotechnology. Open access to PGRs potentially underwritten by open source licenses is an idea that responds to the pervasive colonization of germplasm by intellectual property rights regimes and the ways that those regimes encroach on farmers' freedom to save seeds. Seed saving has been one of the cornerstones of traditional selective breeding. However, with PGRs, the web of proprietary rights spawned over the past two decades continues expanding and there has not yet been a PGR equivalent of the GPL for software.[91]

Second, the open source software movement and the various "farmers' rights" groups have emerged as international movements with the congruent aims of "ensuring open access to a segment of society that has been heavily commoditized under the guise of intellectual property protection."[92] However, multilateral agreements like TRIPS, the CBD, and the ITPGR send conflicting signals as to what is and what is not proprietary with respect to PGRs. As mentioned in the previous chapter, the CBD characterizes PGRs as

---

88. Hope, O/S BIOTECH, *supra* Chapter Four, note 164, at 60.

89. Srinivas, BIOLINUXES, *supra* note 62.

90. Kipp, *Software & Seeds, supra* note 62.

91. For some interesting proposals, *see* Srinivas, BIOLINUXES, *supra* note 62; Felipe Montoya, [*Costa Rica*] *Linux and Seeds, Geeks and Farmers—A Spiritual Link*, A42 (September 11, 2003), *available at* http://www.a42.com/node/view/308; Tom Michaels, *General Public Release for Plant Germplasm: A Proposal by Tom Michaels, Professor of Plant Agriculture, University of Guelph*, v.1, Feb. 1999, *available at* http://www.oac.uoguelph.ca/www/CSRC/pltag/1998-99/gnucrop2.htm.

92. Kipp, *Software & Seeds, supra* note 62; *see also* Larry Ayers, *Software and Plants*, LINUX GAZETTE, No. 31 (1998), *available at* http://linuxgazette.net/issue31/ayers2.html (last visited January 20, 2007).

"sovereign national property." TRIPS mandates that member nations maintain "minimum levels" of intellectual property protection, including some form of proprietary rights in PGRs. While the ITPGR does categorize 64 crops and forages (stored *ex situ* in seed banks) as existing in some type of "limited commons," the implication is that *all* other PGRs not so listed are the property of the nations where they are located, and subject to intellectual propertization.

Third, "farmers' rights" advocates may have the potential to evolve into what the open source software movement has become — a commons-based peer production network that facilitates the sharing of plant genetic information and biotechnological tools.[93] This is where adaptation of GPL from the software context into the PGR context may be useful. As in the software context, opposition to proprietary moves regarding PGRs have been coalescing. One of the most active of these groups is the Philippines-based MASIPAG,[94] an organization that brings together farmers, scientists, and NGOs to engage in agricultural research.[95] To illustrate parallels between trying to ensure free access to PGRs and software source code, consider the following comparisons and contrasts between MASIPAG's version of "farmers' rights" and the GNU/Linux software model.[96] In the context of MASIPAG, Boru Douthwaite writes about

> parallels with the open-source software movement that created Linux. For software, read seed. Some farmers are seed 'hackers.' Although their source code — the DNA coding — is closed to them, nature itself or human intervention generates new 'hacks' by crosses and mutation, and farmers select hacks they judge beneficial. The tantalizing prospect opens up that [participatory plant breeding] might be able to capture the power of the 'bazaar' development model in the same way that the open-source software movement has.... If [participatory plant breeding] can harness the creativity of farmer 'hackers,' wouldn't this be a better and safer way of trying to double rice production in the next twenty years than relying on Big Science to pull off a second Green Revolution?[97]

---

93. Hope, O/S BIOTECH *supra* Chapter Four, note 164, at 180.

94. MASIPAG is an acronyn for Magsasaka at Siyentipiko Para Sa Pag-unlad ng Agrikultura, which translates to "Farmer-Scientist Partnership for Development, Inc.," *available at* http://www.masipag.org; *see also* Boru Douthwaite, ENABLING INNOVATION: A PRACTICAL GUIDE TO UNDERSTANDING AND FOSTERING TECHNOLOGICAL CHANGE at 205 (2002)[hereinafter Douthwaite, INNOVATION] (describing MASIPAG as an example of Participatory Plant Breeding: "MASIPAG was formed in 1985 in Los Banos in the Philippines as a partnership between a group of farmers dissatisfied with he economic and environmental cost of growing [high-yielding varieties] with high levels of chemical inputs; a group of dissident, nationalist crop scientists from the University of the Philippines and some social scientists from an NGO ... The organization began by collecting rice varieties and by 1992, 210 in its breeding stock, of which 87 were [high-yielding varieties]/ At the same time, the scientists trained the farmers in the basics of hybridization, selection and record-keeping.").

95. *Id.*

96. Srinivas, BIOLINUXES, *supra* note 62, at 325 ("A biolinux model can be applied for the development of plant varieties, agro machinery and sharing of information and knowledge. A biolinux model ... [is] as follows. The variety will be made available with a GPL or similar document explicitly stating rights and claims.... There will be no restrictions on using [the variety] to develop new varieties or to experiment with but it is essential that the variety derived from this also be available without restriction on further development.... [An] agency [could] coordinate [to bring] together breeders and farmers.... There could be a common pool to which farmers can contribute [and] ... also exchange materials with others under ... MTAs.").

97. Douthwaite, INNOVATION, *supra* note 94, at 206–07 (2002).

Farmers' Rights and the Open Source Software Model

MASIPAG's list of "Farmers' Rights"[i]	GNU Manifesto
Rights to use save, exchange, multiply, sell and improve genetic resources	Everyone will be permitted to modify and redistribute GNU, but no distributor will be allowed to restrict its further distribution
Right to control seed, including the right to refuse access to seeds and knowledge where such access will be detrimental to farmers	All versions of GNU [shall] remain free [but] GNU is not in the public domain
Right to prevent technologies, policies and institutions that destroy the watershed and [harm] the ability of farmers to produce food and conserve biodiversity[ii]	Copying all or part of a program is as natural to a programmer as breathing, and as productive[iii]

i. Kipp, *Software and Seeds*, *supra* note 62, at 9 ("Like the open source community, farmers' rights groups often have strong international ties. Similarly, the farmers' rights movement consists of many smaller groups of farmers and environmental activists who sometimes work together, just like the open source community where developers work on a variety of different projects which are brought together to make a larger project.").

ii. *Id.*

iii. *Id.*

An open source PGR model would be based on the idea that farmers are both users and developers of different types of agricultural information technology.[98] Such a model might be applied not only to the development of plant varieties via selective breeding, genomics, and genetic manipulation of PGRs but also to the development of related machinery/technology and the sharing of agricultural information, knowledge, and other agricultural know-how.[99]

New plant varieties and related technology developed and created using this participatory process could then be made available to farmers and plant breeders under a GPL-styled license with same "viral" effect—any subsequent modifications must be openly accessible under the GPL terms.[100] Plant varieties and related technologies subject to a GPL-like license would be covered under a license that explicitly conditions the receipt of the plant materials on a contractual promise that there would be no downstream restrictions on the rights of others to experiment, innovate, share or exchange the PGRs.[101]

---

98. Srinivas, BIOLINUXES, *supra* note 62, at 321.

99. Kipp, *Software & Seeds*, *supra* note 62, at 10 ("Where Stallman and the Free Software Foundation seek to ensure that their GNU tools will always be available to programmers, MASIPAG demands that farmers be given the equivalent ability to save their seeds, trade seeds with neighbors, and work separately or together on developing better or different strains in their crops.").

100. *Id.*

101. *Id.*

Currently, seed banks utilize Material Transfer Agreements (MTAs) that PGR recipients must sign in order to receive seeds from the seed bank. Conceivably, MTAs might be reconfigured to contain GPL-like terms. Here is a comparison between an MTA and the GPL:

Material Transfer Agreement (MTA)	General Public License (GPL)
Use permitted for "research purposes only"	Not limited to "research purposes only"
Should research purposes yield commercially viable end results, an obligation arises to shares royalties and profits	No obligation to share royalties
	Permission to copy and distribute programs in the form received provided an acknowledgement is appended
	Obligation not to seek patents
Obligation to share intellectual property rights	No obligation to share intellectual property rights
	Any patent received must be licensed for everyone's free use
Mutual assistance	No provision for mutual assistance

d. Plusses and Minuses of an Open Source PGR Model

The open source model may be a viable option in the PGR context.[102] Thus, it is important to consider the plusses and minuses of this option. On the plus side, historically, farmers have been selecting seeds and selectively breeding crops for centuries in order to create new varieties. However, while farming practices developed around the globe and over millennia, plant breeding as an organized industry has only been in existence for a little over a century, and intellectual property protection for PGRs is an even newer phenomenon. *Chakrabarty* served as a watershed moment when the U.S. Supreme Court opened the door to patenting living organisms.[103] In light of this history, it may make sense to carve out some particular niche, exception, or regulation pertaining to PGRs for food and agriculture.

Also on the plus side is the point that an open source PGR model may lead to increased understanding about PGRs by creating, maintaining, and growing an inclusive user community of farmers, plant breeders and researchers through which

---

102. Note that the open source model for PGRs and related agricultural biotechnology overlaps significantly with the set of approaches that Srinivas, Hope, and Douthwaite call "Participatory Plant Breeding." Srinivas writes that "Farmers have developed seed varieties by experimenting over centuries and sharing the improved varieties with others. Participatory Plant Breeding tries to mix the best in modern science with the wisdom of farmers in order to develop varieties that are both farmer-friendly and meet the needs of different agro-climatic zones." *See* Srinivas, Biolinuxes, *supra* note 62, at 324.

103. *Chakrabarty, supra* Chapter One, note 8.

information and technology may be exchanged freely *via* decentralized commons-based peer-production networks.[104] Such networks would increase the understanding of plant germplasm among individual farmers and researchers thus leading to increased capacity building, rather than treating them as passive consumers of technologically advanced but legally inaccessible crop technology systems. Also, like software programmers, farmers have varying criteria they employ when evaluating seeds, depending on locale, the size of their holdings, etc.[105] An open source PGR model thus would help ensure that farmers in particular local situations would be able to develop and cultivate plant varieties adapted to local climate, soil, and other conditions. This is a different result than the situation wherein multinational agrichemical corporations heavily promote "crop technology systems" that by contrast attempt to adapt local conditions to accommodate their seeds via expensive chemical inputs, rather than adapting a seed to local conditions. Additionally, such corporations are reluctant to invest in any field where the market size is too small or the profitability of the venture is not readily apparent.[106]

Another positive is that an open source PGR model would help prevent further erosion of genetic diversity accelerated by the increasing intellectual propertization and ensuing monoculture of PGRs. The open source model could lead to plant quality improvements because, by analogy in the open source software context, "given enough eyes, all bugs are shallow."[107] An open source PGR model would contribute to increased availability and genetic diversity of PGRs by making germplasm less vulnerable to crop diseases that would be able to wipe out a monoculture crop or the manipulative moves of an increasingly oligopolistic small number of powerful firms.

Like software, seed production is a process with a large fixed cost but that produces a product that can be distributed or copied cheaply.[108] With software, duplication is digital, whereas with seeds, duplication is the result of the self-replicating nature of the seed itself.[109] Moreover, the costs of contribution to an already existing and openly accessible plant variety (as would be a computer program in the software context) is low compared to the cost of starting from scratch if permission cannot be secured to work with materials protected by intellectual property rights.[110]

As mentioned above, an open source PGR model would also serve as a means of spreading risk and sharing costs among farmers, "farmers rights" groups, and other smaller entities involved in the agricultural sector. Under an open source PGR model

104. Srinivas, BIOLINUXES, *supra* note 62, at 327 ("Just as thousands of varieties of rice were made available by the hard work of countless farmers who, over the centuries, enhanced, conserved and created the [genetic] diversity we need ... biolinux and other models will facilitate development on innovations which are not anti-commons."; *See also* Benkler, *Coase's Penguin, supra* Chapter Four, note 164, 371–72 (Describing "commons-based peer production" as a "newly emerging mode of production where individuals work together on projects with a wide range of motivations other than market prices or commands within a hierarchical firm structure."); Benkler, WEALTH OF NETWORKS, *supra* Chapter Four, note 164.

105. Srinivas, BIOLINUXES, *supra* note 62, at 326.

106. *Id.*

107. Raymond, CATHEDRAL & BAZAAR, *supra* note 61, at 41.

108. *See* Kipp, *Software & Seeds, supra* note 62.

109. *Id.*

110. *See* Janet Elizabeth Hope, *Open Source Software as a Business Model, available at* http://rss.anu.edu.au/~janeth/OSBusMod.html (last visited June 28, 2006) [hereinafter HOPE, *Open Source Business Models*]; Janet Hope, O/S BIOTECH, *supra* Chapter Four, note 164.

that promoted participatory open source breeding projects, smaller seed companies would be able to compete with larger companies by lowering research and development costs and farmers would be able to participate in creating new varieties suited to local environments, promoting *in situ* PGR conservation (as opposed to *ex situ* storage in seed banks). *In situ* conservation promotes preservation of traditional farmer know-how as well as promoting genetic diversity.[111] Additionally, the motivations for using an open source model in the PGR context are arguably more profound than in the software area—namely, farmers' survival, PGR preservation, and feeding regional and global populations.[112]

While an open source model for PGRs has attractive aspects, such a model also presents potential problems that need consideration. In the open source software context, the creation and management of a user community is critical.[113] The role of the project leader includes the provision of the basic intellectual content and the addition of new contributions. Other tasks also include the set-up and maintenance of effective community structures to maximize users' motivations to contribute and the keeping up of morale within the user/contributor community.[114]

A problem in the PGR context is that the genetic "information" at issue is far less codified and much more dynamic than in the software context. However, this may be partially addressable by creating an infrastructure for communication of genomic databases between and among farmers, plant breeders, gene bank, newsgroups, and public

---

111. Brush, FARMERS' BOUNTY, *supra* Chapter Two, note 22, at 198–99 (Discussing the benefits of *in situ* conservation and criticism of *ex situ* collections: "First, important elements of crop genetic resources cannot be captured and stored off-site.... *in situ* conservation is dynamic and meant to maintain a living and ever-changing system, thus allowing for both loss and addition of elements of the agroecosystem.... [Second] ... gene bank collections fail to capture real diversity or resources that are generated after the collection has occurred. Recurring collection is rare and limited by many obstacles both within gene banks and outside them.... Third, all forms of conservation are vulnerable, and gene banks are subject to numerous risks—genetic drift within collections, loss of seed viability, equipment failure, security problems, and economic instability.... Finally, service and political reasons bolster *in situ* conservations.... *In situ* conservation has been proffered as an ally of agricultural development for areas bypassed by conventional technology improvement schemes and as a way to achieve development without Green Revolution technology ... [and] can theoretically generate far more diversity and involve farmers in improving local crops through "participatory crop improvement.... improv[ing] food availability and income.").

112. *See generally* Maurer et al., *Open Source Answer, supra* Chapter Four, note 165, (discussing initiatives undertaken by Professor Arti Rai of Duke University Law School to apply open source licensing principles in the pharmaceutical area). *See also* Douthwaite, INNOVATION, *supra* note 94, at 209–10 ("CAMBIA, the Centre for the Applicaion of Molecular Biology to International Agriculture ... is a not-for-profit research institute in Canberra, Australia, which was set up by Richard Jefferson, its executive director, in 1991 to develop and package the novelty generation and selection tools that biotechnology is making possible so that farmers and local researchers can use them and not just scientists working for multinational companies.... CAMBIA is trying to create composite populations of rice plants, but with a difference.... [A CAMBIA biologist said] "If we were designing a rice plant from scratch then we might want to have broad leaves on the lower nodes that quickly cover the ground and suppress weeds. Using our technique we can randomly turn on genes in this part of the plant and, as rice has the genes to grow broad leaves, sooner or later we would get lucky.... Transactivation, the technical term for the technology that creates such novelty, is just one of the tools that CAMBIA is developing ... and delivering its tools through links with farmers and [National Agricultural Research Systems] in developing countries."

113. *See* Hope, *Open Source Business Models, supra* note 110.

114. *Id.*

university institutions such as the Public Intellectual Property Resource for Agriculture (PIPRA) located at the University of California at Davis.[115]

In addition, certain challenges must be overcome for an open source plant germplasm model to succeed. The same challenges with regard to creating, managing, and facilitating communication within the user community may be problems because "qualities" (in the context of "quality control") may not be as readily verifiable as in the software context. Dispute resolution procedures among contributors need to be addressed along with the recruitment, nomination, election, and selection of effective project or group leaders to ensure the long-term viability of such a project.

There are also potential regulatory issues resulting from the CBD, the ITPGR, and TRIPS approach that treats PGRs as "sovereign property."[116] As a result, the movement of PGRs may be restricted across national boundaries, contributing to an "anticommons." As discussed in the previous chapter, the ITPGR currently categorizes the 64 crops and forages listed in Annex I to the Treaty as belonging to a type of "limited commons," therefore PGRs for those crops coming from CGIAR seed banks may not be (intellectual) propertized "in the form received." However, by implication, all PGRs *not* included on the ITPGR Annex are considered "sovereign property" of the nations wherein they exist, and TRIPS mandates that such nations must provide plant variety protection or equivalent *sui generis* intellectual property protection. Additionally, some developing nations may insist, pursuant to the CBD, on compensation (or technology transfer) for appropriation and use of "their" PGRs. These countries will want to issue their "informed consent" in order to secure "equitable benefit sharing."[117] Depending on their terms, such demands may effectively hamper any gains through an open source PGR model by further restricting the free movement of PGRs.

---

115. PIPRA's website states that "PIPRA is an initiative by universities, foundations and non-profit research institutions to make agricultural technologies more easily available for development and distribution of subsistence crops for humanitarian purposes in the developing world and specialty crops in the developed world." Note, however, that PIPRA expressly does *not* engage in open source licensing of its members' technologies. *See* http://www.pipra.org/ (last visited August 30, 2007).

116. It is beyond the scope of this section and this book to address issues raised by genetically engineered crops, but a distinction should be made between transgenic crops, where genes from outside of the particular plant species are inserted into a plant's genome, and non-transgenic crops, where genes from with a species are inserted into a plant genome, as well as the use of new agricultural biotechnology, such as Marker Aided Selection, which dramatically decreases the time necessary via DNA markers and computing power to find and add traits to a particular cultivar from a landrace or a wild and weedy relative. For genetically engineered crops, there are a number regulatory hurdles, at the national and international levels. The Cartegena Biosafety Protocol allows signatory nations to block imports or require labeling on a 'precautionary' basis without firm evidence of scientific harm. *See* Cartegena Protocol of Biosafety to the Convention on Biosafety, 29 Jan. 2000, 39 I.L.M 1027 (2000), *available at* http://www.biodiv.org/biosafety/protocol.asp (last visited March 9, 2007). There is also the FAO's Codex Alimentarius that was established in 1962 to set formal food and hygiene standards. In 1995, the responsibility for Sanitary and Phytosanitary (SPS) food safety standards was assigned to the Codex under the then-new WTO trade regime. In the United States, there is muddled jurisdiction over genetically engineered crops divided amongst the U.S. Agricultural Plant Health Inspector (APHIS), a sub-department of the USDA that regulates field trials of genetically engineered crops, the Environmental Protection Agency (EPA) that regulates pest control in plants, and the Food and Drug Administration (FDA), that regulates food quality which has taken the position that if "substantial equivalence" can be shown be genetically engineered food crops (vitamin, caloric and other criteria) and non-genetically engineered food, genetically engineered crops can get to the market without labeling.

117. John H. Barton & Wolfang E. Siebeck, MATERIAL TRANSFER AGREEMENTS IN GENETIC RESOURCES EXCHANGE — THE CASE OF THE INTERNATIONAL AGRICULTURAL RESEARCH CENTRES, IS-

Yet another challenge to an open source PGR model would be the proliferation of Genetic Use Restriction Technologies (GURTs) and Varietal GURTs (V-GURTs).[118] These could be used by or threatened to be used by corporations seeking to restrict the use of their protected seeds not only by employing the legal system *via* patents, plant breeders' rights, and restrictive licenses but also by technological methods.[119] Thus, not only is the use of protected seed legally prohibited absent an agreement with the seed supplier (with terms skewed in favor of the supplier), it may actually be impossible to replicate such seed since some are designed not to replicate *via* anti-germination technology. On the other side of the issue, there is the question of outcrosses of GURT crops, such as was the case with Bayer CropScience's experimental gene-altered rice "LLRICE601" that had become widespread in the U.S. rice supply.[120]

Finally, there may be issues involving patent misuse in situations where a GPL-like license protects the core feature of the PGR with users permitted to seek proprietary rights on the express condition that they in turn make innovations available not only to other members of the user group but to the public at large, as well.[121] In North America, Robin Feldman has raised concerns as to whether open source practices in the biomedical area amount to patent misuse by seeking to extend their scope beyond the protected technology.[122] Arguably, such concerns may also apply to an open source PGR regime, at least in countries that implement a serious competition of antitrust policy.

SUES IN GENETIC RESOURCES (1994), *available at* http://www.ipgri.cgiar.org/publications/pdf/109 .pdf (last visited August 21, 2006).

118. GURTS and V-GURTs are a form of biotechnological "self-help" that protect genetically engineered crops from unauthorized reproduction and were named "Terminator" seeds by the NGO, RAFI. See Timo Goeschl & Tim Swanson, *The Impact of Genetic Use Restriction Technologies on Developing Countries: A Forecast*, at 181, 182 *in* ECONOMIC & SOCIAL ISSUES, *supra* Chapter Four, note 3 ("[T]he concerns about the potential implications of GURTS are manifold. Some observers worry about the environmental effects of geneflow from crops thus sterilized to other plants, causing potential sterilization of the seeds beyond the confines of the individual field. The redistribution of economic rents between farmers, seed companies and consumers is another area of possibly undesirable consequences. Others are concerned about the impacts of these technologies in the livelihoods of subsistence farmers that predominantly rely on saved seed for replanting their fields.").

119. There are two types of GURTs. V-GURT produces sterile seeds, thus a farmer who purchases seed containing V-GURT technology cannot not save the seed for future use. This technology is restricted to the plant variety level—hence the term V-GURT. T-GURT modifies a crop in such a way that the genetic enhancement engineered into the crop does not function until the crop plant is treated with a chemical that is sold by the biotechnology company. As such, the farmer may save seeds, however they may not take advantage of the advance trait without purchasing the activator compound. It is restricted to the trait level—hence T-GURT. *See* Wikipedia, "Terminator Technology," *available* at http://en.wikipedia.org/wiki/Terminator_Technology (last visited August 21, 2006).

120. Rick Weiss, *Biotech Rice Saga Yields Bushel of Questions for Feds: USDA Approval Shortcut Emerges as Issue*, WASHINGTON POST, A03 (Tuesday, November 6, 2006), ("Federal officials are sill investigating how the experimental 'LLRICE601' escaped from Bayer's test plots after the company dropped the project in 2001 … 'LLRICE601' contains a gene that protects rice from Bayer's Liberty weed killer, allowing farmers to use the chemical without harming their crops. The prospect of widespread cultivation worries many experts, who say the key gene is sure to move via pollen into red rice, a weedy relative of white rice and the No. 1 plant pest for rice farmers in the South. Thus endowed, red rice would become immune to the herbicide, increasing its economic havoc.").

121. Robin Feldman, *Patent Misuse, supra* Chapter Four, note 165.

122. *See id.*

e. Institutional Challenges in Applying an Open Source Model to PGRs

As with GNU/Linux, it would be crucial to create an institutional structure that co-ordinated the activities inherent in an open source PGR model. These activities would include, at minimum: bringing farmers, plant breeders, and public and private researchers together; informing the parties about the uses and abuses of intellectual property law; and educating them on ways that a GPL-like license could be used to facilitate open access to PGRs.[123] Might MASIPAG or similar organizations come to fill the void of replicable models for serving developing countries?

Yet another option is the creation of international- or national-level crop-specific agencies. With the logistical support of the various regional agricultural research centers, national seed banks, and financial backing from the FAO and private foundations, such agencies would either acquire rights to critical bio-patents pertaining to PGRs or negotiate with the patent holders to grant licenses to the public such as the "golden rice" license and dedicate them to the "public domain."[124] These entities would also collect and disseminate information, support innovations, and furnish technical aid to researchers, plant breeders, and farmers.[125]

Professors Anupam Chander and Madhavi Sunder caution that while, in theory, an open access system lacking the restriction of intellectual property rights *should* result in a situation where all parties reap the benefits of a commons-based approach to informational resources. Usually ignored, however, are the distributional consequences of such an approach.[126] Yet differing circumstances such as relative knowledge, wealth, power, access, and ability may render some better able than others to exploit such an open source PGR model. The risk is that the virtues of such a system and its purported benefits to farmers in developing nations may be lost if measures are not taken to ensure that these farmers will be explicitly included in implementing an open source PGR model.[127]

---

123. *Ibid.*
124. *Ibid.*
125. *Ibid.*
126. Chander & Sunder, *Romance of the Public Domain, supra* Chapter Two, note 5.
127. *See id.; see also* Madhavi Sunder, *The Invention of Traditional Knowledge*, DUKE J. L. & CONTEMP. PROB. (forthcoming 2007).

Conclusion

If I am critical of those who seem eager to defend a world of discrete, perfectly bounded cultures that never existed, it is because I am so impressed by the hope and pragmatism of indigenous elders, museum curators, archivists and cultural-resource managers who are negotiating their way to more balanced relationships. They, far more than the activists and academic theorists who set the terms of the debate about cultural ownership, understand that progress will be built on small victories, innovative local solutions, and frequent compromise. They recognize, too, that a world ruled solely by proprietary passions is not a world in which most of us want to live.[1]

One lesson taught by the twentieth [century] and surely applicable to the twenty-first is that there is reason to be wary of totalizing solutions to complex social problems.... Robert Conquest has noted that our times are littered with the ruins of failed utopias that caused untold misery. The alternative is an approach that [he] calls imaginative realism, a willingness to accept a degree of imperfection in the interest of balance 'between the individual and the community, between the desirable and the possible, between our knowledge and our imagination.'[2]

The point of this book is that we need to find balanced solutions to the questions of intellectual property rights in PGRs. From the beginnings of human cultivation up until the last century, the genotype of crops was not seen as susceptible to characterization as property. Crop genetic diversity was developed in a decentralized fashion and plant varieties were closely adapted to local conditions of soil, water, and sunlight. Traditionally, farmers around the world engaged in mass selective breeding, saving the seeds of crops with interesting or desirable characteristics to replant the next season, thereby creating a remarkable cornucopia of genetic diversity within particular crop varieties and within their own fields. When individuals or groups of farmers migrated, they brought their seeds with them, and engaged in selective breeding to try and adapt crops to their new fields.

In the 16th century, the "Columbian Exchange" (courtesy of European colonialism) began to speed up the processes of genetic diffusion around the globe. Competition between colonial powers arose as they vied for plants that would enable their plantation economies. While the genomes of such plants were not claimed as 'property,' the ability to access plant genetic diversity was indeed an important part of national security. Many in the nascent United States were aware of the importance of exotic plants in establishing a robust agricultural economy and the U.S. government became involved in collecting exotic germplasm as well.

---

1. Michael F. Brown, Who Owns Native Culture? 252 (2003).
2. Brown, *supra* note 1, at 8 (citing Robert Conquest, Reflections on a Ravaged Century 18 (2000)).

Anxiety over food supply haunted the 19th century, from the Irish Potato famine to the dark reactionary musings of Thomas Malthus arguing against government subsidy of food to the poor. Although Augustinian monk Gregor Mendel did not contemplate insecurity about food supply and Malthusian nightmares when he began unlocking the secrets of heredity in pea plants in the mid-19th century, his research and findings nonetheless had immense implications in the following century. Mendel published his findings far ahead of the scientific curve; not until the rediscovery of Mendel's work in the early 20th century did plant breeders begin to understand the implications of his findings, then as they began experimenting with hybrid corn.

In 1862, the U.S. Congress passed the Morrill Act, which provided for the creation of state land grant agricultural colleges (LGCs). Government became intimately entwined with the agricultural sector for the remainder of the century. LGCs marked a turn away from the tradition of farmer self-sufficiency: the colleges were able to engage in agricultural research and systemic plant breeding, the results of which would become available to farmers. During this period, members of Congress used their free-franking privilege (at the behest of the USDA) to send out mass mailings of seed samples to encourage farmers' "experimentation." By the turn of the century, the nascent and struggling private seed sector began complaining about unfair competition from public plant breeders who worked for the LGCs.

The development of heterosis, or hybridization, in the second decade of the 20th century marked another major turning point. While the techniques used to create hybrids originated in the public sector at LGCs (where the parent lines were disclosed and were available), by the end of the 1920s private companies such as Pioneer Hi-Bred had begun moving to the fore, keeping their parent lines as proprietary trade secrets. With the development of hybrid crops, private companies were able to profit in the seed industry as they never had before. With traditional seed, farmers were able to save and select seeds, even if they had initially purchased their seed—the means of reproducing the seed was sold along with the seeds. With hybrid crops, farmers who were attracted by higher-yielding crops would have to return season after season, because hybrid vigor did not carry over to subsequent generations of a crop.

As private capital moved into the agricultural sector, public agricultural research emphasis changed. The LGCs began directing their research towards basic (or "pure") research, leaving the development of applied research to private companies; the purpose of public research was seen as supporting private companies, rather than being in competition with them in delivering agricultural innovation directly to farmers.

One unforeseen consequence of this shift of emphasis on agricultural innovation became clear by the middle decades of the 20th century. Seeking ever higher-yielding crop varieties, private seed companies exemplified the attitude that 'one seed could feed the world.' Industrial agricultural systems were developed that required extremely high-inputs of pesticides, herbicides, and fertilizer. By application of expensive inputs, local conditions were made (as much as possible) to adapt themselves to standard crop varieties sold by seed companies—a development which turned out to be environmentally disastrous. Traditional plant breeding and farming techniques were a mirror image, as traditional techniques were focused on adapting the variety to a particular locale's soil, water, and climate. Another cost of this shift toward industrial techniques and plant monoculture was the global loss of plant genetic diversity.

Law has been the handmaiden to these pervasive changes occurring in the global agricultural system. In less than eight decades, we have seen the rise of intellectual property protection, first for a plant's phenotype in the Plant Patent Act (PPA) of 1930 and the European UPOV of the 1960s and the Plant Variety Protection Act (PVPA) of 1970.

Problems with the PPA foreshadowed battles over intellectual property rights at the end of the century. The PPA conferred intellectual property protection to "new" and "distinct" asexually reproduced plants and represented a departure from the requirement that a patentee must describe a patented invention well enough so as to enable an ordinary person skilled in the art to practice the patented invention. Another departure in the PPA was that protection was conferred on a "new" and "distinct" plant that was "invented or *discovered*." The general patent statute excluded items that were discovered (as opposed to invented). Additionally, the PPA protected only the plant itself, not its fruit or flowers.

Forty years later, the U.S. adopted the PVPA of 1970, conferring intellectual property rights in sexually reproduced plant varieties that were "new, distinct, uniform, and stable." The PVPA contained problems similar to those of the PPA, such as a relaxation of the written description requirement. The PVPA also was conceived as similar to the European UPOV, an explicit plant breeders' rights regime. The PVPA was strongly backed by the private seed industry in the U.S. and opposed by public sector plant breeders and farmers group that sought compromise. In the end, the PVPA included important concessions, such as farmer exemptions for seed-saving and seed resale. There was also a research exemption that allowed PVPA-protected varieties to be used as breeding varieties without royalties. One interpretation of the negotiations over the PVPA was that when the final version was enacted into law, Congress had spoken definitively on the subject of intellectual property rights in crop varieties.

Yet the Supreme Court's decisions over the past quarter-century demonstrate that this simply was not the case. The 1980 landmark case, *Diamond v. Chakrabarty*, radically expanded the category of patentable subject matter in U.S. law. *Chakrabarty* held that an oil-eating bacterium was patentable if there was sufficient innovative human agency involved in transforming it from something found in nature into something human-made. This case made it possible for the U.S. Patent and Trademark Office (PTO) to begin issuing utility patents in a genetically modified variety of maize that was upheld in the 1985 *Ex Parte Hibberd* decision. In 1995, the Supreme Court's decision in *Asgrow* substantially narrowed the negotiated farmer seed-saving and resale provisions of the PVPA. Then, in *J.E.M. Ag Supply*, the Court sought to review developments regarding intellectual property rights in plants and ultimately upheld a utility patent that had been granted in a traditionally bred plant variety. There, the Court majority found that there was no inconsistency in allowing *both* utility patent and PVPA protection available for plants meeting the requisite (but different) criteria of both legal regimes. While the PVPA granted protection for a plant's phenotype, under *Chakrabarty* and *J.E.M. Ag Supply*, patent protection could be gained for a plant's genotype, as well as for particular DNA sequences within a particular plant's genome if permitted under the patent statute's criteria.

In a little under a century, then, intellectual property law has pervasively colonized the area of agricultural crops, first with hybridization and trade secrets law, and by the last quarter of the 20th century through transgenic and other genetic manipulation of a plant variety's genotype. By the mid-20th century, the convergence of technology and law had fueled the rise and spread of industrial agriculture, which had in turn created a global crisis: the global erosion of plant genetic diversity, on which global agriculture rests, being taken for granted by seed companies and policymakers alike.

By the 1980s, on the international level, two clusters of legal regimes began emerging. The first was the "intellectual property" regime complex that involved the above-mentioned developments in U.S. patent law, the European UPOV, and multi-lateral talks that eventually crystallized in the Trade Related Aspect of Intellectual Property Agreement (TRIPS) and formation of the WTO in 1995. One of the important parts of TRIPS is that all signatory nations must provide some type of intellectual property protection for plant breeders' rights, whether through utility patent protection, plant variety protection certificates or some other *sui generis* type of legal protection.

The second was the "equity/conservation" regime that sought to address issues of conserving global biodiversity and ameliorating wealth disparities between the developing nations of the global South and the industrialized nation of the global North. The "equity/conservation" regime includes the Consultative Group for International Agricultural Research (CGIAR), an organization created under the auspices of the U.N.'s Food and Agriculture Organization (FAO) and funded by the Rockefeller Foundation. The CGIAR established an international network of "seed banks" in the 1970s to collect, store and facilitate access to disappearing PGRs. Spurring controversy in the 1980s was the FAO's promulgation of the International Undertaking for Plant Genetic Resources of 1983 (IUPGR) that provocatively declared that all PGRs were the "common heritage of mankind" and therefore were freely accessible — including the PVPA and UPOV protected elite cultivars of the U.S. and Europe. Needless to say, the economic powerbroker nations of Europe and North America wanted nothing to do with the FAO's International Undertaking.

The 1992 Rio Conference on Biological Diversity (CBD) represented a turning point in negotiations about the legal characterization of plant genetic resources. Whereas the IUPGR was unsuccessful in characterizing such resources as "common heritage," the CBD was successful in putting forth the idea that plant genetic resources were "sovereign national property" and could not be taken out a country without "informed consent." Then came the multilateral International Treaty for PGRs for Food and Agriculture (ITPGR), which was under negotiation throughout the 1990s. The ITPGR incorporated the CBD's treatment of PGRs as "sovereign property." Ultimately the ITPGR was promulgated in 2001 and went into effect in 2004.

The ITPGR creates a Multilateral System (MLS) that addresses plant genetic resources in three importantly controversial ways. First, such resources are characterized as "sovereign property" and are under the control of the respective signatory nations (and are therefore subject to widely differing treatment). Second, the ITPGR adverts to the idea of "farmers' rights" as a way of recognizing the contributions of anonymous generations of farmers that have contributed to the genetic diversity that underwrites modern agriculture. However, the ITPGR provides no realistic method of valuing such contributions or for compensating "farmers." Third, the ITPGR contains Annex I, that lists 64 crops and forages (from the CGIAR seed banks) for which intellectual property rights are *not* to be sought "in the form received." The bar to seeking intellectual property rights is contained in the Material Transfer Agreement (MTA); anyone receiving material from the CGIAR system must agree to the MTA. An important point about the ITPGR is that presumably, it is permissible to seek intellectual property rights in any crop *not* listed on Annex I.

Thus by the early 21st century, under the CBD and the ITPGR, PGRs are treated as "sovereign property" and under TRIPS, nations are obligated to protect those PGRs as intellectual property. It is becoming clear that because of the convergence of these

Appendix

I. International Agreements

Agreement on Trade-Related Aspects of Intellectual Property Rights (TRIPS)

Article 27: Patentable Subject Matter

1.... Patents shall be available for any inventions[1], whether products or processes, in all fields of technology, provided that they are new, involve an inventive step and are capable of industrial application.... Patents shall be available and patent rights enjoyable without discrimination as to the place of invention, the field of technology and whether products are imported or locally produced.[2]

2. Members may exclude from patentability inventions, the prevention within their territory of the commercial exploitation of which is necessary to protect *ordre public* or morality, including to protect human, animal or plant life or health or to avoid serious prejudice to the environment, provided that such exclusion is not made merely because the exploitation is prohibited by their law.

3. Members may also exclude from patentability:

  (a) diagnostic, therapeutic and surgical methods for the treatment of humans or animals;

  (b) plants and animals other than micro-organisms, and essentially biological processes for the production of plants or animals other than non-biological and microbiological processes. However, Members shall provide for the protection of plant varieties either by patents or by an effective *sui generis* system or by any combination thereof. The provisions of this subparagraph shall be reviewed four years after the date of entry into force of the WTO Agreement.

Convention on Biological Diversity
June 5, 1992

Reaffirming that States have sovereign rights over their own biological resources,

---

1. Subject to the provisions of paragraphs 2 and 3
2. Subject to paragraph 4 of Article 65, paragraph 8 of Article 70 and paragraph 3 of this Article

Reaffirming also that States are responsible for conserving their biological diversity and for using their biological resources in a sustainable manner,

Noting further that the fundamental requirement for the conservation of biological diversity is the *in-situ* conservation of ecosystems and natural habitats and the maintenance and recovery of viable populations of species in their natural surroundings,

Article 1. Objectives

The objectives of this Convention, to be pursued in accordance with its relevant provisions, are the conservation of biological diversity, the sustainable use of its components and the fair and equitable sharing of the benefits arising out of the utilization of genetic resources, including by appropriate access to genetic resources and by appropriate transfer of relevant technologies, taking into account all rights over those resources and to technologies, and by appropriate funding.

. . .

Article 3. Principle

States have, in accordance with the Charter of the United Nations and the principles of international law, the sovereign right to exploit their own resources pursuant to their own environmental policies, and the responsibility to ensure that activities within their jurisdiction or control do not cause damage to the environment of other States or of areas beyond the limits of national jurisdiction.

. . .

Article 6. General Measures for Conservation and Sustainable Use

Each Contracting Party shall, in accordance with its particular conditions and capabilities:

(a) Develop national strategies, plans or programmes for the conservation and sustainable use of biological diversity or adapt for this purpose existing strategies, plans or programmes which shall reflect, *inter alia*, the measures set out in this Convention relevant to the Contracting Party concerned; and

(b) Integrate, as far as possible and as appropriate, the conservation and sustainable use of biological diversity into relevant sectoral or cross-sectoral plans, programmes and policies.

. . .

Article 15. Access to Genetic Resources

1. Recognizing the sovereign rights of States over their natural resources, the authority to determine access to genetic resources rests with the national governments and is subject to national legislation.

2. Each Contracting Party shall endeavour to create conditions to facilitate access to genetic resources for environmentally sound uses by other Contracting Parties and not to impose restrictions that run counter to the objectives of this Convention.

3. For the purpose of this Convention, the genetic resources being provided by a Contracting Party, as referred to in this Article and Articles 16 and 19, are only those that are provided by Contracting Parties that are countries of origin of such resources or by the Parties that have acquired the genetic resources in accordance with this Convention.

4. Access, where granted, shall be on mutually agreed terms and subject to the provisions of this Article.

5. Access to genetic resources shall be subject to prior informed consent of the Contracting Party providing such resources, unless otherwise determined by that Party.

6. Each Contracting Party shall endeavour to develop and carry out scientific research based on genetic resources provided by other Contracting Parties with the full participation of, and where possible in, such Contracting Parties.

7. Each Contracting Party shall take legislative, administrative or policy measures, as appropriate, and in accordance with Articles 16 and 19 and, where necessary, through the financial mechanism established by Articles 20 and 21 with the aim of sharing in a fair and equitable way the results of research and development and the benefits arising from the commercial and other utilization of genetic resources with the Contracting Party providing such resources. Such sharing shall be upon mutually agreed terms.

Article 16. Access to and Transfer of Technology

1. Each Contracting Party, recognizing that technology includes biotechnology, and that both access to and transfer of technology among Contracting Parties are essential elements for the attainment of the objectives of this Convention, undertakes subject to the provisions of this Article to provide and/or facilitate access for and transfer to other Contracting Parties of technologies that are relevant to the conservation and sustainable use of biological diversity or make use of genetic resources and do not cause significant damage to the environment.

2. Access to and transfer of technology referred to in paragraph 1 above to developing countries shall be provided and/or facilitated under fair and most favourable terms, including on concessional and preferential terms where mutually agreed, and, where necessary, in accordance with the financial mechanism established by Articles 20 and 21. In the case of technology subject to patents and other intellectual property rights, such access and transfer shall be provided on terms which recognize and are consistent with the adequate and effective protection of intellectual property rights. The application of this paragraph shall be consistent with paragraphs 3, 4 and 5 below.

3. Each Contracting Party shall take legislative, administrative or policy measures, as appropriate, with the aim that Contracting Parties, in particular those that are developing countries, which provide genetic resources are provided access to and transfer of technology which makes use of those resources, on mutually agreed terms, including technology protected by patents and other intellectual property rights, where necessary, through the provisions of Articles 20 and 21 and in accordance with international law and consistent with paragraphs 4 and 5 below.

4. Each Contracting Party shall take legislative, administrative or policy measures, as appropriate, with the aim that the private sector facilitates access to, joint development and transfer of technology referred to in paragraph 1 above for the benefit of both governmental institutions and the private sector of developing countries and in this regard shall abide by the obligations included in paragraphs 1, 2 and 3 above.

5. The Contracting Parties, recognizing that patents and other intellectual property rights may have an influence on the implementation of this Convention, shall

cooperate in this regard subject to national legislation and international law in order to ensure that such rights are supportive of and do not run counter to its objectives.

Article 17. Exchange of Information

1. The Contracting Parties shall facilitate the exchange of information, from all publicly available sources, relevant to the conservation and sustainable use of biological diversity, taking into account the special needs of developing countries.

2. Such exchange of information shall include exchange of results of technical, scientific and socio-economic research, as well as information on training and surveying programmes, specialized knowledge, indigenous and traditional knowledge as such and in combination with the technologies referred to in Article 16, paragraph 1. It shall also, where feasible, include repatriation of information.

...

Article 19. Handling of Biotechnology and Distribution of its Benefits

1. Each Contracting Party shall take legislative, administrative or policy measures, as appropriate, to provide for the effective participation in biotechnological research activities by those Contracting Parties, especially developing countries, which provide the genetic resources for such research, and where feasible in such Contracting Parties.

2. Each Contracting Party shall take all practicable measures to promote and advance priority access on a fair and equitable basis by Contracting Parties, especially developing countries, to the results and benefits arising from biotechnologies based upon genetic resources provided by those Contracting Parties. Such access shall be on mutually agreed terms.

Article 20. Financial Resources

1. Each Contracting Party undertakes to provide, in accordance with its capabilities, financial support and incentives in respect of those national activities which are intended to achieve the objectives of this Convention, in accordance with its national plans, priorities and programmes.

Article 21. Financial Mechanism

1. There shall be a mechanism for the provision of financial resources to developing country Parties for purposes of this Convention on a grant or concessional basis the essential elements of which are described in this Article. The mechanism shall function under the authority and guidance of, and be accountable to, the Conference of the Parties for purposes of this Convention. The operations of the mechanism shall be carried out by such institutional structure as may be decided upon by the Conference of the Parties at its first meeting. For purposes of this Convention, the Conference of the Parties shall determine the policy, strategy, programme priorities and eligibility criteria relating to the access to and utilization of such resources. The contributions shall be such as to take into account the need for predictability, adequacy and timely flow of funds referred to in Article 20 in accordance with the amount of resources needed to be decided periodically by the Conference of the Parties and the importance of burden-sharing among the contributing Parties included in the list referred to in Article 20, paragraph 2. Volun-

tary contributions may also be made by the developed country Parties and by other countries and sources. The mechanism shall operate within a democratic and transparent system of governance.

...

Article 27. Settlement of Disputes

1. In the event of a dispute between Contracting Parties concerning the interpretation or application of this Convention, the parties concerned shall seek solution by negotiation.

2. If the parties concerned cannot reach agreement by negotiation, they may jointly seek the good offices of, or request mediation by, a third party.

3. When ratifying, accepting, approving or acceding to this Convention, or at any time thereafter, a State or regional economic integration organization may declare in writing to the Depositary that for a dispute not resolved in accordance with paragraph 1 or paragraph 2 above, it accepts one or both of the following means of dispute settlement as compulsory:

   a. Arbitration in accordance with the procedure laid down in Part 1 of Annex II;

   b. Submission of the dispute to the International Court of Justice.

4. If the parties to the dispute have not, in accordance with paragraph 3 above, accepted the same or any procedure, the dispute shall be submitted to conciliation in accordance with Part 2 of Annex II unless the parties otherwise agree.

5. The provisions of this Article shall apply with respect to any protocol except as otherwise provided in the protocol concerned.

International Treaty on Plant Genetic Resources for Food and Agriculture
2001

PREAMBLE

...

The Contracting Parties,

Acknowledg[e] that plant genetic resources for food and agriculture are the raw materi-alindispensable for crop genetic improvement, whether by means of farmers' selection, classical plant breeding or modern biotechnologies, and are essential in adapting to unpredictable environmental changes and future human needs;

Affirming that the past, present and future contributions of farmers in all regions of the world, particularly those in centres of origin and diversity, in conserving, improving and making

available these resources, is the basis of Farmers' Rights;

Affirming also that the rights recognized in this Treaty to save, use, exchange and sell farm-saved seed and other propagating material, and to participate in decision-making regarding, and in the fair and equitable sharing of the benefits arising from, the use of plant genetic resources for food and agriculture, are fundamental to the realization of Farmers' Rights, as well as the promotion of

Farmers' Rights at national and international levels;

...

Recognizing that, in the exercise of their sovereign rights over their plant genetic resources for food and agriculture, states may mutually benefit from the creation of an effective multilateral system for facilitated access to a negotiated selection of these resources and for the fair and equitable sharing of the benefits arising from their use; and

Desiring to conclude an international agreement within the framework of the Food and Agriculture Organization of the United Nations, hereinafter referred to as FAO, under Article

XIV of the FAO Constitution;

Have agreed as follows:

PART I: INTRODUCTION

Article 1 — Objectives

1.1 The objectives of this Treaty are the conservation and sustainable use of plant genetic resources for food and agriculture and the fair and equitable sharing of the benefits arising out of their use, in harmony with the Convention on Biological Diversity, for sustainable agriculture and food security.

1.2 These objectives will be attained by closely linking this Treaty to the Food and Agriculture Organization of the United Nations and to the Convention on Biological Diversity.

Article 2 — Use of terms

For the purpose of this Treaty, the following terms shall have the meanings hereunder assigned to them. These definitions are not intended to cover trade in commodities:

"*In situ* conservation" means the conservation of ecosystems and natural habitats and the maintenance and recovery of viable populations of species in their natural surroundings and, in the case of domesticated or cultivated plant species, in the surroundings where they have developed their distinctive properties.

"*Ex situ* conservation" means the conservation of plant genetic resources for food and agriculture outside their natural habitat.

"Plant genetic resources for food and agriculture" means any genetic material of plant origin of actual or potential value for food and agriculture.

"Genetic material" means any material of plant origin, including reproductive and vegetative propagating material, containing functional units of heredity.

"Variety" means a plant grouping, within a single botanical taxon of the lowest known rank, defined by the reproducible expression of its distinguishing and other genetic characteristics.

"*Ex situ* collection" means a collection of plant genetic resources for food and agriculture maintained outside their natural habitat.

"Centre of origin" means a geographical area where a plant species, either domesticated or wild, first developed its distinctive properties.

"Centre of crop diversity" means a geographic area containing a high level of genetic diversity for crop species in *in situ* conditions.

PART II: GENERAL PROVISIONS

…

Article 5—Conservation, Exploration, Collection, Characterization, Evaluation and Documentation of Plant Genetic Resources for Food and Agriculture

5.1 Each Contracting Party shall, subject to national legislation, and in cooperation with

other Contracting Parties where appropriate, promote an integrated approach to the exploration, conservation and sustainable use of plant genetic resources for food and agriculture and shall in particular, as appropriate:

…

(c) Promote or support, as appropriate, farmers and local communities' efforts to manage and conserve on-farm their plant genetic resources for food and agriculture;

(d) Promote *in situ* conservation of wild crop relatives and wild plants for food production, including in protected areas, by supporting, *inter alia*, the efforts of indigenous and local communities;

…

Article 6—Sustainable Use of Plant Genetic Resources

6.1 The Contracting Parties shall develop and maintain appropriate policy and legal measures that promote the sustainable use of plant genetic resources for food and agriculture.

6.2 The sustainable use of plant genetic resources for food and agriculture may include such measures as:

(a) pursuing fair agricultural policies that promote, as appropriate, the development and maintenance of diverse farming systems that enhance the sustainable use of agricultural biological diversity and other natural resources;

(b) strengthening research which enhances and conserves biological diversity by maximizing intra- and inter-specific variation for the benefit of farmers, especially those who generate and use their own varieties and apply ecological principles in maintaining soil fertility and in combating diseases, weeds and pests;

(c) promoting, as appropriate, plant breeding efforts which, with the participation of farmers, particularly in developing countries, strengthen the capacity to develop varieties particularly adapted to social, economic and ecological conditions, including in marginal areas;

PART III: FARMERS' RIGHTS

Article 9—Farmers' Rights

9.1 The Contracting Parties recognize the enormous contribution that the local and indigenous communities and farmers of all regions of the world, particularly those in the centers of origin and crop diversity, have made and will continue to make for the conservation and development of plant genetic resources which constitute the basis of food and agriculture production throughout the world.

9.2 The Contracting Parties agree that the responsibility for realizing Farmers' Rights, as they relate to plant genetic resources for food and agriculture, rests with national governments. In accordance with their needs and priorities, each Contracting Party should, as appropriate, and subject to its national legislation, take measures to protect and promote Farmers' Rights, including:

(a) protection of traditional knowledge relevant to plant genetic resources for food and agriculture;

(b) the right to equitably participate in sharing benefits arising from the utilization of plant genetic resources for food and agriculture; and

(c) the right to participate in making decisions, at the national level, on matters related to the conservation and sustainable use of plant genetic resources for food and agriculture.

9.3 Nothing in this Article shall be interpreted to limit any rights that farmers have to save, use, exchange and sell farm-saved seed/propagating material, subject to national law and as appropriate.

…

PART IV: THE MULTILATERAL SYSTEM OF ACCESS AND BENEFIT-SHARING

Article 10—Multilateral System of Access and Benefit-sharing

10.1 In their relationships with other States, the Contracting Parties recognize the sovereign rights of States over their own plant genetic resources for food and agriculture, including that the authority to determine access to those resources rests with national governments and is subject to national legislation.

10.2 In the exercise of their sovereign rights, the Contracting Parties agree to establish a multilateral system, which is efficient, effective, and transparent, both to facilitate access to plant genetic resources for food and agriculture, and to share, in a fair and equitable way, the benefits arising from the utilization of these resources, on a complementary and mutually reinforcing basis.

List of Crops Covered under the Multilateral System

Crop	Genus	Observations
Breadfruit	*Artocarpus*	Breadfruit only.
Asparagus	*Asparagus*	
Oat	*Avena*	
Beet	*Beta*	
Brassica complex	*Brassica* et al.	Genera included are: *Brassica, Armoracia, Barbarea, Camelina, Crambe, Diplotaxis, Eruca, Isatis, Lepidium, Raphanobrassica, Raphanus, Rorippa*, and *Sinapis*. This comprises oilseed and vegetable

		crops such as cabbage, rapeseed, mustard, cress, rocket, radish, and turnip. The species *Lepidium meyenii* (maca) is excluded.
Pigeon Pea	*Cajanus*	
Chickpea	*Cicer*	
Citrus	*Citrus*	Genera *Poncirus* and *Fortunella* are included as root stock.
Coconut	*Cocos*	
Major aroids	*Colocasia, Xanthosoma*	Major aroids include taro, cocoyam, dasheen and tannia.
Carrot	*Daucus*	
Yams	*Dioscorea*	
Finger Millet	*Eleusine*	
Strawberry	*Fragaria*	
Sunflower	*Helianthus*	
Barley	*Hordeum*	
Sweet Potato	*Ipomoea*	
Grass pea	*Lathyrus*	
Lentil	*Lens*	
Apple	*Malus*	
Cassava	*Manihot*	*Manihot esculenta* only.
Banana / Plantain	*Musa*	Except *Musa textilis*.
Rice	*Oryza*	
Pearl Millet	*Pennisetum*	
Beans	*Phaseolus*	Except *Phaseolus polyanthus*.
Pea	*Pisum*	
Rye	*Secale*	
Potato	*Solanum*	Section tuberosa included, except *Solanum phureja*.
Eggplant	*Solanum*	Section melongena included.
Sorghum	*Sorghum*	
Triticale	*Triticosecale*	
Wheat	*Triticum* et al.	Including *Agropyron, Elymus,* and *Secale*.
Faba Bean / Vetch	*Vicia*	
Cowpea et al.	*Vigna*	
Maize	*Zea*	Excluding *Zea perennis, Zea diploperennis*, and *Zea luxurians*.

Bonn Guidelines on Access to Genetic Resources and Fair and Equitable Sharing of the Benefits Arising out of their Utilization

I. GENERAL PROVISIONS

A. Key features

1. These Guidelines may serve as inputs when developing and drafting legislative, administrative or policy measures on access and benefit-sharing with particular reference to provisions under Articles 8(j), 10 (c), 15, 16 and 19; and contracts and other arrangements under mutually agreed terms for access and benefit-sharing.

2. Nothing in these Guidelines shall be construed as changing the rights and obligations of Parties under the Convention on Biological Diversity.

...

C. Scope

...

9. All genetic resources and associated traditional knowledge, innovations and practices covered by the Convention on Biological Diversity and benefits arising from the commercial and other utilization of such resources should be covered by the guidelines, with the exclusion of human genetic resources.

...

E. Objectives

...

11. The objectives of the Guidelines are the following:

    a. To contribute to the conservation and sustainable use of biological diversity;

    b. To provide Parties and stakeholders with a transparent framework to facilitate access to genetic resources and ensure fair and equitable sharing of benefits;

    c. To provide guidance to Parties in the development of access and benefit-sharing regimes;

    ...

    k. To contribute to poverty alleviation and be supportive to the realization of human food security, health and cultural integrity, especially in developing countries, in particular least developed countries and small island developing States among them;

...

II. ROLES AND RESPONSIBILITIES IN ACCESS AND BENEFIT-SHARING PURSUANT TO ARTICLE 15 OF THE CONVENTION ON BIOLOGICAL DIVERSITY

A. National focal point

13. Each Party should designate one national focal point for access and benefit-sharing and make such information available through the clearing-house mechanism. The national focal point should inform applicants for access to genetic resources on procedures for acquiring prior informed consent and mutually agreed terms,

including benefit-sharing, and on competent national authorities, relevant in-digenous and local communities and relevant stakeholders, through the clearing-house mechanism.

B. Competent national authority(ies)

14. Competent national authorities, where they are established, may, in accordance with applicable national legislative, administrative or policy measures, be respon-sible for granting access and be responsible for advising on:

    a. The negotiating process;

    b. Requirements for obtaining prior informed consent and entering into mutu-ally agreed terms;

    c. Monitoring and evaluation of access and benefit-sharing agreements;

    d. Implementation/enforcement of access and benefit-sharing agreements;

    e. Processing of applications and approval of agreements;

    f. The conservation and sustainable use of the genetic resources accessed;

    g. Mechanisms for the effective participation of different stakeholders, as appro-priate for the different steps in the process of access and benefit-sharing, in particular, indigenous and local communities;

    h. Mechanisms for the effective participation of indigenous and local communi-ties while promoting the objective of having decisions and processes available in a language understandable to relevant indigenous and local communities.

15. The competent national authority(ies) that have the legal power to grant prior in-formed consent may delegate this power to other entities, as appropriate.

C. Responsibilities

16. Recognizing that Parties and stakeholders may be both users and providers, the following balanced list of roles and responsibilities provides key elements to be acted upon:

    a. Contracting Parties which are countries of origin of genetic resources, or other Parties which have acquired the genetic resources in accordance with the Convention, should:

...

        vi. Establish mechanisms to ensure that their decisions are made available to relevant indigenous and local communities and relevant stakeholders, particularly indigenous and local communities;

        vii. Support measures, as appropriate, to enhance indigenous and local com-munities' capacity to represent their interests fully at negotiations;

    b. In the implementation of mutually agreed terms, users should:

        i.   Seek informed consent prior to access to genetic resources, in conformity with Article 15, paragraph 5, of the Convention;

        ii. Respect customs, traditions, values and customary practices of indige-nous and local communities,

        iii. Respond to requests for information from indigenous and local commu-nities;

iv. Only use genetic resources for purposes consistent with the terms and conditions under which they were acquired;

v. Ensure that uses of genetic resources for purposes other than those for which they were acquired, only take place after new prior informed consent and mutually agreed terms are given;

vi. Maintain all relevant data regarding the genetic resources, especially documentary evidence of the prior informed consent and information concerning the origin and the use of genetic resources and the benefits arising from such use;

vii. As much as possible endeavour to carry out their use of the genetic resources in, and with the participation of, the providing country;

viii. When supplying genetic resources to third parties, honour any terms and conditions regarding the acquired material. They should provide this third party with relevant data on their acquisition, including prior informed consent and conditions of use and record and maintain data on their supply to third parties. Special terms and conditions should be established under mutually agreed terms to facilitate taxonomic research for non-commercial purposes;

ix. Ensure the fair and equitable sharing of benefits, including technology transfer to providing countries, pursuant to Article 16 of the Convention arising from the commercialization or other use of genetic resources, in conformity with the mutually agreed terms they established with the indigenous and local communities or stakeholders involved;

c. Providers should:

i. Only supply genetic resources and/or traditional knowledge when they are entitled to do so;

ii. Strive to avoid imposition of arbitrary restrictions on access to genetic resources.

d. Contracting Parties with users of genetic resources under their jurisdiction should take appropriate legal, administrative, or policy measures, as appropriate, to support compliance with prior informed consent of the Contracting Party providing such resources and mutually agreed terms on which access was granted. These countries could consider, *inter alia*, the following measures:

i. Mechanisms to provide information to potential users on their obligations regarding access to genetic resources;

ii. Measures to encourage the disclosure of the country of origin of the genetic resources and of the origin of traditional knowledge, innovations and practices of indigenous and local communities in applications for intellectual property rights;

iii. Measures aimed at preventing the use of genetic resources obtained without the prior informed consent of the Contracting Party providing such resources;

iv. Cooperation between Contracting Parties to address alleged infringements of access and benefit-sharing agreements;

v. Voluntary certification schemes for institutions abiding by rules on access and benefit-sharing;

vi. Measures discouraging unfair trade practices;

vii. Other measures that encourage users to comply with provisions under subparagraph 16(b) above.

...

IV.STEPS IN THE ACCESS AND BENEFIT-SHARING PROCESS

A. Overall strategy

22. Access and benefit-sharing systems should be based on an overall access and benefit-sharing strategy at the country or regional level. This access and benefit-sharing strategy should aim at the conservation and sustainable use of biological diversity, and may be part of a national biodiversity strategy and action plan and promote the equitable sharing of benefits.

B. Identification of steps

23. The steps involved in the process of obtaining access to genetic resources and sharing of benefits may include activities prior to access, research and development conducted on the genetic resources, as well as their commercialization and other uses, including benefit-sharing.

C. Prior informed consent

24. As provided for in Article 15 of the Convention on Biological Diversity, which recognizes the sovereign rights of States over their natural resources, each Contracting Party to the Convention shall endeavour to create conditions to facilitate access to genetic resources for environmentally sound uses by other Contracting Parties and fair and equitable sharing of benefits arising from such uses. In accordance with Article 15, paragraph 5, of the Convention on Biological Diversity, access to genetic resources shall be subject to prior informed consent of the contracting Party providing such resources, unless otherwise determined by that Party.

25. Against this background, the Guidelines are intended to assist Parties in the establishment of a system of prior informed consent, in accordance with Article 15, paragraph 5, of the Convention.

1. Basic principles of a prior informed consent system

26. The basic principles of a prior informed consent system should include:

    a. Legal certainty and clarity;

    b. Access to genetic resources should be facilitated at minimum cost;

    c. Restrictions on access to genetic resources should be transparent, based on legal grounds, and not run counter to the objectives of the Convention;

    d. Consent of the relevant competent national authority(ies) in the provider country. The consent of relevant stakeholders, such as indigenous and local communities, as appropriate to the circumstances and subject to domestic law, should also be obtained.

2. Elements of a prior informed consent system

27. Elements of a prior informed consent system may include:

a. Competent authority(ies) granting or providing for evidence of prior informed consent;

b. Timing and deadlines;

c. Specification of use;

d. Procedures for obtaining prior informed consent;

e. Mechanism for consultation of relevant stakeholders;

f. Process.

...

Specification of use

34. Prior informed consent should be based on the specific uses for which consent has been granted. While prior informed consent may be granted initially for specific use(s), any change of use including transfer to third parties may require a new application for prior informed consent. Permitted uses should be clearly stipulated and further prior informed consent for changes or unforeseen uses should be required. Specific needs of taxonomic and systematic research as specified by the Global Taxonomy Initiative should be taken into consideration.

35. Prior informed consent is linked to the requirement of mutually agreed terms.

D. Mutually agreed terms

41. In accordance with Article 15, paragraph 7, of the Convention on Biological Diversity, each Contracting Party shall "take legislative, administrative or policy measures, as appropriate (...) with the aim of sharing in a fair and equitable way the results of research and development and the benefits arising from the commercial and other utilization of genetic resources with the Contracting Party providing such resources. Such sharing shall be upon mutually agreed terms." Thus, guidelines should assist Parties and stakeholders in the development of mutually agreed terms to ensure the fair and equitable sharing of benefits.

1. Basic requirements for mutually agreed terms

43. The following elements could be considered as guiding parameters in contractual agreements. These elements could also be considered as basic requirements for mutually agreed terms:

a. Regulating the use of resources in order to take into account ethical concerns of the particular Parties and stakeholders, in particular indigenous and local communities concerned;

b. Making provision to ensure the continued customary use of genetic resources and related knowledge;

c. Provision for the use of intellectual property rights include joint research, obligation to implement rights on inventions obtained and to provide licences by common consent;

d. The possibility of joint ownership of intellectual property rights according to the degree of contribution.

Types of benefits

46. Examples of monetary and non-monetary benefits are provided in appendix II to these Guidelines.

Timing of benefits

47. Near-term, medium-term and long-term benefits should be considered, including up-front payments, milestone payments and royalties. The time-frame of benefit-sharing should be definitely stipulated. Furthermore, the balance among near-term, medium-term and long-term benefit should be considered on a case-by-case basis.

Distribution of benefits

48. Pursuant to mutually agreed terms established following prior informed consent, benefits should be shared fairly and equitably with all those who have been identified as having contributed to the resource management, scientific and/or commercial process. The latter may include governmental, non-governmental or academic institutions and indigenous and local communities. Benefits should be directed in such a way as to promote conservation and sustainable use of biological diversity.

Mechanisms for benefit-sharing

49. Mechanisms for benefit-sharing may vary depending upon the type of benefits, the specific conditions in the country and the stakeholders involved. The benefit-sharing mechanism should be flexible as it should be determined by the partners involved in benefit-sharing and will vary on a case-by-case basis.

50. Mechanisms for sharing benefits should include full cooperation in scientific research and technology development, as well as those that derive from commercial products including trust funds, joint ventures and licences with preferential terms.

...

II. National Legislation

United States

Plant Variety Protection Act
Ch. 57, 7 U.S.C. §2321 (2003)

§ 2401. Definitions and rules of construction

(a) Definitions. As used in this Act:

(1) Basic seed. The term "basic seed" means the seed planted to produce certified or commercial seed.

(2) Breeder. The term "breeder" means the person who directs the final breeding creating a variety or who discovers and develops a variety. If the actions are conducted by an agent on behalf of a principal, the principal, rather than the

agent, shall be considered the breeder. The term does not include a person who redevelops or rediscovers a variety the existence of which is publicly known or a matter of common knowledge.

(3) Essentially derived variety.

    A. In general. The term "essentially derived variety" means a variety that—

        i. is predominantly derived from another variety (referred to in this paragraph as the "initial variety") or from a variety that is predominantly derived from the initial variety, while retaining the expression of the essential characteristics that result from the genotype or combination of genotypes of the initial variety;

        ii. is clearly distinguishable from the initial variety; and

        iii. except for differences that result from the act of derivation, conforms to the initial variety in the expression of the essential characteristics that result from the genotype or combination of genotypes of the initial variety.

    B. Methods. An essentially derived variety may be obtained by the selection of a natural or induced mutant or of a somaclonal variant, the selection of a variant individual from plants of the initial variety, backcrossing, transformation by genetic engineering, or other method.

(4) Kind. The term "kind" means one or more related species or subspecies singly or collectively known by one common name, such as soybean, flax, or radish.

(5) Seed. The term "seed," with respect to a tuber propagated variety, means the tuber or the part of the tuber used for propagation.

(6) Sexually reproduced. The term "sexually reproduced" includes any production of a variety by seed, but does not include the production of a variety by tuber propagation.

(7) Tuber propagated. The term "tuber propagated" means propagated by a tuber or a part of a tuber.

(8) United States. The terms "United States" and "this country" mean the United States, the territories and possessions of the United States, and the Commonwealth of Puerto Rico.

(9) Variety. The term "variety" means a plant grouping within a single botanical taxon of the lowest known rank, that, without regard to whether the conditions for plant variety protection are fully met, can be defined by the expression of the characteristics resulting from a given genotype or combination of genotypes, distinguished from any other plant grouping by the expression of at least one characteristic and considered as a unit with regard to the suitability of the plant grouping for being propagated unchanged. A variety may be represented by seed, transplants, plants, tubers, tissue culture plantlets, and other matter.

§ 2402. Right to plant variety protection; plant varieties protectable

(a) In general. The breeder of any sexually reproduced or tuber propagated plant variety (other than fungi or bacteria) who has so reproduced the variety, or the successor in interest of the breeder, shall be entitled to plant variety protection for the variety, subject to the conditions and requirements of this Act, if the variety is—

1. new, in the sense that, on the date of filing of the application for plant variety protection, propagating or harvested material of the variety has not been sold or otherwise disposed of to other persons, by or with the consent of the breeder, or the successor in interest of the breeder, for purposes of exploitation of the variety—

   A. in the United States, more than 1 year prior to the date of filing; or

   B. in any area outside of the United States—

      i. more than 4 years prior to the date of filing, except that in the case of a tuber propagated plant variety the Secretary may waive the 4-year limitation for a period ending 1 year after the date of enactment of the Federal Agriculture Improvement and Reform Act of 1996 [enacted April 4, 1996]; or

      ii. in the case of a tree or vine, more than 6 years prior to the date of filing;

2. distinct, in the sense that the variety is clearly distinguishable from any other variety the existence of which is publicly known or a matter of common knowledge at the time of the filing of the application;

3. uniform, in the sense that any variations are describable, predictable, and commercially acceptable; and

4. stable, in the sense that the variety, when reproduced, will remain unchanged with regard to the essential and distinctive characteristics of the variety with a reasonable degree of reliability commensurate with that of varieties of the same category in which the same breeding method is employed.

§ 2404. Public interest in wide usage

The Secretary may declare a protected variety open to use on a basis of equitable remuneration to the owner, not less than a reasonable royalty, when the Secretary determines that such declaration is necessary in order to insure an adequate supply of fiber, food, or feed in this country and that the owner is unwilling or unable to supply the public needs for the variety at a price which may reasonably be deemed fair. Such declaration may be, with or without limitation, with or without designation of what the remuneration is to be; and shall be subject to review as under section 71 or 72 [7 USCS § 2461 or 2462] (any finding that the price is not reasonable being reviewable), and shall remain in effect not more than two years. In the event litigation is required to collect such remuneration, a higher rate may be allowed by the court.

§ 2422. Content of application

An application for a certificate recognizing plant variety rights shall contain:

1. The name of the variety except that a temporary designation will suffice until the certificate is to be issued. The variety shall be named in accordance with regulations issued by the Secretary.

2. A description of the variety setting forth its distinctiveness, uniformity, and stability and a description of the genealogy and breeding procedure, when known. The Secretary may require amplification, including the submission of adequate photographs or drawings or plant specimens, if the description is not adequate or as complete as is reasonably possible, and submission of records or proof of ownership or of allegations made in the application. An applicant may add to or correct the description at any time, before the certificate is issued, upon a showing

acceptable to the Secretary that the revised description is retroactively accurate. Courts shall protect others from any injustice which would result. The Secretary may accept records of the breeder and of any official seed certifying agency in this country as evidence of stability where applicable.

3. A statement of the basis of the claim of the applicant that the variety is new.

4. A declaration that a viable sample of basic seed (including any propagating material) necessary for propagation of the variety will be deposited and replenished periodically in a public repository in accordance with regulations to be established hereunder.

5. A statement of the basis of applicant's ownership.

§ 2481. Plant variety protection

(a) If it appears that a certificate of plant variety protection should be issued on an application, a written notice of allowance shall be given or mailed to the owner. The notice shall specify the sum, constituting the issue fee, which shall be paid within one month thereafter.

(b) Upon timely payment of this sum, and provided that deposit of seed has been made in accordance with section 52(3) [7 USCS § 2422(3)], the certificate of plant variety protection shall issue.

(c) If any payment required by this section is not timely made, but is submitted with an additional fee prescribed by the Secretary within nine months after the due date or within such further time as the Secretary may allow, it shall be accepted.

§ 2483. Contents and term of plant variety protection

(a) Certificate.

(1) Every certificate of plant variety protection shall certify that the breeder (or the successor in interest of the breeder)[,] has the right, during the term of the plant variety protection, to exclude others from selling the variety, or offering it for sale, or reproducing it, or importing it, or exporting it, or using it in producing (as distinguished from developing) a hybrid or different variety therefrom, to the extent provided by this Act.

(2) If the owner so elects, the certificate shall—

(A) specify that seed of the variety shall be sold in the United States only as a class of certified seed; and

(B) if so specified, conform to the number of generations designated by the owner.

(3) An owner may waive a right provided under this subsection, other than a right that is elected by the owner under paragraph (2)(A).

(4) The Secretary may at the discretion of the Secretary permit such election or waiver to be made after certificating and amend the certificate accordingly, without retroactive effect.

(b) Term.

(1) In general. Except as provided in paragraph (2), the term of plant variety protection shall expire 20 years from the date of issue of the certificate in the United States, except that—

(A) in the case of a tuber propagated plant variety subject to a waiver granted under section 42(a)(1)(B)(i) [7 USCS § 2402(a)(1)(B)(i)], the term of the plant variety protection shall expire 20 years after the date of the original grant of the plant breeder's rights to the variety outside the United States; and

(B) in the case of a tree or vine, the term of the plant variety protection shall expire 25 years from the date of issue of the certificate.

(2) Exceptions. If the certificate is not issued within three years from the effective filing date, the Secretary may shorten the term by the amount of delay in the prosecution of the application attributed by the Secretary to the applicant.

§ 2531. Ownership and assignment

(a) Subject to the provisions of this title [7 USCS §§ 2531 et seq.], plant variety protection shall have the attributes of personal property.

(b) Applications for certificates of plant variety protection, or any interest in a variety, shall be assignable by an instrument in writing. The owner may in like manner license or grant and convey an exclusive right to use of the variety in the whole or any specified part of the United States.

(c) A certificate of acknowledgment under the hand and official seal of a person authorized to administer oaths within the United States, or in a foreign country, of a diplomatic or consular officer of the United States or an officer authorized to administer oaths whose authority is proved by a certificate of a diplomatic or consular officer of the United States, shall be prima facie evidence of the execution of an assignment, grant, license, or conveyance of plant variety protection or application for plant variety protection.

(d) An assignment, grant, conveyance or license shall be void as against any subsequent purchaser or mortgagee for a valuable consideration, without notice, unless it, or an acknowledgment thereof by the person giving such encumbrance that there is such encumbrance, is filed for recording in the Plant Variety Protection Office within one month from its date or at least one month prior to the date of such subsequent purchase or mortgage.

§ 2541. Infringement of plant variety protection

(a) Acts constituting infringement. Except as otherwise provided in this title [7 USCS §§ 2521 et seq.], it shall be an infringement of the rights of the owner of a protected variety to perform without authority, any of the following acts in the United States, or in commerce which can be regulated by Congress or affecting such commerce, prior to expiration of the right to plant variety protection but after either the issue of the certificate or the distribution of a protected plant variety with the notice under section 127 [7 USCS § 2567]:

(1) sell or market the protected variety, or offer it or expose it for sale, deliver it, ship it, consign it, exchange it, or solicit an offer to buy it, or any other transfer of title or possession of it;

(2) import the variety into, or export it from, the United States;

(3) sexually multiply, or propagate by a tuber or a part of a tuber, the variety as a step in marketing (for growing purposes) the variety;

(4) use the variety in producing (as distinguished from developing) a hybrid or different variety therefrom;

(5) use seed which had been marked "Unauthorized Propagation Prohibited" or "Unauthorized Seed Multiplication Prohibited" or progeny thereof to propagate the variety;

(6) dispense the variety to another, in a form which can be propagated, without notice as to being a protected variety under which it was received;

(7) condition the variety for the purpose of propagation, except to the extent that the conditioning is related to the activities permitted under section 113 [7 USCS § 2543];

(8) stock the variety for any of the purposes referred to in paragraphs (1) through (7);

(9) perform any of the foregoing acts even in instances in which the variety is multiplied other than sexually, except in pursuance of a valid United States plant patent; or

(10) instigate or actively induce performance of any of the foregoing acts.

...

(c) Applicability to certain plant varieties. This section shall apply equally to—

(1) any variety that is essentially derived from a protected variety, unless the protected variety is an essentially derived variety;

(2) any variety that is not clearly distinguishable from a protected variety;

(3) any variety whose production requires the repeated use of a protected variety; and

(4) harvested material (including entire plants and parts of plants) obtained through the unauthorized use of propagating material of a protected variety, unless the owner of the variety has had a reasonable opportunity to exercise the rights provided under this Act with respect to the propagating material.

§ 2542. Grandfather clause

Nothing in this Act shall abridge the right of any person, or the successor in interest of the person, to reproduce or sell a variety developed and produced by such person more than one year prior to the effective filing date of an adverse application for a certificate of plant variety protection.

§ 2543. Right to save seed; crop exemption

Except to the extent that such action may constitute an infringement under subsections (3) and (4) of section 111 [7 USCS § 2541(3) and (4)], it shall not infringe any right hereunder for a person to save seed produced by the person from seed obtained, or descended from seed obtained, by authority of the owner of the variety for seeding purposes and use such saved seed in the production of a crop for use on the farm of the person, or for sale as provided in this section. A bona fide sale for other than reproductive purposes, made in channels usual for such other purposes, of seed produced on a farm either from seed obtained by authority of the owner for seeding purposes or from seed produced by descent on such farm from seed obtained by authority of the owner for seeding purposes shall not constitute an infringement. A purchaser who diverts seed from such channels to seeding purposes shall be deemed to have notice under section 127 [7 USCS §2567] that the actions of the purchaser constitute an infringement.

§2544. Research exemption

The use and reproduction of a protected variety for plant breeding or other bona fide research shall not constitute an infringement of the protection provided under this Act.

§2561. Remedy for infringement of plant variety protection

An owner shall have remedy by civil action for infringement of plant variety protection under section 111 [7 USCS §2541]. If a variety is sold under the name of a variety shown in a certificate, there is a prima facie presumption that it is the same variety.

Canada

Plant Breeders' Rights Act

APPLICATION

Varieties to which Act applies

(1) The varieties of plants in respect of which this Act provides for the granting of plant breeders' rights are restricted to varieties belonging to prescribed categories and found, pursuant to subsection 27(1), to be new varieties.

New varieties

(2) A plant variety is a new variety if it

(a) is, by reason of one or more identifiable characteristics, clearly distinguishable from all varieties the existence of which is a matter of common knowledge at the effective date of application for the grant of the plant breeder's rights respecting that plant variety;

(b) is stable in its essential characteristics in that after repeated reproduction or propagation or, where the applicant has defined a particular cycle of reproduction or multiplication, at the end of each cycle, remains true to its description; and

(c) is, having regard to the particular features of its sexual reproduction or vegetative propagation, a sufficiently homogeneous variety.

Definition of "sufficiently homogeneous variety"

(3) In paragraph (2)(c), "sufficiently homogeneous variety" means such a variety that, in the event of its sexual reproduction or vegetative propagation in substantial quantity, any variations in characteristics of plants so reproduced or propagated are predictable, capable of being described and commercially acceptable.

PLANT BREEDER'S RIGHTS
S.C. 1990, c. 20, s. 5

Nature of plant breeder's rights

§5 (1) Subject to this Act, the holder of the plant breeder's rights respecting a plant variety has the exclusive right

(a) to sell, and produce in Canada for the purpose of selling, propagating material, as such, of the plant variety;

(b) to make repeated use of propagating material of the plant variety in order to produce commercially another plant variety if the repetition is necessary for that purpose;

(c) where it is a plant variety to which ornamental plants or parts thereof normally marketed for purposes other than propagation belong, to use any such plants or parts commercially as propagating material in the production of ornamental plants or cut flowers; and

(d) to authorize, conditionally or unconditionally, the doing of an act described in paragraphs (a) to (c).

Exemption

(2) Paragraph (1)(a) does not apply in respect of the sale of propagating material that is not in Canada when it is sold but, if any such propagating material the sale of which to any person is exempted from that paragraph by this subsection is used as propagating material in Canada by that person, an infringement of the exclusive right conferred by virtue of that paragraph is constituted by the purchase and subsequent use of the propagating material by that person, who shall be liable to be proceeded against in respect of that infringement.

PLANT BREEDER'S RIGHTS

Term of plant breeder's rights

§6. (1) The term of the grant of plant breeder's rights shall, subject to earlier termination pursuant to this Act, be a period of eighteen years, commencing on the day the certificate of registration is issued under paragraph 27(3)(b).

Payment of annual fee

(2) A holder of plant breeder's rights shall, during the term of the grant of those rights, pay to the Commissioner the prescribed annual fee in respect of those rights.

...

APPLICATIONS FOR PLANT BREEDER'S RIGHTS

Entitlement to apply for plant breeder's rights

§7. (1) Subject to section 8, a breeder of a new variety or a legal representative of the breeder may make an application to the Commissioner for the grant of plant breeder's rights respecting that variety if

(a) in the case of a new variety of a recently prescribed category, neither the breeder nor a legal representative of the breeder sold or concurred in the sale of that variety in Canada before the commencement of such period prior to the date of receipt, by the Commissioner, of the application as is prescribed for the purposes of this paragraph;

(b) in any other case, neither the breeder nor a legal representative of the breeder sold or concurred in the sale of that variety in Canada before the effective date of the application; and

(c) subject to any prescribed exemptions, neither the breeder nor a legal representative of the breeder sold or concurred in the sale of that variety outside

Canada before the commencement of such period prior to the date described in paragraph (a) as is prescribed for the purposes of this paragraph.

…

Plant Breeders' Rights Act
COMPULSORY LICENCES

S.C. 1990, c. 20, s. 32

Grant of compulsory licences

§32. (1) Subject to this section and the regulations, the Commissioner shall, on application by any person, where the Commissioner considers that it is appropriate to do so, confer on the person in the form of a compulsory licence rights to do any thing that the holder might authorize another person to do pursuant to paragraph 5(1)(d).

Objectives on granting compulsory licence

(2) In disposing of an application for, and settling the terms of, a compulsory licence pursuant to this section in relation to any plant variety, the Commissioner shall endeavour to secure that

(a) the plant variety is made available to the public at reasonable prices, is widely distributed and is maintained in quality; and

(b) there is reasonable remuneration, which may include royalty, for the holder of the plant breeder's rights respecting the plant variety.

…

Plant Breeders' Rights Act
CIVIL REMEDIES

Infringement

§41. (1) A person who infringes plant breeder's rights is liable to the holder thereof and to all persons claiming under the holder for all damages that are, by reason of the infringement, sustained by the holder or any of those persons and, unless otherwise expressly provided, the holder shall be made a party to any action for the recovery of those damages.

Relief in the event of infringement

(2) In an action for infringement of plant breeder's rights that is before a court of competent jurisdiction, the court or a judge thereof may make any interim or final order sought by any of the parties and deemed just by the court or judge, including provision for relief by way of injunction and recovery of damages and generally respecting proceedings in the action and, without limiting the generality of the foregoing, may make an order

(a) for restraint of such use, production or sale of the subject-matter of those rights as may constitute such an infringement and for punishment in the event of disobedience of the order for that restraint;

(b) for compensation of an aggrieved person;

(c) for and in respect of inspection or account; and

(d) with respect to the custody or disposition of any offending material, products, wares or articles.

Appeals

(3) An appeal lies from any order under subsection (2) under the same circumstances and to the same court as from other judgments or orders of the court in which the order is made.

...

Plant Breeders' Rights Act
OFFENCES

Secrecy

§ 53. (1) Every person commits an offence who wilfully discloses any information with regard to any variety in respect of which an application for plant breeder's rights is made or with regard to the business affairs of the applicant that was acquired by that person in performing any functions under this Act except where the information is disclosed

(a) to the Minister, the advisory committee or the Commissioner or to any other person for the purposes of the performance by that other person of any functions pursuant to this Act or of any duties in an official capacity for enforcement of this Act; or

(b) in compliance with any requirements imposed by or under this Act or by virtue of any power lawfully exercised in the course or for the purposes of any judicial proceedings.

Offences respecting denominations and sales

(2) Every person commits an offence who

(a) wilfully contravenes section 15;

(b) for the purposes of selling any propagating material for propagation or multiplication, wilfully designates the material by reference to

(i) a denomination different from any denomination registered in respect of the plant variety of which the material is propagating material,

(ii) a denomination registered in respect of a plant variety of which the material is not propagating material, or

(iii) a denomination corresponding so closely to a registered denomination as to mislead; or

(c) knowingly, for the purpose of selling any propagating material for propagation or multiplication, represents falsely that the material is propagating material of, or is derived from, a plant variety in respect of which plant breeder's rights are held or have been applied for.

...

Plant Breeders' Rights Act
PLANT BREEDERS' RIGHTS OFFICE

Plant Breeders' Rights Office

§ 56. (1) The Plant Breeders' Rights Office is part of the Canadian Food Inspection Agency established by the Canadian Food Inspection Agency Act.

Commissioner

(2) The President of the Canadian Food Inspection Agency shall designate a Commissioner of Plant Breeders' Rights.

Employees

(3) The President of the Canadian Food Inspection Agency has the authority to appoint the employees of the Plant Breeders' Rights Office.

...

Plant Breeders' Rights Act
RECORDS

Index

§ 62. The Commissioner may prepare an index of names, together with descriptions comprising particulars of distinguishing identifiable characteristics, of such plant varieties in each of the prescribed categories as are ascertainable by the Commissioner to exist as a matter of fact within common knowledge.

Plant Breeders' Rights Act
RECORDS

Register

§ 63. The Commissioner shall keep a register of plant breeders' rights and, subject to the payment of any fee or charge required by or under this Act to be paid in the case of any entry in the register, the Commissioner shall enter in it

(a) the prescribed category to which each new variety belongs;

(b) the denomination of the variety, and any change thereof approved pursuant to subsection 14(5);

(c) the full name and address of the breeder of that variety;

(d) the name and address of the person whom the Commissioner is satisfied, in the manner provided by or under this Act, ought to be registered as the holder of the plant breeder's rights respecting that variety;

(e) the date of the grant of plant breeder's rights respecting that variety;

(f) the date of, and the reason for, any termination or invalidation of plant breeder's rights;

(g) if plant breeder's rights are the subject of a compulsory licence under section 32, a statement to that effect;

(h) the prescribed particulars of each application for the grant of plant breeder's rights and of any abandonment or withdrawal of the application and, where a protective direction is granted, a statement to that effect; and

(i) the prescribed particulars, subject to the provisions of this Act and the regulations, that are considered by the Commissioner to be appropriate for entry in the register.

Plant Breeders' Rights Act
PUBLICATION

Matters to be published

§ 70 (1) The Commissioner shall cause to be published in the Canada Gazette such particulars of the following as are prescribed:

(a) every application that is not rejected pursuant to section 17;

(b) every request included pursuant to subsection 9(1) in an application that is not rejected pursuant to section 17;

(c) every application for a protective direction;

(d) every grant or withdrawal of a protective direction;

(e) every grant or refusal to grant plant breeder's rights;

(f) every assignment of plant breeder's rights of which the Commissioner is informed;

(g) every application for a compulsory licence;

(h) every grant or refusal to grant a compulsory licence and every thing done under subsection 32(4) with respect to a compulsory licence; and

(i) every surrender of plant breeder's rights.

Notice to Department of Industry

(2) The Commissioner shall, on causing particulars of a request referred to in paragraph (1)(b) to be published, give notice of the request to the Department of Industry.

Matters to be published

(3) In addition to the matters referred to in subsection (1), the Commissioner shall cause to be published in the Canada Gazette

(a) such other matters as the Commissioner considers appropriate for public information; and

(b) a notice of every refusal to grant a protective direction and of every annulment under section 34 or revocation under section 35.

III. Cases

United States

Sidney A. DIAMOND, Commissioner of Patents and Trademarks, Petitioner,

v.

Ananda M. CHAKRABARTY et al.

Supreme Court of the United States
65 L.Ed.2d 144, 206 U.S.P.Q. 193
No. 79-136.
Argued March 17, 1980.
Decided June 16, 1980.

Affirmed.

Chief Justice BURGER delivered the opinion of the Court.

We granted certiorari to determine whether a live, human-made micro-organism is patentable subject matter under 35 U.S.C. § 101.

I

In 1972, respondent Chakrabarty, a microbiologist, filed a patent application, assigned to the General Electric Co. The application asserted 36 claims related to Chakrabarty's invention of "a bacterium from the genus *Pseudomonas* containing therein at least two stable energy-generating plasmids, each of said plasmids providing a separate hydrocarbon degradative pathway." This human-made, genetically engineered bacterium is capable of breaking down multiple components of crude oil. Because of this property, which is possessed by no naturally occurring bacteria, Chakrabarty's invention is believed to have significant value for the treatment of oil spills.

Chakrabarty's patent claims were of three types: first, process claims for the method of producing the bacteria; second, claims for an inoculum comprised of a carrier material floating on water, such as straw, and the new bacteria; and third, claims to the bacteria themselves. The patent examiner allowed the claims falling into the first two categories, but rejected claims for the bacteria. His decision rested on two grounds: (1) that microorganisms are "products of nature," and (2) that as living things they are not patentable subject matter under 35 U.S.C. § 101.

II

The Constitution grants Congress broad power to legislate to "promote the Progress of Science and useful Arts, by securing for limited Times to Authors and Inventors the exclusive Right to their respective Writings and Discoveries." Art. I, § 8, cl. 8. The patent laws promote this progress by offering inventors exclusive rights for a limited period as an incentive for their inventiveness and research efforts. *Kewanee Oil Co. v. Bicron Corp.*, 416 U.S. 470, 480–481, 94 S.Ct. 1879, 1885–1886, 40 L.Ed.2d 315 (1974); *Universal Oil Co. v. Globe Co.*, 322 U.S. 471, 484, 64 S.Ct. 1110, 1116, 88 L.Ed. 1399 (1944). The authority of Congress is exercised in the hope that "[t]he productive effort thereby fostered will have a positive effect on society through the introduction of new products and processes of manufacture into the economy, and the emanations by way of increased employment and better lives for our citizens." *Kewanee, supra*, 416 U.S., at 480, 94 S.Ct., at 1885–86.

The question before us in this case is a narrow one of statutory interpretation requiring us to construe 35 U.S.C. § 101, which provides:

"Whoever invents or discovers any new and useful process, machine, manufacture, or composition of matter, or any new and useful improvement thereof, may obtain a patent therefor, subject to the conditions and requirements of this title."

Specifically, we must determine whether respondent's micro-organism constitutes a "manufacture" or "composition of matter" within the meaning of the statute.

III

... this Court has read the term "manufacture" in § 101 in accordance with its dictionary definition to mean "the production of articles for use from raw or prepared materials by giving to these materials new forms, qualities, properties, or combinations, whether by hand-labor or by machinery." *American Fruit Growers, Inc. v. Brogdex Co.*, 283 U.S. 1, 11, 51 S.Ct. 328, 330, 75 L.Ed. 801 (1931). Similarly, "composition of matter" has been construed consistent with its common usage to include "all compositions of two or more substances and ... all composite articles, whether they be the results of chemical union, or of mechanical mixture, or whether they be gases, fluids, powders or solids." *Shell Development Co. v. Watson*, 149 F.Supp. 279, 280 (D.C.1957) (citing 1 A.

Deller, Walker on Patents § 14, p. 55 (1st ed. 1937)). In choosing such expansive terms as "manufacture" and "composition of matter," modified by the comprehensive "any," Congress plainly contemplated that the patent laws would be given wide scope.

The relevant legislative history also supports a broad construction. The Patent Act of 1793, authored by Thomas Jefferson, defined statutory subject matter as "any new and useful art, machine, manufacture, or composition of matter, or any new or useful improvement [thereof]." Act of Feb. 21, 1793, § 1, 1 Stat. 319. The Act embodied Jefferson's philosophy that "ingenuity should receive a liberal encouragement." 5 Writings of Thomas Jefferson 75–76 (Washington ed. 1871). See *Graham v. John Deere Co.*, 383 U.S. 1, 7–10, 86 S.Ct. 684, 688–690, 15 L.Ed.2d 545 (1966). Subsequent patent statutes in 1836, 1870, and 1874 employed this same broad language. In 1952, when the patent laws were recodified, Congress replaced the word "art" with "process," but otherwise left Jefferson's language intact. The Committee Reports accompanying the 1952 Act inform us that Congress intended statutory subject matter to "include anything under the sun that is made by man." S.Rep.No.1979, 82d Cong., 2d Sess., 5 (1952); H.R.Rep.No.1923, 82d Cong., 2d Sess., 6 (1952).

This is not to suggest that § 101 has no limits or that it embraces every discovery. The laws of nature, physical phenomena, and abstract ideas have been held not patentable. See *Parker v. Flook*, 437 U.S. 584, 98 S.Ct. 2522, 57 L.Ed.2d 451 (1978); *Gottschalk v. Benson*, 409 U.S. 63, 67, 93 S.Ct. 253, 255, 34 L.Ed.2d 273 (1972); *Funk Brothers Seed Co. v. Kalo Inoculant Co.*, 333 U.S. 127, 130, 68 S.Ct. 440, 441, 92 L.Ed. 588 (1948); *O'Reilly v. Morse*, 15 How. 62, 112–121, 14 L.Ed. 601 (1854); *Le Roy v. Tatham*, 14 How. 156, 175, 14 L.Ed. 367 (1853). Thus, a new mineral discovered in the earth or a new plant found in the wild is not patentable subject matter. Likewise, Einstein could not patent his celebrated law that $E=mc^2$; nor could Newton have patented the law of gravity. Such discoveries are "manifestations of ... nature, free to all men and reserved exclusively to none." *Funk, supra*, 333 U.S., at 130, 68 S.Ct., at 441.

Judged in this light, respondent's micro-organism plainly qualifies as patentable subject matter. His claim is not to a hitherto unknown natural phenomenon, but to a nonnaturally occurring manufacture or composition of matter—a product of human ingenuity "having a distinctive name, character [and] use." *Hartranft v. Wiegmann*, 121 U.S. 609, 615, 7 S.Ct. 1240, 1243, 30 L.Ed. 1012 (1887). The point is underscored dramatically by comparison of the invention here with that in *Funk*. There, the patentee had discovered that there existed in nature certain species of root-nodule bacteria which did not exert a mutually inhibitive effect on each other. He used that discovery to produce a mixed culture capable of inoculating the seeds of leguminous plants. Concluding that the patentee had discovered "only some of the handiwork of nature," the Court ruled the product nonpatentable:

"Each of the species of root-nodule bacteria contained in the package infects the same group of leguminous plants which it always infected. No species acquires a different use. The combination of species produces no new bacteria, no change in the six species of bacteria, and no enlargement of the range of their utility. Each species has the same effect it always had. The bacteria perform in their natural way. Their use in combination does not improve in any way their natural functioning. They serve the ends nature originally provided and act quite independently of any effort of the patentee." 333 U.S., at 131, 68 S.Ct., at 442.

Here, by contrast, the patentee has produced a new bacterium with markedly different characteristics from any found in nature and one having the potential for significant utility. His discovery is not nature's handiwork, but his own; accordingly it is patentable subject matter under § 101.

IV

Two contrary arguments are advanced, neither of which we find persuasive.

(A)

The petitioner's first argument rests on the enactment of the 1930 Plant Patent Act, which afforded patent protection to certain asexually reproduced plants, and the 1970 Plant Variety Protection Act, which authorized protection for certain sexually reproduced plants but excluded bacteria from its protection.[3] In the petitioner's view, the passage of these Acts evidences congressional understanding that the terms "manufacture" or "composition of matter" do not include living things; if they did, the petitioner argues, neither Act would have been necessary.

We reject this argument. Prior to 1930, two factors were thought to remove plants from patent protection. The first was the belief that plants, even those artificially bred, were products of nature for purposes of the patent law. This position appears to have derived from the decision of the patent office in *Ex parte Latimer*, 1889 Dec.Com.Pat. 123, in which a patent claim for fiber found in the needle of the *Pinus australis* was rejected. The Commissioner reasoned that a contrary result would permit "patents [to] be obtained upon the trees of the forest and the plants of the earth, which of course would be unreasonable and impossible." *Id.*, at 126. The *Latimer* case, it seems, came to "se[t] forth the general stand taken in these matters" that plants were natural products not subject to patent protection. Thorne, Relation of Patent Law to Natural Products, 6 J. Pat.Off.Soc. 23, 24 1923). The second obstacle to patent protection for plants was the fact that plants were thought not amenable to the "written description" requirement of the patent law. See 35 U.S.C. § 112. Because new plants may differ from old only in color or perfume, differentiation by written description was often impossible. See Hearings on H.R.11372 before the House Committee on Patents, 71st Cong., 2d Sess. 7 (1930) (memorandum of Patent Commissioner Robertson).

In enacting the Plant Patent Act, Congress addressed both of these concerns. It explained at length its belief that the work of the plant breeder "in aid of nature" was patentable invention. S.Rep.No.315, 71st Cong., 2d Sess., 6–8 (1930); H.R.Rep.No.1129, 71st Cong., 2d Sess., 7–9 (1930). And it relaxed the written description requirement in favor of "a description ... as complete as is reasonably possible." 35 U.S.C. § 162. No Committee or Member of Congress, however, expressed the broader view, now urged by the petitioner, that the terms "manufacture" or "composition of matter" exclude living things. The sole support for that position in the legislative history of the 1930 Act is found in the conclusory statement of Secretary of Agriculture Hyde,

---

3. The Plant Patent Act of 1930, 35 U.S.C. § 161, provides in relevant part: "Whoever invents or discovers and asexually reproduces any distinct and new variety of plant, including cultivated sports, mutants, hybrids, and newly found seedlings, other than a tuber propogated plant or a plant found in an uncultivated state, may obtain a patent therefor...."

The Plant Variety Protection Act of 1970, provides in relevant part: "The breeder of any novel variety of sexually reproduced plant (other than fungi, bacteria, or first generation hybrids) who has so reproduced the variety, or his successor in interest, shall be entitled to plant variety protection therefor...." 84 Stat. 1547, 7 U.S.C. § 2402(a).

See generally, 3 A. Deller, WALKE ON PATENTS, ch. IX (2d ed. 1964); R. Allyn, THE FIRST PLANT Patents (1934).

in a letter to the Chairmen of the House and Senate Committees considering the 1930 Act, that "the patent laws ... at the present time are understood to cover only inventions or discoveries in the field of inanimate nature." See S.Rep.No.315, *supra*, at Appendix A; H.R.Rep.No.1129, *supra*, at Appendix A. Secretary Hyde's opinion, however, is not entitled to controlling weight. His views were solicited on the administration of the new law and not on the scope of patentablesubject matter—an area beyond his competence. Moreover, there is language in the House and Senate Committee Reports suggesting that to the extent Congress considered the matter it found the Secretary's dichotomy unpersuasive. The Reports observe:

"There is a clear and logical distinction *between the discovery of a new variety of plant and of certain inanimate things*, such, for example, as a new and useful natural mineral. The mineral is created wholly by nature unassisted by man.... On the other hand, a plant discovery resulting from cultivation is unique, isolated, and is not repeated by nature, nor can it be reproduced by nature unaided by man...." S.Rep.No.315, *supra*, at 6; H.R.Rep.No.1129, *supra*, at 7 (emphasis added).

Congress thus recognized that the relevant distinction was not between living and inanimate things, but between products of nature, whether living or not, and human-made inventions. Here, respondent's micro-organism is the result of human ingenuity and research. Hence, the passage of the Plant Patent Act affords the Government no support.

Nor does the passage of the 1970 Plant Variety Protection Act support the Government's position. As the Government acknowledges, sexually reproduced plants were not included under the 1930 Act because new varieties could not be reproduced true-to-type through seedlings. Brief for Petitioner 27, n. 31. By 1970, however, it was generally recognized that true-to-type reproduction was possible and that plant patent protection was therefore appropriate. The 1970 Act extended that protection. There is nothing in its language or history to suggest that it was enacted because § 101 did not include living things.

In particular, we find nothing in the exclusion of bacteria from plant variety protection to support the petitioner's position. See n. 7, *supra*. The legislative history gives no reason for this exclusion. As the Court of Customs and Patent Appeals suggested, it may simply reflect congressional agreement with the result reached by that court in deciding *In re Arzberger*, 27 C.C.P.A. (Pat.) 1315, 112 F.2d 834 (1940), which held that bacteria were not plants for the purposes of the 1930 Act. Or it may reflect the fact that prior to 1970 the Patent Office had issued patents for bacteria under § 101. [FN9] In any event, absent some clear indication that Congress "focused on [the] issues ... directly related to the one presently before the Court," *SEC v. Sloan*, 436 U.S. 103, 120–121, 98 S.Ct. 1702, 1713, 56 L.Ed.2d 148 (1978), there is no basis for reading into its actions an intent to modify the plain meaning of the words found in § 101. See *TVA v. Hill*, 437 U.S. 153, 189–193, 98 S.Ct. 2279, 2299–2301, 57 L.Ed.2d 117 (1978); *United States v. Price*, 361 U.S. 304, 313, 80 S.Ct. 326, 331, 4 L.Ed.2d 334 (1960).

(B)

The petitioner's second argument is that micro-organisms cannot qualify as patentable subject matter until Congress expressly authorizes such protection. His position rests on the fact that genetic technology was unforeseen when Congress enacted § 101. From this it is argued that resolution of the patentability of inventions such as respondent's should be left to Congress. The legislative process, the petitioner argues, is best equipped to weigh the competing economic, social, and scientific considerations involved, and to determine whether living organisms produced by genetic engineering should receive patent protection. In support of this position, the petitioner relies on our recent holding in *Parker v. Flook*, 437 U.S. 584, 98 S.Ct. 2522, 57 L.Ed.2d 451 (1978), and the statement that the judiciary "must proceed cautiously when ... asked to extend patent rights into areas wholly unforeseen by Congress." *Id.*, at 596, 98 S.Ct. at 2529.

.... Nothing in *Flook* is to the contrary. That case applied our prior precedents to determine that a "claim for an improved method of calculation, even when tied to a specific end use, is unpatentable subject matter under § 101." 437 U.S., at 595, n. 18, 98 S.Ct., at 2528, n. 18. The Court carefully scrutinized the claim at issue to determine whether it was precluded from patent protection under "the principles underlying the prohibition against patents for 'ideas' or phenomena of nature." *Id.*, at 593, 98 S.Ct. at 2527. We have done that here. *Flook* did not announce a new principle that inventions in areas not contemplated by Congress when the patent laws were enacted are unpatentable *per se*.

To read that concept into *Flook* would frustrate the purposes of the patent law. This Court frequently has observed that a statute is not to be confined to the "particular application[s] ... contemplated by the legislators." *Barr v. United States*, 324 U.S. 83, 90, 65 S.Ct. 522, 525, 89 L.Ed. 765 (1945). Accord, *Browder v. United States*, 312 U.S. 335, 339, 61 S.Ct. 599, 601, 85 L.Ed. 862 (1941); *Puerto Rico v. Shell Co.*, 302 U.S. 253, 257, 58 S.Ct. 167, 169, 82 L.Ed. 235 (1937). This is especially true in the field of patent law. A rule that unanticipated inventions are without protection would conflict with the core concept of the patent law that anticipation undermines patentability. See *Graham v. John Deere Co.*, 383 U.S., at 12–17, 86 S.Ct., at 691–693. Mr. Justice Douglas reminded that the inventions most benefiting mankind are those that "push back the frontiers of chemistry, physics, and the like." *Great A. & P. Tea Co. v. Supermarket Corp.*, 340 U.S. 147, 154, 71 S.Ct. 127, 131, 95 L.Ed. 162 (1950) (concurring opinion). Congress employed broad general language in drafting § 101 precisely because such inventions are often unforeseeable.

To buttress his argument, the petitioner, with the support of *amicus*, points to grave risks that may be generated by research endeavors such as respondent's. The briefs present a gruesome parade of horribles. Scientists, among them Nobel laureates, are quoted suggesting that genetic research may pose a serious threat to the human race, or, at the very least, that the dangers are far too substantial to permit such research to proceed apace at this time. We are told that genetic research and related technological developments may spread pollution and disease, that it may result in a loss of genetic diversity, and that its practice may tend to depreciate the value of human life. These arguments are forcefully, even passionately, presented; they remind us that, at times, human ingenuity seems unable to control fully the forces it creates—that with Hamlet, it is sometimes better "to bear those ills we have than fly to others that we know not of."

It is argued that this Court should weigh these potential hazards in considering whether respondent's invention is patentable subject matter under § 101. We disagree. The grant or denial of patents on micro-organisms is not likely to put an end to genetic research or to its attendant risks. The large amount of research that has already occurred when no researcher had sure knowledge that patent protection would be available suggests that legislative or judicial fiat as to patentability will not deter the scientific mind from probing into the unknown any more than Canute could command the tides. Whether respondent's claims are patentable may determine whether research efforts are accelerated by the hope of reward or slowed by want of incentives, but that is all.

What is more important is that we are without competence to entertain these arguments—either to brush them aside as fantasies generated by fear of the unknown, or to act on them. The choice we are urged to make is a matter of high policy for resolution within the legislative process after the kind of investigation, examination, and study that legislative bodies can provide and courts cannot. That process involves the balancing of competing values and interests, which in our democratic system is the business of elected representatives. Whatever their validity, the contentions now pressed on us should be addressed to the political branches of the Government, the Congress and the Executive, and not to the courts.

We have emphasized in the recent past that "[o]ur individual appraisal of the wisdom or unwisdom of a particular [legislative] course … is to be put aside in the process of interpreting a statute." *TVA v. Hill*, 437 U.S., at 194, 98 S.Ct., at 2302. Our task, rather, is the narrow one of determining what Congress meant by the words it used in the statute; once that is done our powers are exhausted. Congress is free to amend § 101 so as to exclude from patent protection organisms produced by genetic engineering. Cf. 42 U.S.C. § 2181(a), exempting from patent protection inventions "useful solely in the utilization of special nuclear material or atomic energy in an atomic weapon." Or it may chose to craft a statute specifically designed for such living things. But, until Congress takes such action, this Court must construe the language of § 101 as it is. The language of that section fairly embraces respondent's invention.

Accordingly, the judgment of the Court of Customs and Patent Appeals is

Affirmed.

Mr. Justice BRENNAN, with whom Mr. Justice WHITE, Mr. Justice MARSHALL, and Mr. Justice POWELL join, dissenting.

I agree with the Court that the question before us is a narrow one. Neither the future of scientific research, nor even, the ability of respondent Chakrabarty to reap some monopoly profits from his pioneering work, is at stake. Patents on the processes by which he has produced and employed the new living organism are not contested. The only question we need decide is whether Congress, exercising its authority under Art. I, § 8, of the Constitution, intended that he be able to secure a monopoly on the living organism itself, no matter how produced or how used. Because I believe the Court has misread the applicable legislation, I dissent.

The patent laws attempt to reconcile this Nation's deep seated antipathy to monopolies with the need to encourage progress. *Deepsouth Packing Co. v. Laitram Corp.*, 406 U.S. 518, 530–531, 92 S.Ct. 1700, 1707–1708, 32 L.Ed.2d 273 (1972); *Graham v. John Deere Co.*, 383 U.S. 1, 7–10, 86 S.Ct. 684, 668–690, 15 L.Ed.2d 545 (1966). Given the complexity and legislative nature of this delicate task, we must be careful to extend patent protection no further than Congress has provided. In particular, were there an absence of legislative direction, the courts should leave to Congress the decisions whether and how far to extend the patent privilege into areas where the common understanding has been that patents are not available.[1] Cf. *Deepsouth Packing Co. v. Laitram Corp., supra.*

In this case, however, we do not confront a complete legislative vacuum. The sweeping language of the Patent Act of 1793, as re-enacted in 1952, is not the last pronouncement Congress has made in this area. In 1930 Congress enacted the Plant Patent Act affording patent protection to developers of certain asexually reproduced plants. In 1970 Con-

---

1. I read the Court to admit that the popular conception, even among advocates of agricultural patents, was that living organisms were unpatentable. *See ante*, at 2209, and n. 8.

gress enacted the Plant Variety Protection Act to extend protection to certain new plant varieties capable of sexual reproduction. Thus, we are not dealing—as the Court would have it—with the routine problem of "unanticipated inventions." *Ante*, at 2211. In these two Acts Congress has addressed the general problem of patenting animate inventions and has chosen carefully limited language granting protection to some kinds of discoveries, but specifically excluding others. These Acts strongly evidence a congressional limitation that excludes bacteria from patentability.[2]

First, the Acts evidence Congress' understanding, at least since 1930, that § 101 does not include living organisms. If newly developed living organisms not naturally occurring had been patentable under § 101, the plants included in the scope of the 1930 and 1970 Acts could have been patented without new legislation. Those plants, like the bacteria involved in this case, were new varieties not naturally occurring. Although the Court, *ante*, at 2209, rejects this line of argument, it does not explain why the Acts were necessary unless to correct a pre-existing situation.[3] I cannot share the Court's implicit assumption that Congress was engaged in either idle exercises or mere correction of the public record when it enacted the 1930 and 1970 Acts. And Congress certainly thought it was doing something significant. The Committee Reports contain expansive prose about the previously unavailable benefits to be derived from extending patent protection to plants. H.R.Rep. No. 91-1605, pp. 1–3 (1970), U.S.Code Cong. & Admin.News 1970, p. 5082; S.Rep.No.315, 71st Cong., 2d Sess., 1–3 (1930). Because Congress thought it had to legislate in order to make agricultural "human-made inventions" patentable and because the legislation Congress enacted is limited, it follows that Congress never meant to make items outside the scope of the legislation patentable.

Second, the 1970 Act clearly indicates that Congress has included bacteria within the focus of its legislative concern, but not within the scope of patent protection. Congress specifically excluded bacteria from the coverage of the 1970 Act. 7 U.S.C. § 2402(a). The Court's attempts to supply explanations for this explicit exclusion ring hollow. It is true that there is no mention in the legislative history of the exclusion, but that does not give us license to invent reasons. The fact is that Congress, assuming that animate objects as to which it had not specifically legislated could not be patented, excluded bacteria from the set of patentable organisms.

The Court protests that its holding today is dictated by the broad language of § 101, which cannot "be confined to the 'particular application [s] … contemplated by the legislators.'" *Ante*, at 2211, quoting *Barr v. United States*, 324 U.S. 83, 90, 65 S.Ct. 522, 525, 89 L.Ed. 765 (1945). But as I have shown, the Court's decision does not follow the unavoidable implications of the statute. Rather, it extends the patent system to cover

---

2. But even if I agreed with the Court that the 1930 and 1970 Acts were not dispositive, I would dissent. This case presents even more cogent reasons than *Deepsouth Packing Co.* not to extend the patent monopoly in the face of uncertainty. At the very least, these Acts are signs of legislative attention to the problems of patenting living organisms, but they give no affirmative indication of congressional intent that bacteria be patentable. The caveat of *Parker v. Flook*, 437 U.S. 584, 596, 90 S.Ct. 2522, 2529, 57 L.Ed.2d 451 (1978), an admonition to "proceed cautiously when we are asked to extend patent rights into areas wholly unforeseen by Congress," therefore becomes pertinent. I should think the necessity for caution is that much greater when we are asked to extend patent rights into areas Congress has foreseen and considered but has not resolved.

3. If the 1930 Act's only purpose were to solve the technical problem of description referred to by the Court, *ante*, at 2209, most of the Act, and in particular its limitation to asexually reproduced plants, would have been totally unnecessary.

living material even though Congress plainly has legislated in the belief that § 101 does not encompass living organisms. It is the role of Congress, not this Court, to broaden or narrow the reach of the patent laws. This is especially true where, as here, the composition sought to be patented uniquely implicates matters of public concern

Ex parte Kenneth A. Hibberd, Paul C. Anderson and Melanie Barker.

Board of Patent Appeals and Interferences
August 9, 1985, Heard
September 18, 1985, Decided

OPINION:

Smith, Examiner-in-Chief.

.... The subject matter on appeal relates to maize plant technologies, including seeds, plants and tissue cultures which have increased free tryptophan levels, or which are capable of producing plants or seeds having increased tryptophan content. Claims 239, 249 and 260 are representative of the three groups of rejected claims and are reproduced as follows:

239. A maize seed having an endogenous free tryptophan content of at least about one-tenth milligram per gram dry seed weight and capable of germinating into a plant capable of producing seed having an endogenous free tryptophan content of at least about one-tenth milligram per gram dry seed weight.

249. A maize plant capable of producing seed having an endogenous free tryptophan content of at least about one-tenth milligram per gram dry seed weight, wherein the seed is capable of germinating into a plant capable of producing seed having an endogenous free tryptophan content of at least about one-tenth milligram per gram dry seed weight.

260. A maize tissue culture capable of generating a plant capable of producing seed having an endogenous free tryptophan content of at least about one-tenth milligram per gram dry seed weight, wherein the seed is capable of germinating into a plant capable of producing seed having endogenous free tryptophan content of at least about one-tenth milligram per gram dry seed weight.

There are no rejections based on prior art; rather, claims 239 through 243, 249 through 255 and 260 through 265 are rejected solely under 35 USC 101. It is the examiner's position that the claims drawn to seeds and plants, 239 through 243 and 249 through 255, respectively, comprise subject matter which is inappropriate for protection under 35 USC 101 because the subject matter of plants and seeds is within the purview of the Plant Variety Protection Act of 1970 administered by the U.S. Department of Agriculture, 7 USC 2321 et seq. The examiner's position with respect to claims 260 through 265 drawn to tissue cultures is that such subject matter is inappropriate for protection under 35 USC 101 because it is within the purview of the Plant Patent Act of 1930, 35 USC 161. The examiner asserts that, to the extent that the claimed subject matter can be protected under the Plant Variety Protection Act (PVPA) or the Plant Patent Act (PPA), protection under 35 USC 101 is not available.

We shall not sustain this rejection. Preliminarily, we note that the Supreme Court has interpreted the scope of 35 USC 101 in the recent case of *Diamond v. Chakrabarty,*

447 U.S. 303, 206 USPQ 193 (1980) which involved a rejection of claims to a micro-organism under 35 USC 101 on the ground that Section 101 was not intended to cover living things such as micro-organisms. In determining the scope of Section 101 the Supreme Court began with the language of the statute, interpreted words as taking their ordinary, contemporary, common meaning unless otherwise defined, and was careful not to "read into the patent laws limitations and conditions which the legislature has not expressed." 447 U.S. 308, 206 USPQ 196. The Court noted that the use of the expansive terms "manufacture" and "composition of matter" modified by the comprehensive "any" indicated that Congress "plainly contemplated that the patent laws would be given wide scope." The Supreme Court also noted that the legislative history of Section 101 supports a broad construction and cited the Committee Reports accompanying the 1952 Act which indicate that Congress intended statutory subject matter to "include anything under the sun that is made by man." S. Report No. 1979, 82d Cong., 2d Sess. 5 (1952); H.R. Report No. 1923, 82d Cong., 2d Sess. 6 (1952). Thus, the Court held at 447 U.S. 309, 206 USPQ 197, that the involved micro-organism plainly qualified as patentable subject matter.

The examiner acknowledges in his answer that, in view of the decision in *Diamond v. Chakrabarty, supra*, it appears clear that Section 101 includes man-made life forms, including plant life. Moreover, the examiner's allowance of claims drawn to hybrid seeds and hybrid plants is a further indication that the examiner considers the scope of Section 101 to include man-made plant life. The examiner asserts in his answer, however, that by enacting the PPA in 1930 and the PVPA in 1970 "Congress has specifically set forth how and under what conditions plant life covered by these Acts should be protected." The examiner contends that the only reasonable statutory interpretation is that the PPA and PVPA, which were later in time and more specific than Section 101, each carved out from Section 101, for specific treatment, the subject matter covered by each. Thus, it is the position of the examiner that the plant-specific Acts (PPA and PVPA) are the exclusive forms of protection for plant life covered by those acts.

We disagree with these contentions that the scope of patentable subject matter under Section 101 has been narrowed or restricted by the passage of the PPA and the PVPA and that these plant-specific Acts represent the exclusive forms of protection for plant life covered by those acts. The position taken by the examiner presents a question of statutory construction concerning the scope of patentable subject matter under 35 USC 101, i.e., has the scope of Section 101 been narrowed or restricted by reason of the enactment of the plant-specific Acts.

In cases of statutory construction we begin, as did the Court in Diamond v. Chakrabarty, supra, with the language of the statutes. The language of Section 101 has been set forth, supra, and has been interpreted by the Supreme Court to include everything under the sun that is made by man. The examiner does not point to any specific language in the plant-specific Acts to support his position that the plant-specific Acts restrict the scope of patentable subject matter under Section 101. We have examined the provisions of the PPA and the PVPA and we find, as did appellants, that neither the PPA nor the PVPA expressly excludes any plant subject matter from protection under Section 101. Accordingly, we look next to the legislative histories of the plant-specific Acts to determine whether there is any clear indication of Congressional intent that protection under the plant-specific Acts be exclusive.

The examiner does not refer to the legislative histories of the plant-specific Acts to support his position as to the intent of Congress. Rather, he merely asserts, e.g., at page 2 of his answer, that "... it is clear that Congress intended a 'distinct and new variety of plant' covered by the Plant Patent Act to be something apart from the statutory categories of invention embraced by Section 101" and at page 3 "... the only reasonable statutory interpretation is that each [PPA and PVPA] carved out from Section 101, for specific treatment, the subject matter covered by each." However, as noted by appellants at page 17 of their brief, there is nothing in the legislative histories of the plant-specific Acts from which one could conclude that Congress intended to remove from protection under Section 101 any subject matter already within the scope of that section. Rather, the Senate Committee on the Judiciary concluded on September 29, 1970 in its Report on Senate bill S.3070 in which it recommended passage of the Plant Variety Protection Act that "... it does not alter protection currently available within the patent system."

The Supreme Court in *Diamond v. Chakrabarty*, supra, addressed the legislative history and purpose of the plant-specific Acts and noted that prior to 1930 there were two obstacles to obtaining patent protection on plants. The first was the belief that plants, even those artificially bred, were products of nature not subject to patent protection; the second was the fact that plants were thought not amenable to the "written description" requirement of the patent law. The Supreme Court noted that Congress addressed both of these obstacles in enacting the PPA. Congress explained at length its belief that the work of the plant breeder "in aid of nature" was patentable invention, and it relaxed the written description requirement in favor of a description "as complete as is reasonably possible." In our view, the Supreme Court's analysis of the legislative history of the plant-specific Acts makes it clear that the legislative intent of these acts was to extend patent protection to plant breeders who were stymied by the two noted obstacles.

We find no explicit support in the legislative history for the notion, advanced by the examiner, of an intent to restrict or limit the scope of patentable subject matter available pursuant to 35 USC 101. The examiner tacitly admits such lack of explicit support for his notion of legislative intent by his failure to refer to the legislative history and by the following statement in his Supplemental Examiner's Answer:

When Congress carved out and established distinct forms of protection for certain plants, they implicitly excluded protection of these plants under Section 101. (Emphasis added).

Thus, the examiner's rejection in the final analysis is based on an implied narrowing of Section 101, i.e., an implied partial repeal of Section 101 based on the passage of the plant-specific Acts.

The examiner's contention that Section 101 has been "implicitly" narrowed or partially repealed by implication is not persuasive. The overwhelming weight of authority is to the effect that repeals by implication are not favored and that when there are two acts on the same subject the rule is to give effect to both unless there is such a "positive repugnancy" or "irreconcilable conflict" that the statutes cannot coexist. This "cardinal rule" of statutory construction was set forth by the Supreme Court in *United States v. Borden Co.*, 308 U.S. 189 at 198–99 (1939).

...

In the absence of such "positive repugnancy" or "irreconcilable conflict" that the statutes cannot coexist and we find none, both statutes, i.e., Section 101 and the plant-specific Acts must be given full effect. Indeed, it is our duty to regard each as effective, as the Supreme Court held in *Morton v. Mancari*, 417 U.S. 535 (1973).

These principles of statutory construction were followed in a recent decision of the Court of Appeals, Federal Circuit, *Roche Products, Inc. v. Bolar Pharmaceutical Co.*, 733

F.2d 858, 221 USPQ 937 (Fed. Cir. 1984), *cert. denied*, U.S., 225 USPQ 792 (1984). In *Roche* the Court stated as follows (733 F.2d 864, 221 USPQ 941):

Simply because a later enacted statute affects in some way an earlier enacted statute is poor reason to ask us to rewrite the earlier statute. Repeals by implication are not favored. See, *e.g.*, *Mercantile National Bank v. Langdeau*, 371 U.S. 555, 565, 83 S.Ct. 520, 525, 9 L.Ed.2d 523 (1963). Thus, "courts are not at liberty to pick and choose among congressional enactments, and when two statutes are capable of coexistence it is the duty of the courts, absent a clearly expressed congressional intention to the contrary, to regard each as effective." *Morton v. Mancari*, 417 U.S. 535, 551, 94 S.Ct. 2474, 2483, 41 L.Ed.2d 290 (1974).

The examiner in his answer cited *Bulova Watch Co. v. U.S.*, 365 U.S. 753 (1961) and Morton v. Mancari, supra, for the proposition that a specific statute controls over a general statute where there is a conflict. We find no application of this principle to the facts involved here because before a specific statute can be found to control over a general statute, there must first be an irreconcilable conflict between them, as the Supreme Court made clear in the Morton case. As noted, *supra*, since we find no such irreconcilable conflict, it is our duty to give effect to both Section 101 and the plant-specific Acts.

In an attempt to show a conflict, the examiner points in his answer to provisions of the plant-specific Acts which differ from Section 101. He notes, for example, that (1) the PVPA contains both research (experimental use) and farmer's crop exemptions, while Section 101 does not explicitly contain such exemptions; (2) the PVPA spells out infringement in great detail and includes a compulsory licensing provision, while no such Congressional guidance exists under Section 101 protection; (3) the PVPA limits protection to a single variety, whereas the opportunity for greater and broader exclusionary rights exists under Section 101 protection; (4) under 35 USC 162 (PPA), the applicant is limited to one claim in formal terms to the plant described, whereas there is no such limitation on coverage under Section 101; and (5) under 35 USC 163 (PPA), the plant patent conveys the right to exclude others from asexually reproducing the plant, or selling or using the plant so produced. However, this analysis by the Examiner merely serves to indicate that there are differences in the scope of protection offered by Section 101 and the plant-specific Acts. In our view, such differences fall far short of what would be required to find an irreconcilable conflict or positive repugnancy that would mandate a partial repeal of Section 101 by implication.

Nor does the fact that subject matter patentable under Section 101 overlaps with subject matter protectable under the plant-specific Acts provide a basis for concluding that there is irreconcilable conflict between the statutes. There is ample precedent that the availability of one form of statutory protection does not preclude (or irreconcilably conflict with) the availability of protection under another form. For example, in *In re Yardley*, 493 F.2d 1389, 181 USPQ 331 (CCPA 1974) the Court held that there was an overlap between statutory subject matter under the copyright statute and statutory subject matter under the design patent statute. Such overlap was not found to be an irreconcilable conflict by the Court; rather, the overlap was viewed as an indication that Congress intended the availability of both modes of protection. In so holding the Court stated at 493 F.2d 1395–96, 181 USPQ 336:

The Congress, through its legislation under the authority of the Constitution, has interpreted the Constitution as authorizing an area of overlap where a certain type of creation may be the subject matter of a copyright and the subject matter of a design patent. We see nothing in that legislation which is contradictory and repugnant to the intent of the framers of the Constitution. Congress has not required an author-inventor to elect between the two modes which it has provided for securing exclusive rights on the type of subject matter here involved. If anything, the concurrent availability of both modes of securing exclusive rights aids in achieving the stated purpose of the constitutional provision.

The examiner urges that protection under 35 USC 101 under the circumstances of this case would be a violation of Article 2 of the International Union for the Protection of New Plant Varieties (UPOV). As pointed out by appellants, however, UPOV is an Executive Agreement that has not been ratified by the Senate. Such agreements are not treaties within the Constitution, and are not the Supreme Law of the Land. Valid enactments of Congress, such as Section 101, override conflicting provisions of international executive agreements, irrespective of which came first in point of time. *United States v. Capps*, Inc., 204 F.2d 655 (4th Cir. 1953), aff'd on other grounds, 348 U.S. 296 (1955); Restatement (Second) of the Foreign Relations Law of the United States, §144(1) (1965).

The examiner acknowledges that an executive agreement cannot modify a federal statute, but urges, nevertheless, that the agreement can and should be considered "in interpreting a statute on which it bears." This argument overlooks the fact that the Supreme Court in *Diamond v. Chakrabarty*, supra, has already interpreted this scope of Section 101 to cover everything under the sun made by man.[4] n4 In our view, the examiner is asking for an implied partial repeal of Section 101 on the basis of an executive agreement. To do so would, in our opinion, elevate the agreement to a status superior to an Act of Congress, i.e., Section 101, contrary to the spirit of *United States v. Capps*, Inc., *supra*, and we decline to do so.

In his rejection of claims 260 through 265 drawn to tissue cultures, the examiner contends that the claims to tissue cultures are drawn to "asexual propagating material" and may, therefore, be protected under the PPA under Section 161. We disagree, and the rejection of claims 260 through 265 is, therefore, reversed for the additional reason that tissue cultures are not "plants" within the purview of 35 USC 161. The Court of Customs and Patent Appeals in its decision in *In re Bergy*, 596 F.2d 952, 201 USPQ 352 (CCPA 1979), vacated as moot sub nom. *Diamond v. Chakrabarty*, supra, interpreted the meaning and scope of the term "plant" in the PPA as having its common, ordinary meaning which is limited to those things having roots, stems, leaves and flowers or fruits. In our view, tissue cultures manifestly do not come within the noted "common, ordinary meaning" of the term "plants" and are, therefore, not within the scope of the PPA (35 USC 161).

Motion to Strike

Appellant's motion to strike the Supplemental Examiner's Answer on the ground that there is no provision in the "Patent Laws" or "Rules of Practice" for a paper in rebuttal to Appellant's Reply Brief is denied. In the circumstances presented in this appeal, we consider it desirable to have the complete views of the Examiner and the appellant in the written record.

New Ground of Rejection

The following rejection is made pursuant to the provisions of 37 CFR 1.196(b):

---

4. The record does not reflect whether, or to what extent, the *Chakrabarty* decision was considered when the decision was made to adhere to the international agreement.

Claims 243, 253 and 264 are rejected as unpatentable under the first paragraph of 35 USC 112. The subject matter covered by these claims is described in terms of an assigned accession number for seeds deposited with In Vitro International, Inc. The disclosure is inadequate to enable one skilled in the art to make and use the invention set forth in claims 243, 253 and 264. Assuming that seeds may be deposited in the same manner as micro-organisms to comply with 35 USC 112, there is insufficient evidence in the record as to the availability of the deposited seeds. The depository here, In Vitro International, Inc., is not a recognized public depository, as was the case in *In re Argoudelis*, 434 F.2d 1390, 168 USPQ 99 (CCPA 1970). Nor is there evidence here indicating that In Vitro International, Inc., is under a contractual obligation to maintain the seeds deposited in a permanent collection and to supply samples to anyone seeking them once the patent issues.

The decision of the examiner is reversed.

ASGROW SEED COMPANY, Petitioner

v.

Denny WINTERBOER and Becky Winterboer, dba Deebees.

Supreme Court of the United States
No. 92-2038.
130 L.Ed.2d 682, 63 USLW 4055, 33 U.S.P.Q.2d 1430
Argued Nov. 7, 1994.
Decided Jan. 18, 1995.

Seed company brought action against farmers for alleged violations of Plant Variety Protection Act (PVPA) in connection with sales of protected seeds. The Supreme Court, Justice Scalia, held that: (1) farmers' planting and harvesting of protected seeds was conducted "as a step in marketing" seed company's protected seed varieties for growing purposes, and thus farmers' sales did not fall within crop exemption from PVPA's infringement provision; (2) only protected seed that could be sold by farmer under PVPA crop exemption was seed that had been saved by farmer to replant his own acreage; and (3) exemption requirement, that farmer's "primary farming occupation" was growing of crops, required that selling of crops for other than reproductive purposes constituted preponderance of farmer's business.

Reversed.

Justice Scalia delivered the opinion of the Court.

The Plant Variety Protection Act of 1970, 7 U.S.C. § 2321 *et seq.*, protects owners of novel seed varieties against unauthorized sales of their seed for replanting purposes. An exemption, however, allows farmers to make some sales of protected variety seed to other farmers. This case raises the question whether there is a limit to the quantity of protected seed that a farmer can sell under this exemption.

I

In 1970, Congress passed the Plant Variety Protection Act (PVPA), 84 Stat. 1542, 7 U.S.C. § 2321 *et seq.*, in order to provide developers of novel plant varieties with "adequate encouragement for research, and for marketing when appropriate, to yield for the public the benefits of new varieties," § 2581. The PVPA extends patent-like protection to novel varieties of sexually reproduced plants (that is, plants grown from seed) which parallels the protection afforded asexually reproduced plant varieties (that is, varieties reproduced by propagation or grafting) under Chapter 15 of the Patent Act. See 35 U.S.C. §§ 161–164.

The developer of a novel variety obtains PVPA coverage by acquiring a certificate of protection from the Plant Variety Protection Office. See 7 U.S.C. §§ 2421, 2422, 2481–2483. This confers on the owner the exclusive right for 18 years to "exclude others from selling the variety, or offering it for sale, or reproducing it, or importing it, or exporting it, or using it in producing (as distinguished from developing) a hybrid or different variety therefrom." § 2483.

Petitioner, Asgrow Seed Company, is the holder of PVPA certificates protecting two novel varieties of soybean seed, which it calls A1937 and A2234. Respondents, Dennis and Becky Winterboer, are Iowa farmers whose farm spans 800 acres of Clay County, in the northwest corner of the State. The Winterboers have incorporated under the name "D-Double-U Corporation" and do business under the name "DeeBee's Feed and Seed." In addition to growing crops for sale as food and livestock feed, since 1987 the Winterboers have derived a sizable portion of their income from "brown-bag" sales of their crops to other farmers to use as seed. A brown-bag sale occurs when a farmer purchases seed from a seed company, such as Asgrow, plants the seed in his own fields, harvests the crop, cleans it, and then sells the reproduced seed to other farmers (usually in nondescript brown bags) for them to plant as crop seed on their own farms. During 1990, the Winterboers planted 265 acres of A1937 and A2234, and sold the entire salable crop, 10,529 bushels, to others for use as seed—enough to plant 10,000 acres. The average sale price was $8.70 per bushel, compared with a then-current price of $16.20 to $16.80 per bushel to obtain varieties A1937 and A2234 directly from Asgrow.

Concerned that the Winterboers were making a business out of selling its protected seed, Asgrow sent a local farmer, Robert Ness, to the Winterboer farm to make a purchase. Mr. Winterboer informed Ness that he could sell him soybean seed that was "just like" Asgrow varieties A1937 and A2234. Ness purchased 20 bags of each; a plant biologist for Asgrow tested the seeds and determined that they were indeed A1937 and A2234.

Asgrow brought suit against the Winterboers in the Federal District Court for the Northern District of Iowa, seeking damages and a permanent injunction against sale of seed harvested from crops grown from A1937 and A2234. The complaint alleged infringement under 7 U.S.C. § 2541(1), for selling or offering to sell Asgrow's protected soybean varieties; under § 2541(3), for sexually multiplying Asgrow's novel varieties as a step in marketing those varieties for growing purposes; and under § 2541(6), for dispensing the novel varieties to others in a form that could be propagated without providing notice that the seeds were of a protected variety.

The Winterboers did not deny that Asgrow held valid certificates of protection covering A1937 and A2234, and that they had sold seed produced from those varieties for others to use as seed. Their defense, at least to the §§ 2541(1) and 3) charges, rested upon the contention that their sales fell within the statutory exemption from infringement liability found in 7 U.S.C. § 2543. That section, entitled "Right to save seed; crop exemption," reads in relevant part as follows:

> "Except to the extent that such action may constitute an infringement under subsections (3) and (4) of section 2541 of this title, it shall not infringe any right hereunder for a person to save seed produced by him from seed obtained, or descended from seed obtained, by authority of the owner of the variety for seeding purposes and use such saved seed in the production of a crop for use

on his farm, or for sale as provided in this section: *Provided,* That without re-gard to the provisions of section 2541(3) of this title it shall not infringe any right hereunder for a person, whose primary farming occupation is the grow-ing of crops for sale for other than reproductive purposes, to sell such saved seed to other persons so engaged, for reproductive purposes, provided such sale is in compliance with such State laws governing the sale of seed as may be applicable. A bona fide sale for other than reproductive purposes, made in channels usual for such other purposes, of seed produced on a farm either from seed obtained by authority of the owner for seeding purposes or from seed produced by descent on such farm from seed obtained by authority of the owner for seeding purposes shall not constitute an infringement...."[2]

The Winterboers argued that this language gave them the right to sell an unlimited amount of seed produced from a protected variety, subject only to the conditions that both buyer and seller be farmers "whose primary farming occupation is the growing of crops for sale for other than reproductive purposes," and that all sales comply with state law. Asgrow maintained that the exemption allows a farmer to save and resell to other farmers only the amount of seed the seller would need to replant his own fields—a lim-itation that the Winterboers' sales greatly exceeded. The District Court agreed with As-grow and granted summary judgment in its favor. 795 F.Supp. 915 (1991).

The United States Court of Appeals for the Federal Circuit reversed. 982 F.2d 486 (1992). Although "recogniz[ing] that, without meaningful limitations, the crop exemp-tion [of §2543] could undercut much of the PVPA's incentives," *id.,* at 491, the Court of Appeals saw nothing in §2543 that would limit the sale of protected seed (for reproduc-tive purposes) to the amount necessary to plant the seller's own acreage. Rather, as the Court of Appeals read the statute, §2543 permits a farmer to sell up to half of every crop he produces from PVPA-protected seed to another farmer for use as seed, so long as he sells the other 50 percent of the crop grown from that specific variety for nonre-productive purposes, *e.g.,* for food or feed. The Federal Circuit denied Asgrow's petition for rehearing and suggestion for rehearing en banc by a vote of six judges to five. 989 F.2d 478 (1993). We granted certiorari. 511 U.S. 1029, 114 S.Ct. 1535, 128 L.Ed.2d 189 (1994).

II

It may be well to acknowledge at the outset that it is quite impossible to make complete sense of the provision at issue here. One need go no further than the very first words of its title to establish that. Section 2543 does *not,* as that title claims and the ensuing text says, reserve any "[r]ight to save seed"—since nothing elsewhere in the Act remotely prohibits the saving of seed. Nor, under any possible analysis, is the proviso in the first sentence of §2543 ("*Provided,* That") really a proviso.

With this advance warning that not all mysteries will be solved, we enter the verbal maze of §2543. The entrance, we discover, is actually an exit, since the provision begins by excepting certain activities from its operation: "*Except to the extent that such action may constitute an infringement under subsections (3) and (4) of section 2541 of this title,* it shall not infringe any right hereunder for a person to save seed produced by him ... and use such saved seed in the production of a crop for use on his farm, or for sale as pro-

---

2. Congress has recently amended this section. That amendment has the effect of eliminating the exemption from infringement liability for farmers who sell PVPA-protected seed to other farm-ers for reproductive purposes.

vided in this section...." (Emphasis added.) Thus, a farmer does not qualify for the exemption from infringement liability if he has

"(3) sexually multipl[ied] the novel variety as a step in marketing (for growing purposes) the variety; or (4) use[d] the novel variety in producing (as distinguished from developing) a hybrid or different variety therefrom." 7 U.S.C. §§ 2541(3)–(4).

In 1990, the Winterboers planted 265 acres of Asgrow protected variety seed and collected a harvest of 12,037 bushels of soybeans. The parties do not dispute that this act of planting and harvesting constituted "sexual multiplication" of the novel varieties. See 7 U.S.C. § 2401(f) (defining "sexually reproduced" seed to include "any production of a variety by seed"). The Winterboers sold almost all of these beans for use as seed (*i.e.*, "for growing purposes"), without Asgrow's consent. The central question in this case, then, is whether the Winterboers' planting and harvesting were conducted "as a step in marketing" Asgrow's protected seed varieties for growing purposes. If they were, the Winterboers were not eligible for the § 2543 exemption, and the District Court was right to grant summary judgment to Asgrow.

The PVPA does not define "marketing." When terms used in a statute are undefined, we give them their ordinary meaning. *FDIC v. Meyer*, 510 U.S. 471, 476, 114 S.Ct. 996, 1001, 127 L.Ed.2d 308 (1994). The Federal Circuit believed that the word "marketing" requires "extensive or coordinated selling activities, such as advertising, using an intervening sales representative, or similar extended merchandising or retail activities." 982 F.2d, at 492. We disagree. Marketing ordinarily refers to the act of holding forth property for sale, together with the activities preparatory thereto (in the present case, cleaning, drying, bagging, and pricing the seeds). The word does not require that the promotional or merchandising activities connected with the selling be extensive. One can market apples by simply displaying them on a cart with a price tag; or market a stock by simply listing it on a stock exchange; or market a house (we would normally say "place it on the market") by simply setting a "for sale" sign on the front lawn. Indeed, some dictionaries give as one meaning of "market" simply "to sell." See, *e.g.*, Oxford Universal Dictionary 1208 (3d ed. 1955); Webster's New International Dictionary 1504 (2d ed. 1950). Of course, effective selling often involves extensive promotional activities, and when they occur they are all part of the "marketing." But even when the holding forth for sale relies upon no more than word-of-mouth advertising, a marketing of goods is in process. Moreover, even if the word "marketing" could, in one of its meanings, demand extensive promotion, we see no reason why the law at issue here would intend that meaning. That would have the effect of preserving PVPA protection for less valuable plant varieties, but eliminating it for varieties so desirable that they can be marketed by word of mouth; as well as the effect of requiring courts to ponder the difficult question of how much promotion is necessary to constitute marketing. We think that when the statute refers to sexually multiplying a variety "as a step in marketing," it means growing seed of the variety for the purpose of putting the crop up for sale.[3]

---

3. The dissent asserts that the Federal Circuit's more demanding interpretation of "marketing" is supported by the ancient doctrine disfavoring restraints on alienation of property, see *post*, at 796–797. The wellspring of that doctrine, of course, is concern for property rights, and in the context of the PVPA it is the dissent's interpretation, rather than ours, which belittles that concern. The whole purpose of the statute is to create a valuable property in the product of botanical research by giving the developer the right to "exclude others from selling the variety, or offering it for sale, or reproducing it, or importing it, or exporting it," etc. 7 U.S.C. § 2483. Applying the rule disfavoring restraints on alienation to interpretation of the PVPA is rather like applying the rule disfavoring restraints upon freedom of contract to interpretation of the Sherman Act.

[FN3] Under the exception set out in the first clause of § 2543, then, a farmer is not eligible for the § 2543 exemption if he plants and saves seeds for the purpose of selling the seeds that they produce for replanting

Section 2543 next provides that, so long as a person is not violating either §§ 2541(3) or (4),

"it shall not infringe any right hereunder for a person to *save seed* produced by him from seed obtained, or descended from seed obtained, by authority of the owner of the variety for seeding purposes and use *such saved seed* in the production of a crop for use on his farm, or for sale as provided in this section...." (Emphasis added.)

Farmers generally grow crops to sell. A harvested soybean crop is typically removed from the farmer's premises in short order and taken to a grain elevator or processor. Sometimes, however, in the case of a plant such as the soybean, in which the crop is the seed, the farmer will have a portion of his crop cleaned and stored as seed for replanting his fields next season. We think it clear that this seed *saved for replanting* is what the provision under discussion means by "saved seed"—not merely regular uncleaned crop that is stored for later market sale or use as fodder.

There are two ways to read the provision, depending upon which words the phrase "for sale as provided in this section" is taken to modify. It can be read "production of a crop ... for sale as provided in this section"; or alternatively "use such saved seed ... for sale as provided in this section." The parallelism created by the phrase "*for* use on his farm" followed immediately by "or *for* sale as provided in this section," suggests the former reading. But the placement of the comma, separating "use [of] such saved seed in the production of a crop for use on his farm," from "or for sale", favors the latter reading. So does the fact that the alternative reading requires the reader to skip the lengthy "*Provided,* That" clause in order to find out what sales are "provided [for] in this section"—despite the parallelism between "provided" and "*Provided,*" and despite the presence of a colon, which ordinarily indicates specification of what has preceded. It is surely easier to think that at least some of the sales "provided for" are those that are "Provided" after the colon. (It is, of course, not unusual, however deplorable it may be, for "Provided, That" to be used as prologue to an addition rather than an exception. See *Springer v. Philippine Islands,* 277 U.S. 189, 206, 48 S.Ct. 480, 483–484, 72 L.Ed. 845 (1928); 1A N. Singer, Sutherland on Statutory Construction § 20.22 (5th ed. 1992).)

We think the latter reading is also to be preferred because it lends greater meaning to all the provisions. Under the former reading ("production of a crop ... for sale as provided in this section"), the only later text that could be referred to is the provision for "bona fide sale[s] for other than reproductive purposes" set out in the second sentence of § 2543—the so-called "crop exemption." (The proviso could *not* be referred to, since it does not provide for sale of *crops* grown from saved seed, but only for sale of saved seed itself.) But if the "or for sale" provision has such a limited referent, the opening clause's ("Except to the extent that ...") reservation of § 2541(3) infringement liability (*i.e.,* liability for growing as a step in marketing for reproductive purposes) would be devoid of content, since the provision to which it is attached would *permit* no sales for reproductive purposes. Under the latter reading, by contrast, the farmer may not "use [his] saved seed ... for sale" as the proviso allows *if* the seed was intentionally grown for the purpose of such sale-*i.e.,* "sexually multipl [ied] ... as a step in marketing (for growing purposes) the variety."

A second respect in which our favored reading gives greater meaning to the provision is this: The other reading ("crop ... for sale as provided in this section") causes the "permission" given in the opening sentence to extend only to sales for nonreproductive purposes of the *crops grown* from saved seed, as opposed to sales of the saved seed itself. But no separate permission would have been required for this, since it is already contained within the crop exemption itself; it serves only as a *reminder* that crop from saved seed can be sold under that exemption—a peculiarly incomplete reminder, since the saved seed *itself* can also be sold under that exemption.

To summarize: By reason of its proviso the first sentence of § 2543 allows seed that has been preserved for reproductive purposes ("saved seed") to be sold for such purposes. The structure of the sentence is such, however, that this authorization does *not* extend to saved seed that was grown *for the very purpose* of sale ("marketing") for replanting—because in that case, § 2541(3) would be violated, and the above-discussed exception to the exemption would apply. As a practical matter, since § 2541(1) prohibits all unauthorized transfer of title to, or possession of, the protected variety, this means that the only seed that can be sold under the proviso is seed that has been saved by the farmer to replant his own acreage.[5] (We think that limitation is also apparent from the text of the crop exemption, which permits a farm crop from saved seeds to be sold—for nonreproductive purposes—only if those saved seeds were "produced by descent *on such farm.*" (Emphasis added.) It is in our view the proviso in § 2543, and not the crop exemption, that authorizes the permitted buyers of saved seeds to sell the crops they produce.) Thus, if a farmer saves seeds to replant his acreage, but for some reason changes his plans, he may instead sell those seeds for replanting under the terms set forth in the proviso (or of course sell them for nonreproductive purposes under the crop exemption).

It remains to discuss one final feature of the proviso authorizing limited sales for reproductive purposes. The proviso allows sales of saved seed for replanting purposes only between persons "whose primary farming occupation is the growing of crops for sale for other than reproductive purposes." The Federal Circuit, which rejected the proposition that the only seed sellable under the exemption is seed saved for the farmer's own replanting, sought to achieve some limitation upon the quantity of seed that can be sold for reproductive purposes by adopting a "crop-by-crop" approach to the "primary farming occupation" requirement of the proviso. "[B]uyers or sellers of brown bag seed qualify for the crop exemption," it concluded, "only if they produce a larger crop from a protected seed for consumption (or other nonreproductive purposes) than for sale as seed." 982 F.2d, at 490. That is to say, the brown-bag seller can sell no more than half of his protected crop for seed. The words of the statute, however, stand in the way of this creative (if somewhat insubstantial) limitation.

To ask what is a farmer's "primary farming occupation" is to ask what constitutes the bulk of his total farming business. Selling crops for other than reproductive purposes must constitute the preponderance of the farmer's business, not just the preponderance

---

5. For crops such as soybeans, in which the seed and the harvest are one and the same, this will mean enough seeds for one year's crop on that acreage. Since the germination rate of a batch of seed declines over time, the soybean farmer will get the year-after-next's seeds from next year's harvest. That is not so for some vegetable crops, in which the seed is not the harvest, and a portion of the crop must be permitted to overripen ("go to seed") in order to obtain seeds. One of the *amici* in the Court of Appeals asserted (and the parties before us did not dispute) that it is the practice of vegetable farmers to "grow" seeds only every four or five years, and to "brown bag" enough seed for four or five future crops. A vegetable farmer who sets aside protected seed with subsequent replantings in mind, but who later abandons his plan (because he has sold his farm, for example), would under our analysis be able to sell all his saved seed, even though it would plant (in a single year) four or five times his current acreage.

of his business in the protected seed. There is simply no way to derive from this text the narrower focus that the Federal Circuit applied. Thus, if the quantity of seed that can be sold is not limited as we have described—by reference to the original purpose for which the seed is saved—then it is barely limited at all (*i.e.,* limited only by the volume or worth of the selling farmer's total crop sales for other than reproductive purposes). This seems to us a most unlikely result.

* * *

We hold that a farmer who meets the requirements set forth in the proviso to § 2543 may sell for reproductive purposes only such seed as he has saved for the purpose of replanting his own acreage. While the meaning of the text is by no means clear, this is in our view the only reading that comports with the statutory purpose of affording "adequate encouragement for research, and for marketing when appropriate, to yield for the public the benefits of new varieties." 7 U.S.C. § 2581. Because we find the sales here were unlawful, we do not reach the second question on which we granted certiorari—whether sales authorized under § 2543 remain subject to the notice requirement of § 2541(6).

The judgment of the Court of Appeals for the Federal Circuit is

Reversed.

Justice STEVENS, dissenting.

The key to this statutory puzzle is the meaning of the phrase, "as a step in marketing," as used in 7 U.S.C. § 2541(a)(3) (1988 ed., Supp. V). If it is synonymous with "for the purpose of selling," as the Court holds, see *ante,* at 793, then the majority's comprehensive exposition of the statute is correct. I record my dissent only because that phrase conveys a different message to me.

There must be a reason why Congress used the word "marketing" rather than the more common term "selling." Indeed, in § 2541(a)(1), contained in the same subsection of the statute as the crucial language, Congress made it an act of infringement to "sell the novel variety." Yet, in § 2541(a)(3), a mere two clauses later, Congress eschewed the word "sell" in favor of "marketing." Because Congress obviously could have prohibited sexual multiplication "as a step in selling," I presume that when it elected to prohibit sexual multiplication only "as a step in marketing (for growing purposes) the variety," Congress meant something different.

Moreover, as used in this statute, "marketing" must be narrower, not broader, than selling. The majority is correct that one meaning of "marketing" is the act of selling and all acts preparatory thereto. See *ante,* at 793. But Congress has prohibited only one preparatory act—that of sexual multiplication—and only when it is a step in marketing. Under the majority's broad definition of "marketing," prohibiting sexual multiplication "as a step in marketing" can be no broader than prohibiting sexual multiplication "as a step in selling," because all steps in marketing are, ultimately, steps in selling. If "marketing" can be no broader than "selling," and if Congress did not intend the two terms to be coextensive, then "marketing" must encompass something less than all "selling."

The statute as a whole—and as interpreted by the Court of Appeals—indicates that Congress intended to preserve the farmer's right to engage in so-called "brown-bag sales" of seed to neighboring farmers. Congress limited that right by the express requirement that such sales may not constitute the "primary farming occupation" of either the buyer or the seller. Moreover, § 2541(a)(3) makes it abundantly clear that the unauthorized participation in "marketing" of protected varieties is taboo. If one interprets "marketing" to refer to a subcategory of selling activities, namely, merchandising through farm cooperatives, wholesalers, retailers, or other commercial distributors, the entire statute seems to make sense. I think Congress wanted to allow any ordinary brown-bag sale from one farmer to another; but, as the Court of Appeals concluded, it did not want to permit farmers to compete with seed manufacturers on their own ground, through "extensive or coordinated selling activities, such as advertising, using an intervening sales representative, or similar extended merchandising or retail activities." 982 F.2d 486, 492 (CA Fed.1992).

This reading of the statute is consistent with our time-honored practice of viewing restraints on the alienation of property with disfavor. See, *e.g., Sexton v. Wheaton,* 8 Wheat. 229, 242, 5 L.Ed. 603 (1823) (opinion of Marshall, C.J.). (footnote omitted). The seed at issue is part of a crop planted and harvested by a farmer on his own property. Generally the owner of personal property—even a patented or copyrighted article—is free to dispose of that property as he sees fit. See, *e.g., United States v. Univis Lens Co.,* 316 U.S. 241, 250–252, 62 S.Ct. 1088, 1093–1094, 86 L.Ed. 1408 (1942); *Bobbs-Merrill Co. v. Straus,* 210 U.S. 339, 350–351, 28 S.Ct. 722, 726, 52 L.Ed. 1086 (1908). A statutory restraint on this basic freedom should be expressed clearly and unambiguously. Cf. *Deepsouth Packing Co. v. Laitram Corp.,* 406 U.S. 518, 530–531, 92 S.Ct. 1700, 1708, 32 L.Ed.2d 273 (1972). As the majority recognizes, the meaning of this statute is "by no means clear." *Ante,* at 796. Accordingly, both because I am persuaded that the Court of Appeals correctly interpreted the intent of Congress, and because doubts should be resolved against purported restraints on freedom, I would affirm the judgment below.

J.E.M. AG SUPPLY, INC., et al., Petitioners,
v.
PIONEER HI-BRED INTERNATIONAL, INC.

Supreme Court of the United States
151 L.Ed.2d 508, 70 USLW 4032, 60 U.S.P.Q.2d 1865
Argued Oct. 3, 2001.
Decided Dec. 10, 2001.
Rehearing Denied April 15, 2002.
See 535 U.S. 1013, 122 S.Ct. 1600.

Affirmed.

THOMAS, J., delivered the opinion of the Court, in which REHNQUIST, C.J., and SCALIA, KENNEDY, SOUTER, and GINSBURG, JJ., joined. SCALIA, J., filed a concurring opinion, *post,* p. 606. BREYER, J., filed a dissenting opinion, in which STEVENS, J., joined, *post,* p. 607. O'CONNOR, J., took no part in the consideration or decision of the case.

Justice THOMAS delivered the opinion of the Court.

This case presents the question whether utility patents may be issued for plants under 35 U.S.C. § 101 (1994 ed.), or whether the Plant Variety Protection Act, 84 Stat. 1542, as amended, 7 U.S.C. § 2321 *et seq.,* and the Plant Patent Act of 1930, 35 U.S.C. §§ 161–164 (1994 ed. and Supp. V), are the exclusive means of obtaining a federal statutory right to exclude others from reproducing, selling, or using plants or plant varieties. We hold that utility patents may be issued for plants.

I

The United States Patent and Trademark Office (PTO) has issued some 1,800 utility patents for plants, plant parts, and seeds pursuant to 35 U.S.C. § 101. Seventeen of these patents are held by respondent Pioneer Hi-Bred International, Inc. (Pioneer). Pioneer's patents cover the manufacture, use, sale, and offer for sale of the company's inbred and hybrid corn seed products. A patent for an inbred corn line protects both the seeds and plants of the inbred line and the hybrids produced by crossing the protected inbred line with another corn line. See, *e.g.,* U.S. Patent No. 5,506,367, col. 3, App. 42. A hybrid plant patent protects the plant, its seeds, variants, mutants, and trivial modifications of the hybrid. See U.S. Patent No. 5,491,295, cols. 2–3, *id.,* at 29–30.

Pedigree inbred corn plants are developed by crossing corn plants with desirable characteristics and then inbreeding the resulting plants for several generations until the resulting plant line is homogenous. Inbreds are often weak and have a low yield; their value lies primarily in their use for making hybrids. See, *e.g.,* U.S. Patent No. 5,506,367, col. 6, *id.,* at 43 (describing the traits and applications of the inbred corn line PHP38 by reference to the qualities exhibited in hybrid plants created with PHP38).

Hybrid seeds are produced by crossing two inbred corn plants and are especially valuable because they produce strong and vibrant hybrid plants with selected highly desirable characteristics. For instance, Pioneer's hybrid corn plant 3394 is "characterized by superior yield for maturity, excellent seedling vigor, very good roots and stalks, and exceptional stay green." U.S. Patent No. 5,491,295, cols. 2–3, *id.,* at 29–30. Hybrid plants, however, generally do not reproduce true-to-type, *i.e.,* seeds produced by a hybrid plant do not reliably yield plants with the same hybrid characteristics. Thus, a farmer who wishes to continue growing hybrid plants generally needs to buy more hybrid seed.

Pioneer sells its patented hybrid seeds under a limited label license that provides: "License is granted solely to produce grain and/or forage." *Id.,* at 51. The license "does not extend to the use of seed from such crop or the progeny thereof for propagation or seed multiplication." *Ibid.* It strictly prohibits "the use of such seed or the progeny thereof for propagation or seed multiplication or for production or development of a hybrid or different variety of seed." *Ibid.*

Petitioner J.E.M. Ag Supply, Inc., doing business as Farm Advantage, Inc., purchased patented hybrid seeds from Pioneer in bags bearing this license agreement. Although not a licensed sales representative of Pioneer, Farm Advantage resold these bags. Pioneer subsequently brought a complaint for patent infringement against Farm Advantage and several other corporations and residents of the State of Iowa who are distributors and customers for Farm Advantage (referred to collectively as Farm Advantage or petitioners). Pioneer alleged that Farm Advantage has "for a long-time past been and still [is] infringing one or more [Pioneer patents] by making, using, selling, or offering for sale corn seed of the ... hybrids in infringement of these patents-in-suit." *Id.,* at 10.

Farm Advantage answered with a general denial of patent infringement and entered a counterclaim of patent invalidity, arguing that patents that purport to confer protection for corn plants are invalid because sexually reproducing plants are not patentable subject matter within the scope of 35 U.S.C. § 101 spacing. App. 12–13, 17. Farm Advantage maintained that the Plant Patent Act of 1930 (PPA) and the Plant Variety Protection Act (PVPA) set forth the exclusive statutory means for the protection of plant life because these statutes are more specific than § 101, and thus each carves out subject matter from § 101 for special treatment.[1]

II

The question before us is whether utility patents may be issued for plants pursuant to 35 U.S.C. § 101 (1994 ed.). The text of § 101 provides:

"Whoever invents or discovers any new and useful process, machine, manufacture, or composition of matter, or any new and useful improvement thereof, may obtain a patent therefor, subject to the conditions and requirements of this title." As this Court recognized over 20 years ago in *Chakrabarty,* 447 U.S., at 308, 100 S.Ct. 2204, the language of § 101 is extremely broad. "In choosing such expansive terms as 'manufacture' and 'composition of matter,' modified by the comprehensive 'any,' Congress plainly contemplated that the patent laws would be given wide scope." *Ibid.* This Court thus concluded in *Chakrabarty* that living things were patentable under § 101, and held that a manmade micro-organism fell within the scope of the statute. As Congress recognized, "the relevant distinction was not between living and inanimate things, but between products of nature, whether living or not, and human-made inventions." *Id.,* at 313, 100 S.Ct. 2204.

In *Chakrabarty,* the Court also rejected the argument that Congress must expressly authorize protection for new patentable subject matter.

...

Several years after *Chakrabarty,* the PTO Board of Patent Appeals and Interferences held that plants were within the understood meaning of "manufacture" or "composition of matter" and therefore were within the subject matter of § 101. *In re Hibberd,* 227 USPQ 443, 444, 1985 WL 71986 (1985). It has been the unbroken practice of the PTO since that time to confer utility patents for plants. To obtain utility patent protection, a plant breeder must show that the plant he has developed is new, useful, and non-obvious. 35 U.S.C. §§ 101–103 (1994 ed. and Supp. V). In addition, the plant must meet the specifications of § 112, which require a written description of the plant and a deposit of seed that is publicly accessible. See 37 CFR §§ 1.801–1.809 (2001).

Petitioners do not allege that Pioneer's patents are invalid for failure to meet the requirements for a utility patent. Nor do they dispute that plants otherwise fall within the terms of § 101's broad language that includes "manufacture" or "composition of matter." Rather, petitioners argue that the PPA and the PVPA provide the exclusive means of protecting new varieties of plants, and so awarding utility patents for plants upsets the scheme contemplated by Congress. Brief for Petitioners 11. We disagree. Considering the two plant specific statutes in turn, we find that neither forecloses utility patent coverage for plants.

A

The 1930 PPA conferred patent protection to asexually reproduced plants. Significantly, nothing within either the original 1930 text of the statute or its recodified version in

---

1. Petitioners favor a holding that the PVPA is the only means of protecting these corn plants primarily because the PVPA's coverage is generally less extensive and the hybrid seeds at issue do not have PVPA protection. App. 14. Most notably, the PVPA provides exemptions for research and for farmers to save seed from their crops for replanting. See, *infra,* at 603. Utility patents issued for plants do not contain such exemptions.

1952 indicates that the PPA's protection for asexually reproduced plants was intended to be exclusive.

Plants were first explicitly brought within the scope of patent protection in 1930 when the PPA included "plants" among the useful things subject to patents. Thus the 1930 PPA amended the general utility patent provision, Rev. Stat. § 4886, to provide:

"Any person who has invented or discovered any new and useful art, machine, manufacture, or composition of matter, or any new and useful improvements thereof, or who has invented or discovered and asexually reproduced any distinct and new variety of plant, other than a tuber-propagated plant, not known or used by others in this country, before his invention or discovery thereof, ... may ... obtain a patent therefor." Act of May 23, 1930, § 1, 46 Stat. 376.

This provision limited protection to the asexual reproduction of the plant. Asexual reproduction occurs by grafting, budding, or the like, and produces an offspring with a genetic combination identical to that of the single parent—essentially a clone.[3] [FN3] The PPA also amended Revised Statutes § 4888 by adding: "No plant patent shall be declared invalid on the ground of noncompliance with this section if the description is made as complete as is reasonably possible." *Id.,* § 2, 46 Stat. 376.

In 1952, Congress revised the patent statute and placed the plant patents into a separate chapter 15 of Title 35 entitled, "Patents for plants." 35 U.S.C. §§ 161–164. This was merely a housekeeping measure that did nothing to change the substantive rights or requirements for a plant patent. A "plant patent" continued to provide only the exclusive right to asexually reproduce a protected plant, § 163, and the description requirement remained relaxed, § 162. Plant patents under the PPA thus have very limited coverage and less stringent requirements than § 101 utility patents.

Importantly, chapter 15 nowhere states that plant patents are the exclusive means of granting intellectual property protection to plants. Although unable to point to any language that requires, or even suggests, that Congress intended the PPA's protections to be exclusive, petitioners advance three reasons why the PPA should preclude assigning utility patents for plants. We find none of these arguments to be persuasive.

First, petitioners argue that plants were not covered by the general utility patent statute prior to 1930. Brief for Petitioners 19 ("If the patent laws before 1930 allowed patents on 'plants' then there would have been no reason for Congress to have passed the 1930 PPA ..."). In advancing this argument, petitioners overlook the state of patent law and plant breeding at the time of the PPA's enactment. The Court in *Chakrabarty* explained the realities of patent law and plant breeding at the time the PPA was enacted: "Prior to 1930, two factors were thought to remove plants from patent protection. The first was the belief that plants, even those artificially bred, were products of nature for purposes of the patent law....

The second obstacle to patent protection for plants was the fact that plants were thought not amenable to the 'written description' requirement of the patent law." 447 U.S., at 311–312, 100 S.Ct. 2204. Congress addressed these concerns with the 1930 PPA, which recognized that the work of a plant breeder was a patentable invention and relaxed the written description requirement. See §§ 1–2, 46 Stat. 376. The PPA thus gave patent protection to breeders who were previously unable to overcome the obstacles described in *Chakrabarty*.

---

3. By contrast, sexual reproduction occurs by seed and sometimes involves two different plants.

This does not mean, however, that prior to 1930 plants could not have fallen within the subject matter of § 101. Rather, it illustrates only that in 1930 Congress *believed* that plants were not patentable under § 101, both because they were living things and because in practice they could not meet the stringent description requirement. Yet these premises were disproved over time. As this Court held in *Chakrabarty,* "the relevant distinction" for purposes of § 101 is not "between living and inanimate things, but between products of nature, whether living or not, and human-made inventions." 447 U.S., at 313, 100 S.Ct. 2204. In addition, advances in biological knowledge and breeding expertise have allowed plant breeders to satisfy § 101's demanding description requirement.

Whatever Congress may have believed about the state of patent law and the science of plant breeding in 1930, plants have always had the *potential* to fall within the general subject matter of § 101, which is a dynamic provision designed to encompass new and unforeseen inventions. "A rule that unanticipated inventions are without protection would conflict with the core concept of the patent law that anticipation undermines patentability." *Id.,* at 316, 100 S.Ct. 2204.

Petitioners essentially ask us to deny utility patent protection for sexually reproduced plants because it was unforeseen in 1930 that such plants could receive protection under § 101. Denying patent protection under § 101 simply because such coverage was thought technologically infeasible in 1930, however, would be inconsistent with the forward-looking perspective of the utility patent statute. As we noted in *Chakrabarty,* "Congress employed broad general language in drafting § 101 precisely because [new types of] inventions are often unforeseeable." *Ibid.*

Second, petitioners maintain that the PPA's limitation to asexually reproduced plants would make no sense if Congress intended § 101 to authorize patents on plant varieties that were sexually reproduced. But this limitation once again merely reflects the reality of plant breeding in 1930. At that time, the primary means of reproducing bred plants true-to-type was through asexual reproduction. Congress thought that sexual reproduction through seeds was not a stable way to maintain desirable bred characteristics. Thus, it is hardly surprising that plant patents would protect only asexual reproduction, since this was the most reliable type of reproduction for preserving the desirable characteristics of breeding. See generally E. Sinnott, Botany Principles and Problems 266–267 (1935); J. Priestley & L. Scott, Introduction to Botany 530 (1938).

Furthermore, like other laws protecting intellectual property, the plant patent provision must be understood in its proper context. Until 1924, farmers received seed from the Government's extensive free seed program that distributed millions of packages of seed annually. See Fowler, The Plant Patent Act of 1930: A Sociological History of its Creation, 82 J. Pat. & Tm. Off. Soc. 621, 623, 632 (2000). In 1930, seed companies were not primarily concerned with varietal protection, but were still trying to successfully commodify seeds. There was no need to protect seed breeding because there were few markets for seeds. See Kloppenburg, 71 ("Seed companies' first priority was simply to establish a market, and they continued to view the congressional distribution as a principal constraint").

By contrast, nurseries at the time had successfully commercialized asexually reproduced fruit trees and flowers. These plants were regularly copied, draining profits from those who discovered or bred new varieties. Nurseries were the primary subjects of agricultural marketing and so it is not surprising that they were the specific focus of the PPA. See Fowler, *supra,* at 634–635; Kneen, Patent Plants Enrich Our World, National Geographic 357, 363 (1948).

Moreover, seed companies at the time could not point to genuinely new varieties and lacked the scientific knowledge to engage in formal breeding that would increase agricultural productivity. See Kloppenburg, 77; Fowler, *supra,* at 633 ("Absent significant numbers of distinct new varieties being produced by seed companies, variety protection through something like a patent law would hardly have been considered a business necessity"). In short, there is simply no evidence, let alone the overwhelming evidence needed to establish repeal by implication, see *Matsushita Elec. Industrial Co. v. Epstein,* 516 U.S. 367, 381, 116 S.Ct. 873, 134 L.Ed.2d 6 (1996), that Congress, by specifically protecting asexually reproduced plants through the PPA, intended to preclude utility patent protection for sexually reproduced plants.

Third, petitioners argue that in 1952 Congress would not have moved plants out of the utility patent provision and into § 161 if it had intended § 101 to allow for protection of plants. Brief for Petitioners 20. Petitioners again rely on negative inference because they cannot point to any express indication that Congress intended § 161 to be the exclusive means of patenting plants. But this negative inference simply does not support carving out subject matter that otherwise fits comfortably within the expansive language of § 101, especially when § 101 can protect different attributes and has more stringent requirements than does § 161.

This is especially true given that Congress in 1952 did nothing to change the substantive rights or requirements for obtaining a plant patent. Absent a clear intent to the contrary, we are loath to interpret what was essentially a housekeeping measure as an affirmative decision by Congress to deny sexually reproduced plants patent protection under § 101.

B

By passing the PVPA in 1970, Congress specifically authorized limited patent-like protection for certain sexually reproduced plants. Petitioners therefore argue that this legislation evidences Congress' intent to deny broader § 101 utility patent protection for such plants. Petitioners' argument, however, is unavailing for two reasons. First, nowhere does the PVPA purport to provide the exclusive statutory means of protecting sexually reproduced plants. Second, the PVPA and § 101 can easily be reconciled. Because it is harder to qualify for a utility patent than for a Plant Variety Protection (PVP) certificate, it only makes sense that utility patents would confer a greater scope of protection.

1

The PVPA provides plant variety protection for:

"The breeder of any sexually reproduced or tuber propagated plant variety (other than fungi or bacteria) who has so reproduced the variety...." 7 U.S.C. § 2402(a).

Infringement of plant variety protection occurs, *inter alia,* if someone sells or markets the protected variety, sexually multiplies the variety as a step in marketing, uses the variety in producing a hybrid, or dispenses the variety without notice that the variety is protected.

Since the 1994 amendments, the PVPA also protects "any variety that is essentially derived from a protected variety," § 2541(c)(1), and "any variety whose production requires the repeated use of a protected variety," § 2541(c)(3). See Plant Variety Protection Act Amendments of 1994, § 9, 108 Stat. 3142. Practically, this means that hybrids created from protected plant varieties are also protected; however, it is not infringement to use a protected variety for the development of a hybrid. See 7 U.S.C. § 2541(a)(4).[1]

The PVPA also contains exemptions for saving seed and for research. A farmer who legally purchases and plants a protected variety can save the seed from these plants for replanting on his own farm. See § 2543 ("[I]t shall not infringe any right hereunder for a person to save seed produced by the person from seed obtained, or descended from seed obtained, by authority of the owner of the variety for seeding purposes and use such saved seed in the production of a crop for use on the farm of the person …"); see also *Asgrow Seed Co. v. Winterboer*, 513 U.S. 179, 115 S.Ct. 788, 130 L.Ed.2d 682 (1995). In addition, a protected variety may be used for research. See 7 U.S.C. § 2544 ("The use and reproduction of a protected variety for plant breeding or other bona fide research shall not constitute an infringement of the protection provided under this chapter"). The utility patent statute does not contain similar exemptions.

Thus, while the PVPA creates a statutory scheme that is comprehensive with respect to its particular protections and subject matter, giving limited protection to plant varieties that are new, distinct, uniform, and stable, § 2402(a), nowhere does it restrict the scope of patentable subject matter under § 101. With nothing in the statute to bolster their view that the PVPA provides the exclusive means for protecting sexually reproducing plants, petitioners rely on the legislative history of the PVPA. They argue that this history shows the PVPA was enacted because sexually reproducing plant varieties and their seeds were not and had never been intended by Congress to be included within the classes of things patentable under Title 35.

The PVPA itself, however, contains no statement that PVP certificates were to be the exclusive means of protecting sexually reproducing plants. The relevant statements in the legislative history reveal nothing more than the limited view of plant breeding taken by some Members of Congress who believed that patent protection was unavailable for sexually reproduced plants. This view stems from a lack of awareness concerning scientific possibilities.

Furthermore, at the time the PVPA was enacted, the PTO had already issued numerous utility patents for hybrid plant processes. Many of these patents, especially since the 1950's, included claims on the products of the patented process, *i.e.,* the hybrid plant itself. See Kloppenburg, 264. Such plants were protected as part of a hybrid process and not on their own. Nonetheless, these hybrids still enjoyed protection under § 101, which reaffirms that such material was within the scope of § 101.

2

Petitioners next argue that the PVPA altered the subject-matter coverage of § 101 by implication. Brief for Petitioners 33–36. Yet "the only permissible justification for a repeal by implication is when the earlier and later statutes are irreconcilable." *Morton v. Mancari,* 417 U.S. 535, 550, 94 S.Ct. 2474, 41 L.Ed.2d 290 (1974). "The rarity with which [the Court has] discovered implied repeals is due to the relatively stringent standard for such findings, namely, that there be an irreconcilable conflict between the two federal statutes at issue." *Matsushita,* 516 U.S., at 381, 116 S.Ct. 873 (internal quotation marks omitted).

To be sure, there are differences in the requirements for, and coverage of, utility patents and PVP certificates issued pursuant to the PVPA. These differences, however, do not

---

1. It is, however, infringement of a utility patent to use a protected plant in the development of another variety. See *infra,* at 604–605.

present irreconcilable conflicts because the requirements for obtaining a utility patent under § 101 are more stringent than those for obtaining a PVP certificate, and the protections afforded by a utility patent are greater than those afforded by a PVP certificate. Thus, there is a parallel relationship between the obligations and the level of protection under each statute.

It is much more difficult to obtain a utility patent for a plant than to obtain a PVP certificate because a utility patentable plant must be new, useful, and nonobvious, 35 U.S.C. §§ 101–103. In addition, to obtain a utility patent, a breeder must describe the plant with sufficient specificity to enable others to "make and use" the invention after the patent term expires. § 112. The disclosure required by the Patent Act is "the *quid pro quo* of the right to exclude." *Kewanee Oil Co. v. Bicron Corp.*, 416 U.S. 470, 484, 94 S.Ct. 1879, 40 L.Ed.2d 315 (1974). The description requirement for plants includes a deposit of biological material, for example, seeds, and mandates that such material be accessible to the public. See 37 CFR §§ 1.801–1.809 (2001); see also App. 39 (seed deposits for U.S. Patent No. 5,491,295).

By contrast, a plant variety may receive a PVP certificate without a showing of usefulness or nonobviousness. See 7 U.S.C. § 2402(a) (requiring that the variety be only new, distinct, uniform, and stable). Nor does the PVPA require a description and disclosure as extensive as those required under § 101. The PVPA requires a "description of the variety setting forth its distinctiveness, uniformity and stability and a description of the genealogy and breeding procedure, when known." 7 U.S.C. § 2422(2). It also requires a deposit of seed in a public depository, § 2422(4), but neither the statute nor the applicable regulation mandates that such material be accessible to the general public during the term of the PVP certificate. See 7 CFR § 97.6 (2001).

Because of the more stringent requirements, utility patent holders receive greater rights of exclusion than holders of a PVP certificate. Most notably, there are no exemptions for research or saving seed under a utility patent. Additionally, although Congress increased the level of protection under the PVPA in 1994, a PVP certificate still does not grant the full range of protections afforded by a utility patent. For instance, a utility patent on an inbred plant line protects that line as well as all hybrids produced by crossing that inbred with another plant line. Similarly, the PVPA now protects "any variety whose production requires the repeated use of a protected variety." 7 U.S.C. § 2541(c)(3). Thus, one cannot use a protected plant variety to produce a hybrid for commercial sale. PVPA protection still falls short of a utility patent, however, because a breeder can use a plant that is protected by a PVP certificate to "develop" a new inbred line while he cannot use a plant patented under § 101 for such a purpose. See 7 U.S.C. § 2541(a)(4) (infringement includes "use [of] the variety in producing (as distinguished from developing) a hybrid or different variety therefrom"). See also H.R.Rep. No. 91-1605, p. 11 (1970), U.S.Code Cong. & Admin.News 1970, pp. 5082, 5093; 1 D. Chisum, Patents § 1.05[2][d][i], p. 549 (2001).

For all of these reasons, it is clear that there is no "positive repugnancy" between the issuance of utility patents for plants and PVP coverage for plants. *Radzanower v. Touche Ross & Co.*, 426 U.S. 148, 155, 96 S.Ct. 1989, 48 L.Ed.2d 540 (1976). Nor can it be said that the two statutes "cannot mutually coexist." *Ibid.* Indeed, "when two statutes are capable of coexistence, it is the duty of the courts, absent a clearly expressed congressional intention to the contrary, to regard each as effective." *Morton, supra*, at 551, 94 S.Ct. 2474. Here we can plainly regard each statute as effective because of its different requirements and protections. The plain meaning of § 101, as interpreted by this Court in *Chakrabarty*, clearly includes plants within its subject matter. The PPA and the PVPA are not to the contrary and can be read alongside § 101 in protecting plants.

3

Petitioners also suggest that even when statutes overlap and purport to protect the same commercially valuable attribute of a thing, such "dual protection" cannot exist. Brief for Petitioners 44–45. Yet this Court has not hesitated to give effect to two statutes that overlap, so long as each reaches some distinct cases. See *Connecticut Nat. Bank v. Germain,* 503 U.S. 249, 253, 112 S.Ct. 1146, 117 L.Ed.2d 391 (1992) (statutes that overlap "do not pose an either-or proposition" where each confers jurisdiction over cases that the other does not reach). Here, while utility patents and PVP certificates do contain some similar protections, as discussed above, the overlap is only partial.

Moreover, this Court has allowed dual protection in other intellectual property cases. "Certainly the patent policy of encouraging invention is not disturbed by the existence of another form of incentive to invention. In this respect the two systems [trade secret protection and patents] are not and never would be in conflict." *Kewanee Oil, supra,* at 484, 94 S.Ct. 1879; see also *Mazer v. Stein,* 347 U.S. 201, 217, 74 S.Ct. 460, 98 L.Ed. 630 (1954) (the patentability of an object does not preclude the copyright of that object as a work of art). In this case, many plant varieties that are unable to satisfy the stringent requirements of § 101 might still qualify for the lesser protections afforded by the PVPA.

III

We also note that the PTO has assigned utility patents for plants for at least 16 years and there has been no indication from either Congress or agencies with expertise that such coverage is inconsistent with the PVPA or the PPA. The Board of Patent Appeals and Interferences, which has specific expertise in issues of patent law, relied heavily on this Court's decision in *Chakrabarty* when it interpreted the subject matter of § 101 to include plants. *In re Hibberd,* 227 USPQ 443, 1985 WL 71986 (1985). This highly visible decision has led to the issuance of some 1,800 utility patents for plants.

Moreover, the PTO, which administers § 101 as well as the PPA, recognizes and regularly issues utility patents for plants. In addition, the Department of Agriculture's Plant Variety Protection Office acknowledges the existence of utility patents for plants.

In the face of these developments, Congress has not only failed to pass legislation indicating that it disagrees with the PTO's interpretation of § 101; it has even recognized the availability of utility patents for plants. In a 1999 amendment to 35 U.S.C. § 119, which concerns the right of priority for patent rights, Congress provided: "Applications for plant breeder's rights filed in a WTO [World Trade Organization] member country ... shall have the same effect for the purpose of the right of priority ... as applications for patents, subject to the same conditions and requirements of this section as apply to applications for patents." 35 U.S.C. § 119(f) (1994 ed., Supp. V). Crucially, § 119(f) is part of the general provisions of Title 35, not the specific chapter of the PPA, which suggests a recognition on the part of Congress that plants are patentable under § 101.

IV

For these reasons, we hold that newly developed plant breeds fall within the terms of § 101, and that neither the PPA nor the PVPA limits the scope of § 101's coverage. As in *Chakrabarty,* we decline to narrow the reach of § 101 where Congress has given us no indication that it intends this result. 447 U.S., at 315–316, 100 S.Ct. 2204. Accordingly, we affirm the judgment of the Court of Appeals.

It is so ordered.

Justice O'CONNOR took no part in the consideration or decision of this case.

Justice BREYER, with whom Justice STEVENS joins, dissenting.

The question before us is whether the words "manufacture" or "composition of matter" contained in the utility patent statute, 35 U.S.C. § 101 (1994 ed.) (Utility Patent Statute), cover plants that also fall within the scope of two more specific statutes, the Plant Patent Act of 1930(PPA), 35 U.S.C. § 161 *et seq.* (1994 ed. and Supp. V), and the Plant Variety Protection Act (PVPA), 7 U.S.C. § 2321 *et seq.* I believe that the words "manufacture" or "composition of matter" do *not* cover these plants. That is because Congress intended the two more specific statutes to exclude patent protection under the Utility Patent Statute for the plants to which the more specific Acts directly refer. And, as the Court implicitly recognizes, this Court neither considered nor decided this question in *Diamond v. Chakrabarty,* 447 U.S. 303, 100 S.Ct. 2204, 65 L.Ed.2d 144 (1980). Consequently, I dissent.

I

Respondent and the Government claim that *Chakrabarty* controls the outcome in this case. This is incorrect, for *Chakrabarty* said nothing about the specific issue before us.

. . .

II

The critical question, as I have said, is whether the two specific plant statutes embody a legislative intent to deny coverage under the Utility Patent Statute *to those plants to which the specific plant statutes refer.* In my view, the first of these statutes, the PPA, reveals precisely that intent. And nothing in the later history of either the Utility Patent Statute or the PVPA suggests the contrary.

As initially enacted in 1930, the PPA began by amending the Utility Patent Statute to read as follows:

"Any person who has invented or discovered any new and useful art, machine, manufacture, or composition of matter, or any new and useful improvements thereof, *or who has invented or discovered and asexually reproduced any distinct and new variety of plant, other than a tuber-propagated plant* ... may ... obtain a patent therefor[e]." Rev. Stat. § 4886, as amended by Act of May 23, 1930, § 1, 46 Stat. 376 (language added by the PPA italicized).

This language refers to *all* plants. It says that an inventor—in principle—can obtain a patent on *any* plant (the subject matter of the patent) that meets three requirements. It must be distinct; it must be new; and on one or more occasions it must have been "asexually reproduced," *e.g.,* reproduced by means of a graft.

This last-mentioned "graft" requirement does not separate (1) those plants that can reproduce through grafting from (2) those plants that can reproduce by seed. The two categories are not mutually exclusive. P. Raven, R. Evert, & S. Eichhorn, Biology of Plants 179–180, 255 (6th ed.1999). Many plants—perhaps virtually any plant—can be reproduced "asexually" as well as by seed. S.Rep. No. 315, 71st Cong., 2d Sess., 5 (1930). Rather, the "asexual reproduction" requirement sought to ensure that the inventor was capable of reproducing the new variety "asexually" (through a graft) because that fact would guarantee that the variety's new characteristics had genetic (rather than, say, environmental) causes and would prove genetically stable over time. See *ibid.* ("A plant patent covers only the exclusive right of asexual reproduction, and obviously it would be futile to grant a patent for a new and distinct variety unless the variety had been demonstrated to be susceptible to asexual reproduction"); cf. *Dunn v. Ragin,* 50 USPQ 472, 474, 1941 WL 9724 (1941) noting that asexual reproduction "determine[s] that the progeny in fact possess the characteristic or characteristics which distinguish it as a new variety").

Although the section defining the PPA's coverage does not limit its scope to plants that reproduce primarily through grafting, a later section does so limit the protection that it offers. That section specifies that the patent holder will receive "the exclusive right to asexually reproduce the plant," *e.g.,* the right to reproduce it through grafting, but he will not receive an exclusive right to reproduce the plant sexually, *i.e.,* the right to reproduce it through seeds. 46 Stat. 376. And this is true *regardless* of whether the patent holder could reproduce true to type offspring through seeds. See S.Rep. No. 315, at 4 ("On the other hand, [the PPA] does not give any patent protection to the right of propagation of the new variety by seed, irrespective of the degree to which the seedlings come true to type"). This was a significant limitation because, the Court's contrary claim notwithstanding, *ante,* at 600, and n. 7, it was readily apparent in 1930 that a plant's desirable characteristics *could* be preserved through reproduction by seed. See Fowler, The Plant Patent Act of 1930: A Sociological History of its Creation, 82 J. Pat. & Tm. Off. Soc. 621, 635, 644 (2000).

In sum, the PPA permits patenting of new and distinct varieties of (1) plants that breeders primarily reproduce through grafts (say, apple trees), (2) plants that breeders primarily reproduce through seeds (say, corn), and (3) plants that reproduce both ways (say, violets). See C. Chong, Plant Propagation, reprinted in 1 CRC Handbook of Plant Science in Agriculture 91-92, 94, 104 (B. Christie & A. Hanson eds., 1987); Raven, Evert, & Eichhorn, *supra,* at 179. But, because that statute left plant buyers free to keep, to reproduce, and to sell seeds, the statute likely proved helpful *only* to those in the first category. Both the PPA's legislative history and the earliest patents granted under the Act fully support this interpretation. See S.Rep. No. 315, at 3 explaining that varieties that "resul[t] from seedlings of cross pollenization of two species" were patentable under the Act); Plant Patent Nos. 1–2, 5–6, 8–11 (roses); Plant Patent Nos. 7, 15 (peach trees).

Given these characteristics, the PPA is incompatible with the claim that the Utility Patent Statute's language ("manufacture, or composition of matter") also covers plants. To see why that is so, simply imagine a plant breeder who, in 1931, sought to patent a new, distinct variety of plant that he invented but which he has *never been able to reproduce through grafting, i.e., asexually.* Because he could not reproduce it through grafting, he could not patent it under the more specific terms of the PPA. Could he nonetheless patent it under the more general Utility Patent Statute language "manufacture, or composition of matter?"

Assume the court that tried to answer that question was prescient, *i.e.,* that it knew that this Court, in *Chakrabarty,* 447 U.S., at 311–312, 100 S.Ct. 2204, would say that the Utility Patent Statute language ("manufacture," or "composition of matter") in principle might cover "anything under the sun," including bacteria. Such a prescient court would have said that the Utility Patent Statute did cover plants had the case reached it in 1929, before Congress enacted the more specific 1930 law. But how could any court decide the case similarly in 1931 after enactment of the 1930 amendment? To do so would virtually nullify the PPA's primary condition—that the breeder have reproduced the new characteristic through a graft—reading it out of the Act. Moreover, since the Utility Patent Statute would cover, and thereby forbid, reproduction by seed, such a holding would also have read out of the statute the PPA's more limited list of exclusive rights. Consequently, even a prescient court would have had to say, as of 1931, that the 1930 Plant Patent Act had, in amending the Utility Patent Statute, placed the subject matter of the PPA—namely, plants—outside the scope of the words "manufacture, or composition of matter." See *United States v. Estate of Romani,* 523 U.S. 517, 530–533, 118 S.Ct. 1478, 140 L.Ed.2d 710 (1998) (holding that a later, specific statute trumps an earlier, more general statute).

Nothing that occurred after 1930 changes this conclusion. In 1952, the Utility Patent Statute was recodified, and the PPA language I have quoted was given its own separate place in the Code. See 35 U.S.C. § 161 *et seq.* (1994 ed. and Supp. V). As Pioneer itself concedes, that change was not "substantive." Brief for Respondent 7; see also *ante,* at 599. Indeed, as recodified the PPA still allows a breeder to obtain a patent when he "invents or discovers and asexually reproduces *any* distinct and new variety of plant," 35 U.S.C. § 161 (1994 ed.) (emphasis added), but it only allows the patent holder to "exclude others from *asexually* reproducing the plant or selling or using the plant so reproduced," § 163 (emphasis added).

Nor does the enactment of the Plant Variety Protection Act of 1970 change the conclusion. The PVPA proved necessary because plant breeders became capable of creating new and distinct varieties of certain crops, corn, for example, that were valuable only when reproduced through seeds—a form of reproduction that the earlier Act freely permitted. See S.Rep. No. 91-1246, pp. 2–3 (1970). Just prior to its enactment a special Presidential Commission, noting the special problems that plant protection raised and favoring the development of a totally new plant protection scheme, had recommended that "[a]ll provisions in the patent statute for plant patents be deleted…." President's Commission on the Patent System, To Promote the Progress of Useful Arts, S. Doc. No. 5, 90th Cong., 1st Sess., 20–21 (1967) (hereinafter S. Doc.). Instead Congress kept the PPA while adding the PVPA. The PVPA gave patent-like protection (for 20 years) to plants reproduced by seed, and it excluded the PPA's requirement that a breeder have "asexually reproduced" the plant. 7 U.S.C. §§ 2402, 2483. It imposed certain specific requirements. § 2402 (variety must be new, distinct, uniform, and stable). And it provided the breeder with an exclusive right to sell, offer to sell, reproduce, import, or export the variety, including the seeds. § 2483.

At the same time, the PVPA created two important exceptions. The first provided that a farmer who plants his fields with a protected plant "shall not infringe any right hereunder" by saving the seeds and planting them in future years. § 2543. The second permitted "use and reproduction of a protected variety for plant breeding or other bona fide research." § 2544.

Nothing in the history, language, or purpose of the 1970 statute suggests an intent to reintroduce into the scope of the general words "manufacture, or composition of matter" the subject matter that the PPA had removed, namely, plants. To the contrary, any such reintroduction would make meaningless the two exceptions—for planting and for research—that Congress wrote into that Act. It is not surprising that no party argues that passage of the PVPA somehow enlarged the scope of the Utility Patent Statute.

III

The Court replies as follows to the claim that its reading of the Utility Patent Statute nullifies the PPA's limitation of protection to plants produced by graft and the PVPA's exemptions for seeds and research: (1) The Utility Patent Statute applies only to plants that are useful, novel, nonobvious, and for which the inventor provides an enabling written description of the invention. 35 U.S.C. §§ 101, 102, 103, 112 (1994 ed. and

Supp. V). (2) The PVPA applies to plants that are novel, distinct, uniform, and stable. 7 U.S.C. §2402.(3) The second set of criteria seem slightly easier to meet, as they do not include nonobviousness and a written description (Pioneer does not argue that the "useful" requirement is significant). (4) And Congress could reasonably have intended the planting and research exceptions to apply only to the set of plants that can meet the easier, but not the tougher, criteria.

I do not find this argument convincing. For one thing, it is not clear that the general patent law requirements are significantly tougher. Counsel for Pioneer stated at oral argument that there are many more PVP certificates than there are plant patents. But he added that the major difference in criteria is the difference between the utility patent law's "nonobviousness" requirement and the specific Acts' requirement of "newness"—a difference that may reflect the Patent Office's more "rigorous" examination process. See Tr. of Oral Arg. 26, 30. But see S. Doc., at 20–21 (suggesting little difference because patent office tends to find "nonobviousness" as long as the plant is deemed "new" by the Department of Agriculture).

In any case, there is no relationship between the criteria differences and the exemptions. Why would anyone want to limit the exemptions—related to seedplanting and research—only to those new plant varieties that are slightly less original? Indeed, the research exemption would seem more useful in respect to more original, not less original, innovation. The Court has advanced no sound reason why Congress would want to destroy the exemptions in the PVPA that Congress created. And the Court's reading would destroy those exemptions.

. . .

Those who write statutes seek to solve human problems. Fidelity to their aims requires us to approach an interpretive problem not as if it were a purely logical game, like a Rubik's Cube, but as an effort to divine the human intent that underlies the statute. Here that effort calls not for an appeal to canons, but for an analysis of language, structure, history, and purpose. Those factors make clear that the Utility Patent Statute does not apply to plants.

Nothing in *Chakrabarty* holds to the contrary.

For these reasons, I dissent.

Canada

Percy Schmeiser and Schmeiser Enterprises Ltd., Appellants

v.

Monsanto Canada Inc. and Monsanto Company, Respondents

and

Attorney General of Ontario, Canadian Canola Growers Association (CCGA), Ag-West Biotech Inc., BIOTECanada, Canadian Seed Trade Association, Council of Canadians, Action Group on Erosion, Technology and Concentration, Sierra Club of Canada, National Farmers Union, Research Foundation for Science, Technology and Ecology, and International Centre for Technology Assessment, Interveners

Indexed as: Monsanto Canada Inc. v. Schmeiser
Neutral citation: 2004 SCC 34.
File No.: 29437.
2004: January 20; 2004: May 21.

Present: McLachlin C.J. and Iacobucci, Major, Bastarache, Binnie, Arbour, LeBel, Deschamps and Fish JJ.

on appeal from the federal court of appeal

The judgment of McLachlin C.J. and Major, Binnie, Deschamps and Fish JJ. was delivered by

THE CHIEF JUSTICE AND FISH J. —

I. *Introduction*

1 This case concerns a large scale, commercial farming operation that grew canola containing a patented cell and gene without obtaining licence or permission. The main issue is whether it thereby breached the *Patent Act*, R.S.C. 1985, c. P-4. We believe that it did.

2 In reaching this conclusion, we emphasize from the outset that we are not concerned here with the innocent discovery by farmers of "blow-by" patented plants on their land or in their cultivated fields. Nor are we concerned with the scope of the respondents' patent or the wisdom and social utility of the genetic modification of genes and cells — a practice authorized by Parliament under the *Patent Act* and its regulations.

3 Our sole concern is with the application of established principles of patent law to the essentially undisputed facts of this case.

II. *The Salient Facts*

4 Percy Schmeiser has farmed in Saskatchewan for more than 50 years. In 1996 he assigned his farming business to a corporation in which he and his wife are the sole shareholders and directors. He and his corporation grow wheat, peas, and a large amount of canola.

5 In the 1990s, many farmers, including five farmers in Mr. Schmeiser's area, switched to Roundup Ready Canola, a canola variety containing genetically modified genes and

cells that have been patented by Monsanto. Canola containing the patented genes and cells is resistant to a herbicide, Roundup, which kills all other plants, making it easier to control weeds. This eliminates the need for tillage and other herbicides. It also avoids seeding delays to accommodate early weed spraying. Monsanto licenses farmers to use Roundup Ready Canola, at a cost of $15 per acre.

6 Schmeiser never purchased Roundup Ready Canola nor did he obtain a licence to plant it. Yet, in 1998, tests revealed that 95 to 98 percent of his 1,000 acres of canola crop was made up of Roundup Ready plants. The origin of the plants is unclear. They may have been derived from Roundup Ready seed that blew onto or near Schmeiser's land, and was then collected from plants that survived after Schmeiser sprayed Roundup herbicide around the power poles and in the ditches along the roadway bordering four of his fields. The fact that these plants survived the spraying indicated that they contained the patented gene and cell. The trial judge found that "none of the suggested sources [proposed by Schmeiser] could reasonably explain the concentration or extent of Roundup Ready canola of a commercial quality" ultimately present in Schmeiser's crop ((2001), 202 F.T.R. 78, at ¶ 118).

7 The issues on this appeal are whether Schmeiser infringed Monsanto's patent, and if so, what remedies Monsanto may claim.

III. *Analysis*

A. *The Patent: Its Scope and Validity*

8 Canola is a valuable crop grown in Canada and used to make edible oil and animal feed. The respondents are the licensee and owner, respectively, of Canadian Patent No. 1,313,830. This patent, titled "Glyphosate-Resistant Plants", was issued on February 23, 1993, and expires on February 23, 2010. It discloses the invention of genetically engineered genes and cells containing those genes which, when inserted into plants (in this case canola), dramatically increase their tolerance to herbicides containing glyphosate. Ordinarily, glyphosate inhibits an enzyme essential for plant survival. Most plants sprayed with a glyphosate herbicide do not survive, but a canola plant grown from seed containing the modified gene will survive.

9 Since 1996, canola seed containing the patented gene and cell has been produced in Canada under licence from the respondents; this seed has been marketed to farmers under the trade name "Roundup Ready Canola", reflecting its resistance to the glyphosate herbicide "Roundup" manufactured by the respondents. Roundup can be sprayed after the canola plants have emerged, killing all plants except the canola. This eliminates the need for tillage and other herbicides. It also avoids delaying seeding to accommodate early weed spraying.

10 In 1996, approximately 600 Canadian farmers planted this Roundup Ready Canola on 50,000 acres. By 2000, approximately 20,000 farmers planted 4.5 to 5 million acres—nearly 40 percent of all canola grown in Canada.

11 Monsanto requires a farmer who wishes to grow Roundup Ready Canola to enter into a licensing arrangement called a Technology Use Agreement ("TUA"). The licensed farmers must attend a Grower Enrollment Meeting at which Monsanto describes the technology and its licensing terms. By signing the TUA, the farmer becomes entitled to purchase Roundup Ready Canola from an authorized seed agent. They must, however, undertake to use the seed for planting a single crop and to sell that crop for consumption to a commercial purchaser authorized by Monsanto. The licensed farmers may not sell or give the seed to any third party, or save seed for replanting or inventory.

12 The TUA gives Monsanto the right to inspect the fields of the contracting farmer and to take samples to verify compliance with the TUA. The farmer must also pay a licensing fee for each acre planted with Roundup Ready Canola. In 1998, the licensing fee was $15 per acre.

13 A Roundup Ready Canola plant cannot be distinguished from other canola plants except by a chemical test that detects the presence of the Monsanto gene, or by spraying the plant with Roundup. A canola plant that survives being sprayed with Roundup is Roundup Ready Canola.

14 The trial judge found the patent to be valid. He found that it did not offend the *Plant Breeders' Rights Act*, S.C. 1990, c. 20, and held that the difficulty of distinguishing canola plants containing the patented gene and cell from those without it did not preclude patenting the gene. The trial judge also rejected the argument that the gene and cell are unpatentable because they can be replicated without human intervention or control.

15 The scope of the patent is largely uncontroversial.

16 The trial judge found that "it is the *gene* and *the process for its insertion* ... and *the cell derived from that process*" that comprise the invention (¶ 88 (emphasis added); see also ¶ 26). The Federal Court of Appeal likewise endorsed the claims as being for "genes and cells which are glyphosate-resistant" ([2003] 2 F.C. 165, at ¶ 40).

17 Everyone agrees that Monsanto did not claim protection for the genetically modified plant itself, but rather for the genes and the modified cells that make up the plant. Unlike our colleague, Arbour J., we do not believe this fact requires reading a proviso into the claims that would provide patent protection to the genes and cells only when in an isolated laboratory form.

18 Purposive construction of patent claims requires that they be interpreted in light of the whole of the disclosure, including the specifications: *Whirlpool Corp. v. Camco Inc.*, [2000] 2 S.C.R. 1067, 2000 SCC 67; *Consolboard Inc. v. MacMillan Bloedel (Sask.) Ltd.*, [1981] 1 S.C.R. 504. In this case, the disclosure includes the following:

Abstract of the Disclosure

Plant cells transformed using such genes and plants regenerated therefrom have been shown to exhibit a substantial degree of glyphosate resistance.

Background of the Invention

The object of this invention is to provide a method of genetically transforming plant cells which causes the cells and plants regenerated therefrom to become resistant to glyphosate and the herbicidal salts thereof.

Detailed Description of the Invention

Suitable plants for the practice of the present invention include, but are not limited to, soybean, cotton, alfalfa, canola, flax, tomato, sugar beet, sunflower, potato, tobacco, corn, wheat, rice and lettuce.

19 A purposive construction therefore recognizes that the invention will be practised in plants regenerated from the patented cells, whether the plants are located inside or outside a laboratory. It is difficult to imagine a more likely or more evident purpose for patenting "a method of genetically transforming plant cells which causes *the cells and plants* regenerated therefrom to become resistant to glyphosate" (trial judgment, ¶ 20 (emphasis added)).

20 More particularly, the patented claims are for:

1. A *chimeric gene*: this is a gene that does not exist in nature and is constructed from different species.

2. An *expression vector*: this is a DNA molecule into which another DNA segment has been integrated so as to be useful as a research tool.

3. A *plant transformation vector*: used to permanently insert a chimeric gene into a plant's own DNA.

4. Various species of *plant cells* into which the chimeric gene has been inserted.

5. A *method of regenerating a glyphosate-resistant plant*. Once the cell is stimulated to grow into a plant, all of the differentiated cells in the plant will contain the chimeric gene, which will be passed on to offspring of the plant.

21 The appellant Schmeiser argues that the subject matter claimed in the patent is unpatentable. While acknowledging that Monsanto claims protection only over a gene and a cell, Schmeiser contends that the result of extending such protection is to restrict use of a plant and a seed. This result, the argument goes, ought to render the subject matter unpatentable, following the reasoning of the majority of this Court in *Harvard College v. Canada (Commissioner of Patents)*, [2002] 4 S.C.R. 45, 2002 SCC 76 ("*Harvard Mouse*"). In that case, plants and seeds were found to be unpatentable "higher life forms".

22 This case is different from *Harvard Mouse*, where the patent refused was for a mammal. The Patent Commissioner, moreover, had allowed other claims, which were not at issue before the Court in that case, notably a plasmid and a somatic cell culture. The claims at issue in this case, for a gene and a cell, are somewhat analogous, suggesting that to find a gene and a cell to be patentable is in fact consistent with both the majority and the minority holdings in *Harvard Mouse*.

23 Further, all members of the Court in *Harvard Mouse* noted in *obiter* that a fertilized, genetically altered oncomouse egg would be patentable subject matter, regardless of its ultimate anticipated development into a mouse (at ¶ 3, *per* Binnie J. for the minority; at ¶ 162, *per* Bastarache J. for the majority).

24 Whether or not patent protection for the gene and the cell extends to activities involving the plant is not relevant to the patent's validity. It relates only to the factual circumstances in which infringement will be found to have taken place, as we shall explain below. Monsanto's patent has already been issued, and the onus is thus on Schmeiser to show that the Commissioner erred in allowing the patent: *Apotex Inc. v. Wellcome Foundation Ltd.*, [2002] 4 S.C.R. 153, 2002 SCC 77, at paras. 42–44. He has failed to discharge that onus. We therefore conclude that the patent is valid.

B. *Did Schmeiser "Make" or "Construct" the Patented Gene and Cell, Thus Infringing the Patent?*

25 The *Patent Act* confers on the patent owner "the exclusive right, privilege and liberty of making, constructing and using the invention and selling it to others to be used" (§42). Monsanto argues that when Schmeiser planted and cultivated Roundup Ready Canola seed, he necessarily infringed their patent by making the gene or cell.

26 We are not inclined to the view that Schmeiser "made" the cell within the meaning of §42 of the *Patent Act*. Neither Schmeiser nor his corporation created or constructed the gene, the expression vector, a plant transformation vector, or plant cells into which the chimeric gene has been inserted.

27 It is unnecessary, however, to express a decided opinion on this point, since we have in any event concluded that Schmeiser infringed § 42 by "using" the patented cell and gene.

C. Did Schmeiser "Use" the Patented Gene or Cell, Thus Infringing the Patent?

(1) The Law on "Use"

28 The central question on this appeal is whether Schmeiser, by collecting, saving and planting seeds containing Monsanto's patented gene and cell, "used" that gene and cell.

29 The onus of proving infringement lies on the plaintiff, Monsanto.

30 Infringement is generally a question of fact (see *Whirlpool, supra*). In most patent infringement cases, once the claim has been construed it is clear on the facts whether infringement has taken place: one need only compare the thing made or sold by the defendant with the claims as construed. Patent infringement cases that turn on "use" are more unusual. In those rare cases where a dispute arises on this issue, as in this case, judicial interpretation of the meaning of "use" in s. 42 of the Act may be required.

31 Determining the meaning of "use" under s. 42 is essentially a matter of statutory construction. The starting point is the plain meaning of the word, in this case "use" or "*exploiter*". *The Concise Oxford Dictionary* defines "use" as "cause to act or serve for a purpose; bring into service; avail oneself of ": *The Concise Oxford Dictionary of Current English* (9th ed. 1995), at p. 1545. This denotes utilization for a purpose. The French word "*exploiter*" is even clearer. It denotes utilization with a view to production or advantage: "*tirer parti de (une chose), en vue d'une production ou dans un but lucratif. […] Utiliser d'une manière avantageuse*": *Le Nouveau Petit Robert* (2003), at p. 1004.

32 Three well-established rules or practices of statutory interpretation assist us further. First, the inquiry into the meaning of "use" under the *Patent Act* must be *purposive*, grounded in an understanding of the reasons for which patent protection is accorded. Second, the inquiry must be *contextual*, giving consideration to the other words of the provision. Finally, the inquiry must be attentive to the wisdom of the *case law*. We will discuss each of these aids to interpretation briefly, and then apply them to the facts of this case.

33 We return first to the rule of purposive construction. Identifying whether there has been infringement by use, like construing the claim, must be approached by the route of purposive construction: *Free World Trust v. Électro Santé Inc.*, [2000] 2 S.C.R. 1024, 2000 SCC 66. "[P]urposive construction is capable of expanding or limiting a literal [textual claim]": *Whirlpool, supra*, at ¶ 49. Similarly, it is capable of influencing what amounts to "use" in a given case.

34 The purpose of § 42 is to define the exclusive rights granted to the patent holder. These rights are the rights to full enjoyment of the monopoly granted by the patent. Therefore, what is prohibited is "any act that interferes with the full enjoyment of the monopoly granted to the patentee": H. G. Fox, *The Canadian Law and Practice Relating to Letters Patent for Inventions* (4th ed. 1969), at p. 349; see also *Lishman v. Erom Roche Inc.* (1996), 68 C.P.R. (3d) 72 (F.C.T.D.), at p. 77.

35 The guiding principle is that patent law ought to provide the inventor with "protection for that which he has actually in good faith invented": *Free World Trust, supra*, at ¶ 43. Applied to "use", the question becomes: *did the defendant's activity deprive the inventor in whole or in part, directly or indirectly, of full enjoyment of the monopoly conferred by law?*

36 A purposive approach is complemented by a contextual examination of §42 of the *Patent Act*, which shows that the patentee's monopoly generally protects its business interests. Professor D. Vaver, in *Intellectual Property Law: Copyright, Patents, Trade-marks* (1997), suggests that the common thread among "'making, constructing and using the invention and selling it to others to be used'... is that the activity is usually for commercial purposes — to make a profit or to further the actor's business interests" (p. 151). This is particularly consistent with the French version of §42, which uses the word "*exploiter*".

37 As a practical matter, inventors are normally deprived of the fruits of their invention and the full enjoyment of their monopoly when another person, without licence or permission, uses the invention to further a business interest. Where the defendant's impugned activities furthered its own commercial interests, we should therefore be particularly alert to the possibility that the defendant has committed an infringing use.

38 With respect for the contrary view of Arbour J., this does not require inventors to describe in their specifications a commercial advantage or utility for their inventions. Even in the absence of commercial exploitation, the patent holder is entitled to protection. However, a defendant's commercial activities involving the patented object will be particularly likely to constitute an infringing use. This is so because if there is a commercial benefit to be derived from the invention, a contextual analysis of s. 42 indicates that it belongs to the patent holder. The contextual analysis of the section thus complements — and confirms — the conclusion drawn from its purposive analysis. It is the reverse side of the same coin.

39 We turn now to the case law, the third aid to interpretation. Here we derive guidance from what courts in the past have considered to be use. As we shall see, precedent confirms the approach proposed above and it is of assistance as well in resolving some of the more specific questions raised by this case.

40 First, case law provides guidance as to whether patent protection extends to situations where the patented invention is contained within something else used by the defendant. This is relevant to the appellants' submission that growing *plants* did not amount to "using" their patented *genes* and *cells*.

41 Patent infringement actions often proceed in a manufacturing context. Case law has for that reason focussed on situations where a patented part or process plays a role in production. As Professor Vaver states, *supra*, at p. 152:

> "Use" applies both to patented products and processes, and also to their output. A patent that covers a zipper-making machine or method extends to zippers made by the machine or method. Each zipper sold without authority infringes the patent, even if the zippers themselves are unpatented. This expansive doctrine applies, however, only if the patent plays an important part in production.

42 By analogy, then, the law holds that a defendant infringes a patent when the defendant manufactures, seeks to use, or uses a patented part that is contained within something that is not patented, provided the patented part is significant or important. In the case at bar, the patented genes and cells are not merely a "part" of the plant; rather, the patented genes are present throughout the genetically modified plant and the patented cells compose its entire physical structure. In that sense, the cells are somewhat analogous to Lego blocks: if an infringing use were alleged in building a structure with patented Lego blocks, it would be no bar to a finding of infringement that only the blocks were patented and not the entire structure. If anything, the fact that the Lego

structure could not exist independently of the patented blocks would strengthen the claim, underlining the significance of the patented invention to the whole product, object, or process.

43 Infringement through use is thus possible even where the patented invention is part of, or composes, a broader unpatented structure or process. This is, as Professor Vaver states, an expansive rule. It is, however, firmly rooted in the principle that the main purpose of patent protection is to prevent others from depriving the inventor, even in part and even indirectly, of the monopoly that the law intends to be theirs: only the inventor is entitled, by virtue of the patent and as a matter of law, to the *full* enjoyment of the monopoly conferred.

44 Thus, in *Saccharin Corp. v. Anglo-Continental Chemical Works, Ld.* (1900), 17 R.P.C. 307 (H.C.J.), the court stated, at p. 319:

> By the sale of saccharin, in the course of the production of which the patented process is used, the Patentee is deprived of some part of the whole profit and advantage of the invention, and the importer is indirectly making use of the invention.

This confirms the centrality of the question that flows from a purposive interpretation of the *Patent Act*: did the defendant, by his acts or conduct, deprive the inventor, in whole or in part, directly or indirectly, of the advantage of the patented invention?

45 In determining whether the defendant "used" the patented invention, one compares the object of the patent with what the defendant did and asks whether the defendant's actions involved that object. In *Betts v. Neilson* (1868), L.R. 3 Ch. App. 429 (aff'd (1871), L.R. 5 H.L. 1), the object of the patent was to preserve the contents of bottles in transit. Though the bottles were merely shipped unopened through England, the defendant was held to have used the invention in England because, during its passage through that country, the beer was protected by the invention. Lord Chelmsford said, at p. 439:

> It is the employment of the machine or the article for the purpose for which it was designed which constitutes its active use; and whether the capsules were intended for ornament, or for protection of the contents of the bottles upon which they were placed, the whole time they were in *England* they may be correctly said to be in active use for the very objects for which they were placed upon the bottles by the vendors.

46 In fact, the patented invention need not be deployed precisely for its intended purpose in order for its object to be involved in the defendant's activity. It was not relevant in *Neilson* whether the invention had actually caused bottles to be preserved during shipping, in a situation in which they would otherwise have broken. As a further example, in *Dunlop Pneumatic Tyre Co. v. British and Colonial Motor Car Co.* (1901), 18 R.P.C. 313 (H.C.J.), the defendants placed on display at a car show a car with patented tires which they had intended to remove prior to sale, substituting other tires. The exhibition of the car with the patented tires was nonetheless held to be an infringing use. The common thread is that the defendants employed the invention to their advantage, depriving the inventor of the full enjoyment of the monopoly.

47 Moreover, as Lord Dunedin emphasized in *British United Shoe Machinery Co. v. Simon Collier Ld.* (1910), 27 R.P.C. 567 (H.L.), *possession as a stand-by has "insurance value"*, as for example in the case of a fire extinguisher. The extinguisher is "used" to provide the means for extinguishment should the need arise. This is true, too, of a spare

steam engine which is "intended in certain circumstances to be used for exactly the purpose for which the whole machine is being actually used" (p. 572). Exploitation of the stand-by utility of an invention uses it to advantage.

48 In *Terrell on the Law of Patents* (15th ed. 2000), at ¶ 8.24, the authors observe that "[t]he word 'use'… would … seem to indicate making practical use of the invention itself." In some circumstances, "practical use" may arise from the stand-by utility resulting from mere possession of the invention, or from some other practical employment with a view to advantage. Use, and thereby infringement, are then established.

49 The general rule is that the defendant's intention is irrelevant to a finding of infringement. The issue is "what the defendant does, not … what he intends": *Stead v. Anderson* (1847), 4 C.B. 806, 136 E.R. 724 (C.P.), at p. 736; see also *Hoechst Celanese Corp. v. BP Chemicals Ltd.* (1998), 25 F.S.R. 586 (Pat. Ct.), at p. 598; *Illinois Tool Works Inc. v. Cobra Anchors Co.* (2002), 221 F.T.R. 161, 2002 FCT 829, at paras. 14–17; *Computalog Ltd. v. Comtech Logging Ltd.* (1992), 44 C.P.R. (3d) 77 (F.C.A.), at p. 88. And the governing principle is whether the defendant, by his actions, activities or conduct, appropriated the patented invention, thus depriving the inventor, in whole or part, directly or indirectly, of the full enjoyment of the monopoly the patent grants.

50 However, intention becomes relevant where the defence invoked is possession without use. Where the alleged use consists of exploitation of the invention's "stand-by" utility, as discussed above, it is relevant whether the defendant intended to exploit the invention should the need arise.

51 Thus, possession was found to constitute "use" in *Adair v. Young* (1879), 12 Ch. D. 13 (C.A.), where a ship's master was sued for infringement in relation to the presence of patented pumps on his ship. The ship's owners had fitted the ship with the pumps but were not named in the suit. The master had no power to remove the pumps and had never used them to pump water in British waters. However, the court *held that the master intended to use the pumps if the need arose.* The court thus granted an injunction against use of the pumps to pump water.

52 Similarly, Fox states, *supra*, that "*[m]ere possession of a patented article may amount to infringement* where such possession is unlicensed and *where there is present the intention of user* to the detriment of the patentee, but not if there is no intention to use" (pp. 383–84 (emphasis added; footnotes omitted)).

53 The onus of proving infringement would become impractical and unduly burdensome in cases of possession were the patent holder required to demonstrate the defendant's intention to infringe. As Professor Vaver explains, "[m]ere possession may not be use, but a business that possesses a patented product for trade *may be presumed either to have used it or to intend to use it, unless it shows the contrary*" (*supra*, at p. 151 (emphasis added)).

54 The classic case of *British United Shoe*, *supra*, suggests that mere possession of an object containing a patented ingredient or made by a patented process may not amount to "use" if the defendant can show that the object is held without a view to advancing the defendant's interest. The defendant boot maker owned a machine containing a patented mechanism but was held not to have infringed the patent. The defendants did not use the patented part itself, as it was possible not to bring it into operation unless one wanted to do so. The court noted there was no question of the defendants' honesty (they had returned the patented part willingly when legal action commenced). In the court's view, "[t]he patented part … was … of no use to the Defendants and was put aside by them, and they never thought of using the patented part,

nor was it appropriate to their trade" (p. 571). The court stated that there is a rebuttable presumption or "ordinary inference" that a defendant in possession of an invention had either used it or had it for the future purpose of using it in an infringing manner (p. 571).

55 Commenting on *British United Shoe* in *Pfizer Corp. v. Ministry of Health*, [1965] A.C. 512 (H.L.), Lord Wilberforce observed that "if it can positively be proved that the possession was innocent of any actual use or intention to use, the defendant will not be held to have infringed" (p. 572). Possession requires an "additional ingredient" to make up an infringement (p. 572). In *Pfizer*, according to Lord Wilberforce, use arose from the transportation of patented articles (possession) with a view to trade (the additional ingredient). Where the patent holder shows that the defendant possessed the patented invention, it is up to the defendant to show the absence of the "additional ingredient".

56 Thus, a defendant in possession of a patented invention in commercial circumstances may rebut the presumption of use by bringing credible evidence that the invention was neither used, nor intended to be used, even by exploiting its stand-by utility.

57 The court does not inquire into whether the patented invention in fact assisted the defendant or increased its profits. This is the natural corollary of the finding in *Neilson*, *supra*, that it was not relevant to infringement whether the beer actually was preserved by the invention, and the finding in *Adair*, *supra*, that it was irrelevant whether the ship's master had profited from the presence of the pumps on the ship. The defendant's benefit or profit from the activity may be relevant at the stage of remedy, but not in determining infringement.

58 These propositions may be seen to emerge from the foregoing discussion of "use" under the *Patent Act*:

> 1. "Use" or "*exploiter*", in their ordinary dictionary meaning, denote utilization with a view to production or advantage.
>
> 2. The basic principle in determining whether the defendant has "used" a patented invention is whether the inventor has been deprived, in whole or in part, directly or indirectly, of the full enjoyment of the monopoly conferred by the patent.
>
> 3. If there is a commercial benefit to be derived from the invention, it belongs to the patent holder.
>
> 4. It is no bar to a finding of infringement that the patented object or process is a part of or composes a broader unpatented structure or process, provided the patented invention is significant or important to the defendant's activities that involve the unpatented structure.
>
> 5. Possession of a patented object or an object incorporating a patented feature may constitute "use" of the object's stand-by or insurance utility and thus constitute infringement.
>
> 6. Possession, at least in commercial circumstances, raises a rebuttable presumption of "use".
>
> 7. While intention is generally irrelevant to determining whether there has been "use" and hence infringement, the absence of intention to employ or gain any advantage from the invention may be relevant to rebutting the presumption of use raised by possession.

(2) *Application of the Law*

59 The trial judge's findings of fact are based, essentially, on the following uncontested history.

60 Mr. Schmeiser is a conventional, non-organic farmer. For years, he had a practice of saving and developing his own seed. The seed which is the subject of Monsanto's complaint can be traced to a 370-acre field, called field number 1, on which Mr. Schmeiser grew canola in 1996. In 1996 five other canola growers in Mr. Schmeiser's area planted Roundup Ready Canola.

61 In the spring of 1997, Mr. Schmeiser planted the seeds saved on field number 1. The crop grew. He sprayed a three-acre patch near the road with Roundup and found that approximately 60 percent of the plants survived. This indicates that the plants contained Monsanto's patented gene and cell.

62 In the fall of 1997, Mr. Schmeiser harvested the Roundup Ready Canola from the three-acre patch he had sprayed with Roundup. He did not sell it. He instead kept it separate, and stored it over the winter in the back of a pick-up truck covered with a tarp.

63 A Monsanto investigator took samples of canola from the public road allowances bordering on two of Mr. Schmeiser's fields in 1997, all of which were confirmed to contain Roundup Ready Canola. In March 1998, Monsanto visited Mr. Schmeiser and put him on notice of its belief that he had grown Roundup Ready Canola without a licence. Mr. Schmeiser nevertheless took the harvest he had saved in the pick-up truck to a seed treatment plant and had it treated for use as seed. Once treated, it could be put to no other use. Mr. Schmeiser planted the treated seed in nine fields, covering approximately 1,000 acres in all.

64 Numerous samples were taken, some under court order and some not, from the canola plants grown from this seed. Moreover, the seed treatment plant, unbeknownst to Mr. Schmeiser, kept some of the seed he had brought there for treatment in the spring of 1998, and turned it over to Monsanto. A series of independent tests by different experts confirmed that the canola Mr. Schmeiser planted and grew in 1998 was 95 to 98 percent Roundup resistant. Only a grow-out test by Mr. Schmeiser in his yard in 1999 and by Mr. Freisen on samples supplied by Mr. Schmeiser did not support this result.

65 Dr. Downey testified that the high rate of post-Roundup spraying survival in the 1997 samples was "consistent only with the presence in field number 2 of canola grown from commercial Roundup tolerant seed" (trial judgment, at ¶ 112). According to Dr. Dixon, responsible for the testing by Monsanto US at St. Louis, the "defendants' samples contain[ed] the DNA sequences claimed in claims 1, 2, 5, and 6 of the patent and the plant cell claimed in claims 22, 23, 27, 28 and 45 of the patent" (trial judgment, at ¶ 113). As the trial judge noted, this opinion was uncontested.

66 The remaining question was how such a pure concentration of Roundup Ready Canola came to grow on the appellants' land in 1998. The trial judge rejected the suggestion that it was the product of seed blown or inadvertently carried onto the appellants' land (at ¶ 118):

> It may be that some Roundup Ready seed was carried to Mr. Schmeiser's field without his knowledge. Some such seed might have survived the winter to germinate in the spring of 1998. However, I am persuaded by evidence of Dr. Keith Downey ... that none of the suggested sources could reasonably explain the concentration or extent of Roundup Ready canola of a commercial quality evident from the results of tests on Schmeiser's crop.

67 He concluded, at ¶ 120:

> I find that in 1998 Mr. Schmeiser planted canola seed saved from his 1997 crop in his field number 2 which he knew or ought to have known was Roundup tolerant, and that seed was the primary source for seeding and for the defendants' crops in all nine fields of canola in 1998.

68 In summary, it is clear on the findings of the trial judge that the appellants saved, planted, harvested and sold the crop from plants containing the gene and plant cell patented by Monsanto. The issue is whether this conduct amounted to "use" of Monsanto's invention — the glyphosate-resistant gene and cell.

69 The preliminary question is whether this conduct falls within the meaning of "use" or "*exploiter*". We earlier concluded that these words, taken together, connote utilization with a view to production or advantage. Saving and planting seed, then harvesting and selling the resultant plants containing the patented cells and genes appears, on a common sense view, to constitute "utilization" of the patented material for production and advantage, within the meaning of § 42.

70 We turn next to whether the other considerations relevant to "use" support this preliminary conclusion.

71 In this regard, the first and fundamental question is whether Monsanto was deprived in whole or in part, directly or indirectly, of the full enjoyment of the monopoly that the patent confers. And the answer is "yes".

72 Monsanto's patent gives it a monopoly over the patented gene and cell. The patent's object is production of a plant which is resistant to Roundup herbicide. Monsanto's monopoly enabled it to charge a licensing fee of $15 per acre to farmers wishing to grow canola plants with the patented genes and cells. The appellants cultivated 1030 acres of plants with these patented properties without paying Monsanto for the right to do so. By cultivating a plant containing the patented gene and composed of the patented cells without licence, the appellants thus deprived Monsanto of the full enjoyment of its monopoly.

73 The complementary question is whether the appellants employed or possessed the patented invention in the context of their commercial or business interests. The initial answer must again be "yes".

74 One of the appellants' businesses was growing canola. It used seeds containing the patented qualities in that business. Subject to the appellants' argument discussed below that they did not use the patented invention itself (whether because they used only the plant or because they did not spray with Roundup), the appellants' involvement with the disputed canola is clearly commercial in nature.

75 The answers to the two questions of principle that lie at the heart of "use" under the *Patent Act* both thus suggest that the trial judge and the Court of Appeal were correct in finding that the appellants "used" the protected invention and hence infringed Monsanto's patent. It is helpful as well, however, to consider the insights gained from the case law discussed above and their impact on arguments raised against this conclusion.

76 First, it is suggested that because Monsanto's claims are for genes and cells rather than for plants, it follows that infringement by use will only occur where a defendant uses the genes or cells in their isolated, laboratory form. This argument appears not to have been advanced in any detail at trial or on appeal, but is the position taken by our colleague, Arbour J.

77 It is uncontested that Monsanto's patented claim is only for the gene and cell that it developed. This, however, is the beginning and not the end of the inquiry. The more difficult question—and the nub of this case—is whether, by cultivating plants *containing the cell and gene*, the appellants used the patented components of those plants. The position taken by Arbour J. assumes that this inquiry is redundant and that the only way a patent may be infringed is to use the patented invention in isolation.

78 This position flies in the face of century-old patent law, which holds that where a defendant's commercial or business activity involves a thing of which a patented part is a significant or important component, infringement is established. It is no defence to say that the thing actually used was not patented, but only one of its components.

79 Professor Vaver, *supra*, observes that this is an "expansive doctrine". This is so because otherwise the inventor would be deprived of the full enjoyment of the monopoly that the law of patent confers on him or her. It is rare that patented components or processes are used in isolation; without this principle, an infringer could use the invention to his advantage, and take shelter in the excuse that he or she was not using the invention in isolation.

80 Provided the patented invention is a significant aspect of the defendant's activity, the defendant will be held to have "used" the invention and violated the patent. If Mr. Schmeiser's activities with Roundup Ready Canola plants amounted to use interfering with Monsanto's full enjoyment of their monopoly on the gene and cell, those activities infringed the patent. Infringement does not require use of the gene or cell in isolation.

81 Second, Mr. Schmeiser argued at trial that he should not be held to have "used" Monsanto's invention because he never took commercial advantage of the special utility that invention offered—resistance to Roundup herbicide. He testified that he never used Roundup herbicide as an aid to cultivation. (That he used it in 1996 in his initial gathering of the Roundup Ready seed is clear.)

82 The trial judge dismissed this argument. He pointed out, at ¶ 122, that it "is the taking of the essence of the invention … that constitutes infringement", and that by growing and selling the Roundup Ready crop Mr. Schmeiser took that invention. Consequently, in the judge's view, "whether or not that crop was sprayed with Roundup … [was] not important" (¶ 123).

83 Perhaps the appellants' failure to spray with Roundup herbicide is a way of attempting to rebut the presumption of use that flows from possession. However, the appellants have failed to rebut the presumption.

84 Their argument fails to account for the stand-by or insurance utility of the properties of the patented genes and cells. Whether or not a farmer sprays with Roundup herbicide, cultivating canola containing the patented genes and cells provides stand-by utility. The farmer benefits from that advantage from the outset: if there is reason to spray in the future, the farmer may proceed to do so.

85 Although not directly at issue in this case, cultivating Roundup Ready Canola also presents future revenue opportunities to "brown-bag" the product to other farmers unwilling to pay the licence fee, thus depriving Monsanto of the full enjoyment of their monopoly.

86 Further, the appellants did not provide sufficient evidence to rebut the presumption of use. It may well be that defendant farmers could rebut the presumption by showing that they never intended to cultivate plants containing the patented genes and cells. They might perhaps prove that the continued presence of the patented gene on their

land was accidental and unwelcome, for example, by showing that they acted quickly to arrange for its removal, and that its concentration was consistent with that to be expected from unsolicited "blow-by" canola. Knowledge of infringement is never a necessary component of infringement. However, a defendant's conduct on becoming aware of the presence of the patented invention may assist in rebutting the presumption of use arising from possession.

87 However, the appellants in this case actively cultivated canola containing the patented invention as part of their business operations. Mr. Schmeiser complained that the original plants came onto his land without his intervention. However, he did not at all explain why he sprayed Roundup to isolate the Roundup Ready plants he found on his land; why he then harvested the plants and segregated the seeds, saved them, and kept them for seed; why he next planted them; and why, through this husbandry, he ended up with 1030 acres of Roundup Ready Canola which would otherwise have cost him $15,000. In these circumstances, the presumption of use flowing from possession stands unrebutted.

88 Third, as in their submissions on validity, the appellants seek to rely on the decision of the majority of this Court in *Harvard Mouse*. They contend that the patent should be given a narrow scope for infringement purposes, since the plants reproduce through the laws of nature rather than through human intervention. Thus, they argue, propagation of Roundup Ready Canola without a licence cannot be a "use" by them because plants are living things that grow by themselves.

89 This is also the perspective adopted by Arbour J. In support of the proposition that infringement of gene claims occurs only in a laboratory setting, she cites *Kirin Amgen Inc. v. Hoechst Marion Roussel Ltd.*, [2002] E.W.J. No. 3792 (QL), [2002] EWCA Civ. 1096 (C.A.). That case dealt with a protein useful in the diagnosis and treatment of blood disorders. The English court construed the claims to exclude the naturally occurring form of the DNA sequence in a human cell. However, this was done to accord with the provisions of a regulatory scheme that has no parallel in Canada: Article 5 of the European Parliament's Directive 98/44/EC, which regulates patentability of biotechnological inventions. It states that the discovery of elements of the human body, including genes, is not patentable, although such elements are patentable when isolated or otherwise produced through technical means. The legislature has not enacted a comparable statutory scheme in Canada to narrow the scope of patent construction. Thus, *Kirin Amgen* is not applicable to the case before this Court.

90 The appellants' argument also ignores the role human beings play in agricultural propagation. Farming is a commercial enterprise in which farmers sow and cultivate the plants which prove most efficient and profitable. Plant science has been with us since long before Mendel. Human beings since time immemorial have striven to produce more efficient plants. Huge investments of energy and money have been poured into the quest for better seeds and better plants. One way in which that investment is protected is through the *Patent Act* giving investors a monopoly when they create a novel and useful invention in the realm of plant science, such as genetically modified genes and cells.

91 Finally, many inventions make use of natural processes in order to work. For example, many valid patents have referred to various yeasts, which would have no practical utility at all without "natural forces". See *Re Application of Abitibi Co.* (1982), 62 C.P.R. (2d) 81 (Pat. App. Bd.), in which the inventive step consisted of acclimatizing a known species of yeast from domestic sewage to a new environment, where it would then through its natural operation act to purify waste from pulp plants.

92 The issue is not the perhaps adventitious arrival of Roundup Ready on Mr. Schmeiser's land in 1998. What is at stake in this case is *sowing* and *cultivation*, which necessarily involves deliberate and careful activity on the part of the farmer. The appellants suggest that when a farmer such as Mr. Schmeiser actively cultivates a crop with particular properties through activities such as testing, isolating, treating, and planting the desired seed and tending the crops until harvest, the result is a crop which has merely "grown itself". Such a suggestion denies the realities of modern agriculture.

93 Inventions in the field of agriculture may give rise to concerns not raised in other fields — moral concerns about whether it is right to manipulate genes in order to obtain better weed control or higher yields. It is open to Parliament to consider these concerns and amend the *Patent Act* should it find them persuasive.

94 Our task, however, is to interpret and apply the *Patent Act* as it stands, in accordance with settled principles. Under the present Act, an invention in the domain of agriculture is as deserving of protection as an invention in the domain of mechanical science. Where Parliament has not seen fit to distinguish between inventions concerning plants and other inventions, neither should the courts.

95 Invoking the concepts of implied licence and waiver, the appellants argue that this Court should grant an exemption from infringement to "innocent bystanders". The simple answer to this contention is that on the facts found by the trial judge, Mr. Schmeiser was not an innocent bystander; rather, he actively cultivated Roundup Ready Canola. Had he been a mere "innocent bystander", he could have refuted the presumption of use arising from his possession of the patented gene and cell. More broadly, to the extent this submission rests on policy arguments about the particular dangers of biotechnology inventions, these, as discussed, find no support in the *Patent Act* as it stands today. Again, if Parliament wishes to respond legislatively to biotechnology inventions concerning plants, it is free to do so. Thus far it has not chosen to do so.

96 The appellants argue, finally, that Monsanto's activities tread on the ancient common law property rights of farmers to keep that which comes onto their land. Just as a farmer owns the progeny of a "stray bull" which wanders onto his land, so Mr. Schmeiser argues he owns the progeny of the Roundup Ready Canola that came onto his field. However, the issue is not property rights, but patent protection. Ownership is no defence to a breach of the *Patent Act*.

97 We conclude that the trial judge and Court of Appeal were correct in concluding that the appellants "used" Monsanto's patented gene and cell and hence infringed the *Patent Act*.

D. *Remedy*

98 The trial judge granted injunctive relief and awarded Monsanto an accounting of the profits made by the respondents through growing Roundup Ready Canola, which he ultimately quantified at $19,832. The record is not clear on precisely how this sum was arrived at; that it was awarded by the trial judge on account of profits is, however, undisputed.

99 The Court of Appeal upheld that order on the same basis and the issue is whether it erred in this regard.

100 The *Patent Act* permits two alternative types of remedy: damages and an accounting of profits. Damages represent the inventor's loss, which may include the patent holder's lost profits from sales or lost royalty payments. An accounting of profits, by contrast, is

measured by the profits made by the infringer, rather than the amount lost by the inventor. Here, damages are not available, in view of Monsanto's election to seek an accounting of profits.

101 It is settled law that the inventor is only entitled to that portion of the infringer's profit which is causally attributable to the invention: *Lubrizol Corp. v. Imperial Oil Ltd.*, [1997] 2 F.C. 3 (C.A.); *Celanese International Corp. v. BP Chemicals Ltd.*, [1999] R.P.C. 203 (Pat. Ct.), at ¶ 37. This is consistent with the general law on awarding non-punitive remedies: "[I]t is essential that the losses made good are only those which, on a common sense view of causation, were caused by the breach" (*Canson Enterprises Ltd. v. Boughton & Co.*, [1991] 3 S.C.R. 534, at p. 556, *per* McLachlin J. (as she then was), quoted with approval by Binnie J. for the Court in *Cadbury Schweppes Inc. v. FBI Foods Ltd.*, [1999] 1 S.C.R. 142, at ¶ 93).

102 The preferred means of calculating an accounting of profits is what has been termed the value-based or "differential profit" approach, where profits are allocated according to the value contributed to the defendant's wares by the patent: N. Siebrasse, "A Remedial Benefit-Based Approach to the Innocent-User Problem in the Patenting of Higher Life Forms" (2004), 20 *C.I.P.R.* 79. A comparison is to be made between the defendant's profit attributable to the invention and his profit had he used the best non-infringing option: *Collette v. Lasnier* (1886), 13 S.C.R. 563, at p. 576, also referred to with approval in *Colonial Fastener Co. v. Lightning Fastener Co.*, [1937] S.C.R. 36.

103 The difficulty with the trial judge's award is that it does not identify any causal connection between the profits the appellants were found to have earned through growing Roundup Ready Canola and the invention. On the facts found, the appellants made no profits *as a result of the invention*.

104 Their profits were precisely what they would have been had they planted and harvested ordinary canola. They sold the Roundup Ready Canola they grew in 1998 for feed, and thus obtained no premium for the fact that it was Roundup Ready Canola. Nor did they gain any agricultural advantage from the herbicide resistant nature of the canola, since no finding was made that they sprayed with Roundup herbicide to reduce weeds. The appellants' profits arose solely from qualities of their crop that cannot be attributed to the invention.

105 On this evidence, the appellants earned no profit from the invention and Monsanto is entitled to nothing on their claim of account.

IV. *Conclusion*

106 We would allow the appeal in part, setting aside the award for account of profit. In all other respects we would confirm the order of the trial judge. In view of this mixed result, we would order that each party bear its own costs throughout.

The reasons of Iacobucci, Bastarache, Arbour and LeBel JJ. were delivered by

ARBOUR J. (dissenting in part) —

I. *Introduction*

107 This case was decided in the courts below without the benefit of this Court's decision in *Harvard College v. Canada (Commissioner of Patents)*, [2002] 4 S.C.R. 45, 2002 SCC 76. The heart of the issue is whether the Federal Court of Appeal's decision can stand in light of our decision in that case.

108 More specifically, the trial judge interpreted the scope of the Monsanto patent without the benefit of the holding in *Harvard College* that higher life forms, including plants, are not patentable. Both lower court decisions "allo[w] Monsanto to do indirectly what Canadian patent law has not allowed them to do directly: namely, to acquire patent protection over whole plants" (E. R. Gold and W. A. Adams, "The *Monsanto* decision: The edge or the wedge" (2001), 19 *Nat. Biotechnol.* 587).

109 Such a result is hard to reconcile with the majority decision in *Harvard College*. It would also invalidate the Patent Office's long-standing policy of not granting exclusive rights, expressed in a patent grant, over higher life forms, that was upheld in *Harvard College*: Patent Office, *Manual of Patent Office Practice* (1998 "*Patent Office Manual*"), at ¶ 16.05.

110 The two central issues here, the scope of Monsanto's patent and whether agricultural production of Roundup Ready Canola constitutes an infringing use, are determined by a purposive construction of the patent claims and the proper application of the majority decision in *Harvard College*. Monsanto is on the horns of a dilemma; a narrow construction of its claims renders the claims valid but not infringed, the broader construction renders the claims invalid: *Gillette Safety Razor Co. v. Anglo-American Trading Co.* (1913), 30 R.P.C. 465 (H.L.), at p. 481.

111 In light of *Harvard College*, I conclude that the patent claims here cannot be interpreted to extend patent protection over whole plants and that there was no infringing use. I need not review, and take no issue with the factual overview of the case provided in my colleagues' reasons.

II. *Analysis*

A. *The Decision in Harvard College*

112 The issue in *Harvard College, supra*, was whether a mouse that was genetically modified to make it susceptible to cancer was the valid subject matter for a patent claim. The majority found that higher life forms were not "compositions of matter". Plants were clearly included in the category of higher life forms: *e.g., Harvard College*, at ¶ 199. Accordingly, plants do not fit within the definition of an "invention": *Patent Act*, R.S.C. 1985, c. P-4, s. 2.

113 The majority approved the line drawn by the Patent Office between unpatentable higher life forms, patentable lower life forms, and patentable processes for engineering transgenic higher life forms in the laboratory: *Harvard College*, at ¶ 199. That line is described in the *Patent Office Manual, supra*, at ¶ 16.05:

> Higher life forms are not patentable subject matter. However, a process for producing a higher life form may be patentable provided the process requires significant technical intervention by man and is not essentially a natural biological process which occurs according to the laws of nature....

114 The line was clearly enunciated in *Re Application of Abitibi Co.* (1982), 62 C.P.R. (2d) 81 (Pat. App. Bd.), at p. 89; patents apply to:

> ... all micro-organisms, yeasts, moulds, fungi, bacteria, actinomycetes, unicellular algae, cell lines, viruses or protozoa; in fact to all new life forms which are produced *en masse* as chemical compounds are prepared, and are formed in such large numbers that any measurable quantity will possess uniform properties and characteristics.

115 Thus, in *Harvard College*, claims for a genetically modified plasmid and the process claims to genetically modify a mouse so that it became susceptible to cancer were found to be valid. Claims for the mouse itself were found to be invalid by the Patent Commissioner and that finding was upheld by this Court. No other claims were at issue in *Harvard College*; transgenic mammalian eggs (single cells) were not claimed, although the majority suggested in *obiter* that such a claim may be the valid subject matter of a patent claim: *Harvard College*, at ¶ 162.

B. *The Patent Claims*

116 Monsanto's Canadian Patent No. 1,313,830 is entitled "Glyphosate-Resistant Plants" (see Appendix). The use is evident on the face of the claims, namely glyphosate resistance that a person skilled in the art would understand to mean the conferring of resistance to a glyphosate herbicide, such as "Roundup".

117 The patent contained a series of hierarchical claims. The method claims are separate. The claims in the patent may be split into five general categories:

(1) the chimeric gene, claims 1-7, that does not exist in nature and is constructed, through human intervention, of three components;

(2) the cloning or expression vector, claims 8–14 (a vector is a DNA molecule into which another DNA segment has been integrated);

(3) the plant transformation vector, claims 15–21, 52;

(4) the glyphosate-resistant plant cell containing the chimeric gene, claims 22–28 and claims 43–51; and

(5) the method for constructing (1)–(4) and, in the laboratory, regenerating a plant from the plant cell containing the chimeric gene, claims 29–42.

118 All of the differentiated cells in the regenerated plant contain the chimeric gene, which will be passed to offspring of the plants through natural reproduction. However, as recognized by my colleagues, there is no claim for the regenerated plant or its progeny.

C. *Purposive Construction of the Claims*

119 The first and pivotal step in an infringement action is the purposive construction of the patent claims: *Whirlpool Corp. v. Camco Inc.*, [2000] 2 S.C.R. 1067, 2000 SCC 67, at ¶ 43. The claims construction will set the scope of the patent claims, which, in turn, resolves the two issues in this case: validity and infringing use. However, Monsanto's patent claims cannot be construed with an eye to either infringement or the appellants' defence to infringement, invalidity: *Whirlpool*.

120 Purposive construction delineates the scope of the invention. It identifies what the inventor considered to be the essential elements of the invention: *Whirlpool, supra*, at ¶ 45.

121 My colleagues emphasize the commercial value of the exclusive rights to the patentee as the primary consideration in distilling the "essential elements" of the patent claims. However, commercial interests are not the only considerations. There are three further themes to purposive construction of patent claims. I will address each of these in turn.

(1) *Fairness and Predictability*

122 Fairness to the public is a recurring theme in jurisprudence on claims construction because of the severe economic consequences of patent infringement: *Consolboard Inc.*

v. MacMillan Bloedel (Sask.) Ltd., [1981] 1 S.C.R. 504; *Pioneer Hi-Bred Ltd. v. Canada (Commissioner of Patents)*, [1989] 1 S.C.R. 1623; *Free World Trust v. Électro Santé Inc.*, [2000] 2 S.C.R. 1024, 2000 SCC 66, at ¶41. The scope of the patent protection should be both "fair" and "reasonably predictable": *Whirlpool, supra*, at ¶49; *Consolboard, supra*, at pp. 520–21. "Predictability is achieved by tying the patentee to its claims; fairness is achieved by interpreting those claims in an informed and purposive way": *Free World Trust, supra*, at ¶43.

(2) *What Is Not Claimed Is Disclaimed*

123 The classic rule is "what is not claimed is considered disclaimed": *Whirlpool, supra*, at ¶42. The inventor may not get exclusive rights to an invention that was not part of the public disclosure of the invention. The public must be able to predict the activities that will infringe on the exclusive rights granted to the patentee: *Free World Trust, supra*, at ¶41.

124 So long as the claims are interpreted fairly and knowledgeably, if the patentee has limited the claims, then the public is entitled to rely on that limitation: *Free World Trust, supra*, at ¶51. An inventor cannot enlarge the scope of the grant of exclusive rights beyond that which has been specified: *Western Electric v. Baldwin International Radio of Canada*, [1934] S.C.R. 570. However, the full specification may be looked at to discern the scope of the claims: *Whirlpool, supra*, at ¶49; *Free World Trust, supra*; *Western Electric, supra*, at p. 573; Lindley L.J. in *Needham v. Johnson and Co.* (1884), 1 R.P.C. 49 (H.C.A.), at p. 58. The claims are invalid if they are broader than the disclosures: *Amfac Foods Inc. v. Irving Pulp & Paper Ltd.* (1984), 80 C.P.R. (2d) 59 (F.C.T.D.), at p. 80, citing a long list of authority; *B.V.D. Co. v. Canadian Celanese Ltd.*, [1936] S.C.R. 221.

(3) *The Person Skilled in the Art*

125 Patent claims must be interpreted from the point of view of the hypothetical worker skilled in the art, who has been described by Binnie J. as a

> hypothetical person possessing the ordinary skill and knowledge of the particular art to which the invention relates, and a mind willing to understand a specification that is addressed to him. This hypothetical person has sometimes been equated with the "reasonable man" used as a standard in negligence cases. He is assumed to be a man who is going to try to achieve success and not one who is looking for difficulties or seeking failure.

> (*Free World Trust, supra*, at ¶44, quoting from H. G. Fox, *The Canadian Law and Practice Relating to Letters Patent for Inventions* (4th ed. 1969), at p. 184.)

126 A reasonable person skilled in the art, however, must also be taken to know the state of the law as it relates to the subject matter of his or her invention. For example, in *Lubrizol Corp. v. Imperial Oil Ltd.* (1992), 98 D.L.R. (4th) 1 (F.C.A.), at p. 18, Mahoney J.A. accepted that drafters of patents were able to express their claims with "extreme precision" in order for their claims to stand up to any challenge on validity, that is, they were taken to understand patent law so as to draft claims that accorded with statutory requirements.

127 This interpretation is fair and predictable because the public must equally be entitled to rely on this Court's jurisprudence in determining the scope of patent claims: *Kirin Amgen Inc. v. Hoechst Marion Roussel Ltd.*, [2002] E.W.J. No. 3792 (QL), [2002] EWCA Civ. 1096, at ¶60. In *Kirin Amgen*, the English Court of Appeal considered the testimony of opposing experts (persons skilled in the art) and narrowed a patent claim

over a naturally occurring DNA sequence (EPO gene) so that it excluded that DNA sequence in its natural and therefore unpatentable form. In doing so, the court stated at ¶ 60:

> *The patentee could not monopolise the gene per se as that existed in nature.* The patentee therefore monopolised the DNA sequence encoding for DNA when isolated and in that respect was suitable for use to express EPO in a host cell. As of 1984 such a monopoly would have seemed to give fair protection. To seek to monopolise use of the sequence when not isolated by inserting a construct into a human cell would provide a monopoly not properly supported by the description in the specification. *We also believe that third parties could reasonably expect that if they did not use a DNA sequence for insertion into a host cell, there would be no infringement.* [Emphasis added.]

128 In conclusion, a person skilled in the art, upon filing of Monsanto's patent, could not reasonably have expected that the exclusive rights for gene, cell, vector, and method claims extended exclusive rights over unpatentable plants and their offspring.

(4) *Conclusion on the Scope of Monsanto's Claims*

129 Accordingly, a purposive construction that limits this claim to its "essential elements", considering both the plain language of the claim and the specifications, leads me to the conclusion that the gene patent claims and the plant cell claims should not be construed to grant exclusive rights over the plant and all of its offspring.

130 It is clear from the specification that Monsanto's patent claims do not extend to plants, seeds, and crops. It is also clear that the gene claim does not extend patent protection to the plant. The plant cell claim ends at the point where the isolated plant cell containing the chimeric gene is placed into the growth medium for regeneration. Once the cell begins to multiply and differentiate into plant tissues, resulting in the growth of a plant, a claim should be made for the whole plant. However, the whole plant cannot be patented. Similarly, the method claim ends at the point of the regeneration of the transgenic founder plant but does not extend to methods for propagating that plant. It certainly does not extend to the offspring of the regenerated plant.

131 In effect, the patent claims grant Monsanto a monopoly over the chimeric gene and the cell into which it is inserted and the method for doing so. Therefore, no other biotechnology company can use the chimeric gene to create a glyphosate-resistant plant cell that can then be regenerated into a glyphosate-resistant plant.

D. *Validity*

(1) *The Law on Validity*

132 Claims that would otherwise be valid may be limited by statutory provisions or by jurisprudence: *Commissioner of Patents v. Farbwerke Hoechst Aktiengesellschaft Vormals Meister Lucius & Bruning*, [1964] S.C.R. 49; *Shell Oil Co. v. Commissioner of Patents*, [1982] 2 S.C.R. 536. As stated in *Farbwerke*, at p. 57, "[t]here is no inherent common law right to a patent. An inventor gets his patent according to the terms of the *Patent Act*, no more and no less. If the patent for which he is applying comes within the provisions of § 41(1) [an exemption] of the Act, then he must comply with that section."

133 Subject matters that are specifically precluded by statute from patent protection are natural phenomena, laws of nature, and scientific principles: §27(8). Other subject matter has been excluded by judicial interpretation of §2 definitions of "invention" and "process" and §27(8). For example, the following have been excluded: computer programs if the discovery involved is a method of calculation (*Schlumberger Canada Ltd. v. Commissioner of Patents*, [1982] 1 F.C. 845 (C.A.)); methods of medical treatment (*Tennessee Eastman Co. v. Commissioner of Patents*, [1974] S.C.R. 111); higher life forms (*Harvard College, supra*); business systems and methods and professional skills and methods (*State Street Bank & Trust Co. v. Signature Financial Group, Inc.*, 149 F.3d 1368 (Fed. Cir. 1998)); printed matter producing only an artistic intellectual or literary result (*Re Application of Boussac*, CIPO, Commissioner's Decision No. 143, March 10, 1973); mere human conduct or mental steps, or instructions (*Re Application of Ijzerman*, CIPO, Commissioner's Decision No. 254, July 4, 1975; *Gale's Application*, [1991] R.P.C. 305 (Pat. Ct.), at p. 323); and architectural plans (*Application No. 995 for a Townhouse Building Design (Re)* (1979), 53 C.P.R. (2d) 211 (Pat. App. Bd.)). These examples demonstrate that it is not unusual for courts and the Patent Office to interpret provisions of the *Patent Act* so as to exclude subject matter from patentability.

134 If a claim encompasses subject matter that is precluded from patentability, it is invalid. However, a claim may be interpreted taking into account the exemption. In *Shell Oil, supra*, Wilson J. stated, at p. 553, that "a claim for the compositions in these cases would, it seems to me, extend beyond the scope of the invention and violate §36". Section 36 provides that the specification needs to describe new subject matter in which exclusive property rights are claimed. Following Wilson J.'s reasoning, if any of Monsanto's patent claims had been construed to encompass plants, they would have been invalid.

(2) *Validity of Monsanto's Claims*

135 Applying the purposive construction of Monsanto's product claims, that they do not extend patent protection to plants, all of Monsanto's product claims are valid.

136 Monsanto's process claims are likewise valid. The method claims for making transgenic glyphosate-resistant plant cells should be valid because an invention may be a "process": *Tennessee Eastman, supra*. A process claim may be valid even where the subject matter it manufactures is not patentable, for example, because it is obvious: *F. Hoffmann-Laroche & Co. v. Commissioner of Patents*, [1955] S.C.R. 414; or it constitutes unpatentable subject matter: *Harvard College, supra*.

137 The second part of the method—the regeneration of the plant cell into a plant— may, however, seem more problematic. However, since this process involves substantial human intervention and does not follow the "laws of nature" as would natural asexual or sexual reproduction, I conclude that this part of the process would likewise be patentable. The Patent Commissioner in *Harvard College* found that the process of creating a transgenic cell culture that had the intermediate step of "allowing said embryo to develop into an adult animal" was patentable as a process claim. This conclusion is consistent with the policy of the Patent Office: *Patent Office Manual, supra*, at ¶16.05, and with art. 27(3)(b) of the *Agreement on Trade-Related Aspects of Intellectual Property Rights* (TRIPS), 1869 U.N.T.S. 299 (being Annex 1C of the *Marrakesh Agreement establishing the World Trade Organization*, 1867 U.N.T.S. 3).

E. *Summary and Conclusion on Construction and Validity of the Claims*

138 In short, properly construed, Monsanto's claims both for products and processes are valid. Neither extends patent protection to the plant itself, a higher life form inca-

pable of patent protection. In order to avoid the claim extending to the whole plant, the plant cell claim cannot extend past the point where the genetically modified cell begins to multiply and differentiate into plant tissues, at which point the claim would be for every cell in the plant, i.e., for the plant itself.

139 Therefore, Monsanto's valid claims are solely for genetically modified chimeric genes and cells in the laboratory prior to regeneration—and for the attendant process for making the genetically modified plant.

F. *Infringement*

140 "Infringement" is not defined in the *Patent Act*. To determine what constitutes infringement, recourse must be had to the common law, the statutory provisions that define the grant of rights to the inventor and the recourse to remedies, and, most importantly, the scope of the exclusive rights claimed in the patent: Fox, *supra*, at p. 349. Infringement, in short, is "any act that interferes with the full enjoyment of the monopoly granted to the patentee", if done without the consent of the patentee: Fox, *supra*, at p. 349.

141 The issue at this stage is whether the appellants used the invention so as to interfere with the exclusive rights of the patentee, keeping in mind that the scope of Monsanto's patent does not extend to plants. The public is entitled to rely on the reasonable expectation that unpatentable subject matter falls outside the scope of patent protection and its use does not constitute an infringement: *Kirin Amgen, supra*, at ¶ 60.

142 I will assume, as found by the courts below, that the appellants planted seeds containing Monsanto's patented gene and cell. I agree with my colleagues that the appellants did not make or construct the gene or cell contained in the canola crop and did not use Monsanto's patented process.

(1) *Statutory Interpretation of "Use" in Section 42 of the* Patent Act

143 The relevant statutory provision is § 42 of the *Patent Act* where:

> **42.** Every patent granted under this Act shall contain the title or name of the invention, with a reference to the specification, and shall, subject to this Act, grant to the patentee and the patentee's legal representatives for the term of the patent, from the granting of the patent, the exclusive right, privilege and liberty of making, constructing and using the invention and selling it to others to be used, subject to adjudication in respect thereof before any court of competent jurisdiction.

144 I will use the same three principles of statutory interpretation as did my colleagues to construe the meaning of "use" in § 42 of the *Patent Act*. These are a purposive interpretation of the word "use", a contextual analysis given the surrounding words in the provision, and the case law.

145 A purposive construction of "use" suggests that "use" is limited by the subject matter of the invention, and that any acts for a purpose whether foreseen or not by the inventor may constitute an infringing use. The problem with defining "use" in the manner of my colleagues as commercial use is that the inventor is not obliged to describe the utility of the invention, the inventor must merely describe the invention so as to produce it: *Consolboard, supra*. Utility need not include commercial utility, contrary to my colleagues' opinion. That is determined by the market place: D. Vaver, *Intellectual Property Law: Copyright, Patents, Trade-marks* (1997), at p. 120. An inventor should be entitled to a remedy such as an injunction regardless of whether the infringing use has commercial applications: *Adair v. Young* (1879), 12 Ch. D. 13 (C.A.).

146 Dickson J. (as he then was) in *Consolboard*, *supra*, cited with approval, at p. 526, the following passage, *per* Thorson P. in *The King v. American Optical Co.* (1950), 11 Fox Pat. C. 62 (Ex. Ct.), at p. 85:

> If an inventor has adequately defined his invention he is entitled to its benefit even if he does not fully appreciate or realize the advantages that flow from it or cannot give the scientific reasons for them. It is sufficient if the specification correctly and fully describes the invention and its operation or use as contemplated by the inventor, so that the public, meaning thereby persons skilled in the art, may be able, with only the specification, to use the invention as successfully as the inventor could himself.

147 Although *Consolboard*, *supra*, rejected a need to either claim a utility, or set out the "useful" characteristics of the invention in the disclosure, it did not necessarily eliminate any relationship between infringement and the specification. In *Pioneer Hi-Bred*, *supra*, at p. 1637, Lamer J. (as he then was) held that "[s]ection 36(1) was enacted so competitors could know the limits within which they should avoid infringing the subject of the invention and be aware of their freedom of maneuver when they work in an area related to that of the patentee."

148 This reasoning is essential to a more balanced interpretation of §42. A contextual analysis of that section links the verbs "use", "sell", and "make" to the noun "invention". The definition of "use" in any given circumstances must therefore be limited by the subject matter of the invention. This approach has been followed to interpret "use" in the context of §58, now §56, of the *Patent Act*. Section 56 grants an exemption from infringement for persons who have acquired patentable subject matter prior to the grant of a patent:

> **56.** (1) Every person who, before the claim date of a claim in a patent has purchased, constructed or acquired the subject matter defined by the claim, has the *right to use* and sell to others the *specific article, machine, manufacture or composition of matter patented* [i.e., the invention] and so purchased, constructed or acquired without being liable to the patentee or the legal representatives of the patentee for so doing. [Emphasis added.]

149 In *Libbey-Owens-Ford Glass Co. v. Ford Motor Co. of Canada* (1969), 1 Ex. C.R. 529, at p. 553, in reasoning approved by this Court: *Libbey-Owens-Ford Glass Co. v. Ford Motor Co. of Canada*, [1970] S.C.R. 833, and followed in *Merck & Co. v. Apotex Inc.* (1994), 59 C.P.R. (3d) 133 (F.C.T.D.), the trial judge stated that "the proper approach to the interpretation of §58 [now §56] is to first read its wording, coupled with that of s. 2(*d*) [the definition of invention], in an effort to ascertain its meaning therefrom".

150 Further, the Federal Court of Appeal in *Merck & Co. v. Apotex Inc.*, [1995] 2 F.C. 723, at p. 745, stated:

> It is the intention of the inventor, as inscribed in the patent, which protects the appellant under section 56, given that the law is not one based on form but on the scope of the whole invention....
>
> . . .
>
> This conclusion will, I believe, be strengthened in the subsequent consideration of the composition and use claims of the patent, which will reveal even more clearly the interrelatedness of the whole patent.

151 Therefore "use" and "invention" must be read conjunctively and the scope of "use" must be bounded by the scope of the claims.

152 The test for determining "use" is not whether the alleged user has deprived the patentee of the commercial benefits flowing from his invention, but whether the alleged user has deprived the patentee of his monopoly over the use of the invention as construed in the claims.

153 Applied here, the question is whether the appellants used Monsanto's genetically modified cells and genes as they existed in the laboratory prior to differentiation and propagation—or the process of genetic alteration. The question is not whether the appellants deprived Monsanto of some or all the commercial benefits of their invention.

(2) *The Law on Use*

154 With respect, in my view, the case law does not support my colleagues' interpretation of use. Much of the jurisprudence on "use" and various analogies are unhelpful because of the unique properties of biological materials, especially higher life forms that can self-replicate and spread. The fact that self-replicating materials are difficult to place within the confines of the *Patent Act* was acknowledged by the Federal Court of Appeal, at ¶ 57: "… it seems to me arguable that the patented Monsanto gene falls into a novel category. It is a patented invention found within a living plant that may, without human intervention, produce progeny containing the same invention."

155 It is well established that the use or sale of unpatented subject matter may still infringe a patent where the unpatented subject matter is made employing a patented *process*: *Saccharin Corp. v. Anglo-Continental Chemical Works, Ld.* (1900), 17 R.P.C. 307 (H.C.J.); *F. Hoffmann-Laroche*, supra, at p. 415; *Wellcome Foundation Ltd. v. Apotex Inc.* (1991), 39 C.P.R. (3d) 289 (F.C.T.D.); *American Cyanamid Co. v. Charles E. Frosst & Co.* (1965), 29 Fox Pat. C. 153 (Ex. Ct.). This proposition does not assist the respondent, however. The appellants have not infringed the *process* claim because they have not used the claimed method to produce their canola crop.

156 The real question is whether a patented *product* (the gene or cell) extends patent protection to the unpatentable object into which it is incorporated. The respondents and the intervener, BIOTECanada, further contend that "[i]t is trite law that an unpatentable composition of matter can be an infringement by virtue of it incorporating *patented material*" (joint factum of BIOTECanada and the Canadian Seed Trade Association, at ¶ 39 (emphasis added)), but, like my colleagues, provided no authority on this point. In any event, there is no genuinely useful analogy between growing a plant in which every cell and every cell of all its progeny are remotely traceable to the genetically modified cell and contain the chimeric gene and putting a zipper in a garment, or tires on a car or constructing with Lego blocks. The analogies are particularly weak when it is considered that the plant can subsequently grow, reproduce, and spread with no further human intervention.

157 One option that was urged on us by the appellants was to incorporate a knowledge element into the definition of "use". Such a solution would be broadly applicable to other types of patents and lend uncertainty to a settled issue in Canadian patent law that intention is irrelevant to infringement: *Terrell on the Law of Patents* (15th ed. 2000), at ¶ 8.10; *Hughes and Woodley on Patents* (1984), at § 26; *British United Shoe Machinery Co. v. Gimson Shoe Machinery Co.* (1928), 45 R.P.C. 290 (C.A.), at p. 308; *Computalog Ltd. v. Comtech Logging Ltd.* (1992), 44 C.P.R. (3d) 77 (F.C.A.), at p. 88; *Illinois Tool Works Inc. v. Cobra Anchors Co.* (2002), 221 F.T.R. 161, 2002 FCT 829. Lord Hoffmann in *Merrell Dow Pharmaceuticals Inc. v. H.N. Norton & Co.*, [1996] R.P.C. 76 (H.L.), at p. 92, pointed out that since liability is absolute, the alleged infringer's state of mind is ir-

relevant. "[I]t is and always has been the law in relation to direct infringement that the knowledge or intention of the infringer is irrelevant" (*Terrell on the Law of Patents, supra,* at ¶ 8.08).

158 Most people are not aware of the contents of patents but are effectively deemed to have knowledge. What matters is what the person does. If the person's acts interfere with the exclusive rights granted by the patent, then there is infringement: *Pfizer Corp. v. Ministry of Health,* [1965] A.C. 512 (H.L.). A case such as *British United Shoe Machinery Co. v. Simon Collier Ld.* (1910), 27 R.P.C. 567 (H.L.), that may suggest the contrary is unusual and restricted to its facts: *Pfizer, supra,* or goes to remedy and not infringement: *Terrell on the Law of Patents, supra,* at ¶ 8.09. As pointed out by my colleagues, the presumption of use may only be rebutted in the very rare circumstances, such as in *British United Shoe Machinery Co. v. Simon Collier Ld., supra,* where neither the product nor its stand-by value was used.

159 A truly innocent infringer may be able to rebut the presumption of use. However, that would likely prove difficult once the innocent infringer became aware that the genetically modified crop was present—or was likely to be present—on his or her land and continued to practice traditional farming methods, such as saving seed. The complexities and nuances of innocent bystander protection in the context of agricultural biotechnology should be expressly considered by Parliament because it can only be inadequately accommodated by the law on use.

(3) *Conclusion on Infringement*

160 In the result, the lower courts erred not only in construing the claims to extend to plants and seed, but in construing "use" to include the use of subject matter disclaimed by the patentee, namely the plant. The appellants as users were entitled to rely on the reasonable expectation that plants, as unpatentable subject matter, fall outside the scope of patent protection. Accordingly, the cultivation of plants containing the patented gene and cell does not constitute an infringement. The plants containing the patented gene can have no stand-by value or utility as my colleagues allege. To conclude otherwise would, in effect, confer patent protection on the plant.

161 Uses that would constitute an infringement include using the chimeric gene in its isolated form to create an expression or cloning vector or a transformation vector and using the transformation vector to create a transgenic plant cell. The use claimed for the plant cell extends to the isolated plant cell in a laboratory culture used to regenerate a "founder plant" but not to its offspring.

162 There is no claim for a "glyphosate-resistant" plant and all its offspring. Therefore saving, planting, or selling seed from glyphosate-resistant plants does not constitute an infringing use.

163 Obviously, as was done here, Monsanto can still license the sale of seeds that it produces from its patented invention and can impose contractual obligations on the licencee. Licensing allows the patent owner to impose conditions on the use of the plant, such as a prohibition on saving seeds, with the concomitant ability to sue the farmer for breach of contract if the farmer violates any of the terms of the licence.

G. *The Conclusion Is Consistent With Canada's International Obligations Under the Agreement on Trade-Related Aspects of Intellectual Property Rights*

164 In *Harvard College, supra,* both the majority and the minority called for Parliament's intervention on the issue of patenting higher life forms. As things stand, my conclusion

on the scope of Monsanto's patent claims that is determinative of both validity and infringing use is not contrary to art. 27(1) of TRIPS whereby Canada has agreed to make patents available for any invention without discrimination as to the field of technology.

165 The Canadian Biotechnology Advisory Committee, in *Patenting of Higher Life Forms and Related Issues* (June 2002), suggests that the contrary may, in fact, be the case. The use of biologically replicating organisms as a "vehicle" for genetic patents may overcompensate the patentee both in relation to what was invented, and to other areas of invention. The Canadian Biotechnology Advisory Committee explains the point as follows (at p. 12):

> Because higher life forms can reproduce by themselves, the grant of a patent over a plant, seed or non-human animal covers not only the particular plant, seed or animal sold, but also all its progeny containing the patented invention for all generations until the expiry of the patent term (20 years from the priority date). In addition, much of the value of the higher life form, particularly with respect to animals, derives from the natural characteristics of the original organism and has nothing to do with the invention. In light of these unique characteristics of biological inventions, granting the patent holder exclusive rights that extend not only to the particular organism embodying the invention but also to all subsequent progeny of that organism represents a significant increase in the scope of rights offered to patent holders. It also represents a greater transfer of economic interests from the agricultural community to the biotechnology industry than exists in other fields of science.

166 My conclusion does not violate, and indeed is supported by art. 27(3)(b) of TRIPS, that states:

Article 27

...

3.   Members may also exclude from patentability:

...

(b) plants and animals other than micro-organisms, and essentially biological processes for the production of plants or animals other than non-biological and microbiological processes. However, Members shall provide for the protection of plant varieties either by patents or by an effective *sui generis* system or by any combination thereof....

167 Allowing gene and cell claims to extend patent protection to plants would render this provision of TRIPS meaningless. To find that possession of plants, as the embodiment of a gene or cell claim, constitute a "use" of that claim would have the same effect as patenting the plant. Therefore, my conclusion on both the scope of the claims and the scope of use is consistent with Canada's international obligations under TRIPS.

168 Canada has a *sui generis* system of protection for plants. The *Plant Breeders' Rights Act*, S.C. 1990, c. 20, represents a nuanced statutory regime that takes into consideration the rights of both the developers of new plant varieties and users. There is nothing in the *Plant Breeders' Rights Act* that would exclude genetically modified new plant varieties, such as Roundup Ready Canola, from its purview.

169 While the "rights available under the *Plant Breeders' Rights Act* fall well short of those conferred by patent, both in comprehensiveness and in duration" (*Harvard College, supra*, at ¶61), they may be all that Monsanto is entitled to. Indeed, Professor

Vaver, *supra*, at p. 128, recognizes that patents should not necessarily be available when other, more tailored intellectual property protection exits. Monsanto has since had the opportunity to come within its protection even though the Act was not in force when Monsanto was granted its patent.

170 In light of my conclusion on the issue of infringement, it is unnecessary for me to consider the other issues on appeal.

III. *Disposition*

171 I would allow the appeal with costs to the appellants throughout.

APPENDIX

Patent Document Number 1,313,830: Glyphosate-Resistant Plants

The embodiments of the invention in which an exclusive property or privilege is claimed are defined as follows:

1. A chimeric plant gene which comprises:

(a) a promoter sequence which functions in plant cells;

(b) a coding sequence which causes the production of RNA, encoding a chloroplast transit peptide/5-enolpyruvylshikimate-3-phosphate synthase (EPSPS) fusion polypeptide, which chloroplast transit peptide permits the fusion polypeptide to be imported into a chloroplast of a plant cell; and

(c) a 3' non-translated region which encodes a polyadenylation signal which functions in plant cells to cause the addition of polyadenylate nucleotides to the 3' end of the RNA;

the promoter being heterologous with respect to the coding sequence and adapted to cause sufficient expression of the fusion polypeptide to enhance the glyphosate resistance of a plant cell transformed with the gene.

2. A chimeric gene of Claim 1 in which the promoter sequence is a plant virus promoter sequence.

3. A chimeric gene of Claim 2 in which the promoter sequence is a promoter sequence from cauliflower mosaic virus (CaMV).

4. A chimeric gene of Claim 3 in which the promoter sequence is the CaMV35S promoter sequence.

5. A chimeric gene of Claim 1 in which the coding sequence encodes a mutant 5-enolpyruvylshikimate-3-phosphate synthase (EPSPS).

6. A chimeric gene of Claim 1 in which the EPSPS coding sequence encodes an EPSPS from an organism selected from the group consisting of bacteria, fungi and plants.

7. A chimeric gene of Claim 1 in which the chloroplast transit peptide is from a plant EPSPS gene.

8. A cloning or expression vector comprising a chimeric plant gene of Claim 1.

9. A cloning or expression vector of Claim 8 in which the chimeric plant gene encodes a chloroplast transit peptide of a plant EPSPS gene.

10. A cloning or expression vector of Claim 9 in which the chimeric plant gene comprises a promoter sequence from a plant virus.

11. A cloning or expression vector of Claim 10 in which the promoter sequence is a promoter sequence from cauliflower mosaic virus (CaMV).

12. A cloning or expression vector of Claim 11 in which the promoter sequence is the CaMV35S promoter sequence.

13. A cloning or expression vector of Claim 8 in which the chimeric plant gene comprises a coding sequence encoding a mutant 5-enolpyruvylshikimate-3-phosphate synthase.

14. A cloning or expression vector of Claim 8 in which the coding sequence encodes an EPSPS from an organism selected from the group consisting of bacteria, fungi and plants.

15. A plant transformation vector which comprises a chimeric gene of Claim 1.

16. A plant transformation vector of Claim 15 in which the chimeric plant gene encodes a chloroplast transit peptide of a plant EPSPS gene.

17. A plant transformation vector of Claim 15 in which the chimeric plant gene comprises a promoter sequence from a plant virus.

18. A plant transformation vector of Claim 17 in which the promoter sequence is a promoter sequence from cauliflower mosaic virus (CaMV).

19. A plant transformation vector of Claim 18 in which the promoter sequence is the CaMV35S promoter sequence.

20. A plant transformation vector of Claim 15 in which the chimeric plant gene comprises a coding sequence encoding a mutant 5-enolpyruvylshikimate-3-phosphate synthase.

21. A plant transformation vector of Claim 15 in which the coding sequence encodes an EPSPS from an organism selected from the group consisting of bacteria, fungi and plants.

22. A glyphosate-resistant plant cell comprising a chimeric plant gene of Claim 1.

23. A glyphosate-resistant plant cell of Claim 22 in which the promoter sequence is a plant virus promoter sequence.

24. A glyphosate-resistant plant cell of Claim 23 in which the promoter sequence is a promoter sequence from cauliflower mosaic virus (CaMV).

25. A glyphosate-resistant plant cell of Claim 24 in which the promoter sequence is the CaMV35S promoter sequence.

26. A glyphosate-resistant plant cell of Claim 22 in which the coding sequence encodes a mutant 5-enolpyruvylshikimate-3-phosphate synthase.

27. A glyphosate-resistant plant cell of Claim 22 in which the coding sequence encodes an EPSPS from an organism selected from the group consisting of bacteria, fungi and plants.

28. A glyphosate-resistant plant cell of Claim 22 in which the chloroplast transit peptide is from a plant EPSPS gene.

29. A method for producing a glyphosate-resistant dicotyledonous plant which comprises:

  (a) transforming plant cells using an *Agrobacterium* transformation vector comprising a chimeric plant gene of Claim 1; and

  (b) regenerating glyphosate-resistant plants from said transformed plant cells.

30. A method of Claim 29 in which the chimeric plant gene comprises a plant virus promoter sequence.

31. A method of Claim 30 in which the promoter sequence is a promoter sequence from cauliflower mosaic virus (CaMV).

32. A method of Claim 31 in which the promoter sequence is the CaMV35S promoter sequence.

33. A method of Claim 29 in which the chimeric gene comprises a coding sequence encoding a mutant 5-enolpyruvylshikimate-3-phosphate synthase.

34. A method of Claim 29 in which the coding sequence encodes an EPSPS from an organism selected from the group consisting of bacteria, fungi and plants.

35. A method of Claim 29 in which the coding sequence encodes the chloroplast transit peptide from a plant EPSPS gene.

36. A method for producing a glyphosate-resistant plant cell which comprises transforming the plant cell with a plant transformation vector of Claim 15.

37. A method of Claim 36 in which the chimeric gene comprises a promoter sequence from a plant virus.

38. A method of Claim 37 in which the promoter sequence is a promoter sequence from cauliflower mosaic virus (CaMV).

39. A method of Claim 38 in which the promoter sequence is the CaMV35S promoter sequence.

40. A method of Claim 36 in which the chimeric gene comprises a coding sequence encoding a mutant 5-enolpyruvylshikimate-3-phosphate synthase.

41. A method of Claim 36 in which the coding sequence encodes an EPSPS from an organism selected from the group consisting of bacteria, fungi and plants.

42. A method of Claim 36 in which the coding sequence encodes the chloroplast transit peptide from a plant EPSPS gene.

43. A glyphosate-resistant tomato cell of Claim 22.

44. A glyphosate-resistant tobacco cell of Claim 22.

45. A glyphosate-resistant oil seed rape cell of Claim 22.

46. A glyphosate-resistant flax cell of Claim 22.

47. A glyphosate-resistant soybean cell of Claim 22.

48. A glyphosate-resistant sunflower cell of Claim 22.

49. A glyphosate-resistant sugar beet cell of Claim 22.

50. A glyphosate-resistant alfalfa cell of Claim 22.

51. A glyphosate-resistant cotton cell of Claim 22.

52. Plasmid pMON546, ATCC accession number 53213.

Harvard College
v.
Canada (Commissioner of Patents)

Supreme Court of Canada
Judgment: December 5, 2002
Heard: May 21, 2002
Docket: 28155

The applicant sought to produce animals susceptible to cancer in order to conduct animal carcinogenicity studies. A cancer-prone mouse was produced by using an activated oncogene sequence. A plasmid or carrier was constructed containing the oncogene. The plasmid was injected into a fertilized mouse egg. The injected egg was transferred into a female host mouse and allowed to develop to term. If the resulting mouse had all of its cells affected by the oncogene, it was called a founder mouse. A founder mouse was mated with an uninjected mouse. Fifty per cent of the resulting mice would have all of their cells affected by the oncogene and would be suitable for animal carcinogenic studies. The applicant sought to protect the process by which the oncomice were produced and the end product of the process, being the founder mouse and the offspring whose cells were affected by the oncogene. The Patent Examiner allowed a patent for the process claims but not the product claims. The Commissioner of Patents agreed. The commissioner was of the view that the product claims were outside the definition of "invention" in §2 of the Patent Act. The applicant unsuccessfully appealed to the Federal Court of Canada, Trial Division. The applicant successfully appealed to the Federal Court of Appeal. The Commissioner appealed.

Held: The appeal was allowed.

Per Bastarache J. (L'Heureux-Dubé, Gonthier, Iacobucci and LeBel JJ. concurring): "Correctness" is the standard of review of this decision of the Commissioner of Patents. The court is as well placed as the commissioner to decide whether higher life forms are included in the definition of "invention" in §2 of the Act because the question approaches a pure determination of law having significant precedential value. There is no privative clause in the Act. The Act gives a broad right of appeal. To refuse a patent, the commissioner must be satisfied that the applicant is not "by law" entitled to the patent. Section 40 of the Act does not give the commissioner any discretion to refuse a patent on the basis of public policy considerations independent of any express provision in the Act.

The words of the Act are to be read in their entire context. They are to be read in their grammatical and ordinary sense, harmoniously with the scheme of the Act, the object of the Act and the intention of Parliament. The best reading of the Act supports the conclusion that higher life forms are not patentable.

The sole question was whether the words "manufacture" and "composition of matter" in the context of the Act are sufficiently broad to include higher life forms. The definition of "invention" is broad to encompass unforeseen and unanticipated technology, but is limited to any "art, process, machine, manufacture or composition of matter." "Machine" and "manufacture" do not imply a conscious, sentient living creature. The words "composition of matter" that complete the phrase are restricted to the same genus as the terms preceding, even though a collective term may ordinarily have a much broader meaning. The words "composition of matter" are best read as not including higher life forms. "Matter" captures one aspect of a higher life form. Higher life forms are generally regarded as possessing qualities and characteristics that transcend the particular genetic material of which they are composed. They cannot be conceptualized as mere compositions of matter in the context of the Act. The fact that inventions are unanticipated and unforeseeable does not mean that they are all patentable.

The patentability of higher life forms is a highly contentious matter raising serious practical, ethical and environmental concerns not contemplated by the Act. The issue raises questions of great significance and importance requiring a dramatic expansion of the traditional patent regime. The patenting of higher life forms raises unique concerns not applying to nonliving inventions and which are not addressed by the scheme of the Act. The Act is ill-equipped to deal appropriately with higher life forms. The court does not have the institutional competence to deal with issues of this complexity.

The objects of the Act are the advancement of research and development and the encouragement of broad economic activity. This does not imply that to promote ingenuity is to render all inventions patentable. A product of human ingenuity must fall within the terms of the Act to be patentable.

Given the ambiguity in the law, the substance and form of subsequent legislation such the Plant Breeders' Rights Act are relevant. This special legislation protects plant breeders but does not address other higher life forms. This shows that mechanisms other than the Patent Act may be used to encourage inventors to undertake innovative activity in the field of biotechnology. Many of the issues arising regarding intellectual property protection for plant varieties also arise when considering the patentability of higher life forms. If a special legislative scheme was needed to protect plant varieties, a subset of higher life forms, a similar scheme may also be required to deal with patenting higher life forms in general.

The distinction between lower and higher life forms is not explicit in the Patent Act but is defensible on the basis of the common sense differences between the two. There is a consensus that human life is not patentable but this distinction is not explicit in the Act. If the line between lower and higher life forms is indefensible and arbitrary, then so too is the line between human beings and other higher life forms. It is accepted that lower life forms are patentable but this does not lead to the conclusion that higher life forms are patentable. In part, this is because it is easier to conceptualize a lower life form as a "composition of matter" or "manufacture" than it is to conceptualize a higher life form in these terms. Micro-organisms produced en masse as chemical compounds are prepared and are formed in such large numbers that any measurable quantity will possess uniform properties and characteristics. The same is not true for plants and animals. Several important features possessed by animals distinguish them from both micro-organisms and plants and remove them from being considered a "composition of matter" or a "manufacture." The specific exception for plants and animals in trade agreements shows that a distinction between higher and lower life forms is widely accepted as valid.

Per Binnie J. (dissenting)(McLachlin C.J.C., Major and Arbour JJ. concurring): The oncomouse has been patented in Austria, Belgium, Denmark, Finland, France, Germany, Greece, Ireland, Italy, Luxembourg, The Netherlands, Portugal, Spain, Sweden, the United Kingdom and the United States. A similar patent has been issued in Japan. New Zealand has patented a transgenic mouse that has been genetically modified to be susceptible to HIV infection. The global mobility of capital and technology makes it desirable that comparable jurisdictions with comparable intellectual property legislation have similar legal results. There is no statutory basis to conclude that the oncomouse is not an invention in Canada.

The extraordinary scientific achievement of altering every single cell in the body of an animal which does not in this altered form exist in nature, by human modification of the genetic material of which it is composed is an inventive "composition of matter" within the meaning of §2 of the Act. Acknowledging that the fertilized, genetically altered oncomouse egg is an invention under the Act, there is no basis to conclude that the resulting oncomouse is not itself patentable because it is not an invention. The question is not whether Parliament intended to include "oncomice" or "higher life forms" or biotechnology generally in patent legislation, but whether Parliament intended to protect inventions that were unanticipated when the Act was enacted or at any time before the claimed invention. When enacting the definition of "invention" in 1869, Parliament did not contemplate moon rockets, antibiotics, telephones, e-mail or handheld computers. The definition of "invention" should be read as a whole and expansively with a view to giving protection to what is novel and useful and unobvious. The context and scheme of the Act support a broad interpretation of the words "composition of matter" not confined to inanimate matter. The commissioner has no discretion to refuse a patent on the grounds of morality, public interest, public order or any other ground if the statutory conditions are met. The applicant met the statutory criteria and by law was entitled to the patent.

The adoption of the Plant Breeders' Rights Act does not mean that the subject-matter of patents excludes plants and other higher life forms such as seeds and animals. The rights available under the Plant Breeders' Rights Act fall short of those conferred by patent, both in comprehensiveness and duration. The language of the Patent Act predates Confederation. There was no repeal by implication by the Plant Breeders' Rights Act. The two Acts are not inconsistent.

The lack of a regulatory framework to address the ethical and scientific issues raised by genetic patents is not fatal. The court has no mandate to deny patentability because of the novelty or the potential social, economic or cultural impact of an invention. It is normal that regulation follows rather than precedes the invention. The regulatory regimes for inventions cannot and should not all be placed under the inadequate umbrella of the Patent Act. It is for Parliament to decide whether to make a subject-matter exception for higher life forms and to define it. Neither the commissioner nor the court has the authority to declare a moratorium on higher life patents until Parliament chooses to act.

Binnie J.:

1 The biotechnology revolution in the 50 years since discovery of the structure of DNA has been fuelled by extraordinary human ingenuity and financed in significant part by private investment. Like most revolutions, it has wide ramifications, and presents potential and serious dangers as well as past and future benefits. In this appeal, however, we are only dealing with a small corner of the biotechnology controversy. We are asked to determine whether the oncomouse, a genetically modified rodent with heightened genetic susceptibility to cancer, is an invention. The legal issue is a narrow one and does not provide a proper platform on which to engage in a debate over animal rights, or religion, or the arrogance of the human race.

2 The oncomouse has been held patentable, and is now patented in jurisdictions that cover Austria, Belgium, Denmark, Finland, France, Germany, Greece, Ireland, Italy, Luxembourg, The Netherlands, Portugal, Spain, Sweden, the United Kingdom and the United States. A similar patent has been issued in Japan. New Zealand has issued a patent for a transgenic mouse that has been genetically modified to be susceptible to HIV infection. Indeed, we were not told of any country with a patent system comparable to Canada's (or otherwise) in which a patent on the oncomouse had been applied for and been refused.

3 If Canada is to stand apart from jurisdictions with which we usually invite comparison on an issue so fundamental to intellectual property law as what constitutes "an invention", the respondent, successful everywhere but in Canada, might expect to see something unique in our legislation. However, one looks in vain for a difference in definition to fuel the Commissioner's contention that, *as a matter of statutory interpretation*, the oncomouse is not an invention. The truth is that our legislation is not unique. The Canadian definition of what constitutes an invention, initially adopted in pre-Confederation statutes, was essentially taken from the United States *Patent Act of 1793*, a definition generally attributed to Thomas Jefferson. The United States patent on the oncomouse was issued 14 years ago. My colleague, Bastarache J., acknowledges that the fertilized, genetically altered oncomouse egg is an invention under our *Patent Act,*

R.S.C. 1985, c. P-4 (¶ 162). Thereafter, we part company, because my colleague goes on to conclude that the resulting *oncomouse*, that grows from the patented egg, is not itself patentable because it is not an invention. Subject matter patentability, on this view, is lost between two successive stages of a transgenic mouse's genetically pre-programmed growth. In my opinion, with respect, such a "disappearing subject-matter" exception finds no support in the statutory language.

4 A patent, of course, does not give its holder a licence to practise the invention free of regulatory control (any more than an *un*patented invention enjoys such immunity). On the contrary, the grant of a patent simply reflects the public interest in promoting the disclosure of advancements in learning by rewarding human ingenuity. Innovation is said to be the lifeblood of a modern economy. We neglect rewarding it at our peril. Having disclosed to the public the secrets of how to make or use the invention, the inventor can prevent *unauthorized* people for a limited time from taking a "free ride" in exploiting the information thus disclosed. At the same time, persons skilled in the art of the patent are helped to further advance the frontiers of knowledge by standing on the shoulders of those who have gone before.

5 The issues being thus identified, I think the majority decision of the Federal Court of Appeal was correct. The appeal should be dismissed.

A. Statutory Interpretation

6 The issue, in the words of §2 of the *Patent Act*, is whether the oncomouse that has been produced by a combination of genetic engineering and natural gestation is a "composition of matter" that is new, unobvious and useful. If it is, then the President and Fellows of Harvard University, who funded the research, are entitled to a patent. My colleague, Bastarache J., writes of the oncomouse as follows (at ¶ 163):

The fact that it has this predisposition to cancer that makes it valuable to humans does not mean that the mouse, along with other animal life forms, can be defined solely with reference to the genetic matter of which it is composed. [Emphasis added.]

7 While acknowledging, therefore, that the oncomouse is a "composition of [genetic] matter", my colleague's contention is that the oncomouse is a "composition of [genetic] matter" *plus* something else, undefined. The respondent, however, does not claim to have invented the "plus". Its sole claim is to have modified what my colleague describes as the "genetic matter of which [the oncomouse] is composed", as described in the disclosure portion of the patent application:

(i) the desired oncogene is obtained from the genetic code of a non-mammal source, such as a virus;

(ii) a vehicle for transporting the oncogene into the mammal's chromosomes is constructed using a small piece of circular bacterial DNA referred to as a plasmid; the plasmid is chemically cut and the oncogene is chemically "spliced" into the plasmid;

(iii) the plasmid containing the oncogene is then mechanically injected into fertilized eggs at a site called the male pronucleus;

(iv) the eggs are then implanted in a host mammal or "foster mother";

(v) the eggs are permitted to develop and the offspring are delivered by the foster mother;

(vi) after delivery, the offspring are tested for the presence of the oncogene; the offspring that contain the oncogene are called "founder" animals;

(vii) founder animals are subsequently mated with ordinary animals and the offspring are again tested for the presence of the oncogene before the offspring are used in research.

8 As will be explained more fully below, I believe that the extraordinary scientific achievement of altering every single cell in the body of an animal which does not in this altered form exist in nature, by human modification of "the genetic material of which it is composed", is an inventive "composition of matter" within the meaning of §2 of the *Patent Act*.

9 The position taken by the Commissioner of Patents is, I think, curious. While expressly acknowledging that the oncomouse is new, useful and non-obvious, and therefore meets the usual statutory criteria, the Commissioner of Patents denies that "higher life forms" fall within the *subject matter* contemplated by Parliament as patentable. He says, at ¶51 of his factum:

In 1869, when Parliament first made provision for the patenting of "any new and useful … manufacture, or composition of matter", genetic engineering was unheard of. Thus, Parliament could not at the time of enactment have *intended* that higher life forms would come within the meaning of those words. [Emphasis added.]

10 It is true, of course, that in 1869, when the post-Confederation patent act was passed, Parliament did not contemplate genetically engineered "higher life forms" (*Act respecting Patents of Invention*, S.C. 1869, c. 11). Parliament in 1869 did not contemplate genetically engineered "*lower* life forms" either, although in recent years Canadian patents have regularly been issued for such inventions. (My colleague, Bastarache J., at ¶201, affirms that "lower life" forms will continue to be patentable.) Nor did Parliament in 1869 contemplate moon rockets, antibiotics, telephones, e-mail or hand-held computers. The proper question is not whether Parliament intended to include "oncomice" or "higher life forms" or biotechnology generally in patent legislation, but whether Parliament intended to protect "inventions" that were *not* anticipated at the time of enactment of the *Patent Act*, or indeed, at any time before the claimed invention.

11 I accept, as does my colleague, that the proper approach to interpretation of this statute is to read the words "in their entire context and in their grammatical and ordinary sense harmoniously with the scheme of the Act, the object of the Act, and the intention of Parliament": Driedger, *Construction of Statutes* (2nd ed. 1983), at p. 87. In my opinion, with respect, the context and scheme of the *Patent Act* reinforce the expansive sense of the words "composition of matter" to render the oncomouse patentable. The intent that can properly be attributed to Parliament, based on the language it used and the context of patent legislation generally, is that it considered it to be in the public interest to encourage new and useful inventions without knowing what such inventions would turn out to be and to that end inventors who disclosed their work should be rewarded for their ingenuity. A further indication of Parliament's intent is that the Commissioner of Patents was given *no* discretion to refuse a patent on the grounds of morality, public interest, public order, or any other ground if the statutory criteria are met: *Patent Act*, §40. In my view, the respondent has fulfilled the statutory criteria and "by law" is entitled to the patent.

B. International Scope of Intellectual Property Law

12 Intellectual property has global mobility, and states have worked diligently to harmonize their patent, copyright and trademark regimes. In this context, the Commissioner's approach to this case sounds a highly discordant note. Intellectual property was

the subject matter of such influential agreements as the *International Convention for the Protection of Industrial Property (Paris Convention)* as early as 1883. International rules governing patents were strengthened by the *European Patent Convention* in 1973, and, more recently, the World Trade Organization *Agreement on Trade-Related Aspects of Intellectual Property Rights* (TRIPS) in 1994. Copyright was the subject of the *Berne Convention for the Protection of Literary and Artistic Works* in 1886, revised by the *Berlin Convention of 1908* and the *Rome Convention* of 1928. The *Universal Copyright Convention* was concluded in 1952. Legislation varies of course, from state to state, but broadly speaking Canada has sought to harmonize its concepts of intellectual property with other like-minded jurisdictions.

13 The mobility of capital and technology makes it desirable that comparable jurisdictions with comparable intellectual property legislation arrive (to the extent permitted by the specifics of their own laws) at similar legal results: *Galerie d'art du Petit Champlain inc. c. Théberge*, 2002 SCC 34 (S.C.C.), at ¶ 6.

14 The appellant Commissioner's definition of *un*patentable "higher life forms" includes not only animals but also plants and seeds. Genetically modified foods are controversial, but these are not controversies that should be dealt with by judicial exclusion of "higher life forms" from the definition of "an invention". Parliament itself has clearly signalled its limited view of the role and function of the *Patent Act*. In 1993, it repealed the prohibition in the former §27(3) of the *Patent Act* against patenting "an invention that has an illicit object in view". It thereby made it clear that granting a patent is not an expression of approval or disapproval. At that time, Parliament did *not* add a provision, present in the *European Patent Convention* and in many civil law systems and international agreements, that patents will not be granted for inventions whose use or exploitation would be inconsistent with *ordre public*, public morality, or environmental or health protection. That type of provision would open the door to value judgments in assessing patentability. Parliament did not endorse such an approach, even though the 1993 amendments were introduced to bring Canadian patent law into compliance with various international agreements. Parliament thereby signalled, however passively, that these important aspects of public policy would continue to be dealt with by regulatory regimes outside the *Patent Act*.

15 A more recent indication of the government's approach is the *Assisted Human Reproduction Act*. A discussion paper was placed before the Canadian public in 2000 and a bill placed before Parliament by the Minister of Health as Bill C-56 on May 9, 2002 (re-introduced in the same form as Bill C-13 on October 9, 2002). The bill would prohibit the cloning of human beings, modifying the germ line identity of human beings and the use of human embryos for industrial or commercial purposes. At the same time, Bill C-13 would *not* prevent inventions in that regard from being patented in Canada. This illustrates, again, the fundamental distinction made by Parliament between patentability of an invention and regulation of activity associated with an invention.

E. Patenting Life Forms in Canada

26 My colleague, Bastarache J., comments that "[t]he patentability of lower life forms is not at issue before this Court, and was in fact never litigated in Canada" (¶ 198). However, certain enzyme products (which are living matter) were held to be patentable by this Court 60 years ago in *J.R. Short Milling Co. (Can.) v. George Weston Bread & Cakes Ltd.*, [1942] S.C.R. 187 (S.C.C.), as were engineered micro-organisms used as an antibiotic in *Laboratoire Pentagone Ltée v. Parke, Davis & Co.*, [1968] S.C.R. 307 (S.C.C.).

27 The attempt to patent life forms last came before this Court in *Pioneer Hi-Bred Ltd. v. Canada (Commissioner of Patents)*, [1989] 1 S.C.R. 1623 (S.C.C.). In that case, a patent was sought for a new soybean variety developed from artificial crossbreeding and selection, but cultivated naturally. The applicant's "disclosure" consisted of depositing seed samples with the Patent Office. This Court upheld the rejection of the patent application on the basis that filing a seed sample did not meet the disclosure requirements of § 36(1) of the *Patent Act*, R.S.C. 1970, c. P-4, which then (as now (§ 27(3)) required the inventor to set forth clearly the various steps required to make the "composition of matter, in such full, clear, concise and exact terms as to enable any person skilled in the art or science to which it pertains, or with which it is most closely connected, to make … it". In light of the deficient disclosure, the Court expressly declined to go on to consider whether the new soybean variety could be regarded as an invention within the meaning of § 2.

28 In the course of his reasons for the Court, however, Lamer J. (as he then was) pointed out an important distinction between two approaches to "genetic engineering". The first method (employed by Pioneer Hi-Bred) was hybridization and selection. In this method, "[t]here is thus human intervention … which does not alter the actual rules of reproduction, which continues to obey the laws of nature" (pp. 1632–33).

29 The second method (which was used here to develop the oncomouse) requires change in the genetic material—an alteration of the genetic code affecting all the hereditary material—since in the latter case the intervention occurs inside the gene itself. The change made is thus a molecular one and the "new" gene is thus ultimately the result of a chemical reaction, which will in due course lead to a change in the trait controlled by the gene. While the first method [crossbreeding] implies an evolution based strictly on heredity and Mendelian principles, the second also employs a sharp and permanent alteration of hereditary traits by a change in the quality of the genes. [p. 1633]

30 I do not think Lamer J. expressed any doubt that an "alteration of the genetic code affecting all the hereditary material" produced "an invention" (although he did not decide the point). His doubts seemed rather to be related to whether crossbreeding *without* altering the genetic code using modern variants of techniques that are almost as old as agriculture itself was inventive within the scope of the Act:

The courts have regarded creations following the laws of nature as being mere discoveries the existence of which man has simply uncovered without thereby being able to claim he has invented them. Hi-Bred is asking this Court to reverse a position long defended in the case law. [p. 1634]

The Harvard researchers did not merely "uncover" a naturally occurring oncomouse. The complexity of the genetic splicing did not "follow" the laws of nature, but was a human intervention of a high order. They engineered that part of its genetic code that appears to be responsible for its commercial value.

31 Reference should also be made to *Abitibi Co., Re* (1982), 62 C.P.R. (2d) 81 (Can. Pat. App. Bd. & Pat. Commr.), in which the applicant sought to patent a living organism, namely a "mixed fungal yeast culture system" (p. 83) useful in digesting effluent from wood pulp mills. In holding the subject matter to be patentable, the Patent Appeal Board rejected the Patent Office's somewhat narrow view "derived from a time when the many gradations of living forms were not as fully apprehended as is now possible" (*General Electric Co.'s Application, Re*, [1961] R.P.C. 21, at p. 25, cited in *Abitibi Co.* at p. 85). Somewhat in advance of its time, the Patent Appeal Board in *Abitibi Co.* then commented at p. 90 that "[i]f an inventor creates a new and unobvious insect [i.e., a "*higher*

life form"] which did not exist before (and thus is not a product of nature), and can recreate it uniformly and at will, and it is useful (for example to destroy the spruce bud worm), then it is every bit as much a new tool of man as a micro-organism" and thus, subject to certain conditions as to reproducibility, patentable. In relation to the Abitibi micro-organism at hand, the Patent Appeal Board ruled (at p. 91):

The organism, to be claimed, should not of course have existed previously in nature, for in that event the "inventor" did not create it, and his "invention" is old. It must also be useful, in the sense that it carries out some useful known objective, such as separating oil from sand, producing antibiotics or the like. It cannot be a mere laboratory curiosity whose only possible claim to utility is as a starting material for further research. And it must be sufficiently different from known species that it can be said that its creation involved the necessary element of inventive ingenuity. In the present case we believe the product claims meets these tests, and the [Patent Office] objection should be withdrawn.

32 In *Application for Patent of Connaught Laboratories, Re* (1982), 82 C.P.R. (2d) 32 (Can. Pat. App. Bd. & Pat. Commr.), the Patent Appeal Board allowed that cell lines derived from "higher life forms" were patentable, thus removing another possible dividing line. Not all aspects of "higher life forms" were unpatentable. The Patent Office (now the Canadian Intellectual Property Office) regularly allows patents on human genes, proteins, cells and DNA sequences. Under Canadian law, it is not "life" *per se* which is unpatentable. The issues are, rather, the view taken by the Commissioner to narrow the range of living matter to be considered patentable, and where in the *Patent Act* is there statutory authority for the line the Commissioner wants to draw?

F. Patenting of "Higher Life Forms" in Comparable Jurisdictions

33 In 1873, Louis Pasteur was granted a patent in the United States on a certain yeast, which is a living organism.

34 A patent for the Harvard oncomouse was issued by the United States Patent Office on April 12, 1988 and by the European Patent Office on May 13, 1992, despite the explicit power under the *European Patent Convention* to refuse a patent based on "morality" or "*ordre public*". As mentioned earlier, a similar patent has been issued in Japan, and New Zealand has issued a patent for a transgenic mouse.

35 The appellant Commissioner's principal argument is that to allow the oncomouse patent would be to "expand" the scope of the *Patent Act* (i.e., his factum, paras. 2, 3, 35, 73), but the opposite conclusion reached in so many countries with comparable legislation suggests the contrary. In those jurisdictions, patents for the oncomouse have been issued without any need for legislative amendment, including the United States where the language of our definition of "invention" originated. The Commissioner seeks to *restrict* the legislative definition of invention, and he does so (in my view) for policy reasons unrelated to the *Patent Act* or to its legitimate role and function.

36 The majority of the Federal Court of Appeal in this case found persuasive the interpretative principles applied by the United States Supreme Court in *Diamond v. Chakrabarty*, 447 U.S. 303 (U.S. Sup. Ct. 1980). In that case the inventor, Al Chakrabarty, had genetically engineered bacteria capable of breaking down crude oil spills. The invention was environmentally useful but the bacteria, necessarily, were alive. One of the arguments made by the U.S. Commissioner of Patents and Trademarks, echoed in this appeal before us 22 years later, was that micro-organisms cannot qualify as patentable subject matter until Congress expressly authorizes such protection.

[The Commissioner's] position rests on the fact that genetic technology was unforeseen when Congress enacted § 101. From this it is argued that resolution of the patentability of inventions such as respondent's should be left to Congress. The legislative process, the [Commissioner] argues, is best equipped to weigh the competing economic, social, and scientific considerations involved, and to determine whether living organisms produced by genetic engineering should receive patent protection. [p. 314]

37 Burger C.J.'s answer (at p. 315), also applicable here, was that "[i]t is, of course, correct that Congress, not the courts, must define the limits of patentability; but it is equally true that once Congress has spoken it is 'the province and duty of the judicial department to say what the law is'". The 5-4 majority held at pp. 309–10 that the inventor's micro-organism plainly qualifies as patentable subject matter. His claim is not to a hitherto unknown natural phenomenon, but to a nonnaturally occurring *manufacture or composition of matter*—a product of human ingenuity "having a distinctive name, character [and] use". [Emphasis added.]

The proper distinction was not living *versus* inanimate but between the *discovery* of a product of nature (whether living or not) *versus* a human-made *invention*. Burger C.J. did not subscribe to the notion that patents could be obtained for "anything under the sun that is made by man", quoted as part of his narrative in footnote 6. In fact, at p. 309, he specifically states that "[T]his is not to suggest that [the Act] has no limits or that it embraces every discovery". On the contrary, the patent issued because its subject matter was held to be a "manufacture" or "composition of matter" within the statutory test laid down by Congress. "A rule that unanticipated inventions are without protection would conflict with the core concept of the patent law that anticipation undermines patentability" (*Chakrabarty*, at p. 316).

38 The appellant Commissioner argues that *Chakrabarty* should be rejected because of differences he perceives in the legislative history in Canada and the United States, an allegedly different common understanding of what "composition of matter" meant when the *Patent Act* was passed in 1869, and subsequent legislative action in Canada in 1990 with respect to plant breeders (factum, at paras. 60 and 61). In my view, for reasons given below, these distinctions are not well founded but, in any event, the only interest we have in *Diamond v. Chakrabarty* is the extent to which its reasoning adds persuasive force to the respondent's argument and confirms harmony, broadly speaking, in intellectual property matters among like-minded jurisdictions.

G. The Interpretation of Section 2 of the Patent Act

39 The appellant Commissioner denies that a patent can be obtained in Canada for "anything under the sun that is made by man" and I agree. He says that this expression, used in Congressional hearings in 1952, distinguishes the U.S. legislative history from ours, but this is not so, strictly speaking. A 1952 expression of opinion by a Congressional Committee almost 150 years after the definition was inserted into the U.S. *Patent Act* of 1793 is scarcely *contemporanea expositio*.

40 The check on the indiscriminate grant of patents lies in the established criteria of utility, novelty and non-obviousness. Those are the criteria judged by Parliament to be relevant to its statutory purpose, which is to encourage ingenuity by rewarding its disclosure. The expression "composition of matter" was included in our patent laws prior to Confederation. It appears in 1824 in the Lower Canada statute entitled *An Act to promote the progress of useful Arts in this Province*, 4 Geo. 4, c. 25, and in Upper Canada two years later in *An Act to Encourage the Progress of Useful Arts within this Province*, 7

Geo. 4, c. 5. The 1826 Act included the terms "manufacture" and "composition of matter" in the preamble setting out its object:

Whereas it is expedient for the encouragement of Genius and of Arts in this Province to secure an exclusive right to the Inventor of any New and Useful Art, Machine, Manufacture, or Composition of Matter ...

41 Section 91(22) of the *Constitution Act, 1867*, assigned legislative competence in respect of "Patents of Invention and Discovery" to Parliament which two years later defined patentable subject matter as follows:

Any person ... having invented or discovered any new and useful art, machine, manufacture, or composition of matter, or any new and useful improvement on any art, machine, manufacture or composition of matter, not known or used by others before his invention or discovery thereof, or not being at the time of his application for a patent in public use or on sale in any of the Provinces of the Dominion with the consent or allowance of the inventor or discoverer thereof ... [Emphasis added.]

(*Patent Act*, S.C. 1869, c. 11, §6)

The wording has not changed much in the intervening years, apart from dropping the reference to "discovery". Section 2 of the present *Patent Act* now provides as follows:

"invention" means any new and useful art, process, machine, manufacture or composition of matter, or any new and useful improvement in any art, process, machine, manufacture or composition of matter.

42 It is common ground that to meet the subject matter criteria of the *Patent Act* the oncomouse must qualify as a "composition of matter" or a "manufacture".

(i) "Composition of Matter"

43 "Composition of matter" (*composition de matières*) is an open-ended expression. Statutory subject matter must be framed broadly because by definition the *Patent Act* must contemplate the unforeseeable. The definition is not expressly confined to inanimate matter, and the appellant Commissioner agrees that composition of organic and certain living matter can be patented. In the case of the oncomouse, the modified genetic material is a physical substance and therefore "matter". The fertilized mouse egg is a form of biological "matter". The combination of these two forms of matter by the process described in the disclosure is thus, as pointed out by Rothstein J.A. ([2000] 4 F.C. 528 (Fed. C.A.), at para. 120), a "composition of matter".

44 What, then, is the justification under the *Patent Act* for drawing a line between certain compositions of living matter (*lower* life forms) and other compositions of living matter (*higher* life forms)?

45 My colleague, Bastarache J., quotes from the *Oxford English Dictionary* (2nd ed. 1989) vol. IX, at p. 480, the entry that "matter" is a "[p]hysical or corporeal substance in general...., contradistinguished from immaterial or incorporeal substance (spirit, soul, mind), and qualities, actions, or conditions", but this, of course, depends on context. "Matter" is a most chameleon-like word. The expression "grey *matter*" refers in everyday use to "intelligence"—which is about as incorporeal as "spirit" or "mind". Indeed, the same Oxford editors define "grey matter" as "intelligence, brains" (*New Shorter Oxford English Dictionary* (1993), vol. 1, p. 1142). The *primary* definition of matter, according to the *Oxford English Dictionary*, is "[t]he substance, or the substances collectively, out of which a physical object is made or of which it consists; constituent material" (at p. 479). The definition of "*matière*" in *Le Grand Robert*, quoted by my colleague, is to the

same effect. The question, then, is what, in the Commissioner's view, is the "constituent material" of the oncomouse as a physical entity? If the oncomouse is not composed of matter, what, one might ask, are such things as oncomouse "minds" composed of? The Court's mandate is to approach this issue as a matter (that slippery word in yet another context!) of law, not murine metaphysics. In the absence of any evidence or expert assistance, the Commissioner now asks the Court to take judicial notice of the oncomouse, if I may use Arthur Koestler's phrase, as a "ghost in a machine" but this pushes the scope of judicial notice too far. With respect, this sort of literary metaphor (or its dictionary equivalent) is an inadequate basis on which to narrow the scope of the *Patent Act*, and thus to narrow the patentability of scientific invention at the dawn of the third Millennium.

(ii) Defining the Exception for "Higher Life Forms"

46 The appellant Commissioner says the Federal Court of Appeal erred by allowing a patent on a "higher intelligent life form", but he himself offers no definition of an "intelligent" life form, much less does he identify a dividing line between a "higher" intelligent life form and a "lower" intelligent life form.

47 The *Patent Act* does not distinguish, in its definition of invention, between subject matter that is less complex ("lower life forms") and subject matter that is more complex ("higher life forms"). The degree of complexity is not a criterion found in the Act or in the jurisprudence in determining patentability. The distinction between "lower life forms" and "higher life forms" in its application to s. 2 is the invention of the Patent Office.

48 While refusing to issue a patent for a higher *animal* life form in this case, the Commissioner has issued patents under the *Patent Act* for higher *plant* life forms: see, *e.g.*, Canadian Patent 1,313,830 issued February 23, 1993 for "Round-up Ready Canola", a genetically modified plant, recently before the courts in *Monsanto Canada Inc. v. Schmeiser*, [2002] F.C.J. No. 1209 (Fed. C.A.).

49 The CBAC report says, at p. 6:

The term "higher life form" is not defined in law. In common usage, it includes plants and non-human animals other than single-celled organisms.

The line, on this view, is not drawn between sentient beings and non-sentient beings or intelligent beings and unintelligent beings, but between simple one-cell organisms (such as bacteria) and their more complicated cousins, perhaps as rudimentary as moulds or other fungi.

50 Other approaches abound. In a paper prepared for the Intellectual Property Policy Directorate of Industry Canada, *A Study of Issues Relating to the Patentability of Biotechnological Subject Matter* (1996), J. R. Rudolph offered the following explanation, at pp. 11–12:

Microorganisms are a large and diverse group of organisms consisting of only one cell or cell clusters of prokaryotic or eucaryotic cells. Examples of eukaryotic organisms are algae, fungi, molds and yeasts. An example of prokaryotes is bacteria. An important distinction between single cells or cell clusters which are microorganisms, and single cells or cell clusters which are not microorganisms, is that microbial cells are able to live alone in nature: single animal or plant cells or cell clusters are unable to exist by themselves in nature and can only be successful in either a specialized environment such as a culture system (typically created by man in the laboratory) or as part of a multicellular organism such as a plant or animal. The so-called "higher life forms" are complex multicellular organisms such as simple plants or oysters, for example, which contain thousands or hundreds of thousands of cells. The human, which is a complex multicellular organism, has been estimated to contain at least 1014 cells. [Emphasis added.]

51 My colleague, Bastarache J., takes the view that a key factor is "the unique ability of higher life forms to self-replicate" (para. 170), but in fact self-reproduction is also a fundamental characteristic of "lower life forms". Indeed, one of the most widely held objections to the genetically engineered bacteria in the *Chakrabarty* case was the potential for such unnatural bacteria to escape and reproduce in the wild with unknown consequences for the environment.

52 The various distinctions attempted to be made between "patentable" lower life composition of matter and "*un*patentable" higher life composition of matter, shows, I think, the arbitrariness of the Commissioner's approach. My colleague writes at para. 199:

The distinction between lower and higher life forms, though not explicit in the Act, is nonetheless defensible on the basis of common sense differences between the two.

With respect, there seems to be as many versions of "common sense" as there are commentators:

(1) Some would say all *living* organisms are excluded (e.g., Brennan J. for the dissenters in *Chakrabarty*);

(2) Some would allow micro-organisms but only those that can be produced *en masse with identical features*, like bacteria. In *Abitibi Co., Re, supra*, the Patent Appeal Board recommended that patents extend "to all new life forms which are produced *en masse* as chemical compounds are prepared, and are formed in such large numbers that any measurable quantity will possess uniform properties and characteristics" (p. 89). "Mass" live organisms have a long history of patentability, including food products such as beer and yogurt.

(3) Then there are the proponents of "*higher* life" organisms *versus* "*lower* life" organisms, the latter being defined by the CBAC as having only a single cell.

(4) Others divide the universe between *prokaryotic* cells (e.g., bacteria and certain forms of algae) and *eukaryotic* cells (more complex life forms) and consider "higher" life forms to start only with more "complex" multicellular organisms.

(5) The Patent Appeal Board allowed *multi-celled* organisms such as moulds and fungi in *Connaught Laboratories, supra*.

(6) Some argue that "*complex* life forms" are unpatentable. Nadon J. took this position at trial in this case, [1998] 3 F.C. 510 (Fed. T.D.), at para. 35.

(7) The Commissioner issues patents for genetically modified complex *plants* (*Monsanto Canada Inc., supra*) but refuses to issue a patent for a genetically modified complex mouse.

(8) Others draw the line at *sentient* beings.

(9) Still others draw the line at "*intelligent*" beings.

(10) The Commissioner opened his argument in this case by asking whether "a complex intelligent living being could be considered an invention".

53 In my view, none of these proposed dividing lines arise out of the present text of the *Patent Act*. All of them are policy driven and, if they are to be introduced at all, should be introduced by Parliament.

54 The Federal Court of Appeal and CBAC drew the line at *human* bodies in their entirety at any stage of development, as discussed below. The true basis for the exclusion is not extraneous to the *Patent Act* but lies in an explicit limitation in § 40 which provides that:

40. Whenever the Commissioner is satisfied that an applicant is not by law entitled to be granted a patent, he shall refuse the application ... [Emphasis added.]

40. Chaque fois que le commissaire s'est assuré que le demandeur n'est pas fondé en droit à obtenir la concession d'un brevet, il rejette la demande ... [Je souligne.]

The reference to "by law" is not limited to the *Patent Act* itself (as the French version "*fondé en droit*" makes clear). It has been established for over 200 years that people cannot, at common law, own people: *Somerset v. Stewart* (1772), Lofft 10, (1772), 98 E.R. 499 (Eng. K.B.) . The issue of whether a human being is a "composition of matter" does not, therefore, arise under the *Patent Act*. If further reinforcement is required, §§ 7 and 15 of the *Canadian Charter of Rights and Freedoms* would clearly prohibit an individual from being reduced to a chattel of another individual.

55 The situation here bears some resemblance to *Bishop v. Stevens*, [1990] 2 S.C.R. 467 (S.C.C.), a copyright case, where this Court refused to read an "implied exception to the literal meaning" (p. 480) of the broad rights given to copyright holders in § 3(1)(*d*) of the *Copyright Act* R.S.C. 1985, c. C-42. McLachlin J. (as she then was) stated that "policy considerations suggest that if such a change is to be made to the Act it should be made by the legislature, and not by a forced interpretation" (p. 485). And so it is in this case too.

56 The difference between the Commissioner and the CBAC is that the Commissioner wants the judges to read down the word "matter" to include only a subdivision of "matter" whereas the CBAC is making its proposal to the government, and through the government to Parliament, which is the proper forum in which such restrictions or regulatory structures should be debated and resolved.

(iii) "Manufacture"

57 The inventors argued that the oncomouse falls within the *extended* definition of "manufacture" in § 2. I do not accept that view, but the submission is of significance in terms of the correct approach to the interpretation of the *Patent Act*. The English law of patents finds its root in the *Statute of Monopolies* (1624), which defined the permissible subject matter for a patent in a rather limited way as the "sole working or makinge of any manner of new Manufactures" (§ 6). The definitional approach adopted by my colleague, Bastarache J., leads him to define "manufacture" in the context of the present § 2 of the Act as "a non-living mechanistic product or process" (para. 159). However, the tradition of patent jurisprudence has been expansive, not restrictive. By 1851 the learned text *Godson on Patents* (2nd ed.) noted that the word "manufactures" had received from the English courts "very extended signification. It has not, as yet, been accurately defined; for the objects which may possibly come within the spirit and meaning of that act, are *almost infinite*" (p. 35 (emphasis added)).

58 Of course the word "manufacture" in our statute appears in conjunction with the words "art, ... machine ... or composition of matter" and must be read in context. Nevertheless, it is, I think, worth pointing out the contrast between the expansionist view that has characterized patent jurisprudence to date and the limiting view of the words "manufacture" and "composition of matter" now proposed by my colleague.

59 We should not encourage the Commissioner to try to circle each of the five definitional words with tight language that creates arbitrary gaps between, for example, "manufacture" and "composition of matter" through which useful inventions can fall out of the realm of patentability. To do so would conflict with this Court's earlier expression of a "judicial anxiety to support a really useful invention": *Consolboard Inc. v. MacMillan Bloedel (Sask.) Ltd.*, [1981] 1 S.C.R. 504 (S.C.C.), *per* Dickson J., at p. 521, citing *Hinks & Son v. Safety Lighting Co.* (1876), 4 Ch. D. 607 (Eng. Ch. Div.). The definition of invention should be read as a whole and expansively with a view to giving protection to what is novel and useful and unobvious.

H. Negative Inference from the Plant Breeders' Rights Act

60 The Commissioner argues that we should take from the passage in 1990 of the *Plant Breeders' Rights Act*, S.C. 1990, c. 20, the negative inference that plants were not intended by Parliament to be patentable under the *Patent Act*. (I leave aside, for present purposes, the Commissioner's inconsistency in issuing a patent for Round-up Ready Canola in 1993, three years after the *Plant Breeders' Rights Act* was enacted—see *Monsanto Canada Inc., supra.*) From this questionable premise, the Commissioner reasons that, if plants are not patentable subject matter, the exclusion must also apply to other "higher life forms" such as seeds and animals, all of which are able to reproduce themselves. When *Pioneer Hi-Bred Ltd., supra*, was before the Federal Court of Appeal ([1987] 3 F.C. 8 (Fed. C.A.), at p. 14), Marceau J.A. expressed the view that, if Parliament had intended to include plants in the *Patent Act*, he would have expected that in the definition of invention in §2 "words such as 'strain', 'variety' or 'hybrid' would have appeared".

61 I do not accept this argument. Firstly, there is nothing in the *Plant Breeders' Rights Act* that expressly bars an application under the *Patent Act*, which confers much more exclusive and valuable rights. The *Plant Breeders' Rights Act* grants protection for 18 years on the sale and propagation for sale of enumerated new plant varieties—cultivars, clones, breeding lines, or hybrids that can be cultivated. The plant breeder pays "annual maintenance fees and [must] provide propagating material throughout the term of [protection]. The right does not prevent the development of different varieties from protected plants or the use of seeds taken from protected varieties": D. Vaver, *Intellectual Property Law* (1997), at p. 126. As to the legislative purpose of the *Plant Breeders' Rights Act*, I agree with my colleague, Bastarache J., when he writes, at ¶192:

[I]t may well be that the *Plant Breeders' Rights Act* was passed not out of recognition that higher life forms are not a patentable subject matter under the *Patent Act*, but rather out of recognition that plant varieties deserve some form of intellectual property protection despite the fact that they often do not meet the technical criteria of the *Patent Act*.

The rights available under the *Plant Breeders' Rights Act* fall well short of those conferred by patent, both in comprehensiveness and in duration.

62 Secondly, to address the comment of Marceau J.A., use of specific terms such as "strain" or "hybrid" would undermine the generality that §2 seeks to achieve by use of the term "composition of matter".

63 Thirdly, the *Patent Act* language reaches back (as stated) prior to Confederation. This particular argument suggests that a "negative inference", arising when the plant legislation was enacted in 1990, should somehow be read back to narrow a definition that had at that time been in effect more than a century. This would amount to a repeal by im-

plication, and would necessarily require an inconsistency between the two pieces of legislation. There is no such inconsistency. Rights acquired under both Acts can live together. Similar arguments were rightly rejected by the United States Supreme Court in *J.E.M. AG Supply Inc. v. Pioneer Hi-Bred International Inc.*, 122 S. Ct. 593 (U.S.S.C. 2001).

I. Nature of Rights Granted by a Patent

64 A patent does not exempt the owner from any relevant regulation or prohibition. While § 44 (now § 42) of the *Patent Act* gives the owner, as against the rest of the world, "the *exclusive* right, privilege and liberty of making, constructing and using the invention and selling it to others to be used …" (emphasis added), and in that respect is framed as a positive right, its effect is essentially to prevent others from practising an invention that, but for the patent monopoly, they would be permitted to practise. In exchange for disclosure to the public, the patent protects the disclosed information from unauthorized use for a limited time.

65 The limited nature of the rights conferred by a patent was fully appreciated by CBAC in its Interim Report, *Biotechnology and Intellectual Property: Patenting of Higher Life Forms and Related Issues* (November 2001), at p. vi:

It is crucial for rational debate on questions related to what should or should not be patentable to recognize that patents confer only prohibitive rights. The Canadian patent system is not designed to decide about what uses of technology are permissible nor is the *Patent Act* designed to prevent dangerous or ethically questionable inventions from being made, used, sold or imported. The responsibility and tools for dealing with such matters resides elsewhere (*e.g.*, through regulatory approval or product safety processes). [Emphasis added.]

I agree with this observation. This is not to say that patents are "neutral", or have no link to the ethical and social issues raised by the interveners. It is to say that those issues transcend the narrow question of patentability circumscribed by §§ 2 and 40 of the *Patent Act*.

J. A Working Definition of "Life"

66 The subtext of much of the argument for the appellant Commissioner and his supporters invokes Dolly the cloned sheep and the potential of eugenics and "designer" human beings. However, the scientific notion of life begins at a much lower level. There is a good deal of debate about what constitutes "life" but some consensus about a few of its characteristics. These include the capacity to grow and develop (including reproduction), i.e., a metabolism, the ability of an organism to draw energy from its environment for this purpose, and the ability to respond to stimuli. Other characteristics are sometimes added. For example, the Massachusetts Institute of Technology, in designing its probe for extraterrestrial "life", suggests that the definition of live organisms includes their tendency to ensure self-preservation, and that they be significantly differentiated from their surrounding environment.

67 Life is no less wondrous at the microscopic level, and to think of "life" primarily in terms of dolphins, chimpanzees and blue whales (examples urged by the appellant Commissioner in the oral hearing) is something of an oversimplification.

68 Some of the interveners objected to Harvard claiming credit for inventing a form of life. The Canadian Council of Churches and Evangelical Fellowship of Canada protested that the analysis of Rothstein J.A. "is built on a false premise that this [oncomouse] was

a new form of life. It is not". That is true, of course. Harvard did not construct the mouse from scratch, nor did it create "life". What it did was to modify the genome of the oncomouse so that every cell in its body contained a modified gene. It is not like adding a new and useful propeller to a ship. The oncogene is everywhere in the genetically modified oncomouse, and it is this important modification that is said to give the oncomouse its commercial value, which is what interests the *Patent Act*.

69 The point is that Harvard is not being credited with inventing life. It claims to have modified every cell of a living creature in a new and useful way, and to the extent that modification is a valuable addition to the advancement of learning, Harvard claims only whatever rewards the *Patent Act* entitles it to for its disclosure.

K. The Ongoing Parliamentary Process in Canada

70 The appellant Commissioner of Patents invites the Court to intervene in the debate about a proper legal framework for genetic research (or hasten its conclusion prematurely) that is already underway in the government and in Parliament. None of the parties suggested that the *Patent Act* was an adequate vehicle to deal with biotechnology in general or the ethical issues arising from research into "higher life forms" (however defined) in particular. Patent rights are such a limited aspect of the debate that one would not expect to find such comprehensive regulation jammed into the *Patent Act*.

71 Parliament seems to be of that view. On May 9, 2002, as mentioned, the Minister of Health introduced into Parliament the *Assisted Reproduction Act* based in part on the work of CBAC. In its recent report dated June 2002, the CBAC accepted that life forms come within the definition of "invention" of the present patent legislation, and recommended that life forms *continue* to be patentable, but proposed an express exception in the case of *human* life as follows (*at* p. x):

No patent shall be granted on human bodies at any stage of development.

This, as earlier stated, is consistent with both the common law and the *Charter*. Such an amendment, the CBAC reasoned, *at* p. 9, would apply only to entire human bodies from the zygote to an adult body; DNA sequences, gametes, stem and other cells, or organs will remain patentable. [Emphasis added.]

72 The CBAC emphasized that its proposed exemption related to the "whole human body and not ... its parts" (for example, artificially created human organs), and intended the proposed exception to be "read narrowly" (p. 9). "It is important" opines the CBAC, "not to discourage research on stem cells and the creation of artificial organs" (p. 9). The CBAC recommended *against* extending *non*-patentability to *non*-human animals (which again presumes that under the current *Patent Act* non-human animals are patentable). The *Patent Act* is "not a sufficiently subtle instrument" for those evaluations, and the "dignity of and respect for animals can be better protected through animal welfare and habitat protection measures" (p. 10).

73 The majority of the CBAC also concluded that the "overall public good is best attained by providing patent rights over higher life forms, provided that these rights are no greater in substance than those granted over other inventions, taking into account the particularities of biologically based inventions" (p. 11). Given that one of those particularities is the ability to reproduce, among other characteristics, the CBAC states that this recommendation must be read together with several other recommendations, including the farmers' privilege, protection for innocent bystanders, research and experimental use exception, guidelines for biological inventions, and establishment of an opposition procedure.

74 It is not our job to comment on the CBAC proposals one way or the other except to say that they are directed to the proper destination—the legislators.

L. Policy Arguments Against Granting a Patent for the Oncomouse

75 The appellant Commissioner contends that the Federal Court of Appeal showed no understanding that this case is a "harbinger of a new era". The majority judgment, he says, looked narrowly at the case but failed to consider the broader context. What may have appeared as a small step for the oncomouse was, so to speak, a very large policy leap for patentability. Nevertheless, we must deal with the *Patent Act* as it is. Change ought to come through statutory amendment, not by the Court reading down the *Patent Act* to exclude non-human "higher life forms" from patentability by creative statutory interpretation.

76 The Court heard from a coalition of advocates opposed to the granting of a patent, including religious, environmentalist, agricultural, and non-profit research groups in addition to the concerns voiced by the Commissioner himself.

(i) The Religious Objection

77 Some opponents object to scientists "playing God". A hint, perhaps, of their objection is reflected in the reasons of my colleague, Bastarache J., at para. 163:

Although some in society may hold the view that higher life forms are mere "composition[s] of matter", the phrase does not fit well with common understandings of human and animal life.

78 I do not think that a court is a forum that can properly debate the mystery of mouse life. What we know, in this case, is that the inventors were able to modify a particular gene in the oncomouse genome, and produce a new, useful and unobvious result. That is all we know about the mysteries of oncomouse life and, in my view, it is all we need to know for the purposes of this appeal.

(ii) The "Lack of Regulatory Framework" Objection

79 As already mentioned, much of the Commissioner's argument turned on the lack of the regulatory framework that is necessary, he says, to address the ethical and scientific issues raised by genetic research. The argument is that because in his view genetic patents should be regulated, and because the *Patent Act* fails to do the job, Parliament cannot in 1869 have intended to grant patents for genetically engineered "higher" life forms. My colleague, Bastarache J., accepts this argument at para. 167, where he writes:

... the fact that the *Patent Act* in its current state is ill-equipped to deal appropriately with higher life forms as patentable subject matter is an indication that Parliament never intended the definition of invention to extend to this type of subject matter.

With respect, I do not agree.

80 First, we all probably have strong views that certain activities or things should be regulated. Some say contraceptive devices should not be patented because their use is immoral and unregulated. Others might wish to deny patents to environmentally risky chemical compositions for which, in their view, there is no adequate regulation. On the other hand, others feel that the use of potentially dangerous inventions like explosives and firearms should *not* be regulated. I do not think patents should be denied as a protest against perceived shortcomings in regulatory structures. The opponents of such patents should address themselves to Parliament, not the courts. As Rand J. commented

in *Canada (Commissioner of Patents) v. Winthrop Chemical Co.*, [1948] S.C.R. 46 (S.C.C.), *at* p. 57:

... the intention of a legislature must be gathered from the language it has used and the task of construing that language is not to satisfy ourselves that as used it is adequate to an intention drawn from *general considerations* or to a purpose which might seem to be more reasonable or equitable than what the language in its ordinary or primary sense indicates. [Emphasis added.]

This passage was quoted with approval in a patent context by Pigeon J. in *Tennessee Eastman Co. v. Canada (Commissioner of Patents)* (1972), [1974] S.C.R. 111 (S.C.C.), at p. 121, and again by Lamer J. in *Pioneer Hi-Bred Ltd., supra*, at p. 1643. What I consider to be the Commissioner's misinterpretation of s. 2 of the *Patent Act* proceeds, with respect, from "general considerations" of what he considers to be "reasonable or equitable" regulation of a controversial area of biotechnology. His views may or may not reflect desirable public policy but they have nothing to do with "the language" used by Parliament in § 2 of the *Patent Act*.

81 This is not to deny the importance of context as an aid to statutory construction. It is simply to say that a court has no mandate to deny patentability because of the novelty or the potential social, economic or cultural impact of an invention, whether it be nuclear technology in the 1950s, biotechnology in the 1990s, or reproductive technology in the year 2002.

82 Second, regulation necessarily follows, rather than precedes, the invention. No doubt most people would agree that nuclear technology requires regulation; yet the regulation could hardly have been anticipated in 1869, decades before Ernest Rutherford, while at McGill University, with Frederick Soddy, first formulated the theory of atomic disintegration. Prescription drugs are regulated, but the regulatory structure for new drug approval is not in the *Patent Act*. The grant of a patent does not allow the drug to be marketed. Nor should it. Health and safety are not, and never have been, the preoccupation of intellectual property legislation.

83 It is evident that there are as many areas of potential regulation as there are areas of invention. I think it is also evident that all of these regulatory regimes cannot and should not be put under the inadequate umbrella of the *Patent Act*. Parliament has shown a preference for using more specific statutes altogether outside the framework of patent law. This allows Parliament to tailor the statutory scheme and relevant incentives more precisely to the subject matters involved. Such collateral legislative activity, however, does not justify "reading down" the definition of "invention" in the *Patent Act*, in my opinion.

(iii) The "Laws of Nature" Objection

84 The appellant Commissioner rejected the oncomouse patent in part because the inventors exercised no control over the genetic characteristics of the mouse (hair colour, length of whiskers, etc.) except for the presence of the oncogene. Further, the Commissioner argued, the oncomouse is not reproducible *en masse* like bacteria. The trial judge upheld these objections. The animal resulting from the patented gene insertion process, he said, is "completely unknown and unknowable" because the mouse's "inherent genetic makeup" controls many characteristics and the whole mouse, *with the exception of the oncogene*, is completely independent of human intervention. This is true but not, in my opinion, relevant. The utility of the invention has nothing to do with the length of the mouse's whiskers. Its value, in terms of the patent, appears to reside wholly in the oncogene.

85 My colleague, Bastarache J., as stated, acknowledges that the fertilized genetically modified egg is patentable (¶ 162) but accepts the Commissioner's argument that the oncomouse itself is unpatentable because it develops through the natural process of gestation (which everyone agrees was not invented by Harvard) without further "human intervention" (¶ 162). Rothstein J.A. rejected this argument (at ¶ 121):

Although the natural gestation process is required to allow the fertilized mouse egg to develop, this does not mean the organism ceases to become a "composition of matter" as it develops from the single-cell stage into an oncomouse. The founder oncomouse is therefore itself a composition of matter.

86 Counsel for the Commissioner says there is a world of difference between a fertilized single cell and the animal it becomes, but if the one is allowed, where is the cut-off point? At what point in the process of gestation does the fertilized single cell *cease* to be a "composition of matter"?

87 Counsel for the Commissioner says that growth from a single fertilized cell to the complete mouse has nothing to do with the inventors and everything to do with the "laws of nature". This is true (although each cell of the live mouse contains the genetic modification), but this is scarcely a fatal objection. The "laws of nature" are an essential part of the working of many and probably most patented inventions. Patents on biotechnical processes such as fermentation, wholly dependent on the "laws of nature", were first issued in the early 1800s. Pharmaceutical drugs utilize the normal bodily processes and functions of animals and humans and are not on that account regarded as less patentable. The anti HIV-AIDS drug AZT ingested orally would achieve nothing were it not circulated and processed through the body by the "laws of nature". Indeed, the AZT pill, like the oncomouse, could not be brought into existence without reliance on "the laws of nature" in general and the processes of biochemistry in particular. In *Apotex Inc. v. Wellcome Foundation Ltd.*, 2002 SCC 77 (S.C.C.), released concurrently, we uphold as valid the AZT patent despite the fact that AZT would lack utility (a statutory prerequisite to the issuance of a patent) unless the "laws of nature" arranged for it to "be absorbed into the human blood stream, make its way to the T-cells infected with HIV, enter the T-cells and inhibit the reproduction of the HIV infection without proving toxic to other cells, and demonstrate clinical improvement in the patient" (¶ 20). Such natural processes, before, during and after the construction of the pill, are no more the creation of the AZT inventor than the gestation of an oncomouse (essential to *its* utility) is the creation of the Harvard inventors. An inventor whose invention harnesses the forces of nature is no less an inventor.

(iv) The "De Minimis" Objection

88 The Commissioner rather downplays the inventor's achievement. The implicit objection seems to be, "What's 1 gene in 30,000?". My colleague writes, at ¶ 163:

A person whose genetic make-up is modified by radiation does not cease to be him or herself. Likewise, the same mouse would exist absent the injection of the oncogene into the fertilized egg cell; it simply would not be predisposed to cancer.

89 Such an argument, it seems to me, significantly understates the scientific achievement. The "modification" of the gene is not an add-on. Modification of even a single gene does not, with respect, leave the creature like "him or herself" or "the same mouse". Genetic modification is not like a haircut or a tonsillectomy. Modification or mutation of even a single gene can have colossal consequences. It is instructive, for example, to note the description of Tay-Sachs disease, mentioned earlier, which results in infantile deaths from the mutation of but a *single* gene:

... a familial disease of infancy in which there is a progressive degeneration of nerve cells throughout the whole nervous system and in the retina. It is characterized clinically by progressive muscular weakness and paralysis, mental deterioration and blindness, usually leading to death in coma or convulsions towards the end of the second year.

(*Butterworths Medical Dictionary*, (2nd ed. 1978), *at* p. 1496)

Any suggestion that a child with or without the mutant Tay-Sachs gene is "the same person" would seriously underestimate the power of the science that we are being asked to consider.

(v) Ordre Public or Morality

90 NAFTA and TRIPS each provide that contracting states may *exclude* from patentability inventions the exploitation of which would be contrary to *ordre public* (which seemingly equates to the protection of public security, the physical integrity of individuals as members of society, and the protection of the environment) or morality: *North American Free Trade Agreement Between the Government of Canada, the Government of the United Mexican States and the Government of the United States of America* (1992), Can T.S. 1994 No. 2 (entered into force January 1, 1994), art. 1709(2); *Agreement on Trade-Related Aspects of Intellectual Property Rights* (1994), 25 I.I.C. 209, art. 27(2). The exclusion presupposes a general rule of patentability. Parliament has amended the *Patent Act* to take account of each of these agreements, but has chosen not to include such an exclusion from patentability in the *Patent Act*.

91 The *European Patent Convention* contains an *ordre public* exclusion from patentability, and the corresponding European "oncomouse" patent application was examined having specific regard to this exclusion. In its decision of April 3, 1992, the Examining Division of the European Patent Office stated the issue as follows:

In the case at hand three different interests are involved and require balancing: there is a basic interest of mankind to remedy widespread and dangerous diseases, on the other hand the environment has to be protected against the uncontrolled dissemination of unwanted genes and, moreover, cruelty to animals has to be avoided. The latter two aspects may well justify regarding an invention as immoral and therefore unacceptable unless the advantages, i.e. the benefit to mankind, outweigh the negative aspects.

(*Grant of European patent No. 0 169 762 (Onco-mouse/Harvard)* (1992), OJ EPO 1992, 588, at pp. 591–92)

We do not possess such a "balancing" test in our *Patent Act*, though some thought must have been given to it when Parliament "opened up" the *Patent Act* for NAFTA and TRIPS-related amendments in 1994.

92 The Examining Division of the European Patent Office concluded that issuance of the oncomouse patent was *not* contrary to *ordre public* or public morality and further that "[i]f the legislator is of the opinion that certain technical knowledge should be used under limited conditions only it is up to him to enact appropriate legislation" (*ibid*, p. 591).

93 The European Community Directive on biotechnology (*Directive 98/44/EC of the European Parliament and of the Council of 6 July 1998 on the legal protection of biotechnological invention*) names specific inventions (human cloning, modifying germ line, commercial use of human embryos, and causing suffering to animals without substantial medical benefit to humans or animals) as contrary to *ordre public* or morality. If Parliament thinks it wise to spell out such a policy in the *Patent Act*, it will pass appro-

priate amendments. More likely, as the government has already signalled, such measures will be put into special legislation equivalent to the proposed *Assisted Human Reproduction Act*.

(vi) Unjust Enrichment

94 Other critics take the view that the rewards given by a patent, whether they reflect innovation or not, are unjust. Why, it is asked, should Harvard be rewarded for "inventing" a creature that occurs in its original form in nature? In a scientific laboratory, the wild mouse becomes a research platform. Harvard researchers made an "improvement" by genetic modification, but the remaining unmodified genes contribute to producing the mouse, and shaping its reaction to the laboratory experiments. Why, then, should the whole mouse be considered "patentable"? Why should Harvard appropriate to itself the whole value attributable to the "platform" when all it contributed is an improvement to that platform?

95 Such an argument relates to remedies rather than patentability. A view that the *Patent Act* rewards a patent owner too richly is not a sound basis on which to deny a patent. The inventor of the frisbee (patented in 1967) would also, no doubt, be thought by some critics to have been excessively rewarded.

96 The scientific accomplishment manifested in the oncomouse is profound and far-reaching, and a numerical count of the genes modified and the genes not modified misses the point. Every cell in the animal's body has been altered in a way that is profoundly important to scientific research. If researchers were to discover that cancers were entirely attributable to one gene and then modified individuals so that they were cancer-free, no one would deny that such a modification would be of enormous importance regardless of the fact that only one gene was changed.

97 Researchers who wish to use a wild mouse can catch one in the parking lot. Harvard would have no complaint. It is only if they wish to take advantage of the advances in learning disclosed in the oncomouse patent that they would require authorization from the inventor who made the disclosure they now seek to exploit.

98 If the patent were refused on the oncomouse itself, it would be easy for "free riders" to circumvent the protection sought to be given to the inventor by the *Patent Act* simply by acquiring an oncomouse and breeding it to as many wild mice as desired and selling the offspring (probably half of which will be oncomice) to the public. The weakness of this protection would undermine the incentives intended by the *Patent Act*. I agree with William Hayhurst when he writes:

Some patents for processes may be of little practical value. To discover that a competitor is carrying out the process may be difficult. If a process produces a living organism that reproduces itself, the process may have to be carried out only once: competitors who are able to get their hands on the organism need not repeat the process of producing it. What is needed is a patent for the organism ...

(W. L. Hayhurst, "Exclusive Rights in Relation to Living Things" (1991), 6 *I.P.J.* 171, *at* p. 177)

99 On the other hand, if the oncomouse is patented, and Harvard obtains a judgment for the infringer's profits, the infringer could always contend that the profits should be apportioned between profits attributable to the invention and those profits not attributable to the invention. Harvard will contend that the whole of the laboratory value of the oncomouse is due to its genetic make-up. Others may disagree. Such questions remain, at this stage, entirely premature.

(vii) Animal Rights

100 Animal rights supporters object to the fact that the oncomouse is deliberately designed to cause sentient beings to grow painful malignant tumours. Of course, whatever position is adopted under *patent* law, animals have been and will continue to be used in laboratories for scientific research. Pets are property. Mice are already commodified. Parliament may wish to address animal rights as a distinct subject matter. If the claim for the patent on the oncomouse itself is refused, the result will *not* be that Harvard is denied the opportunity to make, construct, use and sell the oncomouse. On the contrary, the result will be that *anyone* will be able to make, construct, use and sell the oncomouse. The only difference will be that Harvard will be denied the *quid pro quo* for the disclosure of its invention.

(viii) The Commodification of Human Life

101 Some critics argue that life and property rights are incompatible. Patents, they say, treat "life" as a commodity that can be bought and sold, and therefore diminish the respect with which life ought to be regarded. Living entities become "objects".

102 The major concern is that human beings constitute a line that cannot be crossed. The CBAC agrees. But others argue that patenting *any* form of life puts us on a slippery slope. Today the oncomouse; tomorrow Frankenstein's creature. I do not agree. There is a qualitative divide between rodents and human beings. The broadest claim here specifically excepts humans from the scope of transgenic mammals. Moreover, for the reasons already expressed, I do not believe that the issue of patentability of a human being even arises under the *Patent Act*.

(ix) Environmental Protection

103 Environmental concerns include the diversity of the gene pool and potential escape of genetically modified organisms into the environment. These are serious concerns which serious people would expect Parliament to address. The concerns, however, have little to do with the patent system. Patents or no patents, genetically engineered organisms have arrived in our midst. The genie is out of the bottle. As Rothstein J.A. observed, "even if the oncomouse were found not to be patentable, such a decision would not prevent inventors from developing the product or indeed, other genetically engineered living organisms" (at ¶ 197). addresses only the issue of rewarding the inventors for their *disclosure* of what they have done. Larger questions are answered elsewhere.

(x) Globalization

104 Anti-globalization groups object to the impact of broad patentability on developing countries, noting that research dollars and the beneficial effects of patented products are concentrated in developed countries. This criticism is, of course, first a broad attack on intellectual property rights generally and, second, a vote of no confidence in multilateral agreements such as TRIPS. The concerns of developing countries have received wide attention, and rightly so. A countervailing consideration is that the developing world may lose as much benefit as the economically developed world if excessive emphasis is placed on granting equitable access to inventions already made as opposed to continuing to offer adequate incentives for inventions to come. This too is an issue that does not arise for consideration on this appeal.

(xi) Contrary Considerations

105 If a certain subject matter is unpatentable as a matter of law, inventors who do carry on inventing will gravitate toward alternative sources of protection. The most ob-

vious would be trade secrets protection. The problem with this alternative, in terms of the public interest, is that the public would lose the *quid pro quo* of public disclosure that they receive under patent law.

106 Lacking legal protection against unauthorized appropriation of ideas, ingenious people may tend to hide and hoard the products of their ingenuity rather than disclose them for others to build on that knowledge. The "hide and hoard" mentality was the very mischief the *Patent Act* was aimed at.

107 There are, in other words, many policy implications of *excluding* patent protection as well as the policy implications of inclusion relied upon by the appellant Commissioner. The balance between the competing interests is for Parliament to strike.

(xii) Policy Options

108 Parliament may wish to regulate *outside* the framework of the *Patent Act* the creation and use of "higher life forms" (however Parliament chooses to define "higher" life forms) in many ways: ethics boards could be set up to consider "higher life form" patentability on a case-by-case basis, including any patent applications on human genetic material; animal rights legislation might require that all transgenic animal varieties be "engineered" to alleviate or mitigate pain from experimentation; a policy of balancing the potential alleviation of human suffering against animal suffering might be added. Patents on human genetic material, including stem cell research and cloning, might include a provision to exempt all research from patent infringement, or specify compulsory licences for such research.

109 Even a partial listing of the possibilities demonstrates why it should occasion no surprise that such regulatory structures are not crammed into the *Patent Act*, which has always had the more modest and focussed objective of simply encouraging the disclosure of the fruit of human inventiveness in exchange for the statutory rewards.

M. Alleged Deficiencies in the Patent Regime

110 There is much scholarly controversy in Canada over the role of intellectual property in biotechnology: E. R. Gold, *Body Parts: Property Rights and the Ownership of Human Biological Materials* (1996); E. R. Gold, "Making Room: Reintegrating Basic Research, Health Policy, and Ethics Into Patent Law" in T. A. Caulfield and B. Williams-Jones, eds., *The Commercialization of Genetic Research: Ethical, Legal, and Policy Issues* (1999), 63; T. A. Caulfield, "Underwhelmed: Hyperbole, Regulatory Policy, and the Genetic Revolution" (2000), 45 *McGill L.J.* 437; B. M. Knoppers, "Reflections: The Challenge of Biotechnology and Public Policy" (2000), 45 *McGill L.J.* 559; P. R. Mooney, *The Impetus for and Potential of Alternative Mechanisms for the Protection of Biotechnological Innovations*, CBAC (March 2001), *at* p. 13.

111 Some thoughtful critics suggest that patents in this field may in fact deter rather than promote innovation: M. A. Heller and R. S. Eisenberg, "Can Patents Deter Innovation? The Anticommons in Biomedical Research" (1998), 280 *Science* 698; Gold, "Biomedical Patents and Ethics: A Canadian Solution", *supra*.

112 On a more technical level, it is pointed out that a 20-year patent is a very long time in the life cycle of biotechnology. A shorter patent life, with conditions more tailored to the industry, would, it is said, provide sufficient incentive. Then there are those who advocate the "farmers' privilege" to avoid farmers being subject to patent enforcement in the case of the progeny of patented plants and animals. Others advocate protection for "innocent bystanders" who inadvertently make use of a genetically engineered plant or animal, unaware of its being patented.

113 My colleague, Bastarache J., suggests that the *absence* of such provisions supports his conclusion that the oncomouse is unpatentable, but this approach, with respect, simply substitutes the Court's notion of good public policy for the judgment of Parliament, whose members are well aware of these and similar proposals. Parliament has had the *National Biotechnology Strategy* since 1983, renewed as the *Canadian Biotechnology Strategy: An Ongoing Renewal Process* fifteen years later in 1998, the work of the CBAC and *Proceed with Care: Final Report of the Royal Commission on New Reproductive Technologies* (1993).

114 Parliament may find merit in some of the CBAC proposals for legislative reform enumerated by my colleague, Bastarache J., in his judgment at paras. 52 to 58, and 65, but Parliament has not done so to date, and neither the Commissioner of Patents nor the courts have the authority to declare, in effect, a moratorium on life (or "higher" life) patents until Parliament chooses to act. The respondent is entitled to have the benefit of the *Patent Act* as it stands.

N. Conclusion

115 In my view, the oncomouse is patentable subject matter. This does not mean that claims 1 to 12 therefore must be allowed. They ought to be considered by the Commissioner in accordance with the usual patent principles (note, for example, that the European Patent Office ultimately modified claim no. 1 to include only "transgenic rodents" rather than, as claimed, "transgenic non-human mammals": *European Patent Office Press Release*, November 7, 2001).

116 I would therefore have remitted the patent application to the Commissioner to have the specific claims 1 to 12 considered and dealt with.

117 I would dismiss the appeal.

Bibliography of Selected Works

ABA Section on Intellectual Property Law Bulletin January 2005, *available at* http://www
   .abanet.org/intelprop/bulletin/January_2005.doc (last visited February 11, 2005).

Alexander, Gregory. *Dilemmas of Group Autonomy: Residential Associations and Community*, 75 CORNELL L. REV. 1 (1989).

Alker, Daniel and Heidlues, Franz. *Farmers' Rights and Intellectual Property Rights—Reconciling Conflicting Concepts, in* ECONOMIC AND SOCIAL ISSUES IN AGRICULTURAL BIOTECHNOLOGY (R.E. Evenson, V. Santaniello and D. Zilberman eds.) Cambridge, MA: CABI Publishing (2002).

Allcock, Harry M. and Lotz, John W. *Patent Intelligence and Technology—Gleaning Pseudoproprietary Information from Publicly Available Data*, 18 J. CHEM. INFO. & COMP. SCI. 65 (1978).

Allen, Robert C. ENCLOSURE AND THE YEOMAN: THE AGRICULTURAL DEVELOPMENT OF THE SOUTH MIDLANDS, 1450–1850. Oxford: Clarendon Press (1994).

_____. *The Efficiency and Distributional Consequences of Eighteenth Century Enclosure*, 9 ECON. J. 937 (1982).

Alston, Julian M. and Venner, Raymond J. *The Effects of the U.S. Plant Variety Protection Act on Wheat Genetic Improvement*, 31 RESEARCH POL'Y 527 (2002).

Aoki, Keith. *Malthus, Mendel, and Monsanto: Intellectual Property and the Law and Politics of Global Food Supply: An Introduction*, 19 J. ENVTL L. & LITIG. 397 (2004).

_____. *Weeds, Seeds and Deeds: Recent Skirmishes in the Seed Wars*, 11 CARDOZO J. INT'L & COMP. L. 247 (2003).

Asebey, Edgar J. and Kempenaar, Jill D. *The Intellectual Property Perspective on Biodiversity: Biodiversity Prospecting Fulfilling the Mandate of the Biodiversity Convention*, 28 VAND. J. TRANSNAT'L L. 703 (1995).

Ayers, Larry. *Software and Plants*, LINUX GAZETTE, No. 31 (1998), *available at* http://linuxgazette.net/issue31/ayers2.html (last visited February 8, 2007).

Baker, Gladys L., Rasmussen, W.D., Wiser, V., and Porter, J.M. CENTURY OF SERVICE: THE FIRST ONE HUNDRED YEARS OF THE DEPARTMENT OF AGRICULTURE. Washington, DC: United States Department of Agriculture (1963).

Barboza, David. *A Weed Killer is a Block to Build On*, NEW YORK TIMES, August 2, 2001, *available at* http://www.nytimes.com/2001/08/02/business/02CHEM.html (last visited December 17, 2006).

Barrios, Paula. *The Rotterdam Convention on Hazardous Chemicals: A Meaningful Step toward Environmental Protection?*, 16 GEO. INT'L ENVTL L. REV. (2004).

Barron, Nadine and Couzens, Ed. *Intellectual Property Rights and Plant Variety Protection in South Africa: An International Perspective*, 16 (1) J. ENVIRONMENTAL LAW. 19 (2004).

Barton, John H. and Siebeck, Wolfang E. *Material Transfer Agreements in Genetic Resources Exchange — the Case of the International Agricultural Research Centres, Issues in Genetic Resources* (1994), *available at* http://www.ipgri.cgiar.org/publications/pdf/109.pdf (last visited August 21, 2006).

Beck, Robert E. (ed.) WATER AND WATER RIGHTS v. I–III. Charlottesville, VA: The Michie Company (1991).

Beier, F.K. and Strauss, J. *Patents in a Time of Rapid Scientific and Technological Change: Inventions in Biotechnology, in* BIOTECHNOLOGY AND PATENT PROTECTION: AN INTERNATIONAL REVIEW (F.K. Beier, R.S. Crespi and J. Strauss eds.) Paris: OECD (1985).

Benkler, Yochai. THE WEALTH OF NETWORKS: HOW SOCIAL PRODUCTION TRANSFORMS MARKETS AND FREEDOM. New Haven, CT: Yale University Press (2006).

————. *Coase's Penguin, or, Linux and the Nature of the Firm*, 112 YALE L.J. 369 (2002).

————. *Free as the Air to Common Use: First Amendment Constraints on the Enclosure of the Public Domain*, 74 N.Y.U. L. REV. 354 (1999).

Bent, Stephen A. *Protection of Plant Material under the General Patent Statute: A Sensible Policy at the PTO?*, BIOTECH. L. REP. 105 (March 1985).

Berlan, Jean-Pierre and Lewontin, Richard H. *Breeders' Rights and Patenting Life Forms*, 322 NATURE 785 (August 1986).

Bernhardt, Stephanie M. "High Plains Drifting: Wind-Blown Seeds and the Intellectual Property Implications of the GMO Revolution," 4 NW. J. OF TECH. & INTELL. PROP. 1 (Fall 2005).

Bhutani, Shalini and Kothari, Ashish. *The Biodiversity Rights of Developing Nations: A Perspective From India*, 32 GOLDEN GATE U. L. REV. 587 (2002).

Biber-Klemm, Susette, Cullet, Philippe and Peiry, Katharina Kummer. *New Collective Policies, in* RIGHTS TO PLANT GENETIC RESOURCES AND TRADITIONAL KNOWLEDGE: BASIC ISSUES AND PERSPECTIVES. (Susette Biber-Klemm and Thomas Cottier eds.) Cambridge, MA: CABI Publishing (2006).

BIOS — Biological Innovation for Open Society, *available at* http://www.bios.net/daisy/bios/home.html (last visited August 18, 2006).

Bluemel, Eric B. *Substance without Process: Analyzing TRIPS Participatory Guarantees in Light of Protected Indigenous Rights*, 86 J. PAT. & TRADEMARK OFF. SOC'Y 671 (2004).

Boettiger, Sara and Burk, Dan L. *Open Source Patenting* 1 J. INT'L BIOTECH. L. 221 (November/December 2004).

Bollier, David. SILENT THEFT: THE PRIVATE PLUNDER OF OUR COMMON WEALTH. New York and London: Routledge (2002).

Bowles, Elizabeth and Pradesh, Andra. *India as a Case Study in Perspectives on GMO's*, 34 CUMB. L. REV. 415 (2004).

Boyle, James. SHAMANS, SOFTWARE AND SPLEENS: LAW AND THE CONSTRUCTION OF THE INFORMATION SOCIETY. Cambridge, MA: Harvard University Press (1996).

————. *Foreword: The Opposite of Property*, 66 L. & CONTEMP. PROBS. 1 (2003).

_____. *The Second Enclosure Movement and the Construction of the Public Domain*, 66 L. & CONTEMP. PROBS. 33 (2003).

Bragdon, Susan H. and Downes, D.R. *Recent Policy Trends and Developments Related to the Conservation, Use and Development of Genetic Resources: Issues in Genetic Resources*, IPGRSI Paper No. 7, Rome: International Plant Genetic Research Institute, IPGRSI (1998).

Brockway, Lucille H. *Plant Science and Colonial Expansion: The Botanical Chess Game, in* SEEDS AND SOVEREIGNTY: THE USE AND CONTROL OF PLANT GENETIC RESOURCES (Jack R. Kloppenburg, Jr. ed.) Durham, NC: Duke University Press (1988).

_____. SCIENCE AND COLONIAL EXPANSION: THE ROLE OF THE BRITISH ROYAL BOTANICAL GARDENS. New Haven, CT: Yale University Press (1979).

Brown, Michael F. WHO OWNS NATIVE CULTURE? Cambridge, MA: Harvard University Press (2003).

Brush, Stephen B. FARMERS' BOUNTY: LOCATING CROP DIVERSITY IN THE CONTEMPORARY WORLD. New Haven, CT: Yale University Press (2004).

_____. *Genetically Modified Organisms in Peasant Farming: Social Impact and Equity*, 9 IND. J. GLOBAL LEG. STUD.135 (2001).

_____. *Comment: David A. Cleveland and Stephen C. Murray, The World's Crop Genetic Resources and the Rights of Indigenous Farmers*, 38 CURR. ANTHRO. 497 (1997).

_____. *Indigenous Knowledge of Biological Resources and Intellectual Property Rights: The Role of Anthropology*, 95 AMER. ANTHRO. 653 (1993).

Buck, Susan J. THE GLOBAL COMMONS: AN INTRODUCTION. Washington, DC: Island Press (1998).

Burk, Dan L. *Open Source Genomics*, 8 BOSTON U. J. SCI. & TECH. L. 254 (2002).

Busch, Lawrence and Lacy, William B. SCIENCE, AGRICULTURE, AND THE POLITICS OF RESEARCH. Boulder, CO: Westview Press (1983).

Butler, L. J. *Conflicts in Intellectual Property Rights of Genetic Resources: Implications for Agricultural Biotechnology, in* ECONOMIC AND SOCIAL ISSUES IN AGRICULTURAL BIOTECHNOLOGY (R.E. Evenson, V. Santaniello and D. Zilberman eds.) Cambridge, MA: CABI Publishing (2002).

Buttel, Frederick H. and Belsky, Jill M. *Biotechnology, Plant Breeding and Intellectual Property—Social and Ethical Dimensions, in* OWNING SCIENTIFIC AND TECHNICAL INFORMATION, VALUE AND ETHICAL ISSUES (Vivien Weil and John W. Snapper eds.) New Brunswick, NJ: Rutgers University Press (1989).

Byerlee, Derek and Echeverria, Ruben G. AGRICULTURAL RESEARCH POLICY IN AN ERA OF PRIVATIZATION. Cambridge, MA: CABI Publishing (2002).

Cann, Wesley A. Jr. *On the Relationship Between Intellectual Property Rights and the Need of Less-Developed Countries for Access to Pharmaceuticals: Creating a Legal Duty to Supply Under a Theory of Progressive Global Constitutionalism*, 25 U. PA. J. INT'L ECON. L. 755 (1996).

Carson, Rachel. SILENT SPRING. Boston: Houghton Mifflin (1962).

CEAS Consultants (Wye) Ltd. *Final Report for Directorate-General Trade European Commission, Study on the Relationship between the Agreement on TRIPS and Biodiversity Related Issues*. Centre for European Agricultural Studies (September 2000).

Center for Food Safety, MONSANTO V. U.S. FARMERS (2004), *available at* http://per-cyschmeiser.com/MonsantovsFarmerReport/3.05.pdf (last visited February 12, 2007).

Chander, Anupam and Sunder, Madhavi. *The Romance of the Public Domain*, 92 CAL. L. REV. 1331 (2004).

Charles, Daniel. LORDS OF THE HARVEST: BIOTECH, BIG MONEY AND THE FUTURE OF FOOD (2001).

Chen, Jim. *Webs of Life: Biodiversity Conservation as a Species of Information Policy*, 89 IOWA L. REV. 495 (2004).

Chisum, Donald S. CHISUM ON PATENTS: A TREATISE ON THE LAW OF PATENTABILITY, VALIDITY, AND INFRINGEMENT. Dayton, OH: Lexis Publishing (1978).

_____. *The Patentability of Algorithms (Symposium: The Future of Software Production)*. 47 U. PITT. L. REV. 959 (1986).

Chisum, Donald S. and Jacobs, Michael A. UNDERSTANDING INTELLECTUAL PROPERTY LAW. New York: Matthew Bender (1992).

Chon, Margaret. *Intellectual Property and the Development Divide*, 27 CARDOZO L. REV. 2813 (2006).

Chon, Margaret and Ghosh, Shubha. *Joint Comment on the WIPO Draft Report: Intellectual Property Needs and Expectations of Traditional Knowledge Holders* (Fall 2000), *available at* http://www.wipo.int/tk/fr/tk/ffm/ffm-report-comments/msg00008.html (last visited August 22, 2006).

Clark, E. Ann. *The Implications of the Schmeiser Decision*, *available at* http://per-cyschmeiser.com/crime.htm (last visited December 10, 2006).

Cleveland, David A. and Murray, Stephen C. *The World's Crop Genetic Resources and the Rights of Indigenous Farmers*. 38 CURR. ANTHRO. 477 (1997).

Cochrane, Willard. THE DEVELOPMENT OF AMERICAN AGRICULTURE: A HISTORICAL ANALYSIS. Minneapolis, MN: University of Minnesota Press (1979).

Coggins, George Cameron, Wilkinson, Charles F., and Leshy, John D. FEDERAL PUBLIC LAND AND RESOURCES (5th ed.) Westbury, NY: Foundation Press (2002).

Cohen, Julie E. and Lemley, Mark A. *Patent Scope and Innovation in the Software Industry*, 89 CAL. L. REV. 1 (2001).

Commission on Intellectual Property Rights. REPORT OF THE COMMISSION ON INTELLECTUAL PROPERTY RIGHTS: INTEGRATING IPRs AND DEVELOPMENT POLICY (2002), *available at* http://www.iprcommission.org/papers/text/final_report/reporthtmfinal.htm (last visited August 22, 2006).

Conquest, Robert. REFLECTIONS ON A RAVAGED CENTURY. New York: W.W. Norton & Co. (1999).

Convention on Biological Diversity, Third Conference, Conference of the Parties to the Convention on Biological Diversity (UNEP/CBD/COP/3/23) (October 5, 1996), *available at* http://www.iisd.ca/biodiv/cop3/COP3-23-vfinal.htm (last visited February 12, 2007).

Conway, Gordon. THE DOUBLY GREEN REVOLUTION: FOOD FOR ALL IN THE 21ST CENTURY. London: Penguin Books Ltd. (1997).

Coombe, Rosemary J. *Fear, Hope, and Longing for the Future of Authorship and a Revitalized Public Domain in the Global Regime of Intellectual Property*, 52 DEPAUL L. REV. 1171 (2003).

_____. *Intellectual Property, Human Rights and Sovereignty: New Dilemmas in International Law Posed by the Recognition of Indigenous Knowledge and the Conservation of Biodiversity*, 6 IND. J. GLOBAL LEG. STUD. 59 (1998).

Correa, Carlos M. INTELLECTUAL PROPERTY RIGHTS, THE WTO AND DEVELOPING COUNTRIES: THE TRIPS AGREEMENT AND POLICY OPTIONS (Reprinted ed.) London: Zed Books, Ltd. (2000).

_____. *Options for the Implementation of Farmers' Rights at the National Level*, Working Paper No. 8, Trade Related Agenda, Development and Equity (TRADE), South Centre (December 2000), *available at* http://www.southcentre.org/publications/farmersrights/toc.htm (last visited February 8, 2007).

Correa, Carlos M. and Yusuf, Abdulqawi A. (eds.) INTELLECTUAL PROPERTY AND INTERNATIONAL TRADE: THE TRIPS AGREEMENT. London and Boston: Kluwer Law International (1998).

Cottier, Thomas and Panizzon, Marion. *Legal Perspectives on Traditional Knowledge: The Case for Intellectual Property Protection*, 7 J. INT'L ECON. L. 371 (2004).

Crosby, A.W. THE COLUMBIAN EXCHANGE: BIOLOGICAL AND CULTURAL CONSEQUENCES OF 1492. Westport, CT: Greenwood Press (1972).

Crittenden, Ann. *Plan to Widen Plant Patents Stirs Conflict*, NEW YORK TIMES, at A1, (June 6, 1980).

Crump, Andy and Ellwood, Wayne. THE A TO Z OF WORLD DEVELOPMENT. Oxford: New Internationalist Publications (1999).

Cullet, Philippe. *The International Treaty on Plant Genetic Resources for Food and Agriculture*, IELRC, Briefing Paper, No. 2003-2, *available at* http://www.ielrc.org/content/f0302.htm (last visited February 8, 2007).

Cummins, Ronnie. *Hazards of Genetically Engineered Foods and Crops: Why We Need a Global Moratorium*, *available at* http://www.inmotionmagazine.com/geff4.html (last visited February 8, 2007).

Danbom, David B. THE RESISTED REVOLUTION: URBAN AMERICA AND THE INDUSTRIALIZATION OF AGRICULTURE, 1900–1930. Iowa City, IA: Iowa State Press (1979).

Day-Rubenstein, Kelly and Heisey, Paul. *Plant Genetic Resources*, AMBER WAVES 22 (June 2003).

Dedeurwaerdere, Tom. *Bioprospection: From the Economics of Contracts to Reflexive Governance*, *available at* http://www.ucl.ac.uk/bioecon/4th_paper/Dedeurwaedere.doc (last visited August 22, 2006).

Demaine, Linda J. and Fellmeth, Aaron Xavier. *Reinventing the Double Helix: A Novel and Nonobvious Reconceptualization of the Biotechnology Patent*, 55 STAN. L. REV. 303 (2002).

Demsetz, Harold. *The Private Production of Public Goods*, 13 J. L. & ECON. 293 (1970).

Di Bona, Chris, Ockman, Sam and Stone, Mark (eds.) OPEN SOURCES: VOICES FROM THE OPEN SOURCE REVOLUTION. Sebastapol, CA: O'Reilly Media (1999).

Dinwoodie, Graeme and Dreyfus, Rochelle Cooper. *TRIPS and the Dynamics of Intellectual Property Lawmaking*, 36 CASE W. RES. J. INT'L L. 95 (2004).

Douthwaite, Boru. ENABLING INNOVATION: A PRACTICAL GUIDE TO UNDERSTANDING AND FOSTERING TECHNOLOGICAL CHANGE. London: Zed Books, Ltd. (2002).

Dove, Michael R. *Center, Periphery, and Biodiversity: A Paradox of Governance and a Developmental Challenge, in* Valuing Local Knowledge: Indigenous People and Intellectual Property Rights (Stephen B. Brush and Doreen Stabinsky eds.) Washington, DC: Island Press (1996).

Doyle, Jack. Altered Harvest: Agriculture, Genetics, and the Fate of the World's Food Supply. New York: American Book Company (1985).

Drahos, Peter and Braithwaite, John. Information Feudalism: Who Owns the Knowledge Economy? New York: The New Press (2003).

Duall, Elizabeth. *A Liability and Redress Regime for Genetically Modified Organisms under the Cartagena Protocol*, 36 Geo. Wash. Int'l L. Rev. 173 (2004).

Duffy, John F. *Rethinking the Prospect Theory of Patents*, 71 Chi. L. Rev. 439 (2004).

Dutfield, Graham. Intellectual Property Rights, Trade and Biodiversity: Seeds and Plant Varieties. Gland/Geneva and London: Earthscan Publishing Ltd. (2000).

_____. *TRIPS-Related Aspects of Traditional Knowledge*, 33 Case W. Res. J. Int'l L. 233 (2001).

_____. *Indigenous Peoples, Bioprospecting and the TRIPS Agreement: Threats and Opportunities*, *available at* http://www.acts.or.ke/prog/biodiversity/trips/dutfield.doc (last visited August 22, 2006).

East, Edward M. The Relation of Certain Biological Principles to Plant Breeding. Bulletin: Connecticut Agricultural Experiment Station (1907).

East, Edward M. and Jones, Donald F. Inbreeding and Outbreeding: Their Genetic and Sociological Significance. Philadelphia, PA: J.B. Lippincott (1919).

Edie, Asbjørn and Rosa, Allan. *Economic, Social and Cultural Rights: A Universal Challenge, in* Economic, Social and Cultural Rights: A Textbook (Asbjørn Eide et al., eds.) The Hague, The Netherlands: Kluwer Law International (1995).

Elias, Paul. *Saving Seed is Latest Tech Piracy*, Jan. 14, 2005, *available at* http://www.wired.com/news/technology/0,1282,66282,00.html (last visited December 10, 2006).

Ellickson, Robert C. Order Without Law: How Neighbors Settle Disputes. Cambridge, MA: Harvard University Press (1991).

_____. *Cities and Homeowners Associations*, 130 Pa. L. Rev. 1519 (1988).

ETC Group. Communique, *New Enclosures: Alternate Mechanisms to Enhance Corporate Monopoly and Bioserfdom in the 21st Century* (November/December 2001), *available at* http://www.etcgroup.org/documents/NewEnclosuresFinal.pdf (last visited August 22, 2006).

_____. Communique, *2001: A Seed Odyssey* (April 11, 2001), *available at* http://www.etcgroup.org/upload/publication/269/01/com_2001.pdf (last visited August 22, 2006).

_____. Communique, *Bioserfdom, Technology, and the Erosion of "Farmers' Rights" in the Industrialized World* (March 30, 1999) *available at* http://www.etcgroup.org/upload/publication/450/01/raficom53bioserfdom.pdf (last visited August 22, 2006).

_____. Communique, *Seed Industry Consolidation: Who Owns Whom?* (July 30, 1998) *available at* http://www.etcgroup.org/upload/publication/404/01/raficom60seedindustry.pdf (last visited August 22, 2006).

Evenson, Robert E. *Agricultural Research and Intellectual Property Rights, in* International Public Goods and Transfer of Technology under a Globalized In-

TELLECTUAL PROPERTY REGIME (Keith E. Maskus and Jerome H. Reichman eds.) New York: Cambridge University Press (2005).

Evenson, Robert E. and Gollin, D., eds. CROP VARIETY IMPROVEMENT AND ITS EFFECT ON PRODUCTIVITY: THE IMPACT OF INTERNATIONAL RESEARCH. Cambridge, MA: CABI Publishing (2002).

Evenson, Robert E. and Huffman, Wallace E. SCIENCE FOR AGRICULTURE: A LONG TERM PERSPECTIVE. Ames, IA: Iowa State Press (1993).

Ewens, Lara E. *Seed Wars: Biotechnology, Intellectual Property and the Quest for High Yield Seeds*, 23 B.C. INT'L & COMP. L. REV. 285 (2000).

Feibleman, James K. *Pure Science, Applied Science, and Technology: An Attempt at Definitions*, 4 (2) TECH. & CULT. 305 (1961).

Feldman, Robin. *The Open Source Biotechnology Movement: Is It Patent Misuse?*, 6 MINN. J. L. SCI. & TECH. 117 (2004).

Fowler, Cary. UNNATURAL SELECTION: TECHNOLOGY, POLITICS, AND PLANT EVOLUTION. Yverdon, Switzerland: Gordon and Breach Science Publishers (1994).

————. *The Plant Patent Act of 1930: A Sociological History of Its Creation*, 82 J. PAT. & TRADEMARK OFF. SOC'Y 621 (2001).

————. *By Policy or Law? The Challenge of Determining the Status and Future of Agro-Biodiversity*, 3 J. TECH. L. & POL'Y 1 36 (1997).

Fowler, Cary and Mooney, Pat R. SHATTERING: FOOD, POLITICS AND THE LOSS OF GENETIC DIVERSITY. Tucson, AZ: University of Arizona Press (1990).

Frankel, Sir Otto H. *Genetic Resources: The Founding Years—Part One*, 7 DIVERSITY 26 (1985).

————. *Genetic Resources: The Founding Years—Part Two: The Movement's Constituent Assembly*, 8 DIVERSITY 30 (1986).

————. *Genetic Resources: The Founding Years—Part Three: The Long Road to the International Board*, 9 DIVERSITY 30 (1986).

Frug, Gerald E. *Decentering Decentralization*, 60 U. CHI. L. REV. 253 (1993).

Frug, Gerald E., Ford, Richard T. and Barron, David. LOCAL GOVERNMENT LAW (4th ed.) West Publishing (2005).

Fuccillo, Dominic, Sears, Linda, and Stapleton, Paul. BIODIVERSITY IN TRUST: CONSERVATION AND USE OF PLANT GENETIC RESOURCES IN CGIAR CENTRES. New York: Cambridge University Press (1997).

Gabriel, Richard P. and Goldman, Ron. *Open Source: Beyond the Fairytales* (2002), *available at* http://opensource.mit.edu/papers/gabrielgoldman.pdf (last visited August 12, 2006).

GAIA/GRAIN, *TRIPS versus CBD: Conflicts between the WTO Regime of Intellectual Property Rights and Sustainable Biodiversity Management, Global Trade and Biodiversity in Conflict*, 1 GAIA/GRAIN (April 1998), *available at* http://www.grain.org/briefings/?id=24 (last visited August 14, 2006).

Gall, Peter. *What Really Matters—Human Development*, in THE POLITICAL ECONOMY OF DEVELOPMENT AND UNDERDEVELOPMENT (6th ed., Kenneth P. Jameson and Charles K. Wilber eds.) New York: McGraw Hill (1996).

Gana, Ruth L. *Prospects for Developing Countries under the TRIPS Agreement*, 29 Vand. J. Transnat'l L. 735 (1996).

Gasser, C.S. and Fraley, R.T. *Genetically Engineered Plants for Crop Improvement*, 244 Science 1293 (16 June 1989).

Gerhart, Peter M. *Distributive Values and Institutional Design in the Provision of Global Public Goods*, *in* International Public Goods and Transfer of Technology under a Globalized Intellectual Property Regime (Keith E. Maskus and Jerome H. Reichman eds.) New York: Cambridge University Press (2005).

Gervais, Daniel. The TRIPS Agreement: Drafting History and Analysis. London: Sweet and Maxwell (2003).

Ghosh, Shubha. *Traditional Knowledge, Patents and the New Mercantilism (Part II)*, 85 J. Pat. & Trademark Off. Soc'y 885 (2003).

_____. *Pills, Patents and Power: State Creation of Gray Markets as a Limit on Patent Rights*, 14 Fla. J. Int'l L. 217 (2002).

_____. *The Traditional Terms of the Traditional Knowledge Debate*, 11 Cardozo J. Int'l and Comp. L. (2001).

Goeschl, Timo and Swanson, Tim. *The Impact of Genetic Use Restriction Technologies on Developing Countries: A Forecast*, *in* Economic and Social Issues in Agricultural Biotechnology (R.E. Evenson, V. Santaniello and D. Zilberman eds.) Cambridge, MA: CABI Publishing (2002).

Goulet, Denis and Wilber, Charles K. *The Human Element of Development*, *in* The Political Economy of Development and Underdevelopment (6th ed., Kenneth P. Jameson and Charles K. Wilber eds.) New York: McGraw Hill (1996).

Goodwin, James R. Crisis in the World's Fisheries. Stanford, CA: Stanford University Press (1990).

Gordon, H. Scott. *The Economic Theory of a Common-Property Resource: The Fishery*. 62 J. Pol. Econ. 124 (1954).

Grady, Mark F. & Alexander, Jay I. *Patent Law and Rent Dissipation*, 78 Va. L. Rev. 305 (1992).

Graff, Gregory and Zilberman, Dave. *Intellectual Property Clearinghouse, Mechanisms for Agriculture: Summary of an Industry, Academic and International Development Round Table*, 3 IP Strategy Today 15 (2001).

Graziano, Karen M. *Biosafety Protocol: Recommendations to Ensure the Safety of the Environment*, 7 Colo. J. Int'l Envtl L. & Pol'y 179 (1995).

Grubb, Michael, Koch, Matthias, Munson, Abby, Sullivan, Francis and Thomson, Koy. The Earth Summit Agreements: A Guide and Assessment. London: Earthscan Publications Ltd. (1993).

Gruner, Richard S. *Intangible Inventions: Patentable Subject Matter for an Information Age*, 35 Loy. L.A. L. Rev. 355 (2002).

Guzman, Andrew T. *International Antitrust and the WTO: The Lesson from Intellectual Property*, 43 Va. J. Int'l L. 933 (2003).

Halbert, Debora. *Intellectual Property in the Year 2025*, 49 J. Copyright Soc'y U.S.A. 225 (2001).

Halewood, Michael. *Indigenous and Local Knowledge in International Law: A Preface to Sui Generis Intellectual Protection*, 44 McGill L. J. 953 (1999).

Hamilton, Neil D. *Who Owns Dinner: Evolving Legal Mechanisms for Ownership of Plant Genetic Resources*, 28 Tulsa L. J. 587 (1993).

Hanning, Mark. *An Examination of the Possibility to Secure Intellectual Property Rights for Plant Genetic Resources Developed by Indigenous People of NAFTA States: Domestic Legislation Under the International Convention for Protection of New Plant Varieties*, 13 Ariz. J. Int'l & Comp. L. 175 (1996).

Hardin, Garrett. *The Tragedy of the Commons*, 162 Science 1243 (1968).

Harlan, Jack. *Genetics of Disaster*, 1 J. Envtl Quality 213 (1977).

Harris, Donald P. *TRIPS' Rebound: An Historical Analysis of How the TRIPS Agreement Can Ricochet Back Against the United States*, 25 Nw. J. Int'l L. & Bus. 99 (2004).

Helfer, Laurence R. *Using Intellectual Property Rights to Preserve the Global Genetic Commons: The International Treaty on Plant Genetic Resources for Food and Agriculture, in* International Public Goods and Transfer of Technology under a Globalized Intellectual Property Regime (Keith E. Maskus and Jerome H. Reichman eds.) New York: Cambridge University Press (2005).

_____. *Regime Shifting: The TRIPS Agreement and New Dynamics of International Intellectual Property Lawmaking*, 29 Yale J. Int'l L. 1 (2004).

Heller, Michael A. *The Tragedy of the Anticommons: Property in the Transition from Marx to Markets*, 111 Harv. L. Rev. 622 (1998).

Heller, Michael A. and Eisenberg, Rebecca S. *Can Patents Deter Innovation? The Anticommons in Biomedical Research*, 280 Science 698 (1998).

Henderson, David. *International Agencies and Cross-Border Liberalization: The WTO in Context, in* The WTO as an International Organization (Anne O. Kreuger ed.) Chicago and London: University of Chicago Press (1998).

Hennig, Mark. *An Examination of the Possibility to Secure Intellectual Property Rights for Plant Genetic Resources Developed by Indigenous Peoples of the NAFTA States—Domestic Legislation Under the International Convention for Protection of New Plant Varieties*, 13 Ariz. J. Int'l & Comp. L. 175 (1996).

Hess, Charlotte and Ostrom, Elinor. *Ideas, Artifacts, and Facilities: Information as a Common Pool Resource*, 66 L. & Contemp. Probs. 111 (2003).

Hettinger, Edwin C. *Justifying Intellectual Property*, 18 Phil. & Pub. Aff. 31 (1989).

Hightower, Jim. Hard Tomatoes, Hard Times: A Report of the Agribusiness Accountability Project on the Failure of America's Land Grant College Complex. Cambridge, MA: Schenkman Publishing Company (1973).

Himanen, Pekka. The Hacker Ethic and the Spirit of the Information Age. New York: Random House (2001).

History of Monsanto's Glyphosate Herbicides, available at http://www.monsanto.com/monsanto/content/products/productivity/roundup/back_history.pdf (last visited August 21, 2006).

Holwick, Scott. *Developing Nations and the Agreement on Trade-Related Aspects of Intellectual Property Rights*, 11 Colo. J. Int'l Envtl L. & Pol'y 183 (2000).

Hope, Janet Elizabeth. *Open Source Software as a Business Model, available at* http://rsss
.anu.edu.au/~janeth/OSBusMod.html (last visited June 28, 2006).

————. Open Source Biotechnology (doctoral thesis), *available at* http://rsss
.anu.edu.au/~janeth/OpenSourceBiotechnology27July2005.pdf (last visited June
28, 2006).

————. *Open Source Initiative, available at* http://www.opensource.org/ (last visited
August 12, 2006).

Hubbard, Amanda. *Comment, The Convention on Biological Diversity's Fifth Anniversary: A General Overview of the Convention — Where Has It Been and Where is It
Going?*, 10 Tul. Envtl L. J. 415 (1997).

Hyde, Lewis. The Gift: Imagination and the Erotic Life of Property. New York:
Random House (1979).

Innes, N.L. *Patents and Plant Breeding*, 298 Nature 786 (August 1982).

Intergovernmental Committee on Intellectual Property and Genetic Resources, Tradi-
tional Knowledge and Folklore, Second Sess. (10–14 Dec. 2001), *Operational
Principles for Intellectual Property Clauses of Contractual Agreements Concerning
Access to Genetic Resources and Benefit Sharing*, WIPO/GRTKF/1C/2/3 94 (10
Sept. 2001).

International Center for Technology Assessment, *available at* http://www.icta.org/intel-
prop/FarmAdAnalysis.pdf (last visited August 21, 2006).

Jain, Meetali. *Global Trade and the New Millennium: Defining the Scope of Intellectual
Property Protection of Plant Genetic Resources and Traditional Knowledge in India*, 22
Hastings Int'l & Comp. L. Rev. 777 (1999).

Janis, Mark A. and Kesan, Jay P. *U.S. Plant Variety Protection: Sound and Fury ... ?*, 39
Hous. L. Rev. 727 (2002).

Jaszi, Peter and Woodmansee, Martha. *Beyond Authorship: Refiguring Rights in Traditional Culture and Bioknowledge, in* Scientific Authorship: Credit and Intellectual Property in Science (Mario Biagoli and Peter Galison eds.) New York
and London: Routledge (2001).

Juma, Calestous. The Gene Hunters: Biotechnology and the Scramble for Seed
(African Centre for Technology Studies Research Series, No. 1). Princeton,
NJ: Princeton University Press (1989).

Kadidal, Shayana. *Plants, Poverty and Pharmaceutical Patents*, 103 Yale L. J. 223 (1993).

Kameri-Mbote, Annie Patricia and Cullet, Philippe. *The Management of Genetic Resources: Developments in the 1997 Sessions of the Commission on Genetic Resources
for Food and Agriculture*, 1997 Colo. J. Int'l Envtl L. & Pol'y 78 (1997).

Kane, Eileen M. *Splitting the Gene: DNA Patents and the Genetic Code*, 71 Tenn. L. Rev.
707 (2004).

Kaul, Inge, Grunberg, Isabelle, and Stern, Marc. Global Public Goods: International Cooperation in the 21st Century. New York: Oxford University Press
(1999).

Keohane, Robert O. *Comment: Norms, Institutions and Cooperation, in* International
Public Goods and Transfer of Technology under a Globalized Intellec-
tual Property Regime (Keith E. Maskus and Jerome H. Reichman eds.) New
York: Cambridge University Press (2005).

Kershen, Drew L. *Of Straying Crops and Patent Rights*, 43 WASBURN L. J. 575 (2004).

Keystone Center. *Final Consensus Report of the Keystone International Dialogue Series on Plant Genetic Resources: Madras Plenary Session*. Keystone, CO: Keystone Center (1990).

Kipp, Margaret E. I. *Software and Seeds: Open Source Methods*, *available at* http://www .firstmonday.org/issues/issue10_9/kipp/ (last visited Jun 18, 2006).

Kirkendall, Richard S. SOCIAL SCIENTISTS AND FARM POLITICS IN THE AGE OF ROO-SEVELT. Columbia, MO: University of Missouri Press (1966).

Kitch, Edmund W. *The Nature and Function of the Patent System*, 30 J. L. & ECON. 265 (1977).

Kitch, Edmund W. and Perlman, Harvey S. LEGAL REGULATION OF THE COMPETITIVE PROCESS (3d ed.) Westbury, NY: Foundation Press (1986).

Klinenborg, Verlyn. *Biotechnology and the Future of Agriculture*, NEW YORK TIMES, at A18 (December 8, 1997).

Kloppenburg, Jack R., Jr. FIRST THE SEED: THE POLITICAL ECONOMY OF PLANT BIOTECHNOLOGY, 1492–2000. New York: Cambridge University Press (1988).

Kloppenburg, Jack R., Jr. and Kleinman, Daniel. *Preface, Plant Genetic Resources: The Common Bowl, in* SEEDS AND SOVEREIGNTY: THE USE AND CONTROL OF PLANT GE-NETIC RESOURCES (Jack R. Kloppenburg, Jr. ed.) Durham, NC: Duke University Press (1988).

————. *Seed Wars: Common Heritage, Private Property, and Political Strategy*. 95 SO-CIALIST REV. 6 (1987).

Klose, Norman. AMERICA'S CROP HERITAGE: THE HISTORY OF FOREIGN PLANT INTRO-DUCTION BY THE FEDERAL GOVERNMENT. Ames, IA: Iowa State College Press (1950).

Krimsky, Sheldon. SCIENCE IN THE PRIVATE INTEREST: HAS THE LURE OF PROFITS CORRUPTED BIOMEDICAL RESEARCH? Lanham, MD: Rowman & Littlefield (2003).

Kruger, Maria. *Harmonizing TRIPs and the CBD: A Proposal from India*, 10 MINN. J. GLOBAL TRADE 169 (2001).

Lange, David. *Recognizing the Public Domain*, 44 L. & CONTEMP. PROBS. 147 (1981).

Lappé, Francis Moore. DIET FOR A SMALL PLANET. New York: Ballantine Books (1971).

Lappé, Francis Moore, Collins, Joseph, and Fowler, Cary. FOOD FIRST: BEYOND THE MYTH OF SCARCITY. Boston: Houghton Mifflin Publishing (1977).

Leahy, Stephen. *Monsanto's 'Seed Police' Watching Farmers*, *available at* LEXIS, IPS-Inter Press Service (January 14, 2005).

Lehman, Karen and Krebs, Al. *Control of the World's Food Supply, in* THE CASE AGAINST THE GLOBAL ECONOMY AND FOR A TURN TOWARD THE LOCAL. (Jerry Mander and Edward Goldsmith eds.) San Francisco, CA: Sierra Club Books (1997).

Leskien, Dan and Flinter, Michael. *Intellectual Property Rights and Plant Genetic Re-sources: Options for a Sui Generis System, Issues in Genetic Resources*, No. 6 INTER-NATIONAL PLANT GENETIC RESOURCES INSTITUTE, ROME (June 1997).

Lesser, W. and Masson, R. AN ECONOMIC ANALYSIS OF THE PLANT VARIETY PROTEC-TION ACT. Washington DC: American Seed Trade Association (1985).

Lessig, Lawrence. THE FUTURE OF IDEAS: THE FATE OF THE COMMONS IN A NET-WORKED WORLD. New York: Random House (2001).

Levy, Steven. HACKERS: HEROES OF THE COMPUTER REVOLUTION. New York: Double-day (1984).

Lewontin, Richard. *Agricultural Research and the Penetration of Capital*, 14 SCI. FOR THE PEOPLE 12 (1982).

Litman, Jessica. DIGITAL COPYRIGHT: PROTECTING INTELLECTUAL PROPERTY ON THE INTERNET. Amherst, NY: PROMETHEUS BOOKS (2001).

_____. *The Public Domain*, 39 EMORY L. J. 965 (1990).

Long, Doris Estelle. *The Impact of Foreign Investment on Indigenous Culture: An Intellectual Property Perspective*, 23 N.C. J. INT'L L. & COM. REG. 61 (1998).

Lopez, Carlos Scott. *Intellectual Property Reform for Genetically Modified Crops: A Legal Imperative*, 20 J. CONTEMP. HEALTH & POL'Y 367 (2004).

Mansfield, Edwin. *How Rapidly Does New Industrial Technology Leak Out?*, 34 J. INDUS. ECON. 217 (1985).

Marco, Alan C. and Rausser, Gordon C. *Mergers and Intellectual Property in Agricultural Biotechnology*, *in* ECONOMIC AND SOCIAL ISSUES IN AGRICULTURAL BIOTECHNOL-OGY (R.E. Evenson, V. Santaniello and D. Zilberman eds.) Cambridge, MA: CABI Publishing (2002).

Marx, Karl. CAPITAL, VOL. I: A CRITIQUE OF POLITICAL ECONOMY (Ben Fowkes trans.) New York: Penguin Books (1992).

Mas-Colell, Andreu, Whinston, Michael D., and Green, Jerry R. MICROECONOMIC THE-ORY. New York: Oxford University Press (1995).

Maskus, Keith E. and Reichman, Jerome H. *The Globalization of Private Knowledge Goods and the Privatization of Global Public Goods*, 7 J. INT'L ECON. L. 279 (2004).

Maurer, Stephen M., Rai, Arti and Sali, Andrej. *Finding Cures for Tropical Diseases: Is Open Source an Answer?*, 6 MINN. J. L. SCI. & TECH. 169 (2004).

Mayr, Ernst. THE GROWTH OF BIOLOGICAL THOUGHT: DIVERSITY, EVOLUTION, AND IN-HERITANCE. Cambridge, MA and London: Belknap Press (1982).

McClellan, Traci L. *The Role of International Law in Protecting the Traditional Knowledge and Plant Life of Indigenous People*, 19 WIS. INT'L L. J. 249 (2001).

McGowan, David. *Legal Implications of Open-Source Software*, 2001 U. ILL. L. REV. 241 (2001).

McManis, Charles R. *The Interface between International Intellectual Property and Environmental Protection: Biodiversity and Biotechnology*, 76 WASH. U. L.Q. 255 (1998).

Mekouar, Ali. *A Global Instrument on Agrobiodiversity: The International Treaty on Plant Genetic Resources for Food and Agriculture*, FAO Legal Papers Online # 24 (January 2002), *available at* http://www.fao.org/Legal/prs-ol/lpo24.pdf (last visited February 10, 2007).

Mendelson, Joseph III. *Patently Erroneous: How the U.S. Supreme Court's Decision in Farm Advantage Ignores Congress and Threatens the Future of the American Farmer*, 32 ENVTL L. REV. 10698 (June 2002).

Merges, Robert P. *As Many as Six Impossible Patents for Breakfast,* 14 BERKELEY TECH. L.J. 579 (1999).

Merges, Robert P., Menell, Peter S., and Lemley, Mark A. INTELLECTUAL PROPERTY IN THE NEW TECHNOLOGICAL AGE (4th ed.) New York: Aspen Publishers (2006).

Mgbeoji, Ikeihi. *Patents and Traditional Knowledge of the Uses of Plants: Is a Communal Patent Regime Part of the Solution to the Scourge of Biopiracy,* 9 IND. J. GLOBAL LEG. STUD. 163 (2001).

Michaels, Tom. *General Public Release for Plant Germplasm: A Proposal by Tom Michaels* (Professor of Plant Agriculture, University of Guelph), v.1, 1, 26 (February 1999), *available at* http://www.oac.uoguelph.ca/www/CSRC/pltag/1998-99/gnucrop2.htm

Moglen, Eben. *Anarchism Triumphant: Free Software and the Death of Copyright,* 4 FIRST MONDAY 8 (Aug. 2, 1999), *available at* http://firstmonday.org/issues/issue4_8/moglen/index.html (last visited February 12, 2007).

Monsanto Canada: Products: Roundup Ready, available at http://www.monsanto.ca/products/roundupready/index.shtml (last visited December 10, 2006).

Monsanto Co., Achievements in Plant Biotechnology—Evaluation: Canola, available at http://www.biotechknowledge.com/biotech/bbasics.nsf/biotech01_canola.html (last visited December 10, 2006).

Montoya, Felipe. *[Costa Rica] Linux and Seeds, Geeks and Farmers—A Spiritual Link,* A42 (September 11, 2003), *available at* http://www.a42.com/node/view/343 (last visited February 10, 2007).

Moody, Glyn. REBEL CODE: THE INSIDE STORY OF LINUX AND THE OPEN SOURCE REVOLUTION. New York: HarperCollins (2001).

Mooney, Pat R. THE LAW OF THE SEED, DEVELOPMENT DIALOGUE, VOL. 1, NO. 2. London: Zed Books, Ltd. (1983).

————. SEEDS OF THE EARTH: A PRIVATE OR PUBLIC RESOURCE? London: International Coalition for Development Action (1979).

Mossoff, Adam. *What is Property? Putting the Pieces Back Together,* 45 ARIZ. L. REV. 371 (2003).

Murphy, Sean D. *Biotechnology and International Law,* 42 HARV. INT'L L. J. 47 (2001).

Myers, Norman. A WEALTH OF WILD SPECIES. Boulder, Co: Westview Press (1983).

Myers, W.M. *Germ Plasm Control as it Would Affect Variety Improvement and Release of Field Crops, in* PLANT BREEDERS' RIGHTS. American Society of Agronomy ed. (1964).

Nabhan, Gary P. *Sharing the Benefits of Plant Resources and Indigenous Scientific Knowledge, in* VALUING LOCAL KNOWLEDGE: INDIGENOUS PEOPLE AND INTELLECTUAL PROPERTY RIGHTS (Doreen Stabinsky and Stephen B. Brush eds.) Washington, DC: Island Press (1996).

National Research Council (NRC), *Managing Global Genetic Resources: The U.S. National Plant Germplasm System,* Committee on Managing Global Genetic Resources: Agricultural Imperatives, Board on Agriculture, National Research Council. Washington, DC: National Academy Press (1991).

Neagly, C.H., Jeffery, D.D., and Diepenbrock, A.R. *Genetic Engineering Patent Law Trends Affecting Development of Plant Patents,* 4 GENETIC ENGINEERING NEWS 10 (April 1984).

Noble, David F. *The Corporation as Inventor*, in AMERICA BY DESIGN: SCIENCE, TECHNOLOGY, AND THE RISE OF CORPORATE CAPITALISM. New York: Galaxy Books (1977).

Nottenburg, Carol, Pardey, Philip, and Wright, Brian. *Accessing Other Peoples' Technology for Non-Profit Research*, 46 AUSTRALIAN J. AGR. RESOURCE ECON. 389 (2002).

Ntambirweki, John. *Biotechnology and International Law within the North-South Context*, 14 TRANSNAT'L. LAW 103 (2001).

Nwabreze, Remigius N. *Ethnopharmacology, Patents and the Politics of Plants' Genetic Resources*, 11 CARDOZO J. INT'L & COMP. L. 585 (2003).

Odek, James O. *Bio-Piracy: Creating Proprietary Rights in Plant Genetic Resources*, 2 J. INTELL. PROP. L. 141 (1993).

Okediji, Ruth L. *Public Welfare and the Role of the WTO: Reconsidering the TRIPS Agreement*, 17 EMORY INT'L L. REV. 819 (2003).

_____. *The International Relations of Intellectual Property: Narratives of Developing Country Participation in the Global Intellectual Property System*, 7 SING. J. INT'L & COMP. L. 315 (2003).

Olson, Mancur. The LOGIC OF COLLECTIVE ACTION: PUBLIC GOODS AND THE THEORY OF GROUPS. Cambridge, MA: Harvard University Press (1965).

Onwoekwe, Chika B. *The Commons Concept and Intellectual Property Rights: Whither Plant Genetic and Traditional Knowledge*, 2 PIERCE L. REV. 65 (2004).

Opderbeck, David W. *The Penguin's Genome, or Coase and Open Source Biotechnology*, available at http://ssrn.com/abstract=574804 (2004).

Ostrom, Elinor. GOVERNING THE COMMONS: THE EVOLUTION OF INSTITUTIONS FOR COLLECTIVE ACTION. New York: Cambridge University Press (1990).

Ostrom, Elinor and Keohane, Robert (eds.) LOCAL COMMONS AND GLOBAL INTERDEPENDENCE: HETEROGENEITY AND COOPERATION IN TWO DOMAINS. London: Sage Publishing (1994).

Panjabi, Ranee K. L. *Idealism and Self-Interest in International Environmental Law: The Rio Dilemma*, 23 CAL. W. INT'L L. J. 177, 191 (1992).

Patel, Kirit K. *"Farmers' Rights" Over Plant Genetic Resources in the South: Challenges and Opportunities*, in INTELLECTUAL PROPERTY RIGHTS IN AGRICULTURAL BIOTECHNOLOGY (2d ed., F.H. Erbisch and K.M. Maredia eds.) Cambridge, MA: CABI Publishing (2003).

Pepa, Stevan. *Research and Trade In Genetics: How Countries Should Structure for the Future*, 17 Med. & L. 437, 441 (1998).

Peet, Richard and Hardwick, Elaine. THEORIES OF DEVELOPMENT. New York: The Guilford Press (1999).

Petit, Michel, Fowler, Cary, Collins, Wanda, Correa, Carlos, and Thornström, Carl-Gustaf. WHY GOVERNMENTS CAN'T MAKE POLICY: THE CASE OF PLANT GENETIC RESOURCES IN THE INTERNATIONAL ARENA. Lima, Peru: CIP (2001).

Pistorius, Robin and van Wijk, Jeroen. THE EXPLOITATION OF PLANT GENETIC INFORMATION: POLITICAL STRATEGIES IN CROP DEVELOPMENT. Cambridge, MA: CABI Publishing (1999).

Plucknett, Donald L. and Smith, Nigel. GENE BANKS AND THE WORLD'S FOOD SUPPLY. Princeton, NJ: Princeton University Press (1987).

Posey, Darrel A. and Dutfield, Graham. BEYOND INTELLECTUAL PROPERTY: TOWARDS TRADITIONAL RIGHTS FOR INDIGENOUS PEOPLES AND LOCAL COMMUNITIES. Ottawa, Canada: International Development Research Centre (1996).

_____. *International Agreements and Intellectual Property Rights Protection for Indigenous Peoples, in* INTELLECTUAL PROPERTY RIGHTS FOR INDIGENOUS PEOPLES: A SOURCEBOOK (Tom Greaves ed.) Oklahoma City, OK: Society for Applied Anthropology (1994).

Preston, Hilary. *Drift of Patented Genetically Engineered Crops: Rethinking Liability Theories*, 81 TEX. L. REV. 1153 (2003).

Profile of Percy and Louise Schmeiser, available at http://percyschmeiser.com/profile.htm (last visited December 10, 2006).

Quinn, Miriam Latorre. *Protection for Indigenous Knowledge: An International law Analysis*, 14 ST. THOMAS L. REV. 287 (2001).

Radin, Margaret Jane. CONTESTED COMMODITIES. Cambridge, MA: Harvard University Press (1996).

Rai, Arti K. and. Eisenberg, Rebecca S. *Bayh-Dole Reform and the Progress of Biomedicine*, 66 L. & CONTEMP. PROBS. 289 (2003).

Rajagopal, Balakrishnan. INTERNATIONAL LAW FROM BELOW: DEVELOPMENT, SOCIAL MOVEMENTS, AND THIRD WORLD RESISTANCE. New York: Cambridge University Press (2003).

Raustiala, Kal and Victor, David G. *The Regime Complex for Plant Genetic Resources*. 32 (2) INT'L ORG. 147 (April 2004).

Raymond, Eric S. THE CATHEDRAL AND THE BAAZAR: MUSINGS ON LINUX AND OPEN SOURCE BY AN ACCIDENTAL REVOLUTIONARY. Sebastapol, CA: O'Reilly Media (1999).

Reichman, J.H. *From "Free Riders" to "Fair Followers": Global Competition under the TRIPS Agreement*, 29 NYU J. INT'L L. & POL'Y 11 (1996–97).

Relationship between the TRIPS Agreement and the Convention on Biological Diversity: Summary of Issues Raised and Points Made by the WTO Secretariat, IP/C/W/368 (Aug. 8, 2002).

RESTATEMENT (THIRD) OF UNFAIR COMPETITION, §§38–45 (1995).

Riley, Angela R. *Recovering Collectivity: Group Rights to Intellectual Property in Indigenous Communities*, 18 CARDOZO ARTS & ENT. L.J. 175 (2000).

Rittich, Kerry. *The Future of Law and Development: Second Generation Reforms and the Incorporation of the Social*, 26 MICH. J. INT'L L. 199 (2004).

Robinson, Raoul A. RETURN TO RESISTANCE: BREEDING CROPS TO REDUCE PESTICIDE DEPENDENCE. Ottawa, Canada: International Development Research Centre (1996).

Rodriguez, Silvia and Camacho, Maia Antnieta. *Bioprospecting in Costa Rica: Facing New Dimensions of Social and Environmental Responsibility, in* THE GREENING OF BUSINESS IN DEVELOPING COUNTRIES: RHETORIC, REALITY, AND PROSPECTS (Peter Utting ed.) London: Zed Books, Ltd. (2002).

Roht-Arriaza, Naomi. *Of Seeds and Shamans: The Appropriation of the Scientific and Technical Knowledge of Indigenous and Local Communities*, 17 MICH. J. INT'L L. 919 (1996).

Rose, Carol M. PROPERTY AND PERSUASION: ESSAYS ON THE HISTORY, THEORY AND RHETORIC OF OWNERSHIP. Boulder, CO: Westview Press (1994).

_____. *Romans, Roads and Romantic Creators: Traditions of Public Property in the Information Age*, 66 L. & CONTEMP. PROBS. 89 (2003).

_____. *The Several Futures of Property: Of Cyberspace and Folk Tales, Mission Trades and Ecosystems*, 83 MINN. L. REV. 129 (1998).

_____. *The Comedy of the Commons: Custom, Commerce, and Inherently Public Property*, 53 U. CHI. L. REV. 711 (1986).

Rose, Gregory. *International Law of Sustainable Agriculture in the 21st Century: The International Treaty on Plant Genetic Resources for Food and Agriculture*, 15 GEO. INT'L ENVTL L. REV. 583 (2003).

Rosenberg, Charles E. NO OTHER GODS: ON SCIENCE AND AMERICAN SOCIAL THOUGHT. Baltimore, MD: Johns Hopkins Press (1976).

Ruby, Steven M. *Note, The UPOV System of Protection: How to Bridge the Gap Between 1961 and 1991 in Regard to Breeders' Rights*, 2 OKLA. J. L. & TECH. 19 (2004).

Ryan, Michael P. KNOWLEDGE DIPLOMACY: GLOBAL COMPETITION AND THE POLITICS OF INTELLECTUAL PROPERTY. Washington, DC: Brookings Institution Press (1998).

Safrin, Sabrina. *Hyperownership in a Time of Biotechnological Promise: The International Conflict to Control the Building Blocks of Life*, 98 AM. J. INT'L L. 641 (2004).

Samuelson, Pamela. *Benson Revisited: The Case against Patent Protection for Algorithms and Other Computer Program-Related Inventions*, 39 EMORY L. J. 1025 (1990).

Sarma, Lakshmi. *Note, Biopiracy: Twentieth Century Imperialism in the Form of International Agreements*, 13 TEMP. INT'L & COMP. L. J. 107 (1999).

Seay, Nicholas O. *Protecting the Seeds of Innovation: Patenting Plants*, 16 A.I.P.L.A. Q. J. 418 (1989).

Seabrook, John. *Sowing for Apocalypse*, THE NEW YORKER 60 (August 27, 2007).

Sedjo, Roger A. *Property Rights and the Protection of Plant Genetic Resources, in* SEEDS AND SOVEREIGNTY: THE USE AND CONTROL OF PLANT GENETIC RESOURCES (Jack R. Kloppenburg, Jr. ed.) Durham, NC: Duke University Press (1988).

Sell, Susan K. PRIVATE POWER: THE GLOBALIZATION OF INTELLECTUAL PROPERTY. New York: Cambridge University Press (2003).

_____. *Post-TRIPS Developments: The Tension between Commercial and Social Agendas in the Context of Intellectual Property*, 14 FLA. J. INT'L L. 193 (2002).

Shand, Hope. FATAL HARVEST: THE TRAGEDY OF INDUSTRIAL AGRICULTURE. Washington, DC: Island Press (2002).

_____. *There is a Conflict between Intellectual Property and the Rights of Framers in Developing Countries*, 4 J. AGRIC. & ENVTL ETHICS 131 (1991).

Shiva, Vandana, Bhar, Radha Holla, and Jafri, Afsar H. CORPORATE HIJACK OF BIODIVERSITY. New Dehli: Navdanya (2002).

Shiva, Vandana. BIOPIRACY: THE PLUNDER OF NATURE AND KNOWLEDGE. Cambridge, MA: South End Press (1997).

_____. THE VIOLENCE OF THE GREEN REVOLUTION: THIRD WORLD AGRICULTURE, ECOLOGY, AND POLITICS. London: Zed Books, Ltd. (1992).

Simma, Bruno. *The Implemenation of the International Covenant of Economic, Social and Cultural Rights*, in THE IMPLEMENTATION OF THE INTERNATIONAL COVENANT OF ECONOMIC, SOCIAL AND CULTURAL RIGHTS: INTERNATIONAL AND COMPARATIVE ASPECTS (Engel Verlag ed.) Kehl am Rhein, Germany: NP Engel (1991).

Simmonds, Norman W. PRINCIPLES OF CROP IMPROVEMENT. London: Longman Publishing (1979).

Singer, Joseph W. PROPERTY LAW: RULES, POLICIES AND PRACTICES (4th ed.) New York: Aspen Publishers (2005).

_____. THE EDGES OF THE FIELD. Boston, MA: Beacon Press (2000).

_____. ENTITLEMENT: THE PARADOXES OF PROPERTY. New Haven, CT: Yale University Press (2000).

Sneep, J. Murray, B.R., and Utz, H.F. *Current Breeding Methods*, in PLANT BREEDING PERSPECTIVES (J. Sneep, A.J.T. Hendrickson, and O. Holbek eds.) Wageningen, The Netherlands: Centre for Agricultural Publishing and Documentation (1979).

Southwest Farm Press. *Biodiversity Treaty Signed*, SOUTHWEST FARM PRESS, April.15, 2004, *available at* http://southwestfarmpress.com/mag/farming_biodiversity_treaty _signed/index.html (last visited Mar. 9, 2005).

Special Report: *The WTO under Fire: The Doha Round*, THE ECONOMIST (U.S. Edition), September 18, 2003, at 26.

Srinivas, K. Ravi. *Innovations, Commons and Creativity: Open Source, Bio Linux and Seeds*, *available at* http://www.wacc.org.uk/wacc/content/pdf/634 (last visited June 27, 2006).

_____. *The Case for Biolinuxes and Other Pro-Commons Innovations*, THE SARAI READER 2002: THE CITIES OF EVERYDAY LIFE (2002), *available at* http://www.sarai .net/journal/02PDF/10infopol/09biolinux.pdf (last visited August 19, 2006).

Srinivasan, C.S. and Thirtle, Colin. *Impact of Terminator Technologies in Developing Countries: A Framework for Economic Analysis*, in ECONOMIC AND SOCIAL ISSUES IN AGRICULTURAL BIOTECHNOLOGY (R.E. Evenson, V. Santaniello and D. Zilberman eds.) Cambridge, MA: CABI Publishing (2002).

Stallman, Richard. *The GNU Operating System and the Free Software Movement*, in OPEN SOURCES: VOICES FROM THE OPEN SOURCE REVOLUTION (Chris DiBona, Sam Ockman and Mark Stone eds.) Sebastapol, CA: O'Reilly and Associates, Inc. (1999).

_____. *GNU Manifesto* (1985), *available at* http://www.gnu.org/gnu/manifesto.html (last visited August 19, 2006).

_____. THE GNU LIBRARY GENERAL PUBLIC LICENSE (VERSION 2, JUNE 1991), *available at* http://www.gnu.org/copyleft/library.txt (last visited February 10, 2007).

Steele, Leonard. The *Hybrid Corn Industry in the United States*, in MAIZE, BREEDING AND GENETICS (D.B. Walden ed.) New York: John Wiley & Sons (1978).

Steiner, Henry J. and Alston, Philip (eds.). INTERNATIONAL HUMAN RIGHTS IN CONTEXT: LAW, POLITICS, MORALS (2d ed.) New York: Oxford University Press (2000).

Stenson, Anthony J. and Gray, Tim S. The Politics of Genetic Resource Control. Hampshire, London: Palgrave McMillan (1999).

Stiglitz, Joseph E. Economics of the Public Sector (3d ed.) New York: W.W. Norton & Co. (2000).

Strachan, J.M. *Plant Variety Protection in the U.S.A.*, *in* Intellectual Property Rights in Agricultural Biotechnology (2d ed., F.H. Erbisch, & K. M. Maredi eds.) London: Oxford University Press (2004).

Su, Evelyn. *The Winners and the Losers: The Agreement on Trade-Related Aspects of Intellectual Property Rights and Its Effects on Developing Countries*, Hous. J. Int'l L. 169 (2000).

Summary of the First Session of the Governing Body of the International Treaty on Plant Genetic Resources for Food and Agriculture, 12–16 June 2006, *available at* http://www.iisd.ca/vol09/enb09369e.html (last visited August 14, 2006).

Sunder, Madhavi. *The Invention of Traditional Knowledge*, __ Duke J. L. & Contemp. Prob. __ (2007).

Taylor, Michael R. and Cayford, Jerry. *American Patent Policy, Biotechnology, and African Agriculture: The Case for Policy Change*, 17 Harv. J. L. & Tech. 321 (2004).

Tejera, Valentina. *Tripping Over Property Rights: Is It Possible to Reconcile the Convention on Biological Diversity With Article 27 of the TRIPS Agreement?*, 33 New Eng. L. Rev. 967 (1999).

Terry, Dickson. The Stark Story: Stark Nurseries 150th Anniversary. St. Louis, MO: Missouri Historical Society (1966).

Tilford, David. *Saving the Blueprint: The International Legal Regime for Plant Resources*, 30 Case W. Res. J. Int'l L. 373 (1998).

Tinker, Catherine J. *Introduction to Biological Diversity: Law, Institutions and Science*, 1 Buff. J. Int'l L. 1 (1994).

Thomas, John R. *The Patenting of the Liberal Professions*, 40 B.C. L. Rev. 1139 (1999).

Thomas, Phil. *Outcrossing between Canola Varieties—A Volunteer Canola Control Issue*, *available at* http://mindfully.org/GE/Outcrossing-Canola-Alberta.html (last visited February 10, 2007).

Thompson, Carol B. *International Law of the Sea/Seed: Public Domain versus Private Commodity*, 44 Nat. Res. J. 841 (2004).

Torvalds, Linus. *The Linux Edge*, *in* Open Sources: Voices from the Open Source Revolution (Chris DiBona, Sam Ockman and Mark Stone eds.) Sebastapol, CA: O'Reilly and Associates, Inc. (1999).

Travis, Hannibal. *Pirates of the Information Infrastructure: Blackstonian Copyright and the First Amendment*, 15 Berkeley Tech. L. J. 777 (2000).

U.N. Food and Agriculture Organization, Plant Genetic Resources: Report of the Director General, Document C, at 6 (August 23, 1983).

U.N. High Commissioner for Human Rights, Intellectual Property Rights and Human Rights, Sub-commission on Human Rights Resolution 2000/07 (August 17, 2000), *available at* http://www.unhchr.ch/Huridocda/Huridoca.nsf/0/c462b62cf8a07b13c1 2569700046704e?Opendocument (last visited August 14, 2006).

Urbano, Cynthia C. *Gene Splicing: How Does It Work and What Can It Do?*, AM. NURS-ERYMAN 44 (Oct. 15, 2004).

Vaidhyanathan, Siva. COPYRIGHTS AND COPYWRONGS: THE RISE OF INTELLECTUAL PROPERTY AND HOW IT THREATENS CREATIVITY. New York: NYU Press (2001).

Van Cleve, George. *Regulating Environmental and Safety Hazards of Agricultural Biotechnology for a Sustainable World*, 9 WASH. U. J.L. & POL'Y 245 (2002).

Vogel, Joseph Henry. GENES FOR SALE: PRIVATIZATION AS A CONSERVATION POLICY. London: Oxford University Press (1994).

Vogt, David B. *Protecting Indigenous Knowledge in Latin America*, 3 OR. REV. INT'L L. 12 (2001).

von Lewinski, Silke (ed.). INDIGENOUS HERITAGE AND INTELLECTUAL PROPERTY: GENETIC RESOURCES, TRADITIONAL KNOWLEDGE, AND FOLKLORE. London and Boston: Kluwer Law International (2004).

Watal, Jayashree. INTELLECTUAL PROPERTY RIGHTS IN THE WTO AND DEVELOPING COUNTRIES (Jayashree Watal ed.) New Delhi: OUP (2001).

Wayner, Peter. FREE FOR ALL: HOW LINUX AND THE FREE SOFTWARE MOVEMENT UNDERCUT THE HIGH-TECH-TITANS. New York: Harper Business (2000).

Weber, Steven. THE SUCCESS OF OPEN SOURCE. Cambridge, MA: Harvard University Press (2004).

Weiss, Rick. *The World's Agricultural Legacy Gets a Safe Home*, WASHINGTON POST, A01 (Monday, June 19, 2006).

_____. Biotech Rice Saga Yields Bushel of Questions for Feds: USDA Approval Shortcut Emerges as Issue. WASHINGTON POST, A03 (Tuesday, November 6, 2006).

West, Joel. *How Open is Open Enough? Melding Proprietary and Open Source Platform Strategies*, 32(7). RESEARCH POL'Y 1259 (2003).

Wilkes, H. Garrison. *Current Status of Crop Plant Germplasm*, I (2) CRIT. REV. PLANT SCI. 133–181 (1983).

_____. *Plant Genetic Resources Over Ten Thousand Years: From a Handful of Seed to the Crop-Specific Mega-Gene Banks*, in SEEDS AND SOVEREIGNTY: THE USE AND CONTROL OF PLANT GENETIC RESOURCES (Jack R. Kloppenburg, Jr. ed.) Durham, NC: Duke University Press (1988).

_____. *The World's Crop Germplasm—An Endangered Resource*, 33 BULL. ATOM. SCI. 8 (1977).

Williams, Sam. FREE AS IN FREEDOM: RICHARD STALLMAN'S CRUSADE FOR FREE SOFTWARE. Sebastapol, CA: O'Reilly and Associates, Inc. (2002).

Williams, Sidney B. *Protection of Plant Varieties as Intellectual Property*, 225 SCIENCE 18 (July 6, 1984).

White, Katherine E. *An Efficient Way to Improve Patent Quality for Plant Varieties*, 3 NW. J. TECH. & INTELL. PROP. 79 (2004).

Woodmansee, Martha and Jazsi, Peter (eds.) THE CONSTRUCTION OF AUTHORSHIP: TEXTUAL APPROPRIATION IN LAW AND LITERATURE (POST-CONTEMPORARY INTERVENTIONS). Durham, NC: Duke University Press (1994).

World Intellectual Property Organization (WIPO) Report on Fact-finding Missions on Intellectual Property and Traditional Knowledge (1998–1999), INTELLECTUAL PROPERTY NEEDS AND EXPECTATIONS OF TRADITIONAL KNOWLEDGE HOLDERS

(2001), *available at* http://www.wipo.int/tk/en/tk/ffm/report/index.html (last visited February 12, 2007).

Yelling, J.A. COMMON FIELD AND ENCLOSURE IN ENGLAND, 1450–1850. London: Macmillan Publishers Ltd. (1977).

Zahl, Adrian. *Patenting of "Higher Life Forms" in Canada*, 23 BIOTECH. L. REP. 556 (2004).

Zirkle, Conrad. *Plant Hybridization and Plant Breeding in Eighteenth Century America*, 55 (1) AGR. HIST. 25 (1969).

Index